A MILTON ENCYCLOPEDIA

A MILTON ENCYCLOPEDIA

VOLUME 4 Ho–La

Edited by

William B. Hunter, Jr., *General Editor*

John T. Shawcross *and* John M. Steadman, *Co-Editors*

Purvis E. Boyette and Leonard Nathanson,
Associate Editors

Lewisburg
Bucknell University Press
London: Associated University Presses

© 1978 by Associated University Presses, Inc.

Associated University Presses, Inc.
Cranbury, New Jersey 08512

Associated University Presses Ltd.
Magdalen House
136–148 Tooley Street
London SE1 2TT, England

A Milton encyclopedia.
Includes bibliographical references.
1.   Milton, John, 1608–1674—Dictionaries, indexes, etc.
I.   Hunter, William Bridges, 1915–
PR3580.M5   821'.4   75–21896
ISBN 0–8387–1837–X

SHORT FORMS USED
IN THIS ENCYCLOPEDIA

AdP	Ad Patrem
Animad	Animadversions upon the Remonstrant's Defense
Apol	An Apology
Arc	Arcades
Areop	Areopagitica
BrM	Bridgewater Manuscript
BN	Brief Notes upon a Late Sermon
Brit	The History of Britain
Bucer	The Judgement of Martin Bucer
CarEl	Carmina Elegiaca
Carrier 1, 2	On the University Carrier; Another on the Same
CB	Commonplace Book
CharLP	Character of the Long Parliament
Circum	Upon the Circumcision
CD	Christian Doctrine
CM	Columbia Edition of Milton's *Works*
Colas	Colasterion
CivP	A Treatise of Civil Power
DDD	The Doctrine and Discipline of Divorce
1Def	Pro Populo Anglicano Defensio
2Def	Defensio secunda
3Def	Pro se Defensio
Educ	Of Education
Eff	In Effigiei ejus Sculptorem
Eikon	Eikonoklastes
El	Elegia
EpDam	Epitaphium Damonis
Epistol	Epistolarum Familiarium
EpWin	Epitaph on the Marchioness of Winchester
FInf	On the Death of a Fair Infant

French,	
Life Records	J. Milton French. *The Life Records of John Milton*
Hire	Considerations touching the likeliest Means to Remove Hirelings from the Church
Hor	The Fifth Ode of Horace
Idea	De Idea Platonica
IlP	Il Penseroso
L'Al	L'Allegro
Literae	Literae Pseudo-Senatus Anglicani Cromwellii
Lyc	Lycidas
Logic	Artis Logicae
Mask	A Mask ("Comus")
Masson, *Life*	David Masson. *The Life of John Milton*
May	Song : On May Morning
Mosc	A Brief History of Moscovia
Nat	On the Morning of Christ's Nativity
Naturam	Naturam non pati senium
NewF	On the New Forcers of Conscience
Parker, *Milton*	William R. Parker. *Milton : A Biography*
Peace	Articles of Peace
PL	Paradise Lost
PR	Paradise Regained
PrelE	Of Prelatical Episcopacy
PresM	The Present Means
Prol	Prolusion
Ps	Psalm
QNov	In Quintum Novembris
RCG	Reason of Church Government
Ref	Of Reformation
Rous	Ad Ionnem Rousium
SA	Samson Agonistes
Shak	On Shakespeare
SolMus	At a Solemn Music
Sonn	Sonnet
StateP	State Papers
Tenure	The Tenure of Kings and Magistrates
Tetra	Tetrachordon
Time	On Time
TM	Trinity Manuscript
TR	Of True Religion
Vac	At a Vatican Exercise
Variorum Commentary	*A Variorum Commentary on the Poems of John Milton.* 3 vols. to date (New York : Columbia University Press, 1970–).
Way	The Ready and Easy Way to Establish a Free Commonwealth
Yale *Prose*	*Complete Prose Works of John Milton.* 6 vols. to date. (New Haven, Conn. : Yale University Press, 1953–).

A MILTON ENCYCLOPEDIA

SYSTEM OF REFERENCES

Organization of the material in this Encyclopedia is alphabetical with cross-referencing achieved in two ways. First, a subject may appear as an entry in the main alphabet, with citation of another entry under which that subject is treated. Second, subjects mentioned in an entry that are also discussed in other entries are marked with asterisks, with the exception of certain ones appearing too frequently for such treatment to be practical: the titles of all of Milton's works, each of which has a separate entry; the various named characters who appear in the works; and the names of Milton and his family, including his wife Mary Powell and her family, and his sister Anne Phillips and her family.

Titles of articles in serials have been removed, as have the places of publication of modern books. The titles of Milton's various works have been uniformly abbreviated in forms to be found in the front matter, as have references to the major modern editions and biographical works. All quotations of his writing are taken, unless otherwise indicated, from the complete edition published by the Columbia University Press (1931–1938).

HOBBES, THOMAS (1588–1679), English philosopher. Two basic motivations underlie Hobbes's political thinking: a desire for peace and order, and a low estimate of human nature. In both attitudes he was diametrically opposed to Milton, for whom the achievement of an ideal society required the dynamic intellectual interaction of men equally endowed by their Creator with moral judgment.

From the age of forty, Hobbes supported the idea of an absolute monarchy, gradually fortifying this position with a mechanistic psychology*. His earliest publication was a translation of Thucydides (1628), upon the failures of democracy. In *De Cive* (1642) he sought to establish the purpose and extent of civil authority and to strengthen the relationship of the church and state. *De Corpore Politico* (written in 1640 but published in 1650) was an appeal for kingship based upon psychology rather than divine right.

His most important work, *Leviathan* (1651), completed his theory of human behavior based upon mechanical determinism and from this position demonstrated the need for absolute monarchy. From Milton's side of the political debate he accepted the principle that magistracy originated with the consent of the governed, but he denied Milton's view that the consent was revocable; neither would he accept Milton's idea in *Tenure* that all men, "being the image of God himself, . . . were . . . born to command, and not to obey."

In *Questions Concerning Liberty Necessity, and Chance* (1657), Hobbes argued for psychological determinism, a view directly counter to Milton's central belief in free will*. *Behemoth* (completed 1668) interpreted the history of the period 1640–1660 in accordance with Hobbes's mechanistic view and his absolutist ideal for society, which he finally yoked with an implied adherence to the doctrine of the divine right of kings.

Hobbes's views on religion* seem to have grown out of his wishes for the state. He was mainly concerned that religion should not be a source of discord, a desire that led him to place "true religion" between Catholic authoritarianism and such extreme individualism as Milton endorsed in regarding each man as potentially his own church. His reliance on Scripture was not so literal as Milton's, and unlike Milton he characteristically saw faith as coming from listening to true pastors appointed by the sovereign rather than from individaul interpretation of Scripture. In fact, though he believed in God as creator and in the existence of "true religion," his pronouncements on the subject have an ironic tone and suggest that he was skeptical about much doctrine, if not about the main idea. [EFD]

HOBSON, JOHN. Hobson (or Hopson) was the husband of Lady Margaret Ley*; they were married on December 30, 1641, at St. Giles, Cripplegate. At the same time that Milton resided there, they lived in Aldersgate Street in St. Botolph's parish. Friendship is inferred because of this closeness of residence and *Sonn* 10, which is addressed to Lady Margaret.

Hobson was born around 1597 at Ningwood on the Isle of Wight. His first wife was Anne Bromfield, widow, by whom he had a daughter Margery. When he died on January 13, 1656, being buried in St. Botolph's, he left a third wife, Rachel, and three daughters, Elizabeth, Margaret (Margery?), and Mary. He had been a commissioned captain of the trained bands of Ningwood, volunteered for service with the Parliamentarian army, and was appointed Lieutenant Colonel of the Westminster Regiment before March 1644. For a while he was attached to Sir William Waller's army. [JTS]

HOBSON, THOMAS: *see* ON THE UNIVERSITY CARRIER.

HOG(G), WILLIAM (b. 1652?), translator. A Scotsman from Gowrie, Perthshire, Hog (or Hogaeus in Latin) translated five of Milton's poems into Latin verse in the last decade of the seventeenth century. *Paraphrasis Poetica in Tria ata, viz. Paradisum Amissum, Paradisum Recuperatum, et Samson Agonisten* (London: John Darby, 1690) translates the ten-book version of the first edition of *PL*, with the arguments gathered preceding the poem, the first full Latin translation*; then *PR*, the first translation of that poem, and *SA*, also the first translation of that poem. It was reprinted in 1699 in Rotterdam. In 1694 appeared *Paraphrasis Latina in duo Poemata,* translations of *Lyc* (the first) and John Cleveland's elegy to Edward King from *Justa Edovardo King naufrago** (1638). The printer was Hugh Newman, as an advertisement in the catalogue for Michaelmas term, 1694, attests. In 1698 Hog's version of *Mask* appeared as *Comoedia Joannis Miltoni, Viri Clarissimi (Quae agebatur in arce ludensi) Paraphrastice Reddita,* the first translation of the poem.

In 1747 and again in 1750 William Lauder*, in "An Essay on Milton's Imitations of the Moderns," inserted lines taken from Hog's translation of *PL* into passages from Hugo Grotius's* *Adamus Exul,* Jacopo Masenius's *Sarcotis,* and some of Staphorstius's poems in an effort to discredit Milton's reputation. The forgery was discovered by John Douglas and exposed in his *Milton Vindicated From the Charge of Plagiarism, Brought against him by Mr. Lauder* (1751). [JTS]

HOLINESS. Holiness in general is the quality of any person or object that it derives from its close relationship to God. In the strictly supernatural order, that closeness in the case of a person derives from his incorporation in Christ through sanctifying grace*. This incorporation in time* involves a union with God through the three supernatural virtues of faith*, hope*, and charity*; and, as St. Paul says, the greatest of these is charity. In eternity the beatific union with God will be by charity or love alone. It is this concept of holiness that Spenser* allegorizes in Book 1 of the *Faerie Queene* in the adventures of the Red Cross Knight. We recall that his final education in the House of Holiness was by Fidelia, Speranza, and Charissa (Faith, Hope, and Charity). This is also the concept of holiness that operates in much of Milton's writings, which he makes clear in his own definition of holiness in *CD* (1:xxi). Holiness is there identified with "being ingrafted in Christ." One of the effects of this ingrafting or incorporation in Christ through grace Milton sees as "love or charity, arising from a sense of the divine love shed abroad in the hearts of the regenerate by the Spirit, whereby those who are ingrafted in Christ being influenced, become dead to sin, and alive again unto God, and bring forth good works spontaneously and freely. This is also called holiness." And he goes on to say that "the love here intended is not brotherly love . . . , nor even the ordinary affection which we bear to God, but one resulting from a consciousness and lively sense of love wherewith he hath loved us, and which in theology is reckoned the third after faith and hope. . . . This is the offspring, as it were, of faith, and the parent of good works. . . . It is described

1 Cor. xiii and 1 John iv. 16." He further remarks that "in consequence of this love or sanctity all believers are called saints. Philipp. iv, 21, 22. 'salute every saint in Christ Jesus'; and to the same effect in other passages. The holiness of the saints is nevertheless imperfect in this life." [MBM]

HOLINSHED, RAPHAEL. Reginald Wolfe, Queen's printer, employed Holinshed (d. 1580?) to assist with a projected history and cosmography of the world. After Wolfe's death, Holinshed and his assistants persevered, producing the *Chronicles of England, Scotland, and Ireland* in two folios, 1577. William Harrison wrote the memorable Description of England; Holinshed the History of England and (by redaction) Scotland; Stanyhurst and Campion did Ireland. Upon Holinshed's death, John Hooker ("Vowell") directed the continuations and enlargements of the *Chronicles* by Abraham Fleming and others. Milton, like Shakespeare*, used this second edition, 3 volumes, 1586–87. *CB* shows that Milton read Holinshed closely between 1639–1641, taking most of his numerous notes from volume 3, containing "The Historie of England" from William the Conqueror to 1586. Milton turned to the British historians for material for poetry, but his notes have immediate relevance to the political issues of his day: charters of popular liberty, the common law, the responsibilities of kings measured against their tyrannies, the corruption of the clergy. In *TM* (1640–41) Milton acknowledges Holinshed's *Chronicles* as his source for at least six of the projected British tragedies. He soon had occasion to use Holinshed among other sources in his first antiprelatical tract, *Ref.* Later in the 1640s, writing *Brit,* Milton shows that he valued history strictly for the "naked truth." He is critical, if not testy, when he finds "Fables" offered as facts. He is impatient with the credulous, circumstantial narrations he has plowed through in Holinshed and other British historians. Milton no doubt kept Holinshed, Speed*, Stow*, and other chroniclers at hand to collate and sift, but he preferred the medieval historians such as Geoffrey of Monmouth*, Gildas*, and William of Malmesbury*, despite monkish shortcomings. *See* HISTORIOGRAPHY, MILTON AND SEVENTEENTH-CENTURY. [TLH]

HOLLINGWORTH, RICHARD: *see* EIKON BASILIKE.

HOLSTE (HOLSTENIUS), LUKAS. A German scholar who worked for three years at Oxford and was later patronized by Cardinal Barberini*, Holste (1596–1661) met Milton during one of his two stays in Rome at the Vatican library where Holste was to become librarian. In *Epistol* 9 (from Florence, March 30, 1639) Milton thanked him for his politeness and helpfulness during Milton's stay in Rome, and apologized for not being able to supply copies of some material Holste had requested from the Laurentian Library in Florence (since the Library forbade copying any of its manuscripts without special permission). The letter survives in the Vatican Library, and was reproduced in photographic facsimile in *Publications of the Modern Language Association,* 68, between pages 622 and 623. Milton mentioned in *2Def* that while in Rome he enjoyed the society "of Lucas Holstenius and of many other learned and superior men." However, in a letter to Nicolas Heinsius* in 1653, Holste mentions that Milton was disliked by some in Italy because of his "over strict morals" and because "he disputed freely about religion." [WM]

HOMER. Racine, the only seventeenth-century poet whose knowledge of and debt to Greek literature matched that of Milton, left extensive traces of his study of Greek tragedy in his annotations of Sophoclean and Euripidean plays, and the sophistication and concreteness of his critical marginalia are an invaluable guide to the scholar in interpreting his allusions and determining the limits to which they may be pushed. The student of Milton receives virtually no help from biographical evidence in assessing Milton's debt to Homer. Our knowledge of the St. Paul's School* curriculum permits the inference that Milton must have first come across Homer no later than 1624, when he was fifteen years old (Parker, *Milton,* pp. 13–14). In the second elegy, written "anno aetatis 17" when he was a Cambridge student, he showed off his knowledge of Homer by some allusions to the *Iliad* (*El*2:14, 15, 19; *Iliad* 24. 334ff., 1. 320ff., 18. 104), which, unlike the vaguer references to Homer and Circe in the first elegy (*El*1 : 23, 87–88), imply a knowledge of specific passages. But despite our knowledge of the editions and commentaries that Milton did use or could have used (*see* HOMER, PARADISE LOST AND THE RENAISSANCE), there is no evidence to allow reconstruction of the process by which Milton acquired and maintained the remarkably extensive and intimate knowledge of the Homeric poems, and especially of the *Iliad,* to which *PL* bears witness. It is impossible to determine whether the scattered remarks by the early biographers* rest on facts or are extrapolations based on the evidence of the poems. Toland* reports that Milton "could almost repeat without book" the *Iliad* and the *Odyssey,* but then as now such a reputation could be acquired by a knowledge of a few carefully chosen lines. Richardson* reports that Milton was "put upon translating Homer" and extols his qualifications for the job. Perhaps we are on more solid ground with John Ward's* summary of an interview with Milton's daughter Deborah when she was an old woman : "Isaiah, Homer, and Ovid's* Metamorphoses were books which they were often called to read to their father" (French, 5 : 110). We seem to catch a glimpse of an idiosyncratic preference in this remark, which contrasts refreshingly with the wooden manner in which Milton in his prose refers to Homer in the context of the epic tradition, notably in *RCG* : "that Epick form whereof the two poems of *Homer,* and those other two of *Virgil**

and *Tasso** are a diffuse, and the book of *Job* a brief model" (3 : 237). This is as impersonal as and no more helpful than the homage to Greek tragedy in the different context of the preface to *SA* : "the three Tragic Poets unequall'd yet by any, and the best rule to all who endeavour to write Tragedy." Nor can one attach much weight to Milton's frequent allusions to Homer in his role as the archetypal poet, for instance the mention in the sixth elegy that he drank water and ate sparingly (*El*6 : 71).

Casual allusions to the Homeric poems occur throughout Milton's poetry. The flies swarming about the milk pail (*Iliad* 2. 469–73, 16. 641–43) attracted his attention as early as *QNov* (lines 178–80) and as late as *PR* (4. 15–17), and both times he solved the problem of Homer's apparent breach of epic* decorum by using the simile with a pejorative intent it did not have in the *Iliad.* The fall of Hephaestus (*Iliad* 1. 590–94), which inspired the famous lines in *PL* 1. 740–46, had already attracted him in *Naturam* (lines 23–24). And *Vac* has an arresting description of the effect of Demodocus's "solemn songs" on "sad Ulysses' soul" (lines 48–52). But Homeric allusions play an extensive structural and thematic role only in *Mask* and in *PL,* and even in the former the use of the Circe myth depends much more heavily on the mythographical and allegorical* tradition of the Renaissance than on the specific features of the Homeric story, although Milton was clearly familiar with the Circe passages of the *Odyssey* (*Mask* 636–37, 651; *Odyssey* 10. 277–301.

In discussing *PL* as an epic one should resist the temptation to derive such general features of Milton's work as its scope, sublimity, or even "spirit" from either Homer or Virgil, depending on one's preferences. In truth, Milton's sensibility was most un-Homeric, whatever one may understand by that, and it was, if anything, even less Virgilian in its profound aversion to the rituals of authority, whether secular or religious. It seems best to forgo speculations about the spiritual affinities of *PL,* to accept its irrepressibly Miltonic voice, and to restrict the discussion of Milton's relationship with Homer to those verbal, thematic, and structural aspects of the *Iliad* and *Odyssey,* which are recalled in the text of *PL* through a process of allusion and which require explication if the text is to yield its full meaning.

In order to do so one must describe, however sketchily, the peculiarities of Milton's use of epic allusions. Virgil provided later epic poets not only with a model to imitate; his use of Homer also established a method of imitation. It has been too readily assumed that Milton followed that method and that, by and large, he used Homer and Virgil in the same manner in which Virgil used Homer. In fact, Milton's use of epic material is highly idiosyncratic. Virgil counterpointed his revaluation of Homeric values with a scrupulous imitation of the formal conventions and plot patterns of the Homeric epics. The *Aeneid* aims at including all the significant actions of both *Iliad* and *Odyssey* within the confines of one epic: it is in the likeness of Homeric actions that Virgilian characters reveal their utter difference from the world of Achilles or Odysseus. The fluidity of Virgil's historical material enabled him to shape it according to the constraints imposed by his formal aims. Milton, on the other hand, was faced not only with a richer and more diverse literary heritage that inevitably weakened the claim of any single work to serve as a formal model, but, more important, with the scriptural claim to literal and absolute truth, which ruled out any accommodation of the subject matter to the constraints of his formal model. It was the form that had to give.

One sees this difference very clearly where Virgil and Milton make use of the same Homeric passage. In the *Aeneid* the description of the shield follows the Iliadic model (*Aeneid* 8. 370–453, 608–731; *Iliad* 18. 369–617). The hero's mother visits the god of fire and requests a shield for her son. It is manufactured by the god and delivered by the goddess. The significant

differences emerge on the basis of these and other detailed resemblances. Whereas the Homeric shield gives, in Chapman's words, a timeless picture of the "universall world," the Virgilian shield portrays history moving toward its fulfillment in the Augustan empire. Homer's shield is described as it is made; in Virgil the hero contemplates the events embossed on the shield, which he does not recognize as the consequences of his actions but interprets as a good omen for the future.

Milton used the shield of Achilles in Michael's prophetic survey of human history. Scripture, Milton's primary source, recorded no detailed incidents between the murder of Abel and the Flood to illustrate the fact that "the wickedness of man was great in the earth" (Gen. 6 : 5). Milton filled this gap in the biblical narrative by using elements from the shield of Achilles to form a tableau demonstrating the corruption of the world and justifying the Flood. Homer's wedding (*Iliad* 18. 491–96) provides the details for the marriage of the sons of God with the daughters of men (*PL* 11. 580–92). There are other correspondences, the most striking being the transformation of the court scene in which a homicide case is settled by the judge with the "straightest opinion" (*Iliad* 18. 497–508) into the Miltonic council scene in which the feuding parties turn violently on the one man who "spake much of Right and Wrong, / Of Justice, of Religion, Truth and Peace, / And Judgment from above" (*PL* 11. 666–68). The thematic purpose of these allusions is apparent. Homer's celebration of a world that despite the inclusion of struggle and violence has order and beauty is transformed into an unmasking of the world's corruption. Equally apparent is the destruction of the formal model : the narrative context of the shield description itself is broken up into parts that will fit the narrative structure of Genesis.

Epic allusions, however brilliant or complex, play an ancillary role in the design of *PL.* Milton's imitation of the Bible* establishes the pattern that governs the use of epic allusions. Structurally they have less in common with Virgil's use of Homer than with Virgil's use of nonepic sources. Whereas Virgil respects what might be called the "narrative syntax" of his epic model, Milton makes use of fragments as they fit into a design that transcends both the formal and thematic limits of the genre. For this reason, it is much harder in *PL* than in the *Aeneid* to delimit the context a given allusion intends, and the search for wider and more detailed contextual implications than individual allusions can bear has been one of the commonest critical errors in the discussion of Milton's use of epic sources (e.g., D. P. Harding*, *The Club of Hercules*).

The thematic function of epic allusions is often to magnify Milton's subject by belittling or disparaging the epic "source." This technique is part of the competitive nature of the epic tradition in which each new work aims at "overgoing" or replacing its predecessors (Propertius 2. 34. 65–66). For the Christian poet such competition easily turned into outright rejection, as it does in Milton's dismissal of the subject matter of previous epics and romances (*PL* 9. 13–41). A very peculiar kind of rejection operates in Milton's portrayal of Hell*, where epic allusions amount to an interpretation of the classical world, which is unmasked as the process of allusion establishes its true derivation.

On the other hand, the moral intent of an allusion rarely exhausts its poetic effect. Allusions are subject to the paradoxes of poetic denial, which cannot obliterate the presence of that which is denied and may even enhance it, as is manifestly the case in Milton's beautiful simile :

> Not that faire field
> Of *Enna,* where *Proserpin* gathering flours
> Her self a fairer Flour by gloomie Dis
> Was gatherd, which cost *Ceres* all that pain
> To seek her through the world . . .
> (*PL* 4. 268–72)

And on a lower level, allusions, however destructive or pejorative in intent, perpetuate the continuity of the genre by

their mere presence.

Some of Milton's most effective allusions simply add to a passage the emotional poignancy of the original. A good example is the allusion to Hector's return to Troy (*Iliad* 6. 237–41) in *PL* 10. 26–29. In the words of an anonymous eighteenth-century critic : "Here the Circumstance of the Guardian Angels making no Answer to those Questions they were asked about Man, is imitated from the 6th Lib. of the ILIAD, where, on Hector's Arrival from Battle, the *Trojan* Women flock about him, enquiring concerning their Husbands, Sons, and Brothers, who, in the same Manner passes on, without giving an Answer. As the great Beauty of this Passage consists in the Affection and Concern the Angels had for mankind; so I think we have a clearer Notion of that, by taking Notice of the Imitation. The Imitation of this Passage seems to insinuate this Concern and Tenderness of the Angels to be equal to that of a fond Woman for Husband, or Son" (*Essay Upon Milton's Imitations of the Ancients,* pp. 41–42). More striking still is the description of Adam's waiting for Eve's return and his reaction to her fall, which receives much of its effect from the allusions to the scene in which Andromache learns of Hektor's death (*Iliad* 22. 440–46, 461, 466–76; *PL* 9. 838–95; cf. *Comparative Literature Studies* 6 : 298–99, 312–13).

Milton's use of the messenger topos is a very sophisticated example of such "atmospheric" allusions. If the Homeric Hermes carried out his mission to Calypso in a leisurely and social manner, the curtness of the Virgilian Mercury is intended to contrast with it, and this contrast is underscored by differences in the setting of the messenger's journey. Although there are some Virgilian allusions in the description of Raphael's voyage (*PL* 5. 266–67; *Aeneid* 4. 253), it is apparent that this visit by the "sociable spirit" primarily recalls Hermes' visit to Calypso, whereas the more austere Michael speaks with the harsher voice of Virgil's Mercury (*PL* 11. 251, 263–65; *Aeneid* 4. 265, 279–80). Here the indubitable fact that senior archangels are superior to junior Olympians is incidental to the different moods the allusions are intended to evoke.

Iliadic allusions in *PL* not only outnumber Odyssean allusions by a wide margin, as might be expected from Milton's systematic use of the *Iliad* in the War in Heaven*; they also tend to have greater individual weight. Iliadic allusions are among the most striking examples of Milton's frequent practice of alluding to the same passage in different places. Thus the Iliadic formula stating that without divine intervention disaster would ensue (*Iliad* 8. 130, 11. 310) appears three times in *PL* (3. 222–26, 4. 990–97, 6. 669–74). Double allusions are often intentional: from the perspective of the common source emerges a significant connection between two Miltonic passages. Pope* already remarked that Milton made good use of the scandalous lovemaking of Zeus and Hera (*Iliad* 14. 346–51) when he undercut the lovemaking of Adam and Eve after the Fall through an allusion to that notorious passage (9. 1039–41). When in Book 4 Adam smiles on Eve "with superior Love, as *Jupiter* / On *Juno* smiles, when he impregns the Clouds / That shed *May* Flowers" (4. 499–501), the allusion is not to the Iliadic passage itself, but to its chaste moralization. The connection underscores the contrast between the fallen and unfallen world; an element of foreshadowing, however, is also present. At the end of Book 1 the Satanic armies appear so grand that by comparison all armies of mythology and history could not "merit more than that small infantry/ Warr'd on by Cranes" (1. 575–76). This alludes to the pygmies and cranes simile at the opening of *Iliad* 3, which serves as the model for the clash of Satan's and Michael's armies in the War in Heaven. But in that context the "banded powers" of Satan do not even deserve the name of an army and are dwarfed by the quiet and order of the angelic host. The motif of the unanswered challenge (*Iliad* 7. 92ff.) establishes a contrast between the manner in which Satan and the Son* volunteer

for their heroic missions (*PL* 2. 417–29; 3. 217–26).

Beyond the level of specific allusions there are structural and thematic resemblances that relate *PL* more closely to the *Iliad* than to any other epic. Perhaps this is the reason for the very prominent Iliadic allusions in the proemium of *PL*. "Man's first disobedience" is syntactically almost identical with the first line of the *Iliad*. In both epics the noun is qualified by a relative clause describing the sufferings caused by the central actions of "anger" and "disobedience" (cf. *PL* 1. 33–34; *Iliad* 1. 8–9, for further resemblances). This emphasis on a destructive action sets the *Iliad* and *PL* apart from the *Odyssey* and the *Aeneid,* which move toward a homecoming and the founding of a city. At the same time, the theme of destruction is counterpointed in both works by a theme of reconciliation that mitigates the tragic effect. The epic that announces as its theme the disastrous anger of Achilles ends with the ceremonious meeting of Achilles and Priam. Similarly the title of *PL* does only partial justice to its content. The slow process of learning obedience is a crucial part of the epic of "man's first disobedience." Renaissance theories of the heroic poem required that its subject be some great enterprise of prosperous design. It could be argued that *PL* moves toward such an event in the anticipation of Christ's central triumph over Satan. But this final history is no more the subject of *PL* than the Achaean triumph over the Trojans is the subject of the *Iliad*. The anger of Achilles and the disobedience of Adam are both apparent setbacks in the larger struggle, but paradoxically they make the final victory all the more certain. The main concern of both poets was not with the splendor of that triumph, but with the bitterness of the disastrous event that impeded, and by impeding necessitated, the final success.

In both *PL* and the *Iliad* the material of a large narrative cycle is organized around a central event, which is only an episode in that cycle. The Trojan War is to the tragedy of Achilles, Patroklos, and Hektor, what the "Celestial Cycle" is to the Fall* of Adam and Eve. The episode that becomes the central action is chosen because it is an individual crisis in which the poet's vision of human experience is crystallized. In both works the total narrative is organized in such a manner as to frame the central plot and throw into fuller relief its representative and universal nature. In the *Iliad* this frame consists of two gigantic montages that set beginning against end. The duel of Paris and Menelaos and the breaking of the truce reenact the *casus belli*; the death of Hektor foreshadows the fall of Troy.

Similarly, the first two and last two books of *PL* are clearly montages of the fallen world in an analytical and historical mode respectively. They point inward toward the Fall and show its universal consequences. As in the *Iliad,* the central action occupies only a fraction of the narrative. In the *Iliad* the scenes of general fighting separate the scenes of the Achilleid; in *PL* the story of Adam and Eve is divided into two groups of scenes by the narrative of the War in Heaven and the Creation*. In both works the total structure that results from the interlacing of the central story with episodes and from the framework of corresponding montages maintains a chronological semblance, but it is not based on sequential narrative as the organizing principle. The poet's intention was to achieve patterns that would develop the central theme in multiple variations.

It is possible, though somewhat speculative, to argue that the causal structure of Milton's central action owes something to the relationship of the Patrokleia to the Achilleid in the *Iliad*. Milton was apparently the first poet to make Adam responsible for the situation in which Eve confronts the Serpent by herself. If the tragedy of Adam is "triggered" by the tragedy of Eve, the latter is indirectly the result of Adam's ill-advised concessions. This causal relationship between the two falls is exactly analogous to the inter-dependence of the Achilleid and the Patrokleia. The death of Patroklus causes that of Achilles, but Achilles is responsible for the death of Patroklus because he permitted him to fight an adversary whom he should have faced himself. Against their better judgment both Achilles and Adam yield to the requests of the weaker partner; both times their explicit warnings are fatally disregarded. Thus both Adam and Achilles are ultimately responsible for the disasters that befell them. The analogue, although not confirmed by concrete verbal allusions, offers at least a possible source for the unprecedented scene in which Adam allows Eve to work by herself.

Although allusions to the *Odyssey* are far fewer in number and generally less striking than Iliadic allusions, one of the most obvious epic features of *PL,* the flashback narrative, is specifically Odyssean, despite the Virgilian allusions in Raphael's opening words (5. 563–64; *Aeneid* 2, 3). Whereas in the *Aeneid* the flashback narrative is moved toward the beginning with the result that apart from Book 1 the events of the epic follow a chronological order, in both *PL* and the *Odyssey* the chronological continuity of the narrative is interrupted by the flashback narrative, which occupies the physical middle of the poem. As in the *Odyssey,* Raphael's narrative introduces the listener to a world of a different order; moreover, Paradise* stands between the supernatural world of Heaven* and Hell* and the real world, just as the country of the Phaeacians stands between wonderland and Ithaca. The setting for the flashback narrative, which merges Hermes' visit to Calypso with Odysseus's stay at the court of the Phaeacians, is also Odyssean.

Some critics have pushed the Phaeacian allusions harder than they will go. Satan's voyage is said to be modeled on Odysseus's voyage to Scheria; Odysseus's address to Nausikaa (6. 149–85) is seen as the model for Satan's speech to Eve (9. 532–48), who is identified with Nausicaa through the Delia image of 9. 386–92

(*Odyssey* 6. 102–8). This may be a case of wrongly interpreting Miltonic images as if they were contextual allusions in the manner of Virgil. Satan and Eve "historically" precede their literary ancestors. As the daring adventurer, Satan is the prototype of such men as the Argonauts and Odysseus, who are explicitly named rather than alluded to in 2. 1017–20. Far from implying that the quest of Satan is modeled on the wanderings of Odysseus, such open naming may even be argued to rule out an allusive relationship. The portrait of Satan is the composite of his partial identification with his "descendants," none of whom has a privileged position. Similarly Eve is not identified with Nausicaa any more closely than she is with Dido or any other of her daughters. The Delia simile is a convention associating her with all epic heroines, but not with any one in particular. The wider context of the simile, which recalls Dido (*Aeneid* 1. 498–502) as much as Nausicaa, does not primarily invite the reader to see either Nausicaa or Dido through Delia. Rather, the simile is one in a series of divine identifications establishing Eve as a nature goddess. Delia joins Pales, Pomona, and Ceres. If it is legitimate to single out one allusion from this cluster as establishing a dominant context, it should be the final one to "*Ceres* in her Prime, / Yet Virgin of *Proserpina* from *Jove*" (9. 395–96), which links up with the Proserpina allusion of 4. 268–72 to provide an allusive context with a much more precise degree of correspondence than the encounter of Odysseus and Nausicaa provides.

If the convention of the flashback narrative is clearly Odyssean, the substance and manner of that narrative are, at least on the surface, the most Iliadic features of *PL*. The poet's peculiar use of Homeric features in this part of his work shows his self-conscious and ironic attitude toward the tradition of his genre. Whereas in the *Odyssey* the hero tells his own adventures, the hero of *PL* listens to the adventures of a different hero. Adam listens to an epic about the Son. The War

in Heaven is the only part of *PL* in which the action is systematically based on a formal model, the fighting in the *Iliad*. As in the first scene of Iliadic fighting, the march of the opposing armies toward each other (6. 61–98; *Iliad* 3. 1–9) is followed by an indecisive duel in which Satan and Abdiel play the roles of Paris and Menelaos (6. 103; *Iliad* 3. 29), though the details of Satan's retreat (6. 193–95) allude to the wounding of Hector by Diomedes (*Iliad* 11. 354–56). The splintered sword of Menelaus (*Iliad* 3. 361–63; cf. *Aeneid* 12. 731–41) appears in a second version of that duel, the encounter of Satan and Michael at the end of the first day of fighting (6. 323–27). Again the wounding of Satan (6. 335–43) alludes in considerable detail to a scene in which Hector is wounded (*Iliad* 14. 424–32). At night the victorious angels camp on the battlefield (6. 410–14); their "cherubic waving fires" (6. 413) recall the famous tableau of the Trojans camping outside the walls of the city at the end of the second day of fighting (*Iliad* 8. 553–65). Meanwhile the devils, like the defeated Achaeans, hold a nocturnal strategy session, whose outcome, the invention of artillery, of course, owes nothing to Homer (6. 413–523; *Iliad* 9. 1–172). The marshaling of the angelic army on the second day (6. 541–44) is closely modeled on Agamemnon's exhortation to his troops (2. 382–84); otherwise the cosmic chaos of the second day bears no resemblance to Homeric fighting. But the third day is epic again. The Son abandons the role of the absent hero, and like Achilles, he prevents the angelic army from joining in his fight against Satan (6. 801–23; *Iliad* 22. 205–7; cf. *Aeneid* 12. 760–62). Milton uses the epic motif to illustrate the biblical notion that vengeance belongs to the Lord (Romans 12 : 19). The very appearance of the Son causes panic among the devils, as does the appearance of the unarmed Achilles among the Trojans (18. 203–29). The description of the rout itself (6. 834–66) follows the routing of the Achaeans by Apollo (*Iliad* 15. 318–27).

In Milton's radical theology the perfection of epic heroism* could be attributed only to the Son. The contrast between the triumph of the perfect hero and the tragedy of the human listener was an inspired way of putting literary conventions in the service of theology by expressing the typological contrast of the Son and Adam through the traditional opposition of epic and tragic hero. On the other hand, this use of literary conventions also puts their validity in doubt. Epic conventions are in fact used by Milton wherever the action moves away from the immediacy of human experience. The very conventionality of the War in Heaven is an ironic device to arouse the reader's skepticism about the literal truth of the story. The more serious Michael replies to Adam's questions about the time and place of the Son's final victory over Satan: "Dream not of thir fight / As of a Duel, or the local wounds / Of head or heel" (12. 386–88).

What is true of the "image" of the Son is also true of Satan, his idol or hideous double. He too acts within the conventions of the epic. We may note here an important difference between *PL* and other epics. Whereas in the epics of Homer, Virgil, and their successors the divine action runs parallel to the human action and epic conventions govern the action on both levels, in *PL* epic conventions are by and large restricted to the divine sphere and serve to separate it from the human sphere. The Son and Satan do indeed reenact the divine conflict of the epic tradition, which is most clearly represented by the antagonism of Jupiter and Juno, but their conflict is cast in terms of that of Turnus and Aeneas. The patterns of the opposing gods and of the opposing heroes are merged in the conflict of Satan and the Son.

The opposition of epic conventions (the Son and Satan) and tragic conventions (Adam and Eve) is part of the "Iliadic" structure of *PL,* with its focus on a central action that is merely an episode in a larger struggle. Their op-position expresses the typographical contrast of the Son and Adam. The total structure of *PL* transcends the limits of the epic because for Milton the creation of a Christian epic with its necessary revaluation of classic heroic ideals entailed a radical departure from the formal conventions of the tradition. Christian orthodoxy led to literary heresy; but that the product of this act of heresy should bear an astonishing resemblance to the structure of the *Iliad* and constitute in a sense a return to the origin of the epic tradition is one of the ironies of literary history. [MMu]

HOMER, PARADISE LOST AND THE RENAISSANCE. As Harris Fletcher has shown, Milton knew intimately the great Renaissance edition of Homer's* *Works* by Jean de Sponde (Johannes Spondanus), first published in 1583. This edition is notable for its extensive commentary and for its verbatim hexameter Latin translation that parallels the Greek text. The commentary, which is interspersed between sections of text, is mainly directed at ethical* and stylistic* aspects of Homer, with occasional etymological derivations of Greek words, sometimes rather fanciful. The focus of the commentary is, then, primarily humanistic and ethical, but these interests are from time to time betrayed by that bane of Renaissance criticism, the allegorical* interpretation. Spondanus draws heavily on the famous commentary of Eustathius, Archbishop of Thessalonica (fl. 1180), on the *Moralia* of Plutarch*, on Plato* and Aristotle*, and occasionally on the sometimes far-fetched exegeses of the *Allegoriae Homericae* of an otherwise obscure Heraclitus and the *Mythologiae* of Natale Conti (Natalis Comes*).

In general Spondanus's interpretations of Homer seem to be characterized by good sense. He points out again and again the purity and simplicity of manners in Homer, the elegance of his insights, the aptness of his similes, and the profoundly moral and even Christian spirit of the whole. When he is troubled by what he regards as lapses from such high standards, as in the seduction of Zeus by Hera in *Iliad* 14, he resorts to a naive allegorical explanation from natural philosophy —Zeus is the air and Hera is the ether and Homer is, in this troublesome incident, conveying under a cloud the scientific views of his age. But these extravagant divagations are rare : most of the time Spondanus has his eye fixed clearly on the text.

Milton's other main Homeric sources were Eustathius's commentary and the *Thesaurus* of Henri Estienne (Henricus Stephanus). Eustathius's prose commentary in Greek exceeds in bulk the *Iliad* and the *Odyssey* : it was reprinted in the nineteenth century in five folio volumes. It consists of a running commentary, often line-by-line, offering an enormous variety of interpretations. The book is obviously a compilation of all the extant Homeric criticism the scholarly Archbishop could lay his hands on in the twelfth century. Alexander Pope* had the good fortune to prevail on Parnell to extract and translate the most significant and relevant portions of Eustathius, who is quoted generally with respect on almost every page of this Augustan commentary on Homer. For those who are daunted by several thousand pages of dense Greek prose Pope's Homer seems to provide a back door for getting at this valuable critical compendium. Another back door to both Spondanus and Eustathius is the spirited and learned commentary of Anne Dacier, Pope's French counterpart. Between Pope's Homer and that of Mme. Dacier, Eustathius's exegetical labors are well represented. The *Thesaurus* of Henricus Stephanus, a Greek-Latin dictionary in five enormous folios, is also a triumph of Renaissance scholarship. It is generally free from those fanciful and wrongheaded etymologies that badly misled passionate devotees of Homer like George Chapman, who seemed to make a point of seeking them out in the inferior *Lexicon* of Johannes Scapula.

These, then, are the principal tools Milton used in studying Homer. Thanks to the Homeric allusions in *PL* compiled in the index of *CM,* we can readily see that here was no casual acquaintance, but an intimate, profound, and extensive knowledge of the *Iliad* and the *Odyssey.* Milton had read Greek from an early age and, as we can see from his marginalia on Euripides as well as his allusions to Homer and his own original Greek poems, had achieved a mastery of the language and literature that was extremely rare in seventeenth-century England.

Milton's expertise in Greek thus freed him from a dependence on Latin translations, mythologies, and florilegiae. His knowledge of Homer was firsthand, minute, and perspicuous.

The relation of *PL* to its predecessors in the epic* and romance traditions has been exhaustively studied and documented. The best recent scholarship on Milton and the heroic* tradition has pursued the innumerable classical allusions in the poem and explored the ways in which Milton has modified his borrowings. Usually, as Steadman, Willey, Tillyard, Lewis, and many others show, Milton employs the allusion to denigrate classical heroism and romantic *fortezza* by assigning them to his villainous characters while at the same time praising the "deeds beyond heroic" of Christian charity and self-sacrifice. On the other hand, his systematic "critique" of the heroic values—fortitude, sapience, leadership, *amor,* magnanimity, etc.—has been emphasized at the expense of a due appreciation of the ways Milton adapted heroic themes, motifs, incidents, and characters in a positive way to enhance his heroic vision. His "critique" has been misunderstood through stress on only one side of a highly complex process of adaptation. For while it is true that Milton's epic was more comprehensive, more moral, and more spiritual than Homer's, he was deeply aware of an indebtedness to the spiritual and moral qualities of Homer; and while the "dreams of guile and violence" that are alleged to be the "dreams of grandeur praised by Homer" are an integral part of the Homeric vision, they are no more to be identified as being endorsed by Homer than the guile and violence of Iago are to be thought of as being "praised" by Shakespeare*; and while it is true that Milton systematically alludes to Odysseus in his account of Satan's flight through Chaos, invasion of Paradise, and seduction of Eve, thus emphasizing the Archangel's fortitude, ingenuity, and guile, the pattern is crossed by another pattern of subtler and more implicit allusions to Homer (to the *Odyssey,* especially), which have a totally opposite effect. If Satan's titanic adventure suggests an Odyssean strength and self-reliance and if his disguises and enticements suggest the stratagem of the Wooden Horse and the destruction of Troy, the other pattern continually suggests by contrast the ways in which Satan fails to live up to some of Odysseus's virtues.

A look at Satan's encounter with Eve will illustrate. As she leaves Adam for the first time in Book 8, seeing him bent on "thoughts abstruse" in his conversation with Raphael, Milton describes her thus:

Her Husband the Relater she preferr'd
Before the Angel, and of him to ask
Chose rather: hee, she knew, would intermix
Grateful digressions, and solve high dispute
With conjugal Caresses, from his Lip
Not Words alone pleas'd her. O when meet now
Such pairs, in Love and mutual Honour joyn'd?
With Goddess-like demeanour forth she went;
Not unattended, for on her as Queen
A pomp of winning Graces waited still,
And from about her shot Darts of desire
Into all Eyes to wish her still in sight.
(52–63)

The index to *CM* refers the third and fourth lines from the end of this passage to the *Iliad* 3. 142, where Helen, setting forth from her hall to view the combat of Menelaus and Paris from the walls of Troy is "not alone, for two handmaidens accompanied her." As she stands near the Scaean gate, the elders of Troy gathered about Priam are struck by her seductive beauty and agree that the Trojans and Achaeans can hardly be blamed for suffering such woes for such a woman because "she looks wonderfully like one of the immortal goddesses" (156–58).

This identification of Eve and Helen, whom the old men finally think of as "a bane to us and our children after us," clearly anticipates Eve's later separation from Adam in Book 9 (for which this is a kind of rehearsal) to become mother of "all our woes" and, of course, mother of the ruinous Helen. Eve's separation from Adam to encounter the flashy, smooth-talking serpent is likewise assimilated to Helen's abandonment of Menelaus for Paris. The allusions then suggest Eve's potential and impending role as a greater and more destructive Helen. The Index fails to catch another instance where the key Homeric line, "not alone, but accompanied by handmaidens," occurs, and that is in a totally different context, in the sixth book of the *Odyssey,* where the innocent Nausicaa, with thoughts of marriage very much on her mind, sets forth with her companions in a mule-drawn cart to do the family wash and picnic beside a stream near which the shipwrecked Odysseus is sleeping in a thicket. In Book 9 of *PL,* when Eve, after the famous debate with her husband, sets forth on her own, Milton enforces the comparison to Nausicaa by comparing her to "Delia," another name for Artemis, who was born with her twin brother, Apollo, under a palm tree on Delos:

Thus saying, from her Husbands hand her hand
Soft she withdrew, and like a Wood-Nymph light,
Oread or *Dryad,* or of *Delia's* Traine,
Betook her to the Groves, but *Delia's* self
In gate surpass'd and Goddess-like deport . . .
(385ff.)

When Odysseus emerges naked from the thicket, modestly concealing his sexual organs with an olive branch, he tactfully enquires of Nausicaa whether she is a goddess or a mortal and goes on to say that if she is a goddess she must be Artemis and that she reminds him in her grace and stature of the beautiful palm tree he once saw on Delos, where the goddess was born (Homer has already compared her to Artemis in an elaborate simile beginning at 6. 102).

Since Nausicaa's motives and behavior during the whole incident are innocent and unexceptionable, we must then admit that the double Homeric identification makes Eve a potential Nausicaa as well as a potential Helen, or, to put it another way, that Milton is presenting Eve as the future mother not only of the unfaithful and ruinous Helen but of the virtuous Nausicaa. The Homeric identification is thus richly ambiguous and inclusive and entirely appropriate to Eve's present freedom to obey or disobey, to stand or fall, to be an archetypal Helen or a Nausicaa.

This doubleness also applies to the way in which Milton uses the allusions to Odysseus in the following encounter. The "crafty and honeyed words" that Satan uses in addressing Eve ("a Goddess among Gods") are directly derived from Homer's description of Odysseus's speech to Nausicaa. Before jumping to the conclusion that Milton is simply denigrating thereby the heroic criterion "sapience," we should remember that Odysseus's wiles are directed at the honorable goals of self-preservation and the preservation of Nausicaa's virgin modesty (Joyce has described him here as "the first gentleman of Europe"). Ravenous, naked, and exhausted, Odysseus emerges from the thicket with sufficient presence of mind and tact to reassure the princess, concluding his appeal for food and clothing with a blessing on her, her family, and most of all her future husband, and a remarkable encomium on the happiness of a good marriage. Far from being a seducer, Odysseus ignores Nausicaa's rather pointed remarks about what a fine husband he would make.

While the more obvious pattern of Homeric allusions throughout the temptation scene suggest that Satan is another disingenuous, smooth-talking flatterer like Odysseus, the Nausicaa identification suggests the ways in which Satan contravenes the values that Odysseus embodies. Mil-

ton, in a memorable simile in Book 4, compares him to a rapacious wolf invading a sheepfold, thus adapting Homer's simile at the moment when his hero emerges from the thicket, like a ravening lion prowling around a steading for cattle or sheep, "for need drives him." Resolved to ruin Eve's "harmless innocence," Satan, "with Necessity, / The Tyrant's plea, excus'd his devilish deeds." The resemblance between the situations of Odysseus and Satan is enforced by the possible influence on Milton's wording of Spondanus's translation, "Necessitas enim urgebat." Yet surely the point of the comparison is that Odysseus is *not* Satan, and Satan is not Odysseus. It is much nearer the truth to think of Satan as misapplying and perverting the gifts and virtues of Odysseus,

> So little knows
> Any, but God alone, to value right
> The good before him, but perverts best things
> To worst abuse, or to thir meanest use.
> (4. 201ff.)

One final indication that Milton is not using allusions to the *Odyssey* only in a pejorative way is to be found in the vivid descriptive passage immediately preceding Satan's assault on Eve:

> Neerer he drew, and many a walk travers'd
> Of stateliest Covert, Cedar, Pine, or Palme,
> Then voluble and bold, now hid, now seen
> Among thick-wov'n Arborets and Flours
> Imborderd on each Bank, the hand of *Eve*:
> Spot more delicious than those Gardens feign'd
> Or of reviv'd *Adonis,* or renown'd
> *Alcinous,* host of old *Laertes'* Son
> Or that, not Mystic, where the Sapient King
> Held dalliance with his fair *Egyptian* Spouse.
> (9. 434ff.)

Two points are significant: (1) When Milton calls Paradise "Spot more delicious than those Gardens feign'd / Or of reviv'd *Adonis,* or renown'd / *Alcinous*" (thus alluding compactly to the entire tradition in epic and romance of the *locus amoenus*), he is not denigrating either the garden of Alcinous or the garden of Adonis but using their beauty to evoke the even greater beauty of Eden. (2) When Milton, in this prologue to his Odyssean tempter's first address to Eve, refers to "old Laertes' Son," the affectionate reference to Odysseus at this moment must be a reminder that we are *not* to take certain points of comparison between Satan and Odysseus as constituting a simple identification. Roy Daniells has spoken of Milton's power to "hold in one tense equilibrium his own strong instinct for individualistic revolt and his Christian submission to reasoned doctrine, to the revealed will of God." There is evidence, in Milton's Odyssean allusions in his presentation of Satan and in his allusions through Eve to both Helen and Nausicaa, of a larger equilibrium than any simple anti-heroic conception of him would allow.

In many ways the final and greatest flowering of the Renaissance in England, *PL* in one important respect represents a major departure from the epic tradition of the Renaissance, especially in its unallegorical and anti-allegorical nature. From post-Homeric times through the Middle Ages and well into the late Renaissance in England, allegory dominated critical views about how heroic poetry had been written and how it must be read. The notion that the epic poem served to convey mystically truths concealed from the vulgar had been for over twenty centuries a critical commonplace, culminating in such descriptions as Spenser's* "good discipline clowdilly enwrapped in Allegoricall devises" and Chapman's suggestion that wherever the narrative seems fantastic or impossible we must dive for allegorical meaning : "if the Bodie (being the letter, or historie) seems fictive, and beyond Possibilitie to bring into Act, the sence then and Allegorie (which is the Soule) is to be sought which intends a more eminent expressure of Vertue, for her lovelinesse, and of Vice for her uglinesse, in their severall effects, going beyond the life than any Art within life can possibly delineate."

J. W. H. Atkins has shown how the allegorical interpretation of Homer began in the sixth century B.C. with Theagenes and Anaxagoras as a defense against charges of impiety and immorality, the most famous of which was, of course, to be Plato's* attack on the poets in the *Republic*. Atkins implies that there was something casuistical in this reaction : "Philosophy, which had led the attack, provided also the main line of defence. Already among philosophers the idea had obtained currency that the earlier poets in their myths had concealed profound wisdom in enigmatic and symbolic fashion; and that by means of an allegorical interpretation it was possible to arrive at the real significance of the myths concerned" (*Literary Criticism in Antiquity* [1937], 1 : 14). According to Domenico Comparetti, Homer bore the brunt of this approach :

> Allegory was applied by the ancients to mythology generally and to the language of the poets particularly, as these latter formed, in the absence of a religious code, the only written authority for the common faith. . . . For those who were anxious to find documentary authority for the common beliefs, no other writers could have the weight of Homer, whether on account of his prehistoric antiquity or the marvellous power of his genius or the character and national importance of his poems. (*Virgil in the Middle Ages* [1895].)

In the Christian era pagan literature continued to be read (there was no orthodox literature, except the Bible, of equal quality and interest), and the allegorical approach continued to preserve it from censure. Ovid* was an especially interesting case, as Davis Harding has shown, because it was believed that in his accounts of the creation of the world in *Metamorphoses* 1 he had in some way had access to a version of Genesis. In this way Ovid became *moralisé*. But there were impieties in Homer that no scriptural authority could explain away, such as the seduction of Zeus by Hera in *Iliad* 14. Pope has summed up the attempts to save this passage by an allegorical approach :

> In the next place, if we have recourse to Allegory (which softens and reconciles everything) it may be imagin'd that by the

Congress of *Jupiter* and *Juno,* is meant the mingling of the *Aether* and the *Air* (which are generally said to be signify'd by these two Deities). The Ancients believ'd the *Aether* to be Igneous, and that by its kind influence upon the Air it was the Cause of all Vegetation: putting forth her Flowers immediately upon this Congress.

PL is founded on a wholly different conception of truth from that embodied in the allegorical tradition. Throughout the poem Milton insists on the reality of the events he is telling as distinguished from the "feigned" truths of his epic predecessors. As Basil Willey puts it, the fact that Milton "was able to believe in his own subject matter as 'real' as well as 'typical' was due . . . to his sharing of Protestant confidence in the authority of Scripture. That he did so believe in his own high argument is evident . . . from the fact that the poem as a whole does not read like allegory."

Oddly enough Milton's "materialism" puts him much closer to Homer than to most of the intervening epic writers, including Virgil, Ovid, Ariosto*, Tasso*, and Spenser. Milton's world has a "solidity of specification" that we certainly do not find in these others, not even in the steady Roman, whose apparently solid world is repeatedly shaken by the most extravagant kinds of magic (namely, the metamorphosis of Aeneas's ships or the attack by the Harpies or the strange wonders of the bleeding cornel plant into which Polydorus has been transformed). Perhaps Homer's gods are more solidly anthropomorphic than those of subsequent epic writers; at any rate Homer's mortals exhibit a degree of realism and psychological verisimilitude that brings us very close to Milton. The predominant pattern of allusions in *PL* is Homeric and Milton himself, in *CD,* suggested that the issue of *PL,* man's freedom and his moral responsibility, is also the central issue of the *Odyssey*:

Whoever has paid attention to what has been urged, will easily perceive that the difficulties respecting this doctrine have arisen from want of making the proper

distinction between the punishment of hardening the heart and the decree of reprobation; according to Prov. xix. 3. *the foolishness of man perverteth his way, and his heart fretteth against Jehovah.* For such things do in effect impugn the justice of God, however vehemently they may disclaim the intention; and might justly be reproved in the words of the heathen Homer:

> . . . they perish'd self-destroy'd
> By their own fault.

And again, in the person of Jupiter:

> Perverse mankind! whose wills, created free,
> Charge all their woes on absolute decree:
> All to the dooming gods their guilt translate,
> And follies are miscall'd the crimes of fate.
> (14:175)

The implications of this reference at the center of Milton's discussion of man's free will* and moral responsibility are momentous. For one thing, it shows that Milton saw the *Odyssey* as a theodicy, justifying the ways of God to men, and in this he followed Spondanus, who observed of the words of Zeus quoted by Milton,

This passage is elegant and worthy not only of a Gentile but of a Christian man. Under the guise of Jove's speech the poet declares that the cause of the evils which befell men is not to be traced to God but to the iniquities and dishonesties in man himself.

(Zeus's words occur at the divine conclave with which the action of the *Odyssey* begins. Such a conscious allusion as this, furthermore, shows that Milton was much less systematically anti-heroic than recent excellent studies of Milton's anti-heroic attitudes would suggest. The balance needs to be redressed to permit us to see the many ways in which Milton adapted the heroic tradition to express or enhance various moral and spiritual values at the heart of *PL.* This has been done in the cases of Ovid and Virgil by Davis Harding and others, but the Miltonic view of Homer requires fuller and more precise exploration. [GdeFL]

HOOKER, RICHARD. Hooker (ca. 1554–1600) was the author of *The Laws of Ecclesiastical Polity,* the principal sixteenth-century defense of the Elizabethan Settlement and "the first great original prose work in English" (J. W. C. Wand, *Anglicanism in History and Today*). Hooker pursued a quiet career, first as a professor of Hebrew at Corpus Christi College, Oxford, and later in holy orders. His appointment as Master of the Temple initiated the most significant incident of his life, a theological dispute with Walter Travers, Calvinist* afternoon lecturer at the Temple. Travers was silenced by Archbishop Whitgift for the extremism of his position, but the greater popularity of Travers's arguments constrained Hooker to develop the position of the Church of England in *The Laws of Ecclesiastical* Polity (Bks. 1–4, 1594; 5, 1597; 6 and 8, 1648; 7, 1662).

The general principles of this work accord more closely with the pronouncements of Milton than do some of its specific elaborations. Hooker's belief in free will* and the general importance of right reason* coincides almost exactly with Milton's. On the importance of obedience* of creatures to the law of nature*, with its implication of hierarchy, Milton differs only in denying the inevitable and sanctified position of rulers.

In the establishment of church doctrine Hooker gives a somewhat less exclusive authority to Scripture than Milton, finding less scriptural treatment of issues. Milton comments that "Scripture is the sole judge of controversies," and pointedly supplies scriptural quotation for almost all his statements. Hooker, on the other hand, finds Scripture occasionally not explicit, whereupon he turns to reason. Milton uses reason alongside Scripture but asserts that in "sublime" matters "above our reason" "belief must be founded, not on mere reason, but on the word of God exclusively" (14 : 217). Hooker finds authority also in the practice of antiquity (5 : vii), whereas Milton says that "the opinions of our forefathers" are not to be trusted (16 : 281).

Hooker believes in the subordination of local churches to the bishops (3 : 14, 18) and is an Erastian*, whereas Milton believes in the independence of these churches, placing them under the authority of "lay elders and ordained pastors, free both of bishops and state control." This position, taken in the antiprelatical pamphlets, gives way ultimately to an emphasis on the rightful duty of the individual to search Scripture (16 : 265) and in effect to become his own church (16 : 241). On incidental matters of church service Hooker takes a traditional stance, whereas Milton is either silent or Puritan.

Significantly, though Hooker was an apologist for Tudor political absolutism, his conception of the law of nature led him to the principle of contract and the right of the people to call their princes to account. Though he never carried this so far as Milton's argument that tyrants might be deposed, his ultimate political influence was in the direction of liberalism. [EFD]

HOPE. Hope, according to traditional teachings derived from St. Paul, is the second of the theological virtues* (1 Cor. 13 : 13), a virtue that is based on the first : "Now faith* is the substance of things hoped for, the evidence of things not seen" (Heb. 11 : 1). In his *Christian Dictionary* (1612) Thomas Wilson gave his definition of hope as "a certaine and undoubted expectation or looking for of al promised good thinges which bee to come, but namely of heavenly blessednes, being freely given us of God, and grounded upon his infinit mercies, and Christs merites alone." Wilson gave a distinctly Protestant note to his definition in stating that "Christians build their Hope upon the mercies of God in Christ; Papists, upon Gods grace* and their owne merits." Milton in *CD* treats of hope in the course of his discussion of the virtues concerned with internal worship; such worship is defined as the acknowledgment of the one true God and the cultivation of "devout affections" toward him, the latter consisting of love of God, trust, hope, gratitude, fear, humility, patience, and obedience*. The discussion is highly compressed, but it has traces of the traditional teachings concerning the progression from faith to hope and charity*. After explaining the nature of the love of God, Milton refers to what he has said elsewhere about faith and then proceeds to consider trust and hope. The distinction between the two seems to lie in the fact that the former is the immediate effect of love of God whereby we "repose" in him, while hope is a further development to which certitude is added: "Hope is that by which we expect with certainty the fulfillment of God's promises" (17 : 57). Of the other "devout affections," patience has some aspects traditionally associated with hope, including as it does a confident reliance on divine providence* rather than mere trust in oneself.

Hope is opposed by despair*, a sin that arises from sloth in the face of a spiritual or moral imperative. Don Cameron Allen sees despair, along with unbelief and hatred of God, as among Satan's master sins; despair receives a preponderant amount of attention because it is the sin* that is most likely to infect man. Satan reveals his despair in the initial exchanges with Beelzebub (1. 125–26, 183–91) and at the opening of the infernal council (2. 6–10)—a fact commented upon by the Father* (3. 85). This despair again comes to the fore at his first sight of Eden (4. 32–113, especially 4. 23–24, 73–78, and the authorial comment in 4. 115, 155–56). Despair is aroused when he views the Son approaching in battle (6. 785–87). Satan's principal followers share his despair, as is obvious in the case of Moloch (2. 45, 92–93) and unacknowledged but equally present in Belial and Mammon. Despair is among the reactions of Adam and Eve when called to account by God (10. 111–13). Adam gives way to a death wish (10. 771–78) and Eve suggests suicide (10. 1001–6), but eventually the pair develop a Christian response to their guilt. In *SA* the temptation to despair and the triumph of Christian hope is a dominant theme (*The Harmonious Vision* [1954], pp. 71–94). [RF]

HOPKINS, GERARD MANLEY (1844–1889), English Jesuit poet. Hopkins was strongly influenced by Milton. Sister M. Aquinas Healy (*University of Toronto Quarterly* 22 : 18–25) points out that no fewer than seventy-four references to Milton exist in Hopkins's letters, journal, notebooks, and papers, almost all of which concern the poetic excellency and particular versification* techniques of Milton. Although Hopkins thought Milton "a very bad man" (because of his views on divorce*), he recognized the poet's greatness, placing him above Homer*, Dante*, and Shakespeare*. Partly in *PL*, more fully in *PR* ("an advance in his art"), and most fully in the choruses* of *SA*, Hopkins saw Milton employing counterpoint ("two different coexisting scansions"). To him Milton was only one step from simple sprung rhythm, a step he could not take because of critics and previous poetic practice. Of the choruses, Hopkins says: "In reality, they are sprung, but Milton keeps up a fiction of counterpointing the heard rhythm . . . upon a standard rhythm which is never heard but only counted and therefore really does not exist" (*Letters to Robert Bridges*, pp. 45–46). Although Hopkins says he strove for a "more balanced and Miltonic style," critics have been split on the question of influence. Charles Williams thought Milton the best key to an understanding of Hopkins, but others, such as E. E. Phare and Terence Heywood, have seen no relation at all between the two. The question seems to be whether Hopkins read Milton through the eyes of a student or a critic. [WM]

HOPKINS, JOHN: *see* ADAPTATIONS.

HOPKINSON, FRANCIS: *see* MILTON IN AMERICA.

HORACE. The son of a freedman, Quintus Horatius Flaccus (65 B.C.–8 B.C.)

was born at Venusia in southern Italy and educated at Rome and Athens. Despite his championship of the republican cause during the civil wars (he was an officer at the battle of Philippi), he subsequently enjoyed the friendship and/or patronage of prominent members of the emperor's circle : Maecenas, Agrippa, Messalla, Pollio. It was to the first of these that he owed his Sabine farm. His literary friends included Virgil* and Tibullus. His principal works were the *Sermones* (or Satires), the *Odes* and *Epodes* (many of them reflecting a close study of Greek lyric poets and their metrical conventions), the *Epistles,* the *Carmen Saeculare,* and the *Epistula ad Pisones* (the *Ars Poetica*). As a theorist he advocated the judicious imitation of Greek models, careful observation of decorum in matter and style, and the addition of conscious art and industry to natural talent or inspiration. Arguing that the poet could be (as Homer* was) a more effective teacher of morality than the philosophers of the schools, he maintained that the best poet combines utility and pleasure. His own poetry exemplifies many of these principles, including his dictum that it is "art to conceal art."

As a moralist, Horace frequently exploits both Epicurean and Stoic *topoi* —utilizing both with such restraint that they do not appear inconsistent. Extolling strenuous virtue and condemning ignoble ease in one poem, he may celebrate the tranquil enjoyment of rural, yet learned, leisure in the next. Speaking with both a public and a private voice, he can exalt civic patriotism, the martial and political virtues, and the destiny of Rome or (alternatively) the superiority of a quiet mind to the cares of city and camp. He often takes the simpler, traditional mores of ancient Rome as a standard for censuring contemporary society. He writes (like Milton) for a select audience, despising the crowd ("profanum vulgus").

Horace was a standard author in many English grammar schools of the Renaissance. Erasmus* had included him in the course of study outlined in the *De ratione studii,* which John Colet chose as a plan for St. Paul's School*. The library at St. Paul's contained a copy of Lambinus's annotated edition, and Milton could, as D. L. Clark suggests in *John Milton and St. Paul's School,* have read Horace in this text or possibly in the edition by John Bond.

References to Horace or echoes of his poetry recur throughout Milton's poetry and prose. In *Educ* he includes Horace among authorities on the sublime art of poetry. From the *Ars Poetica,* as from Aristotle's* *Poetics* and the commentaries of Italian Renaissance critics, students may learn the laws of the poetic genres, the cardinal principle of decorum, and "what religious, what glorious and magnificent use might be made of Poetry both in divine and humane things" (4 : 286). In *PR* 4.345, the condemnation of the poetry of Greece as "thin sown with aught of profit or delight" recalls the "prodesse aut delectare" of the *Ars Poetica.* The statement in the preface to *SA,* "It suffices if the whole Drama be found not produc't beyond the fift Act," similarly recalls the *Ars Poetica,* "Neve minor neu sit quinto productior actu/ Fabula," though this concept had, of course, become a Renaissance critical commonplace.

Milton's translation of *Odes* 1. v (*Quis multa gracilis te puer in Rosa*) was first printed in the 1673 edition of his *Poems.* Estimates of its date of composition range from about 1626 to 1653; see the discussions by John Shawcross in *Studies in English Literature* 3 and Douglas Bush in *Variorum* 2. In this translation (1 : 69) Milton endeavored to render the Latin original "almost word for word without Rhyme according to the Latin Measure, as near as the Language will permit." In *Apol* he translates passages from Horace's *Satires* 1. i and x. *El* 6 mentions Horace as the Roman poet who drenched his songs in wine and sang of Glycera and Chloe. *Areop* emphasizes the fact that the "satirical sharpness or naked plainness" (4 : 301) of Horace and other Latin satirists had not been prohibited by any official order. Direct quotations from Horace occur in 7 *Prol, CPow, CD, Famil,* and all three *Defences.* The allusion to Canidia in 1 *Prol* recalls *Epodes* 3, 5, and 17.

Horatian echoes have been noted by Merritt Y. Hughes and other commentators in *El4, EpDam, AdP, May, Mask, Rous,* and *Shak,* as well as in *PL, PR,* and *SA.* It has been suggested that Belial's phrase "His red right hand" (*PL* 2. 174) has been derived from Horace's "rubente dextera" (*Odes* 1. ii), and thus involves a conscious parallel between Jehovah and Jove. Analogies between the vine-and-elm imagery of both poets and their accounts of Empedocles' suicide in hope of being "deemd / A God" may involve indirect allusion to Horace, though they are, in fact, commonplaces. More significant are the Horatian themes, attitudes, and mannerisms that characterize several of Milton's sonnets, especially those addressed to Fairfax, Cromwell, Vane, Lawrence, and Cyriack Skinner (*Sonn* 15, 16, 17, 20, 21). In the opinion of John S. Smart (*The Sonnets of Milton*) *Sonn* 20 and 21 suggest "the Horatian ode as a literary model." Marjorie Nicolson (*John Milton: A Reader's Guide*) detects in *Sonn* 20 the form of "invitation to a friend" in the pattern established by Horace in *Epistles* 1. ix, and in *Sonn* 21 she finds the Horatian "pattern of admonition to the young. . . ." (She also regards *Nat* as "more Horatian than Pindaric or Anacreontic. . . ."). [RCF]

HORACE, THE FIFTH ODE OF:
Milton's sixteen-line translation from Horace's first book of odes first appeared in *Poems, &c. upon Several Occasions* (1673). Scholars disagree as to its date of composition, with suggestions ranging from Milton's grammar-school period to 1646–1648. In his biography of Milton, William Riley Parker assigned it, albeit tentatively, to 1629 on the ground that its subject matter of unrequited love harmonized with other poems that Milton was writing at that time (*Milton,* 2 : 745–46). More convincing is John

Shawcross's attempt at dating. The poem's omission from the 1645 edition of Milton's works; its Latin text, which does not seem to have appeared before 1636; and especially its place in the order of the poems in the 1673 edition—all suggest to Shawcross late composition, probably around 1646–1648 (*Studies in English Literature* 3 : 77–84). Parker objected to these dates on the ground that he could not imagine "the mature Milton, in his first years of parenthood, fascinated by Pyrrha and her fatal charms. If the translation was done by a man who in 1648 . . . was translating psalms for spiritual consolation, then perhaps some of the continental Miltonians have been right in considering him a good subject for psychoanalysis" (*Milton,* p. 745). Shawcross's explanation, however —that the poem represents the same kind of metrical rendering that Milton was doing in those translations of the psalms— is not unreasonable (p. 81). Quite simply, Milton may have undertaken the translation because of the technical problems involved rather than because of the subject matter of youthful love.

The poem examines the plight of a youth enamored of the lovely Pyrrha and unaware—as is the older, more experienced author—of the fickle nature of women and the stormy course of love. Its nature as a translation and the technical problems that Milton faced are indicated by the headnote that he appended to it: *"Rendered almost word for word without Rhyme according to the Latin Measure, as near as the Language will permit."* He attempted, in other words, the extremely difficult task of writing English verse while using the rules of Latin prosody; and to a remarkable degree he succeeded, although in places he sacrificed sense to sound.

Critics in general have given the ode high praise. "Remarkably ingenious," "almost unbelievable perfection," "more Horatian . . . than Horace himself"—such phrases are representative of the critical reaction. Parker, on the other hand, considered it "a much overpraised poem" that "fails to catch the tone of the original and, worse, is poor poetry in its own right" (*Milton*, p. 57). Perhaps the most perceptive criticism of it is Davis P. Harding's, which examines both its fidelity as a translation and its foreshadowing of the metrical strategies of *PL*. In the ebb and flow of its verse, in its deliberate blurring of syntactical relationships, Harding finds clearly revealed "the degree of classical influence on Milton's mature style" (*The Club of Hercules* [1962], p. 128). [ERG]

HORTON, BUCKINGHAM, a country area about seventeen miles west of Westminster, where Milton's father resided from 1635 to 1641. Milton's mother died and was buried here in April 1637, and about a year later Milton went abroad and then resided in London upon his return. There is no evidence that he took up residence in London toward the end of 1637, although he had considered doing so. Frequently, however, he was in London during the years of his being in Horton. His brother Christopher and his wife, Thomasine, joined Milton's father at Horton around the end of 1637 and by spring 1638. In the past the Horton period of Milton's life was thought to have begun in 1632 after his graduation from Christ's College* and thus the location of his writing such poems as *Sonn* 7, *Arc* and *Mask*. Since this dating has been shown to be in error, the only poem that can be assigned to the Horton period with certainty is *Lyc* (November 1637). However, *Mask* seems to have been revised in autumn–winter 1637 and perhaps other works can be reassigned to this period of apparently renewed creativity. Further, if *AdP* dates in early 1638, it too falls into the Horton period. These years carry on the "studious retirement" begun at Hammersmith* in 1632–1635, and suggest that *CB* was begun during the Horton phase. It has likewise been argued that a more definite move toward the creative life occurred late in this period. Thus the Horton period represents in Milton biography a time of study, probably some definite planning for the future, and possibly action to insure success for such plans. [JTS]

HORWOOD, ALFRED J. (1821–1881). In 1874, Horwood discovered among the papers of Sir Frederick Graham a manuscript of the *CB* of Milton. He edited it, and published it in 1876 (Camden Society Publications) in facsimile and print, revising it in 1877. In his introduction, he deals with such problems as the various handwritings of the manuscript, a history of the document, and the text itself. Unfortunately, as James Holly Hanford pointed out, Horwood did his work with "little care" and left it incomplete in many particulars. While the text is fairly accurate, the "editorial work is in the highest degree unsatisfactory." Horwood failed to identify many of the works and authors cited; his list of parallels with Milton's published work is scanty. He did not distinguish the various amanuenses* properly, and, finally, he gave no idea of a chronology* of the individual entries, which Hanford in his essay attempts to do. [WM]

HOTMAN, FRANCIS (1524–1590), French jurist and Protestant who fled to Switzerland after the St. Bartholomew Massacre. Milton mentions Hotman's *Franco-Gallia* (1573) in *CB* (ca. 1642–1644), although he apparently had not seen it firsthand (he gives Thuanus's* *Historia* as his source). However, in *1Def* (and later *2Def*), he cites Hotman's work directly as an authority in arguing for limitation of power of kings. [WM]

HOWARD, SIR ROBERT: *see* ASSOCIATES, PERSONAL.

HOWARD, WILLIAM: *see* ADAPTATIONS.

HUGHES, MERRITT YERKES (1893–1971), important modern editor of Milton. Having received his doctorate from Harvard in 1921, Hughes soon became a member of the faculty at the University of Wisconsin, where he helped lead the English graduate program into national prominence. His most important contributions are editorial summaries that show wide learning and sound judgment, especially as they appear in his editions of *PL* (1935), the other poems (1937), the prose (1947), and finally the *Complete Poems and Major Prose* (1957), the most comprehensively annotated editions of their day and for many years the standard in the United States. The text that he established is probably at present the most frequently quoted one for the poetry. His scholarship is meticulous, and he never became identified with any one critical school. He was editor for volume 3 of the Yale *Prose*, including *Tenure, Peace,* and *Eikon*. He also was general editor of the Variorum Commentary on Milton's poems, and at the time of his death he had almost completed the work for the commentary on *PL*. [WBH]

HUMANISM, MILTON AND CHRISTIAN.

Like Renaissance, baroque*, and mannerism* (in literary criticism), humanism is one of those terms which open up a Pandora's box of disagreement among scholars, cultural historians, and literary critics. As with the terms mentioned above, there is no universal agreement on the precise nature, qualities, definition, and applicability of humanism, although there is general agreement on its broad nature. (The literal meaning of the term causes little controversy, unlike the literal meaning of baroque, for example, where even such minimal agreement cannot be taken for granted.) With Christian humanism the difficulties are compounded rather than diminished by an apparently qualifying adjective. For some scholars, all Renaissance humanism is essentially Christian (if not Catholic) and the prefatory adjective, Christian, is therefore superfluous, even redundant; for others, humanism is essentially pagan and the prefatory adjective is therefore misleading, fallacious, and a contradiction; for still others, it is neither pagan nor Christian, but "secular." In order to set Milton and his

position in perspective, therefore, this entry will be divided into two sections: 1) the historical and critical background and meaning of *humanism* in the Renaissance, together with an attempt to isolate what may be understood by *Christian humanism*, or a humanism that is inherently, even more than specifically, Christian; 2) Milton's place in the Christian humanist movement.

In the now dated but still classic study, *Early Tudor Poetry* (1920), John Berdan defined humanism as "a revival of interest in classical life and in classical literature" (p. 230). Berdan, of course, was concerned with humanism in its most basic sense as manifested in England during that "transitional" period signaled by the coming-to-power of the house of Tudor; but his definition will serve as a basic starting point.

Humanism, as we understand the word today in connection with that broad cultural/intellectual movement which is usually traced to fourteenth-century Italy and which came to England somewhat later (the late fifteenth century marks its beginnings in England, although its golden age in literature is generally thought of as the middle and late sixteenth century), had little or no currency as a meaningful term until the nineteenth century. Originally, the Italian term *umanista* (or *humanista*) merely meant a teacher of Latin whose particular emphasis was on the rhetorical aspects of the language. The implications of the term, however, were more extensive. Paul Oskar Kristeller, one of the foremost students of Italian Renaissance culture and philosophy, sees humanism, as it originated in Italy during the Italian Renaissance, as a cultural and literary movement that was not in its substance philosophical, but that had important philosophical implications and consequences (*Renaissance Thought, I: The Classic, Scholastic, and Humanist Strains* [1961]). This is not at variance with Berdan's brief definition cited above; for, according to Kristeller, what these early Italian humanists had in common was a belief in the "value of man" (a key notion, if an ambiguous one) as well as a belief in the revival of ancient learning.

As an educational movement one cannot properly label humanism Christian or non-Christian; it could be either, or even anti-Christian. There is nothing in the interest in the best of classical literature and Greek and Roman thought that need be inherently anti-Christian. Petrarch*, sometimes called the first humanist (if any one can properly be labeled "first" in such a movement), for example, was indeed interested in the literature and thought of Rome and Greece, in the recovery and preservation of manuscripts of these literatures. He even records his first meeting with Laura in his favorite copy of Virgil so that it may be in a place frequently perused; yet, Virgil shares a place with Augustine as his favorite author, and he objects to the Aristotelians of Padua not only because of their rough Latin (a cardinal sin for a true classical humanist) but because of their apparent atheism. Humanist and classicist that he was, Petrarch remained clearly, sometimes painfully, Christian.

What must be recognized about humanism, as it originally flourished in fourteenth- and fifteenth-century Italy—if one is to have a clear picture of Milton's place in the movement in England—is its essential character as an educational movement based on the study and the ideals of the literature and thought of ancient Greece and Rome. The early humanists believed that there was something to be learned about man and his place in the world—about man as man— from two of the great civilizations of the past, civilizations that were among the fountainheads of Western civilization itself. To say that the movement started primarily as an educational one (self-educational as well as "socially" educational) is not to say that it did not grow from this origin to take on other aspects. One of the most important points to recognize about humanism is that it did not, even in the Renaissance, mean exactly the same thing everywhere.

In Italy, at first, humanism focused on something as basic as the acquiring and preserving of classical manuscripts; it extended to the study of the works contained in these manuscripts, with a cultivation of the disciplines necessary to make such study meaningful; it expressed itself in a genuine concern to establish authentic texts, and, ultimately, it extended to a consideration and adaptation of the ideas and attitudes discernible in the classical writers, ideas not only about literature and composition, rhetoric* and poetry, but about life and living, and about the nature of life. If we are to follow the argument of Georg Voigt, whose classical study of humanism has been somewhat eclipsed by the work of the famous Jacob Burckhardt, the study of classical literature stimulated a self-consciousness in the early humanists and a concern with the meaning and value of human experience as individual rather than as collective experience. In Italy this study of classical values was frequently channeled into political and social theory and practice as much as possible, as well as into educational theory.

One factor about humanism as it began in Italy perhaps needs to be placed in perspective. Given the natural Italian temperament, the affinity for the sensuous, if not the sensual, one need not be surprised that one dominant direction of Italian humanism was toward the hedonistic, perhaps not so much toward what the moralist would label the immoral as toward the amoral. This is the understanding of humanism that frequently dominates in the popular conception; and in this sense the "value of man" as man was as a more or less purely physical being. It is a somewhat simplified notion to suggest that the difference between the Middle Ages and the Renaissance is the difference between the otherworldly view of man and a this-worldly view of man, between a sacred or religious and a secular outlook on life; simplified, because even in the Renaissance and through the Reformation the clear-cut distinction and categorization between secular and sacred, which is an accepted aspect of modern thought, was not so clear-cut, although the process of separation was underway. Nevertheless, if we recognize the simplification for what it is, this concise formula does describe the essential difference. For some—particularly in Italy—in the wake of the new-found interest in classical values and thought, the satisfaction of the flesh, the indulgence in the senses, particularly as seen in the more lavish periods of the Roman Empire, were the be-all and end-all of humanism. Humanism thus became an emphasis on the "human" in the most basic sense.

But this is by no means the whole story of humanism; and others saw a different definition for the "value of man" and for the meaning of being "human." Again, a classic example is Petrarch, who was a humanist, but whose inclinations, as he exercised them, were not in the direction of the hedonistic indulgence often facilely equated with Italian humanism in popular thought. At least—to qualify that a bit—his inclinations toward such indulgence were tempered by modifying influences that we might sum up under the heading "concern for the *relation* of present to transcendent values." The history of his love for Laura as celebrated in the *Rime* is the history of his psychological journey toward that reconciliation between the desires of the flesh and the needs of the spirit. This is manifest even in the patriotic and political poems interspersed throughout the *Rime;* for, in Petrarch, the humanist spirit finds utterance not only in the personal attitude but in the public man who shows his concern for political and social ethics, for the combination of the active and the contemplative lives. Just as Laura herself becomes the human who leads him, perhaps, to spiritual values, the state—the political realm—is the earthly city that one needs to make as perfect as possible.

What this reveals is a humanism that is not a cloistered virtue, a thing unto itself, but something that informs the self and *re-forms* it, so that it may affect the external world and teach it the way.

This, too, is humanism, and it has been summed up by a contemporary critic in terms not inapplicable to the Renaissance and Milton:

> a humanist is anyone who rejects the attempt to describe or account for man wholly on the basis of physics, chemistry, and animal behavior. He is anyone who believes that will, reason, and purpose are real and significant; that value and justice are aspects of a reality called good and evil and rest upon some foundation other than custom; that consciousness is so far from being a mere epiphenomenon that it is the most tremendous of actualities; that the unmeasurable may be significant; or, to sum it all up, that those human realities which sometimes seem to exist only in the human mind are the perceptions, rather than merely the creations of that mind. (Joseph Wood Krutch, *Human Nature and the Human Condition* [1959], p. 197).

In essence, this implies a reliance on an objective standard of conduct and the good, knowable by the human intellect and enforcible by the human will.

To sum up briefly: traditionally, humanism is regarded as an intellectual movement that found its first outlet in education and educational reform. Its spirit was drawn from a new and different interest in the literature and thought of ancient Greece and Rome, partly stimulated by the discovery of new, long-neglected texts and manuscripts. In general, it was an a-religious rather than an anti-religious manifestation, and even this generalization needs to be accepted with caution, for humanism may be seen as taking several forms, only one of which is the hedonistic, amoral approach to life that has often dominated the popular notion about Renaissance humanism in Italy.

As a balance to this popular conception, however, it might be well to remember that men such as Ficino and Pico della Mirandola were humanists; and perhaps in their work we see that strain which was to dominate in transalpine and English humanism, and which was so important for Milton. For these men, humanism represented education in a "re-integrative" sense, an infusion of the pagan past with the Christian present. Pico's analysis of the "value of man" shows us the direction in which humanism can and did go with Milton. It occurs most strikingly in his famous (undelivered) *Oration on the Dignity of Man*. Man, Pico tells us, has the power from God to degenerate into a beast or to be regenerated into higher, divine forms. This power comes from the judgment of man's soul ("ex tui animi sententia regenerari" is the original Latin). Later, Pico stresses that human contemplation of the world should recognize the Creator in the creature, and the creature in the Creator. What is most significant in this speech, however, and the issue that gives these remarks focus, is that it is basically a celebration of man's power of reason* as the divine gift or spark through which he elevates (or degrades) himself *willfully* (it is in this sense that we must understand the phrase "ex tui animi sententia"). To see creation* as a manifestation of God was hardly a new idea, even in the Renaissance; its origins go back to medieval thought, at least. To find the idea celebrated by Pico serves to emphasize not only the syncretic nature of his thought, but the technique of pouring old wine into new bottles, which is one aspect of humanism in the Renaissance. It is precisely this kind of continuity, with amplification, that gives substance to the view of those scholars who see the Renaissance as not so much a sharp break from the Middle Ages as a continuation and a development.

In stressing the role of will* and reason Pico is stressing an issue important for Renaissance humanism. As an educational movement, humanism was quite naturally concerned with some kind of reform. Education was to lead to reform (as well as constituting a reform in itself), and this was to be accomplished through the cultivation of human reason by knowledge; knowledge, in turn, was to move the will to action. In its concern with the past humanism also became, rather paradoxically, both a progressive

and a retrogressive movement, both liberal and conservative. For its concern was, in some sense, a *restoration* of things as they once were at their best—what Jan Huizinga has called "a return to old perfection and purity" (*In the Shadow of Tomorrow* [1936]). The humanists were concerned with acquiring and applying ancient wisdom and virtue to modern situations and reforms, for guidance and instruction. Humanism, by nature, involves a veneration of the past, but a veneration that seeks to apply the best of the past, the permanent and unchanging principles of human nature, to the present and the future; hence, Pico and Ficino see in Plato*, in the Cabbala, in the myths of the pagan gods, a wisdom not incompatible with Christian truth and wisdom. If we want a perfect encapsulation of the humanist creed, with a very explicit expression of the "value of man" with which it is concerned (and which Milton would have held), we need only look in the most famous play ever written: "What a piece of work is man! How noble in reason! how infinite in faculties! in form and moving how express and admirable! in action how like an angel! in apprehension how like a god! the beauty of the world, the paragon of animals" [*Hamlet* 2. 2].

Hamlet's famous statement raises the question of distinguishing humanism as Christian. In this, much depends on what one takes to be the true nature of man, what it means to be "human." For the kind of Renaissance thinker who saw the essential nature of man in terms similar to Hamlet's—that is, a *human* is a being who is part matter, part spirit, whose spiritual element is his better part and provides his link to God—then any education, any "thought" that ignored or neglected this aspect was *nonhumanistic, inhumane*. The spiritual element in man was evident in his power to reason, a function of his soul, God's "viceroy" in man, as Donne called reason in one of his sonnets. This is why "reason" became such an important consideration for those humanists whom we label "Christian."

Perhaps Jacques Maritain best describes this kind of humanism in contrast with the more popular notion of humanism as hedonistic, when he distinguishes two kinds of humanism: a theocentric or Christian humanism, which recognizes that God is the center of man (God who manifested himself *as* man in Christ and thus demonstrated that man's corruption was capable of redemption); and an anthropocentric humanism, in which man believes that man is the center of man and of all things (*Integral Humanism, Temporal and Spiritual Problems of a New Christendom* [1968]). These are at least two species of the genus *humanism*; both draw their inspiration from the literature and thought of classical times, at least in part. Whereas the latter concentrates on that literature and thought as a code of externals, a prescription for enjoying the body and the flesh (hence, one definition of *human-ism*) for its own sake, the former, or Christian humanism, saw such literature and thought in a new light: as part of the unbroken tradition of "reason" in the world. True, it represents reason without the privilege of revelation, but it was an aspect of reason nevertheless. For this brand of humanism, reason was the key to education, and hence classical literature and thought were important. They showed what reason could achieve without revelation, thus demonstrating the essential spiritual source of such reason. With the addition of revelation, man should be capable of much more, if he was capable of so much without it. Education, through reason, was a way, an intellectual discipline (and *intellectual* discipline was uniquely *human*) by which man could improve his corrupt nature.

Humanism in its Christian manifestation is perhaps more specifically (though not exclusively) a northern phenomenon. While it is orthodox to trace the beginnings of humanism to Renaissance Italy, it is customary to see this humanism given its most Christian emphasis when it crossed the Alps. The important figure in this respect—important for European humanism and for Milton in general—is Erasmus*. If any one person has been credited with integrating a potentially nonreligious (or nonethical) movement with Christian tradition and values, or —if one accepts the thesis, to be described below, that humanism is by nature Christian and basically a continuation of a medieval synthesis—with bringing out the essential relation between humanism and Christianity, it is Erasmus. In the face of the crumbling unity of Christendom that he beheld, Erasmus felt that only a Christianized classical learning could restore any semblance of unity. His theory centered on the Roman notion of the classical period, that an education based on the finest in literature and thought led to virtue or "integrity of life." Erasmus attempted to Christianize this theory by bringing together sacred and *humane* literature in the educative experience, by showing that classical literature, properly understood, contained a truth basically harmonious with Christian truth, in much the same way as the Florentine Neoplatonists* attempted to show that Plato*, Plotinus*, and such exotic and esoteric writers as Hermes Trismegistus*, contained a truth that demonstrated the essential truth of Christianity. These earlier writers—before revelation and the coming of Christ—were steps along the way, enlightened attempts; as such, they were clear demonstrations of the power of reason as an enlightened and enlightening force—that power which most made man *human*—for truth. The pagan writers of antiquity, then, were far from being models, in their writings, for a hedonistic life-style. The true humanist was the man who could study their writings in an effort to find their exact meaning, just as he was to try to study the Bible. If he interpreted them accurately, he would derive from them the true philosophy of Christ. What the true humanist could find from pagan classical literature was an assertion, even an exemplification, of the dignity of man. It was this concern, this focus, that made a humanist Christian. James Holly Hanford has stated it succinctly:

The essential character of that humanism is its assertion of the spiritual dignity of man, its recognition of the degree to which his higher destinies are in his own hands, its repudiation of the claim of his lower nature to control his higher or of any force or agency external to his own mind and will to achieve for him salvation. This humanism is sharply and irreconcilably at odds with mediaeval thought. It discards, first of all, the ascetic principle and releases for enjoyment and use all the agencies of self-realizing perfection. It proposes, moreover (and this is its essential character) to achieve its goal through the study not of God but of man and it trusts the human reason as well as intuition and revealed truth as the instrument of its knowledge. It turns, therefore, to Scripture for the best record of man's nature in its relation to the God of righteousness and love, then to the *litterae humaniores* of antiquity, where it finds a wider revelation of man as an individual and a citizen, this latter source constituting no denial but a completion of the data afforded by the former (*John Milton Poet and Humanist* [1966], pp. 179–80).

Although not every analyst of Christian humanism would accept Hanford's contention that it is "sharply and irreconcilably at odds with medieval thought," most would agree, at least, that the difference between Renaissance thought and medieval thought on this point is centered in the turn from asceticism, from an emphasis on God and spirit to the neglect of man and the flesh, to an emphasis on man and the flesh *as they look toward God and spirit.*

While the *Christian* aspect of *Christian humanism* should now be obvious, at least in the abstract, one cannot oversimplify. As was suggested earlier, not every scholar accepts humanism as a Christian phenomenon in any sense; some (as already indicated) accept Christian humanism as one aspect of the whole, larger spectrum of humanism. There is one group, however, that sees humanism as inherently Christian and, in fact, as representing not a break with the Middle Ages (as Hanford states) but a continuity of one line of development in the Middle Ages, perhaps a fulfillment of that line in which Milton is the last great exponent. The

principal figure in this group is Douglas Bush, closely followed, though not in every detail, by Herschel Baker and Hiram Haydn, among others. In *The Renaissance and English Humanism* (1939) Bush, following to some extent the lead of the Italian scholar Giuseppe Toffanin (who saw humanism as essentially Christian, and as old as the Church Fathers), sees Renaissance humanism as an extension of medieval thought, medieval Christian thought: ". . . in the Renaissance the ancient pagan tradition (which does not mean neo-paganism), with all its added power, did not overthrow the medieval Christian tradition; it was rather, in the same way if not quite to the same degree as in the Middle Ages, absorbed by the Christian tradition" (p. 34).

Bush's definition of Christian humanism (which, for him, is synonymous with *humanism* itself) is famous: "Humanism in the Renaissance normally means Christian faith in alliance with God-given reason, which is the most human faculty and thought which keeps man in union with God and above the biological level. It opposes both the irreligious scientific rationalism which would separate man from the divine, and the ethical or unethical naturalism—often the eldest child of rationalism—which would link him with the beasts" (pp. 54–55). In Bush's view, Renaissance humanism is a carryover of what he calls the medieval fusion of classical wisdom with Christian faith. The only real change he sees between the Middle Ages and the Renaissance and later is that, starting in the Renaissance, the classical element, philosophically and aesthetically, became a less inferior partner.

Bush has been followed in his thesis about humanism as an essentially Christian phenomenon representative of a continuity rather than a break with the Middle Ages, by Hiram Haydn and Herschel Baker. Haydn's not uncontroversial position (in *The Counter-Renaissance* [1950]) labels what is called above the hedonistic or anthropocentric version of humanism (including the irreligious, naturalistic tendencies), the "Counter-Renaissance," thus reserving, as Bush does, the term *humanism* for the intellectual movement that wedded reason and faith*, philosophy* and religion*; and that Haydn too suggests does not represent an open revolt from medieval tradition but a continuation with a shift in the major areas of interest. This shift, according to Haydn, was away from abstract logic* and theorizing to a focus on humane letters, which were to promote an ethical* education "intended to develop virtuous men and rounded citizens, rather than a theological education directed to the contemplation of the wonders of God's creation and the exposition of his universal laws." This "practical learning . . . found its final good in the exercise of right reason in virtuous action on this earth." In relation to this last point, it is Haydn who most explicitly and concisely makes the distinction between that kind of humanism we can label *Christian* and the non-Christian variety. Christian humanism relates man's activities here on earth, that is, his *human* activities, to a transcendent end. The *humanistic* aspect of the total concept lies in finding human, earthly, activities good and valuable (unlike the trend of medieval asceticism); but—and this is an important qualification—that it finds them good and valuable not simply for their own sake but ultimately for the sake of man's spiritual, eternal destiny is the Christian dimension of such humanism : Christian, because this eternal destiny and its relation to man was seen in terms of the act whereby God became man in the person of Christ and thus, in effect, gave a new sanction to humanity and human reason that it had not enjoyed since the Fall*. Again, the strong emphasis is on the use of right reason.

For the Christian humanist, not only classical literature, but all literature became part of the educative process, a means to an end. Broadly, that end was to promote morality, "right living," or, in other words, proper *human* behavior

now in the perspective of the eternity that would face one *then*. Sidney, himself a Christian humanist of considerable influence, perhaps encapsulated the aesthetic of the Christian humanist's attitude toward literature and its function in his discussion of the "right" poet; and Spenser*, whom Milton thought a better teacher than Aquinas*, not only exemplifies Sidney's "program," but illustrates *how* a poet can teach through literature, in a way that Milton was to admire and imitate to some degree. The knights, and most of the characters in *The Faerie Queene,* in spite of its allegorical* structure, do not simply *stand for* abstraction and virtues; they are exemplifications of *human* characters in action in the world; and their behavior illustrates, actively, the nature of man as a creature part spirit, part beast. What we watch, and are moved by, is active virtue in operation in the journey of life. This is a type of literature, the function of which is not at odds with that of humanistic education : education taught the principles of virtuous action; "right" literature illustrated those principles in convincing action so as to move the soul, to enlighten the reason to the possibilities of right choice.

What Christian humanists, both as thinkers and authors of imaginative literature, emphasized most strongly in their concentration on reason was the idea of choice. The right choice was important; and toward helping man to *know* the right choice and to make that choice, the Christian humanist aimed all of his intellectual, imaginative, persuasive, and rhetorical powers. Literature was, indeed, to give *pleasure,* but right literature gave pleasure not only (or merely) as a kind of sensual titillation, but as an intellectual, rational stimulation that was to appeal to that which made man man, or human: in particular, to his reason, which not only enabled him to understand, to some degree, the purposes and nature of God, but also empowered him to choose the patterns of life on this earth that were consistent with "virtue," with an objective and transcendent standard of good and evil* for which he would be rewarded or punished in the next life. In this sense, all of the literature of Christian humanism was "didactic."

In brief and general fashion, let us now attempt to establish Milton's place in the tradition of Christian humanism, as described above, with an overview of his work and career. Many of the characteristics of Christian humanism are obvious in Milton's career and work : the wide range of reading and learning in both classical and biblical/theological literature. Indeed, he may well be the most formally "learned" of all English poets (if such distinctions are of any importance); and he never seemed to cease to extend his learning in line with the humanistic sense that learning and knowledge lead to virtue. Something of this humanistic attitude may be seen, for example, in his letter to Lukas Holste* in 1639 (*Epistol* 10). Writing to this scholar to thank him for his kindness during a trip to the Vatican, Milton talks with that fervor and love of manuscripts and books which was one of the characteristics of basic humanism as early as Petrarch. He is thankful for being permitted to browse through numerous Greek authors in manuscript—some of them still not in print—and annotated by Holste. The letter is infused with that spirit of reverence, not for books as physical objects, but as records of human thought and wisdom. Milton's *CB*, too, particularly under such entries as "Of the Knowledge of Literature," reveals the wide-ranging interest of the humanist both in his reading and in his concerns for those aspects of life which are focused on human conduct and values in relation to virtue. Virtually all of Milton's prose, polemical in character and spirit as it is, is an attempt to promote what we might call humanistic reform in a broad sense : an education in "right" attitudes and public, civic conduct. In every case these treatises are attempts to posit, through a reasoned

examination of facts and attitudes, some kind of objective norm of conduct, whether in personal life or political/public life, that is in line with a standard of "virtue."

Even *CD*, doctrinal as it may seem to be, is a genuine attempt to use enlightened reason and knowledge as applied to biblical texts—interestingly enough, much of the strength of *CD* (originally in Latin, the standard language of humanist Europe) comes from its application of the mind to a consideration of the *text* of the Bible. Not unlike Erasmus before him, Milton is not only making a case for applying human knowledge to the word of God, but he is simultaneously examining critically what is taken for the word. What is the real text is a question implicitly raised in *CD*. The attempt to decide on an authentic text of the Scripture—so important an issue with earlier humanists, and particularly with Erasmus—is part of an attempt at an enlightened examination of the meaning and implications of that text. The polemics that occupied such an important period of Milton's life and constitute a major area of his total literary work are, on the whole, examples of Christian humanism in action, not so much in an attempt to establish God's kingdom on earth (though he may have had some sort of hope in that direction before his disillusionment with the Commonwealth) —as a true Christian humanist, Milton realized God's kingdom could no longer be established on earth—as in an attempt to institute a God-*like* kingdom on earth.

If the polemical, reformatory (by intention, at least) prose was a direct call for personal and institutional reform consistent with the Christian humanistic concern for a return to true, enduring values, Milton's poetry is never less than an attempt to establish, through the aesthetic experience, the true "value of man," both to mankind in general and to the individual reader in particular; to give some vision of himself and the possibilities open to him as a "human" under the eternal law of providence. Few poets have had such a self-conscious sense of mission and of the poet's role as an instrument of reform and truth through art. His whole life, his sense of vocation, and the direction of his poetry, even from the earliest paraphrases of the Psalms, are an embodiment of the Christian humanist sense that art has a direction, a purpose—a Christian purpose. Call it social reform through affective means, or self-reform through the cultivation of a rational sensibility, but it all had to do with helping man to realize his place and his role in the scheme of creation, and more specifically, in the dispensation offered by the coming of Christ.

This is not to suggest that Milton wrote religious or theological tracts in the guise of poetry, but to say that the very nature and texture of his poetry, its *end,* involve an assertion of the spiritual nature and dignity of man. As Hanford says:

> He retains . . . certain fundamental postulates and assurances in common with mediaeval Christianity. He is convinced of God, of the fact of evil, of the inevitableness of retribution, and of the hope of Heaven. These postulates are the postulates not of Puritanism alone but of the total humanism of the Renaissance. They are absolutely vital to Milton's thought . . .

> The real "system" which Milton erects is not a theology but an interpretation of experience, based on the bed rock of human freedom, and formulated under the guiding influence of the Bible, the ancients, and the thinkers and poets of the preceding generation. (p. 180)

Milton gives voice to his Christian humanism in rather explicit terms in *RCG* when, speaking of his literary and polemical career, he compares himself to the writers of the past, but makes an important addition:

> I apply'd my selfe to that resolution which *Ariosto* follow'd against the perswasions of *Bembo,* to fix all the industry and art I could unite to the adorning of my native tongue; not to make verbal curiosities the end, that were a toylsom vanity, but to be an interpreter & relater of the best and sagest things among mine own Citizens throughout this Iland in the mother dialect. That what the greatest and choycest wits of *Athens, Rome,* or modern *Italy,* and those Hebrews of old did for their country, I, in my proportion *with this over and above, of being a Christian, might doe for mine.* (3:236; italics added)

Later, in the same work, he talks about poetry and inspiration, making the point that the kinds of ability discernible in inspired, divine poetry are characteristic of all *good* poetry because it has a specific function:

> But those frequent songs throughout the law and prophets beyond all these, not in their divine argument alone, but in the very critical art of composition may be easily made to appear over all the kinds of Lyrick poesy, to be incomparable. These abilities, wheresoever they be found, are the inspired guift of God rarely bestowed, but yet to some (though most abuse) in every Nation: and are of power beside the office of pulpit, to inbreed and cherish in a great people the seeds of virtu and publick civility, to ally the perturbations of the mind, and set the affections in right tune, to celebrate in glorious and lofty Hymns the throne and equipage of God's Almightinesse, and what he works, and what he suffers to be wrought with high providence in his Church, to sing the victorious agonies of Martyrs and Saints, the deeds and triumphs of just and pious Nations, doing valiantly through faith against the enemies of Christ, to deplore the general relapses of Kingdoms and States from justice and Gods true worship. Lastly, whatsoever in religion is holy and sublime, in virtu amiable, or grave, whatsoever hath passion or admiration in all the changes of that which is call'd fortune from without, or the wily suttleties and refluxes of mans thoughts from within, all these things with a solid and treatable smoothnesse to paint out and describe. Teaching over the whole book of sanctity and virtu through all the instances of example with such delight to those especially of soft and delicious temper who will not so much as look upon Truth herselfe, unlesse they see her elegantly dresst, that whereas the paths of honesty and good life appear now rugged and difficult, though they be indeed easy and pleasant, they would then appeare to all men both easy and pleasant though they were rugged and difficult indeed. (3:338–39)

The echoes of Spenser's letter to Ralegh, at the beginning of *The Faerie Queene,* in the final sentences above should not cause surprise. This describes precisely the humanistic methodology —the Christian humanistic methodology—that made Spenser a better teacher than Aquinas for Milton. In general, this passage asserts Milton's sense of the high function and end of poetry not simply as an expression of humanity, but as an expression of that humanity in the perspective of divine providence. This sense of poetry as a human educative instrument, in a broad sense, as an essential means of communicating divine wisdom in enlightening man's reason—no more evident than in the manner in which it infuses *PL*—may be seen as early as *AdP*, a poem that describes the function of the poet as a humanistic one. Literature —poetry—is a form of knowledge that shows us something of our spiritual nature :

> Nec tu vatis opus divinum despice carmen,
> Quo nihil aetheros ortus, et semina caeli,
> Nil magis humanam commendat origine mentem,
> Sancta Prometheae retinens vestigia flammae.
> Carmen amant superi, tremebundaque Tartara carmen
> Ima ciere valet, divosque ligare profundos,
> Et triplici duros Manes adamante coercet.
>   (17–23)

> (Do not despise divine song, the work of the poet-prophet,
> than which nothing preserves its heavenly origins, and
> the vestiges of heaven, nor more commends the human
> mind to its heavenly origin, retaining holy vestiges
> of the Promethean fire. The gods above love poetry,
> and poetry has the power to shake the trembling Tartaran
> deep, and to bind the gods of the deep, and to restrain
> the obstinate Shades of the dead with triple adamant.)

The young man who devotes a portion of his youth to retirement and study to prepare for a "mission" of poetry, a vocation by which he clearly expects to make a mark on society—to "educate"—is thus concerned with poetry (we might say, literature in general) as an affective instrument of control and reform in the context of the Christian culture (through classical expression) that is an essential part of his being. This is the very essence of Christian humanism as conceived in the Renaissance.

There are, however, three prose works that most clearly establish Milton's Christian humanism as a general aspect of his thought : *Prol* 7 (a defense of learning and knowledge), *Educ* (his own program for education), and *Areop,* which, in dealing with censorship and books, emphatically makes some assertions about man and his right to knowledge as well as his right of choice in using that knowledge.

In its contention that God gave man a divine spirit, an immortal, imperishable part of Himself, which is to return to heaven, Milton's *Prol* 7 takes its place next to Pico's *Oration* as a basic statement of the Christian humanistic position. But, more significant for the *humanistic* aspect of Christian humanism, is the position taken in that Prolusion that *both* the everlasting life *and* our life on earth must be taken into account in any consideration of human happiness. For Milton, in this Prolusion, there is an essential relation between life here on earth and Art, by which he means to some extent, learning and study, which enable man to know something about and to contemplate eternal life. With the notion that learning or knowledge is integrally connected with happiness in this life as well as in the next, that one is related to the other, Milton shows himself in the tradition of Christian humanism. The desire for knowledge Milton equates with a longing put into the human mind by God, a longing that is part of the great design that is to lead us to God's glory. What is essentially at issue here is the sense, characteristic of Christian humanism, that knowledge is virtue, or leads to virtue.

When—in this same Prolusion—Milton says that proper learning, approved by God for His glory and as a guide to happiness, must be joined with "integrity of life" and good character, he is voicing the Christian humanist idea of the artist as reformer through his art. The "voice" through which *PL* is transmitted is this character "of upright heart and pure" who is thus qualified and privileged to make us see things invisible to mortal sight. Milton recognizes the relationship between intellect and will in the achievement of virtue, a relationship codified at least as early as Aquinas, implicit in Sidney's* theory of the function of right poetry, and integral to Christian humanist thought: the Intellect illuminates and guides the Will, so that the right choice through knowledge is superior and more "human" than the right choice through ignorance. At an early and formative period in his career, this academic exercise suggests, Milton was firmly in the tradition of Christian humanism, and already saw his function as poet-prophet (as well as polemicist) to guide the will through enlightening the intellect.

The theory articulated in *Prol 7* is given a more practical turn in *Educ*. In its famous formulation of the purpose of education (or learning), this pamphlet takes into account man's twofold nature and the relation between life on earth and the life beyond:

> The end then of Learning is to repair the ruines of our first Parents by regaining to know God aright, and out of that knowledge to love him, to imitate him, to be like him, as we may the neerest by possessing our souls of true virtue, which being united to the heavenly grace of faith makes up the highest perfection. *But because our understanding cannot in this body found it self but on sensible things, nor arrive so clearly to the knowledge of God and things invisible, as by orderly conning over the visible and inferior creature, the same method is necessarily to be follow'd in all discreet teaching.* (4:277; italics added)

Education (and, like all Christian humanists, Milton considers literature as part of education) is not a useless program of acquiring facts for their own sakes. It is, according to Milton, essentially a liberal and *liberating* procedure in which the acquirement of true knowledge has a purpose commensurate with man's place in the scheme of creation. Its function is, in part, to nourish, through the powers of the intellect and the will, that divine spark, the soul, which God put in man.

While *Areop* is not a document that proclaims educational methodology and purposes in the explicit sense that *Educ* does, in the broad sense that it deals with man's right to know, to use his intellect to acquire knowledge through books, and his will to judge, to accept or to reject that knowledge, it *is* concerned with education. To rehearse the arguments of this classic defense of freedom of the press is not to the point here. What is to the point are the assumptions about the nature and purpose of knowledge that inform *Areop*. One of the basic premises of the work—indeed, the premise on which the argument against the impracticality of really attempting to suppress evil, is built—is the recognition of the fact of a fallen world. In such a world, evil is a fact of life that one cannot wish away. One learns to deal with it, to recognize it, to overcome it. The fact of a fallen world, one of the basic tenets of Christian humanism, is not one that leads to pessimism; instead, it leads to that desire to "reform" inherent in Sidney's conception of "right" poetry and its function, and in Spenser's *Faerie Queene*. Milton merely represents the most concentrated, most explicitly dedicated exponent of this notion: "what wisdom can there be to choose, what contenence to forbear, without the knowledge of evil? He that can apprehend and consider vice with all her baits and seeming pleasures, and yet abstain, and yet distinguish, and yet prefer that which is truly better, he is the true warfaring Christian." This is what makes man *man;* this is what makes him *human* for the Christian humanist: the ability to distinguish with knowledge (hence the value of learning), and most of all the ability to *choose,* "that he might see and know, and yet abstain." Proper choice is dependent on reason:

Many there be that complain of divin Providence for suffering *Adam* to transgress, foolish tongues! when God gave him reason, he gave him freedom to choose, for reason is but choosing. . . . We our selves esteem not of that obedience, or love, or gift, which is of force: God therefore left him free, set before him a provoking object, ever almost in his eyes; herein considered his merit, herein the right of his reward, the praise of his abstinence. Wherefore did he creat passions within us, pleasures round about us, but that that these rightly tempered are the very ingredients of virtu? (4:319)

PL represents the literary culmination of this spirit of Christian humanism. In a sense, it is a polemical poem, "to justify the ways of God to man"; and it is, too, a visionary view of history, man's earliest, most basic history: in fact, the history that made him "man." In both of these senses, it is a humanistic work: that is to say, a work with a serious purpose. We might see this serious purpose as a presentation not only of our origins, but of the origin of evil, of the reason for our "reason," and of the importance of that reason and choice. What the poem presents in the "fiction" of an inspired vision is not simply the fact of evil but the nature of evil. It is a work, then, that is to make us aware of evil, of its forms, of the reasons for our plight, and of the possibilities open to the human spirit even after evil is a fact of existence.

There are two crucial moments in the poem that bring this issue home and show us what, in the Christian humanistic view, is the essential nature of man; these passages define man's *value* for Milton. The first occurs in Book 5 during the long interview between Adam and Raphael, before the Fall, when the angel tells Adam of the destiny planned for him (*PL* 5. 467–505):

O *Adam,* one Almightie is, from whom
All things proceed, and up to him return,
If not deprav'd from good, created all
Such to perfection, one first matter all,
Indu'd with various forms, various degrees
Of substance, and in things that live, of life;
But more refin'd, more spiritous, and pure,
As neerer to him plac't or neerer tending

Each in thir several active Sphears assignd,
Till body up to spirit work . . .

(469–78)

The second comes in the last book (12) when Michael describes man's redemption through Christ (*PL* 12. 386–465):

Dream not of thir fight,
As of a Duel, or the local wounds
Of head or heel; not therefore joynes the Son
Manhood to God-head, with more strength to foil
Thy enemie; nor so is overcome
Satan, whose fall from Heav'n, a deadlier bruise,
Disabl'd not to give thee thy deaths wound:
Which hee, who comes thy Saviour, shall recure,
Not by destroying *Satan,* but his works
In thee and in thy Seed: nor can this be,
But by fulfilling that which thou didst want,
Obedience to the Law of God, impos'd
On penaltie of death, and suffering death,
The penaltie to thy transgression due,
And due to theirs which out of thine will grow:
So onely can high Justice rest appaid.
The Law of God exact he shall fulfill
Both by obedience and by love, though love
Alone fulfill the Law; thy punishment
He shall endure by coming in the Flesh
To a reproachful life and cursed death,
Proclaming Life to all who shall believe
In his redemption . . .

(386–408)

Both of these are passages that confront the nature of man and his possibilities; the first explains man's original destiny before the Fall—a process of progressive refinement and spiritualization whereby body would become, or, more properly, blend into, spirit; the second explains the possibilities open to man after the Fall, the hope for Adam's progeny in the destruction of Satan's works by the "one greater Man" whose presence looms large throughout the poem. As recounted in *PR,* at least a sequel to *PL* in this sense, the destruction of Satan's works comes about by the acts of *choice* made by the Son* as Christ. These are fulfillments of his original choice, made in Book 3 of *PL,* in heaven, to redeem man. The one choice made in heaven in *PL* is fulfilled in *PR* through several "human" choices: the choice not to yield to the temptations of Satan (as Adam had through Eve), and the choice to die on the cross for Adam's choice. Both *PL* and *PR* are essentially embodiments of the central point of Christian humanism, the concern with man and his relation to the spirit, the concern with the "value of man" in a universe where morality and virtue are recognized as objective, unchanging values. These poems are attempts to deal with the heart of the matter as Milton saw it, to explain why we are where we are, how we got there, what we must do to move on, why the right choice or choices are important, and why we must make those choices with knowledge. As such, they are poems that educate, that attempt to reform; they are poems, too, that are "learned" as part of their designs: we are to presume that we are listening to an inspired, informed master.

There is one crucial passage in *PR* (4. 285ff.)—Christ's rejection of the literature and culture of ancient civilizations, particularly Greece—which seems to represent (in the eyes of many) Milton's rejection of the corpus of works and ideas that form the very foundation of humanism and humanistic thought in the Renaissance. But this rejection is only apparent, and it must be seen in its perspective. One needs to consider the dramatic situation and context in which this rejection occurs. The great eulogy of ancient civilization and thought has just come from the mouth of Satan, and it comes as one of Christ's temptations, a temptation to "knowledge" for its own sake. It is a temptation to "backward" knowledge in this context; for Satan, in this situation, is asking Christ, not to use ancient wisdom as the basis for supplementary enlightenment, but as a substitute for the wisdom that has come since. Christ's rejection of this is not a rejection of classical culture *per se,* but a rejection of that culture for its own sake, as the be-all and end-all of wisdom when something better is available. Classical culture has been enlightened by grace:

Think not but that I know these things, or think
I know them not; not therefore am I short
Of knowing what I aught; he who receives
Light from above, from the fountain of light,
No other doctrine needs, though granted true;
But these are false, or little else but dreams,
Conjectures, fancies, built on nothing firm.
(*PR* 4. 286–92)

What Christ is defining here is the difference between natural and supernatural truth. From his perspective, from the perspective of one who comes from the source of essential truth, what could classical or pagan wisdom represent but gropings in the dark? Even if we forget for a minute the dramatic appropriateness of this scene in the poem, and assume that it literally represents Milton's own position, there is nothing anti-Christian humanist about it. Indeed, this was essentially the Christian humanist's position. Classical thought, at its best, represented man as using his intellect and his will to reach a truth of which he had but some pale glimmerings. Only with the coming of Christ, with the coming of the age of grace*, was it possible to see things clearly, to put those early, somewhat tentative and conjectural moves toward truth in perspective. This is what Christian humanists like Ficino and Pico were doing in their translations, interpretations of and commentaries on Plato, Virgil, the Cabbala, Hermes Trismegistus: supplementing, from their position in time, in the age of grace, the unclear, indirect movements toward truth that they saw in the writings of the past. Still, they used these writings with a sense of the continuity of human thought, thought peculiar to man and representative of his dignity as the highest of creatures; thought, which displayed the reason, by which man examined alternatives, and the will, by which he accepted or rejected those alternatives. In his ability to choose lay his freedom; but in his ability to choose rightly, to follow an objective norm of virtue, no matter how difficult, lay his most *human, humanistic,* and therefore nearly divine, potential. For the Christian humanist the coming of Christ and the Christian tradition made the nature of the choices clearer than they had been before. To help us to know the right choices, to clarify, to illustrate and exemplify the choices and possibilities, to remind us of the objective norms that would make us most human and therefore most nearly divine, to make us concerned for the relation of present values to transcendent values, were essentially the basis of almost everything Milton ever wrote, in prose or verse. This is the essence of Milton's Christian humanism. [ARC]

HUME, PATRICK. All that is known about "P. H." is that he produced the first set of annotations to an English poem, but a more learned and thorough set of notes is difficult to imagine. Usually identified at Patrick Hume (although Parker queries whether it should be Philip), the author compiled "Explanatory Notes on Each Book of the Paradise Lost," which was published in many copies of Tonson's 1695 edition, although advertised on all 1695 title pages. Because of these notes, Hume has also been credited with " A Table of the most remarkable Parts . . . Under the Three Heads of Description, Similies, and Speeches," although there is no proof that "P. H." was responsible for it. "A Table" appears in some copies of the 1695 edition, sometimes with and sometimes without the "Explanatory Notes."

The notes stress etymological and analogous materials. They are a major contribution to an understanding of the areas of learning that went into the making of *PL,* and they aid often in answering questions of historical meaning, in tracing the history of ideas, and in giving directions for a full study of Milton's sources of knowledge. The notes were extensively plagiarized in the eighteenth century without any kind of acknowledgment; for example, see John Callander's edition of *Milton's Paradise Lost, Book I* (Glasgow, 1750). [JTS]

HUMOURS, THEORY OF THE: *see* SCIENCE, MILTON AND.

HUNT, THOMAS: *see* ADAPTATIONS, PROSE.

HYDE, EDWARD: *see* CLARENDON, EARL OF.

HYPOCRISY. By *hypocrisy* is meant a false pretense with regard to belief or conduct. In *CD* there are scattered texts dealing with the nature, cause and manifestations of this vice. Hypocrisy consists of deeds that "though plausible, are not good, or if good, are not done with a good design" (17 : 45). The hypocrite is motivated by the desire to extort greater praise for his own merits* (239). Hypocrisy occurs in religious worship when external forms are duly observed but without an accompanying affection of the mind (77–79); even the act of offering in public prayers designed for private use is hypocritical (93). Hypocrisy can assume the mask of virtue, that is, of patience as in "the flagellations of the modern Papists" (253) and of charity when there is a public display of almsgiving (259). Archimago in *The Faerie Queene* is a famous example.

With one exception, the explicit references to hypocrisy in *PL* have to do with Satan. As the "artificer of fraud," he is "the first / That practis'd falsehood under saintly shew" (4. 121–22). Gabriel correctly terms him a "sly hypocrite" in claiming to be a patron of liberty (4. 957–60). His vice is so subtle that "neither Man nor Angel can discern / Hypocrisie, the only evil that walks / Invisible, except to God alone" (3. 682–84). The only mention of hypocrisy not directly applied to Satan occurs in Milton's comment as Adam and Eve retire to the nuptial bower : "Whatever Hypocrites austerely talk / Of puritie of place and innocence . . ." (4. 744ff.). Even here, hypocrisy as a diabolical vice is suggested, for the passage alludes to St. Paul's prophecy that some shall depart from the faith, "giving heed to seducing spirits, and doctrines of devils"; they shall speak "lies in hypocrisy . . . forbidding to marry" (1 Tim. 4 : 1–3). [RF]

ICONOGRAPHY identifies the themes and motifs, and the most basic concepts and ideas conveyed by visual images or pictorial representations, whereas iconology provides a more profoundly symbolic interpretation (see Erwin Panofsky, *Meaning in the Visual Arts* [1955]). In studying the works of art of the Italian Renaissance (for example, Mantegna's *Triumph of Wisdom over Vice*), an iconographer would identify the helmeted figure of Minerva as the personification of Wisdom. In this painting the chaste Diana is assisting Wisdom in the struggle against Venus, who personifies lust and who is depicted as the mother of many vices, including Dalliance, Sloth, Hate, Suspicion, and Avarice. Having recognized that Mantegna's painting was a conventional representation of the *psychomachia* in which pagan figures personify the conflict between Virtues and Vices, an iconographer would classify the painting with similar works of art, like Perugino's *Combat of Love and Chastity* and Badinelli's *Combat of Ratio and Libido*. An iconologist, however, would use philosophy*, psychology*, theology, history, or literature to define more precisely the milieu in which a work of art was conceived and executed and to clarify the depth of an artist's intended meaning. But sometimes an iconologist would elicit meaning beyond, and different from, an artist's intention. Thus Mantegna's pictorial representation of water may be profoundly symbolic to the iconologist who adopts a Freudian or a Jungian perspective in order to interpret the stagnant pool in which the mother Venus keeps her brood of Vices.

If an iconologist chose to interpret the *Triumph of Wisdom over Vice* in relation to selected works of literature that also depict the *psychomachia,* then Milton's *Mask* would serve his purpose. In this work Venus (line 124) signifies not only lust but most of the vices associated with Intemperance, whereas the "unblemish't form of Chastity" (line 214) and "Wisdoms self" (line 374) are the opposing virtues, as Mantegna had depicted them. Similarly, because the Lady in *Mask* personifies Chastity* and Wisdom*, she is clad metaphorically (line 420) in the armor that is evident in numerous pictorial representations of Diana and Minerva, including Mantegna's. The stagnant pool in *Triumph of Wisdom over Vice* could be contrasted with the "translucent wave" (line 860), "silver lake" (line 864), and "fountain pure" (line 911) where Sabrina dwells and from which she emerges to assist the Lady.

Much as iconologists use other disciplines, especially literature, to interpret the visual arts, so also literary scholars may employ the visual arts to interpret symbolism in literature. When an author alludes to classical mythology* or develops themes from the Christian tradition (for example, the Fall*, the Redemption, Atonement*, Regeneration), his work may be analyzed with reference to the visual arts. And when authors like Spenser* and Milton synthesize classical mythology and the Christian tradition, their work virtually requires this kind of analysis. In a resemblance cited above between *Mask* and Mantegna's painting, the armor of Wisdom and Chastity has Christian as well as classical significance. St. Paul (Eph. 6 : 10–22) describes the armor worn by every Christian struggling against the "wiles of the devil." Spenser's Redcrosse Knight is clad in this armor; and in Carpaccio's *St. George Slaying the Dragon,* another work of the Italian Renaissance, the armor is visible indeed as protection against the onslaught of the devil, who is visualized as the dragon or Leviathan* mentioned in the Old and New Testaments—in Isaiah, Ezekiel, and Job on the one hand and in the Book of Revelation on the other. Medieval sculptures depict Christ as the dragon-killer with a dragon or basilisk underfoot, and numerous icons of Christ trampling the serpent dramatize an apocalyptic* vision of the Book of Revelation—that Leviathan will finally be slain. Thus the dialectic between the Lady and Comus enacts Christ's struggle against Satan, St. George's combat against the devil, and every Christian's contest against the onset of evil*. This *imitatio Christi* makes the Lady a hero.

Classical mythology and Christian themes in Milton's work may be interpreted in relation to the visual arts, but the undertaking is a major effort. The visual arts especially relevant to an interpretation of Milton are numerous and diverse: illuminated manuscripts (including psalters, Bibles, books of hours, missals, breviaries, lectionaries, sacramentaries, block books); illustrated medieval and Renaissance editions, translations, or interpretations of the classics; illustrated medieval and Renaissance dictionaries*, manuals, or encyclopedias of classical antiquity; emblem books; various sculptures and paintings (cathedral porches, chapel cupolas, palace vaulting, statuary, bas-reliefs, frescoes, terra-cotta friezes, stained-glass windows); decorative and ornamental work (engraved metals, medallions, cameos, intaglios, wooden crosiers, reliquary covers). This enumeration is not meant to imply that the means of expression are separate and unrelated; on the contrary, images depicting a pagan divinity or a tableau of Christian figures may be remarkably similar across different visual media. A complex tradition interrelates not only the several visual arts but also literature and the visual arts, and this tradition must be discussed concurrently with an analysis of Milton. This tradition involves the transmission of knowledge of classical fables, legends, and myths through the Middle Ages and into the Renaissance, as well as an account of the allegorical* and sometimes Christian interpretation of the classics. At least three studies have recently attempted to define this tradition: Erwin Panofsky's *Studies in Iconology: Humanistic Themes in the Art of the Renaissance* (1939), Jean Seznec's *The Survival of the Pagan Gods: The Mythological Tradition and Its Place in Renaissance Humanism and Art* (1953), and Don Cameron Allen's *Mysteriously Meant: The Rediscovery of Pagan Symbolism and Allegorical Interpretations in the Renaissance* (1970). Though authors in the Renaissance may have studied the classics firsthand, it seems more probable that they learned of classical antiquity by studying commentaries and interpretations. Even in the later period of classical antiquity (during the fourth and fifth centuries), Servius's commentary on Virgil, Capella's *Nuptiae Mercurii et Philologiae,* and Fulgentius's *Mitologiae* interpreted the classics allegorically. In the Middle Ages the trend toward allegorizing the classics was continued by the mythographers and encyclopedists, including Orosius*, Isidore of Seville, Bede*, and Rabanus Maurus. About 1160 Peter Comestor wrote his *Historia scholastica,* a compilation of certain previous commentaries. His compilation was a principal source for Vincent of Beauvais's thirteenth-century *Speculum historiale.* Of course, some of the Church Fathers had been ingeniously allegorical in viewing certain persons and events of the Old Testament as prefigurations of the New Dispensation, and they were just as ingenious in establishing parallels between classical antiquity and the Christian theology. Renaissance humanists* also subjected the classics to mythological exegesis, which became a cultural phenomenon. For some commentators pagan divinities personified virtues and vices; others elicited *philosophia moralis* from pagan fables, legends, and myths; still others paralleled pagan antiquity with the Bible, so that Hercules was likened to Christ, Atlas to the Four Evangelists, and the relationship between Pyramus and Thisbe to the affection of Christ for the soul of man. Beginning in the Middle Ages and continuing through the Renaissance, numerous interpretations of Ovid* were published. Boccaccio's fourteenth-century *Genealogy of the Gods* was another compendium that transmitted the commentary of the Middle Ages to the Renaissance. The Italian Neoplatonists* of the fifteenth century, continental and British emblematists of the Renaissance, and Italian encyclopedists perpetuated the tradition. Illustrated encyclopedias—Giraldi's *The History of the Gods* (1548), Conti's* *Mythology* (1551), and Cartari's *The Images of the Gods* (1556)—were principal sources of information about antiquity. These compilations were used, in turn, by Cesare Ripa for his *Iconologia,* which Emile Mâle (in *L'Art religieux après le concile de Trente*) views as "the key to the painted and sculptured allegories of the seventeenth century." Scholars and authors of the Renaissance relied on the Italian encyclopedias for allegorical interpretations of pagan antiquity. Much of Goulart's commentary (1583) on mythological allusions in Du Bartas's* *Sepmaine* is derived from Giraldi, Conti, and Cartari, all of whom he mentions. In England, Bacon*, Burton*, Chapman, and Marston, among others, used the Italian encyclopedias; Ben Jonson* and Inigo Jones, in conceiving characters for their masques, in planning the action, and in designing costumes and sets, used Ripa's *Iconologia* and emblem books. The encyclopedic and emblematic tradition was so pervasive that manuals of painting were derived from it. These manuals explained how pagan divinities were to be portrayed and how the details of their visual images were to be interpreted.

This is the tradition in which Milton was schooled from boyhood. Dictionaries, encyclopedias, lexicons, thesauri, and commentaries that interpreted and illustrated the classics were commonplace academic and reference texts from grammar school through the university. Milton's knowledge of these texts is easily demonstrated, for he seems to have owned the thesauri prepared and published in the sixteenth century by Henry and Robert Stephanus, the French classical scholars. In his marginalia on Aratus's* *Phoenomena,* Milton refers to Henry Stephanus's *Thesaurus Graecae Linguae* (18 : 327); and two early biographers* of Milton, John and Edward Phillips, mention the poet's efforts in compiling his own thesaurus, which was to have been modeled after Robert Stephanus's *Thesaurus Linguae Latinae.* The Stephani used the Italian encyclopedias and continental emblem books in preparing their thesauri; and Milton, while doing research for his own compilation, no doubt reviewed the classics firsthand but also studied illustrated commentaries. Milton's allusions to classical mythology are countless, and it is futile to attempt to determine specific indebtedness for a given allusion. Later commentaries were derived from earlier ones, so that similar intrepretations of a pagan fable, legend, or myth were very common and, of course, "traditional." It is the tradition to which Milton was indebted. In *Arc,* for example, Milton's description of the Fates or "daughters of *Necessity*" (line 69), who "turn the Adamantine spindle round" (line 66), may have been derived from the tenth book of the *Republic* or from commentaries on Plato. Cartari's *The Images of the Gods* excerpts some details from Plato, omits others, and adds more; and Cartari's illustrations of the Fates emphasize the large size of the spindle turned by them. Actually Milton's description of the Fates and the Sirens (lines 63–73) differs in some details from Plato's, but to determine specific indebtedness for these differences is virtually impossible. *Arc* begins with a long description of the goddess *Fama;* and here, as in another reference to *Fama* in *QNov,* Milton may have used the *Aeneid* (4. 173–87) or the *Metamorphoses* (12. 39–63) directly; or he may have relied on encyclopedias and emblem books that describe and depict *Fama* ensconced on a throne and emitting beams of light.

In *L'Al* Milton personifies Mirth or Gladness as Euphrosyne, one of the three sister Graces. He traces her parentage to Bacchus and Venus; and though he may have recalled Servius's commentary on the *Aeneid* (line 724), he could have learned of Euphrosyne's genealogy through at least ten Renaissance encyclopedias, including Giraldi's, Conti's, and Cartari's. She is also described in Charles Stephanus's *Dictionarium,* and she is, moreover, Ripa's *Allegrezza.* In encyclopedias and in Renaissance and Baroque* art, she is depicted as a beautiful woman naked or clad in simple garments—"fair and free" as Milton describes her (line 11). She is dancing among Spenser's* "daughters of delight" (*The Faerie Queene* 6. 10), and she appears in many of Jonson's masques, either alone or with her sister Graces or accompanied by Sport, Laughter, and Revel. She was frequently interpreted as *nuda virtus* and *nuda Veritas,* and for the Italian Neoplatonists she represented the ideal as opposed to the the sensible. Her allegorical and Neoplatonic meaning suffuses Milton's poem.

Nat and *Mask* contain numerous classical allusions that are assimilated into a Christian context. In the Nativity poem Christ is explicitly likened to Pan (line 89), who is the "guardian of flocks" in Virgil's* *Georgics* (line 17). Pan was described and sometimes depicted as a prefiguration of Christ, the Good Shepherd. Another identification, implicitly suggested, is between Christ and Hercules (lines 221–28). Much as the infant Hercules overcame the onslaught of the serpents and the adult Hercules struggled (in his second labor) against the Hydra, so also Christ's "dredded . . . hand" will rout the pagan gods, "*Typhon* huge ending in snaky twine," and the entire "damned crew." Hercules as a prefiguration of Christ was a common icon, and Hercules's conquest of the serpents and the hydra signified the defeat of Leviathan envisioned in the Book of Revelation and alluded to in *Nat* : "Th'old Dragon under ground / In straiter limits bound" (lines 168–69). In *Nat* (and especially in Book 1 of *PL*) Milton's catalogue of pagan gods provides detailed description of their grotesque idols and of the religious rites performed in their honor. The Renaissance encyclopedias, especially Cartari's, illustrate and comment on the Egyptian, Syrian, Assyrian, Phoenician, Libyan, and Scythian gods that Milton describes; and visual details of their appearance are interpreted. Numerous other sources, of course, did the same thing. Several of the allegorical personifications in the Nativity poem were common icons: Peace, Harmonia, Concord, Truth, Justice, Mercy. Milton's description of Peace—"meekey'd," "crown'd with Olive green," holding a "mirtle wand," and accompanied by a turtle dove (lines 46–51)—accords with numerous pictorial representations. When interpreted in a Christian context, Peace (in iconographic depictions and in Milton's poem) signifies the coming of Christ, the beginning of the New Dispensation, and the inception of the Christianized Golden Age during which Christ will reestablish rapport between heaven and earth, between God and mankind.

The classical framework in *Mask* must likewise be interpreted in a Christian context. The visual appearance of the characters, an interpretation of their significance, stage directions, and action onstage are derived, in part, from the iconographic tradition. The underlying classical myth is from the tenth book of the *Odyssey,* which describes Ulysses' encounter with Circe. In the *Metamorphoses* (14. 223–311) the myth is repeated with minor variation. All interpreters agree that submission to Circe represents the degradation of sensual indulgence. The *philosophia moralis* to be elicited from *Mask* is best summed up by Milton in *Apol* (3 : 305). From having read Plato and Xenophon*, Milton asserts that he has learned "of chastity and love, I meane that which is truly so, whose charming cup is only vertue which she bears in her hand to those who are worthy." Others "are cheated with a thick intoxicating potion which a certaine Sorceresse the abuser of loves name carries about." Furthermore, love "begins and ends in the soule, producing those happy twins of her divine generation knowledge and vertue." Milton calls these philosophical truths "abstracted sublimities." These excerpts from the prose treatise concisely summarize the Neoplatonic view that the spiritualization of man results from the exercise of knowledge, love, and virtue, which is precisely what the Lady in *Mask* accomplishes. Indeed, man's potential for heavenly ascent is prominent in *Mask* (and is, too, the topic of many of Raphael's disquisitions in *PL*). But man's potential for depravity, for descent to the level of the beasts, is likewise prominent. These philosophical truths are rendered concrete in *Mask*. Milton inventively ascribes Comus's parentage to Bacchus and Circe; but Comus's wand, his "baneful cup" (line 524), and his crew of men with beasts' heads were all part of the iconographic tradition that developed through interpretation and depiction of the Circe myth. For instance, George Sandys's *Ovid's Metamorphosis, Englished, Mythologiz'd and Represented in Figures* (1632) exhibits numerous parallels with Milton's rendition of the Circe myth. Emblem books also likened men to beasts when depicting man's submission to sensual indulgence. The Lady, however, resists Comus's seduction, and she witnesses and exemplifies the Platonic ideals of Virtue. Her clear-sighted vision of "pure-ey'd Faith"; "white-handed Hope, / Thou hovering Angel girt with golden wings"; and "thou unblemish't form of Chastity" (lines 212–14) includes descriptive details that typify allegorical personifications of these virtues. The use of lighting and dancing to emphasize visually the contest between Virtues and Vices establishes an affinity with the numerous masques (especially Ben Jonson's) that relied on the iconographic tradition as a source for visual details. But the classical myth, allegorical personifications, and Neoplatonic philosophy are indeed reconciled with the Christian theology because the Lady in *Mask* is Milton's first sustained portrait of a Christian hero. The Lady's elder brother asserts "that which mischief meant most harm, / Shall in the happy trial prove most glory" (lines 590–91); and the Attendant Spirit, after the Lady and her brothers have reached Ludlow Castle, sings "Heav'n hath timely tri'd their youth, / Their faith, their patience." They were "sent . . . through hard assays / With a crown of deathless Praise" (lines 969–72). Milton's definition

of good temptation in *CD* (15 : 86–89) accords with the Lady's experiences in *Mask*. That is, good temptation is "for the purpose of exercising or manifesting . . . faith or patience." To support his definition, Milton quotes from 1 Peter 1 : 7 and James 1 : 12: "that the trial of your faith . . . might be found unto praise"; and "blessed is the man that endureth temptation; for when he is tried, he shall receive the crown of life."

Like Milton's earlier poetry, *PL* may be interpreted iconographically. The synthesis of classical mythology and the Christian tradition is prevalent throughout the epic; equally important, however, is Milton's reliance on distinctively Christian iconography, a tradition of pictorial representation that unites the Old and New Testaments. A notable example of the synthesis of classical myth and the Christian tradition is the allegory of Satan, Sin, and Death. In the *Theogony* Hesiod recounts how Pallas Athene emerged from Zeus's brain, and in *PL* Sin is described as having sprung like "a Goddess arm'd" from an opening on the left side of Satan's head (2. 755–59). Though she was "once deemd so fair" (2. 748), Sin was seduced by her father Satan, who viewed his own "perfect image" in her (2. 764). The ensuing incestuous relationship resulted in the birth of Death. This painful birth deformed Sin, so that her "nether shape" (2. 784) became serpentine. "Inflam'd with lust" (2. 791) at birth, Death immediately copulated with his mother, begetting the "yelling Monsters" (2. 795) that surround her and gnaw at her entrails. As Milton's description indicates, the myth of the birth of Athene is fused with Ovid's account of the transformation of Scylla (*Met.* 13. 734–37), who was a beautiful woman, like Milton's Sin, so long as she remained "chaste in thought, and in body unspotted" (as George Sandys comments). When a woman is lascivious, she submits to the degradation of sensuality, and Sandys observes that man's potential for depravity, for affinity with bestial impulses, is visualized in Scylla's serpentine shape from the waist down and in the dogs and wolves that surround her waist. Conti's *Mythology* illustrates Scylla as woman, dog, and serpent; and these juxtaposed images traditionally suggest concupiscence and ensuing spiritual death. Interpretation of the lascivious relationship of Satan, Sin, and Death is also traceable to James 1. 14–15: "Every man is tempted, when he is drawn away by his own lust, and enticed"; and "when lust hath conceived, it bringeth forth sin; and sin, when it is finished, bringeth forth death." The icons depicting these verses stress that lust, which means both pride* (or inordinate ambition) and concupiscence, is the cause of the Fall* of Mankind and that sin and death are consequences of the Fall. Accordingly, Francis Quarles's* illustration (*Emblems,* 1635) of James 1. 14 depicts Eve alongside the Tree of Knowledge of Good and Evil, around which the serpent is entwined. The serpent's seduction speech, which Quarles composed to accompany the illustration, resembles Satan's appeal to Eve in Book 9 of *PL.* That is, the serpent appeals to Eve's pride but also accomplishes a sexual seduction after having aroused his own and Eve's concupiscence. In fact, the verses immediately below Quarles's illustration emphasize that the liaison between Eve and the serpent resulted in the "fatal Birth" of "all the Ills that Man sustains on Earth." To be sure, Sin and Death, as in *PL,* are among these ills; but as importantly, Eve forfeits her conjugal chastity, as she does in Milton's account of the Fall. Both rabbinic and Patristic commentaries describe the Fall as an act of adultery, and Cain's birth is often ascribed to Eve's sexual union with Satan. In illustrating James 1 : 15, Quarles depicts a spherical earth (described as a "chaste and pregnant womb" in his accompanying poem) through which various animals' heads, including dogs and wolves, are pushing forth. Quarles describes the earth, after the Fall of Mankind, as a "base adulteress" giving birth to monsters that "make a trade to kill." After Adam and

Eve have committed Original Sin, Milton explains that the earth "trembl'd from her entrails, as again / In pangs, and Nature gave a second groan" (9. 1000–1001). The disharmony engendered in Nature by the Fall indicates the effect of Original Sin on the entire natural order. Thus Milton's description of Satan's archetypal sin, involving first pride and then lasciviousness, is adapted from classical myth, scriptural texts, and iconography. Satan's seduction of Eve infuses her with pride and lasciviousness, and the birth of the murderer Cain is Eve's enactment of Sin's having mothered Death. The birth of monsters from the earth, as Quarles depicts and interprets them, is Nature's similar experience with the anguish of breeding progeny called Death.

Milton's account of the Fall reflects a distinctively Christian iconographic tradition that correlates persons and events from the Old Testament with counterparts from the New. This tradition, first employed by Paul in the New Testament, was further developed from commentary of the Church Fathers, and it was depicted with little variation throughout the Middle Ages in the *Biblia Pauperum,* the *Speculum Humanae Salvationis,* the *Speculum Sanctae Mariae Virginus,* and in countless other illustrated manuscripts (including Bibles, books of hours, missals, block books, emblem books). This typological association means that a person from the Old Testament (Moses, for instance) was viewed as a type or prefiguration of Christ. In *CD* (15 : 286–87) Milton views Moses as a type of Christ; and in other prose treatises, like *RCG* and *Hire,* and in *PL* (12. 300–306), Milton develops similar typological relationships. Throughout Books 11 and 12 of *PL,* as Adam is experiencing the vision of the future, various Old Testament personages who have faithfully served God become prefigurations of Christ : Abel, Enoch, Noah, Abraham, Isaac, Moses, Joshua, David. This kind of typological association is sometimes modified by Milton to highlight an ironic relationship between an Old Testament personage or event and a

New Testament counterpart. This ironic relationship, which is traceable to the same Christian iconographic tradition, is nowhere better exemplified than in Book 9 of *PL*, where Milton's account of the Fall is related implicitly to the manner by which mankind is to be saved. In books of hours (for example, Catherine of Cleves's and Jean, Duke of Berry's) and in emblem books, like Henry Hawkins's *Partheneia Sacra,* Eve is depicted along with the Virgin Mary. Frequently, Eve is shown on the left side of the Tree of Knowledge of Good and Evil, and the Virgin Mary is at the right side holding Christ. Eve's experience with "a fatal birth" (to use Quarles's phrase) is contrasted with Mary's giving birth to Christ, the source of Eternal Life. Throughout Adam's vision of the future in *PL,* the prophecy is repeated that "womans seed," which alludes to Christ's birth from the Virgin Mary, will bruise the serpent's head. Christ's victory over Death, which is accomplished at the Resurrection—"Death his deaths wound shall then receive" (3. 252)—begins the liberation of mankind from the fatal consequences of the Fall, but Christ's final victory over Satan, envisioned in the Book of Revelation, is to be achieved at the Second Coming. The ironic typological* association between Eve and the Virgin Mary is ingeniously developed in iconography. The virginal conception, for instance, is believed to have occurred at the Annunciation. Paintings, sculpture, and illustrated manuscripts depict Gabriel saluting Mary at the Annunciation. Above Mary is a dove from which beams of light, which signify divine insemination, descend onto her head. Gabriel is sometimes holding a lily, which represents both virginal purity and the undefiled birth of Christ. Often a closed door is in the background, and the *porta clausa* image suggests the Virgin's inaccessibility to evil. The entire setting is an enclosed garden (*hortus conclusus*). In the *Biblia Pauperum* the Annunciation is visually juxtaposed with a scene of Eve at the Tree of Knowledge in order to contrast the Vir-

gin's chastity, fidelity, and humility on the one hand with Eve's pride and act of adultery on the other. Whereas Satan penetrates the Garden of Eden and seduces Eve, he is unable to gain access to the Virgin, who is harboring Christ. Eve's accessibility to Satan is stressed in *PL,* and the seduction is metaphorically consummated when the serpent's words "Into her heart too easie entrance won" (9. 734). In the first illustration of Christopher Harvey's *Schola Cordis* (1647), an emblem book that traces the heart's separation from God and its eventual return, Eve is offering her heart to the serpent while she stands under the Tree of Knowledge. The "darkness" of the fallen heart and the onset of evil are illustrated in successive emblems, and the parallelism with Milton's description of the effects of the Fall is striking.

Eve's pride and her concupiscence, both of which are stressed in Milton's conception of the Fall, are likewise stressed in iconography. Her susceptibility to pride and sinful vanity is depicted iconographically when she accepts a mirror proffered by the tempter, and in *PL* her Narcissistic urge was evident while she gazed at her own image reflected from the stream and "pin'd with vain desire" (4. 466). Furthermore, the serpent is sometimes visualized with Eve's head (for example, in Jean, Duke of Berry's *Très Riches Heures*), and Eve is tempted by her own image that appears high in the Tree. Her susceptibility to concupiscence is reflected in icons that depict the serpent with the genitals of a man or with the head of a handsome young man.

The typological association that ironically relates the Tree of Knowledge with the crucifix is highlighted when these visual images are actually fused. A commonplace icon depicts Christ crucified in the branches of the Tree of Knowledge; and in the poetry of Robert Southwell, of George Herbert, and of several other devotional lyricists, Christ is imagized as the "fruit" restored to the Tree in order that divine justice can be satisfied. In numerous legends of the cross, in the

Cursor Mundi, in the *Somme le Roi,* in the *Biblia Pauperum,* and throughout the Middle Ages, the cross is typologically associated and visually related not only to the Tree of Knowledge but also to Moses' rod and Jacob's ladder, both of which are described in *PL.* Across the panorama of the epic, the metamorphosis of the image of the cross continually calls attention to the necessity of Christ's sacrifice for man's salvation. *SA* and *PR* also reflect Christocentric iconography, and together with *PL* they comprise a traditional iconographic triptych that shows an Old Testament prefiguration of Christ, man's Fall as the cause of Christ's sacrifice, and the life of Christ as a historical verity. [ACL]

IDOLATRY. In Book Two of *CD* Milton states that "IDOLATRY consists in THE MAKING, WORSHIPPING, OR TRUSTING IN IDOLS WHETHER CONSIDERED AS REPRESENTATIONS OF THE TRUE GOD, OR A FALSE ONE" (17 : 135). The fact that this broad definition comes under the general subject of "WORSHIP or LOVE of GOD" coupled with the fact that Milton considers worship as both internal and external ("nor are they ever separated, except by the impiety of sinners." 17: 73, 75), indicates that he understands the representations of idolatry ("OF THE TRUE GOD, OR A FALSE ONE") to be internal and external perversions of worship : perversions of the love and trust owed to God. In this understanding Milton reflects, more or less faithfully, the beliefs of his age.

A brief survey of some of these beliefs will clarify the relationship between the inner and the outer act of idolatry. In the *Institutes of the Christian Religion* Calvin* sees idolatry beginning internally; he says that the mind of man is "a perpetual manufactory of idols" (ed. John Allen [1813], 1 :105). As he describes the process, "the mind of man, being sunk in stupidity, and immersed in profound ignorance, imagines a vain and ridiculous phantom instead of God" (p. 98). Sub

sequently, "men attempt to express in the work of their hands such a deity as they have imagined in their minds." This view was generally accepted by Reformed churches.

The Devil was thought to use idolatry as his chief weapon for undermining and perverting true worship. In *An Arrow Against Idolatrie* (London 1611), Henry Ainsworth says: "The old Serpent, called the *Devil & Satan,* hath frō the beginning fought to draw men from the service of God, to the service of himself : and this he hath doon as by other synns, so cheefly by idolatry, which therefore above all other, is called and counted the worship & service of Divils" (p. 3). In such temptations, idolatry adulterates the "Church and People of God" with the tempting "allurements of false worship." In *CB* (1639?) Milton, quoting from Tertulian's *De Spectaculis,* illustrates the principle underlying the Devil's representations : "In moral evil there can be mixed much of good and that with cunning skill . . . ; so the Devil flavors his fatal concoctions with the most pleasing gifts of God" (17 : 128).

John Lightfoot, commenting on Revelation 20 in *A Sermon Preached Before the Honorable House of Commons* (London, 1647), delineates two historical phases of idolatry. In the first phase, *"Heathenisme"* (p. 7), Satan could create new oracles and idols at will, and he did so through the proliferation of nature or fertility cults. But the advent of Christ, the incarnation, put a sudden stop to heathenism (Milton's *Nat* celebrates, with the silencing of the pagan oracles, this event). The second phase of idolatry, *"Antichristianisme"* (p. 7), comes about through the activities of the Antichrist in Revelation, what Thomas Taylor in *Christs Victorie over the Dragon: or Satans Downfall* (London, 1633) calls the "great wrath," that is, "the sly stealing of the Antichrist upon the world by a Catholic apostacy" (p. 693). Likewise, Milton believed that "the great enemy of the Church is called 'Antichrist,' who according to prediction

[2 Thess. 2 : 3f.] is to arise from the church itself" (16 : 315).

In the Protestant interpretation of the Antichrist the Pope is consistently identified with him, seated in Rome at the center of all Antichristian idolatry. In his early poems on the Gunpowder Plot Milton adjures the Pope, the "monster skulking on the seven mountains," to use his "hellish powder" to drive "to the skies loathsome cowls, and as many insensate gods as Rome profane possesses." He sees pagan cultic practices hidden in the rituals of Rome. In *QNov* (1628) he describes the Feast of St. Peter in terms of the licentious practices associated with the pagan festival of Dionysius : "The uproar of the chanters time and again filled the empty, vaulted chambers, and the void spaces with such noises as [is heard] when Bromius [Dionysius] howls, and Bromius's squadrons, as they chant their orgiastic hymns in Echionian Aracynthus."

Milton's judgment of Roman Catholicism as idolatrous remained constant. In *TR* (1673) he gives his final views: "Popery" is "the worst of superstitions, and the heaviest of all Gods Judgements" (6 : 180). Of the secret idolatries of Rome, he writes : "when men sin outragiously," and "will not be admonisht," God "gives over chastizing them . . . by Pestilence, Fire, Sword, or Famin . . . and takes up his severest punishments, hardness, besottedness of heart, and Idolatry, to their final perdition. Idolatry brought the Heathen to hainous Transgressions. . . . And hainous Transgressions oft times bring the slight professors of true religion*, to gross Idolatry" (p. 179).

Earlier, Milton had argued that some of the practices of Rome had adulterated the Anglican Church. In *Ref* (1641) he says that the English church retains the "senceless *Ceremonies*" of Rome to serve "either as mist to cover nakedness where true *grace** is extinguisht; or as an Enterlude to set out the *pompe* of *Prelatisme*" (3 : 6). In *Apol* (1642) he tells us that the English prelates did as the Israelites who, "figur'd under the names of Aholah and Aholibah," went "a whoring after all the heathen inventions," because "they saw a religion gorgeously attir'd and desirable to the eye" (3 : 355). Milton's main accusation against the prelates is that they were obsessed with externals, with the material trappings of religion that are the substance from which idolatry develops. In *Ref* he charges: "what an excessive wast of Treasury hath beene within these few yeares in this Land not in the expedient, but in the Idolatrous erection of Temples beautified exquisitely to out-vie the Papists, the costly and deare-bought Scandals, and snares of Images, Pictures, rich Coaps, gorgeous Altar-clothes" (p. 54). Such materialism is Antichristian : "If the splendor of *Gold* and *Silver* begin to Lord it once againe in the Church of *England,* wee shall see *Antichrist* shortly wallow heere, though his chiefe Kennell be at Rome" (pp. 54–55).

Milton traces the history of prelatical idolatry to the union of church and state made possible by the Donation of Contantine*, a fiction that he wholeheartedly accepted. Constantine's wealth allowed prelates to indulge in material benefits, and accordingly it was "at this time," Milton says, that *"Antichrist* began first to put forth his horne" (p. 25), although as a matter of fact Constantine seems to have taken a leading role in banishing image worship. Milton hints in *CB* that the Emperor's motive for banishing image worship was euhemeristic; he alludes to uncited authorities for proof that Constantine was the first of the Roman emperors to allow himself to be worshiped (18 : 173) and makes no mention of Constantine as an iconoclast. He does, however, give that honor to *"Phillippicus* and *Leo,"* who "with divers other Emperours after them, not without the advice of their *Patriarchs,* and at length of a whole Easterne Counsell of 3. hundred thirty eight *Bishops,* threw the Images out of Churches as being decreed idolatrous" (3 : 43).

In *Eikon* (1649) Milton sees Charles I* as a type of Constantine (see 5 : 261) who chooses instead of violence "a more mystical way, a newer method of Antichristian fraud . . . to undermine and weare out the true Church by a fals Ecclesiastical policy" (5 : 227). With respect to the supposed idolatry of Charles I, Milton saw himself in the role of the iconoclast, zealous in his attempt to destroy the King's Image, the *Eikon Basilike**, which is "a Romish guilded Portrature" that can give no "better Oracle then a Babylonish gold'n Image" (p. 215). In debunking *Eikon Basilike,* Milton aligns himself with the long tradition of iconoclasm : "Iconoclastes" was "the famous Surname of Many Greek Emperors, who in thir zeal to the command of God, after long tradition of Idolatry in the Church, took courage, and broke all superstitious Images to peeces" (p. 68). However, Milton never advocated the kind of wanton and indiscriminate destruction of stained glass and religious statuary carried out during the winter of 1643–44 by the notorious William Dowsing and his deputy Francis Jessups acting in accordance with an ordinance of Parliament issued on August 26, 1643, which decreed that "all Crucifixes, Crosses, and all Images and Pictures of Saints . . . shalbe taken away and defaced."

Idolatry expresses itself in materialistic terms, their paradigm tracing to the time when Satan was still in Heaven. His self-exaltation on the Mount of Congregation and later on the throne of Pandaemonium* prefigures all earthly examples. His "Royal seat" is built "High on a Hill, far blazing, as a Mount / Rais'd on a Mount, with Pyramids and Towrs / From Diamond Quarries hew'n, and Rocks of Gold, / The Palace of great *Lucifer*" (*PL* 5 : 757–60). As Arnold Stein points out, Satan attempts to "possess the power of spirit by means of matter" (*Answerable Style,* p. 36). Moreover, in imitating "that Mount whereon / *Messiah* was declar'd in sight of Heav'n" (5. 764–65), Satan is explicitly opposing himself to the Son* and assuming the role of the Antichrist, material against spiritual. In Hell* the devils pursue with new zeal the manipulation of the material begun in Satan's Antichristian service in Heaven. The same

techniques employed in the invention of Satan's artillery are now employed in the building of Pandaemonium. In Heaven Satan builds to rival the power of the Son, in Hell to maintain his illusory power over the fallen angels*. And again materialistic ostentation fills the void of spiritual impotence :

Anon out of the earth a Fabrick huge
Rose like an Exhalation, with the sound
Of Dulcet Symphonies and voices sweet,
Built like a Temple, where *Pilasters* round
Were set, and Doric pillars overlaid
With Golden Architrave, nor did there want
Cornice or Freeze, with bossy Sculptures
    grav'n;
The Roof was fretted Gold. Not *Babilon*
Nor great *Alcairo* such magnificence
Equal'd in all thir glories, to inshrine
Belus or *Serapis* thir Gods, or seat
Thir Kings when *Egypt* with *Assyria* strove
In wealth and luxurie.

                                                    (1. 710–22)

By describing Pandaemonium as a "Fabric huge" rising "like an Exhalation," Milton suggests that there is something fantastic about the material splendor of Satan's infernal temple; it swells into being blown up by Satan's pride, his self-love. Indeed, it is filled and sustained by Satan's "proud Imaginations" (2. 10). Pandaemonium is the prototype of various earthly buildings that may lead men into idolatry and that are sustained by the corrupt imaginations of their worshipers.

With the Fall* of Adam and Eve, earth and Pandaemonium are united in a single Kingdom ruled over by Satan's phantasms or *eidola*, Sin and Death. His whole effort in *PL* is to "confound the race / Of mankind in one root, and Earth with Hell / To mingle and involve" (2. 382–83). To accomplish this, Satan begins by tampering with the mind of Eve in a dream, for she is inclined to be fascinated with her own *eidolon**, her own physical perfection (as Satan is fascinated with his own spiritual perfection before the fall from Heaven), which she discovered reflected in the lake of Eden. Satan takes advantage of this weakness by intruding narcissistic images into the pure mirror of her imagination so as to flatter Eve's vanity with a dream-image of herself as the idol of all Nature. Later, in the daylight temptation, Eve is easily fascinated by the gorgeous appearance and the obsequious flattery of a "specious object" (9. 361), the specious miracle of the talking snake. And she is easily convinced by serpent logic of the possibility of rising in the scale of being: "That ye should be as Gods, since I as Man, / Internal Man, is but proportion meet, / I of brute human, yee of human Gods" (9. 710–12). Such sinful idolatry of herself is subjective rather than objective.

Thus, for Milton idolatry is finally a technique of allurement invented by Satan to pervert and adulterate spiritual realities, and as such, it is primarily an internal phenomenon that carnalizes the imagination by focusing it on material entities. Satan's kingdom, or the mystery of iniquity, is begotten in this world when the mind of man reduplicates the "proud imaginations" of Pandaemonium. [TAB]

IGNATIUS OF ANTIOCH (ca. 50–ca. 107), earliest of the Church Fathers of whom there is any written record (Eusebius, *Historia Ecclesiastica* 3. 36). Ignatius was Bishop of the church at Antioch, and under the anti-Christian reign of Trajan was transported in chains to Rome, where he was killed by lions in the arena. During the long trek from Syria to Italy he wrote seven letters that have survived. During the Reformation these letters formed a part of the controversy over the suitability of the Episcopal versus the Presbyterian* form of church organization (J. B. Lightfoot, "The Ignatian Epistles," in *Essays on The Work Entitled 'Supernatural Religion,'* [1889]). Milton is aware of the importance of the Ignatian letters to the Presbyterian cause, and he addresses the controversy surrounding the letters in two polemical works. In *Ref* 1641 Milton cites Ignatius's letter to the Philadelphians as evidence that bishops must be elected by their church, that early bishops did not have dioceses, but rather could move from place to place (3:18), and that the

early Fathers urged their churches to refer all controversies directly to the Scriptures (3 : 30). On the other hand, *PrelE*, printed in the same year, treats Ignatius quite differently. Milton hints that Ignatius may not have really existed (3 : 82); implies that none of his letters can be trusted since there exist five other letters purportedly by Ignatius that are known to be false (3 : 88); and finally charges that the letters were written by the "Perkin Warbeck of Ignatius," that is, a pseudo-Ignatius (3 : 102).

There are several possible reasons for Milton's ambivalent treatment of Ignatius. One is that selective citation was a common polemical device in the seventeenth century. In *Ref* Ignatius provided important evidence for some of the organizational practices of the early apostolic church that the reformers wished to institute in England. In *PrelE,* arguing against episcopacy, Milton found in Ignatius's letters strong support for the idea of the ascendancy of bishops over the church as a whole, which thus made him a target for Milton's destructive polemics. A second possible reason for Milton's treatment of Ignatius is that in 1641 the only versions of the letters available were those in which there were obvious interpolations by later commentators. The purer Greek version of the letters was not published until three years later (James Ussher, *Polycarpi et Ignatii Epistolae,* Oxford, 1644). Milton thus had grounds to reject the letters on internal evidence. Even so, we can assume that, for a polemicist, the chance to use one of his opponents' chief sources against them, as he does in *Ref,* may have been too tempting to pass up.

Milton cites Ignatius's view of marriage* from the 1623 Geneva edition of *S. Ignatii Antiocheni & Martyriis Quae Exstant Omnia* in *CB.* [RCR]

ILLUSTRATORS. William Riley Parker has observed that the story of Milton's "after-fame" may be told by the bibliographer, by the literary or cultural historian, or by the critic—either of Milton or of another phase of literary endeavor. The story of Milton's "after-fame" may also be told by the student of the vast body of illustrations that Milton's poetry has steadily accumulated. Two situations in our own century, however, have tended to obliterate the efficacy of such an approach. First of all, literary criticism, despite all its advances, has become regimented and formalized; in the process, illustration has been pushed beyond the very boundaries that used to contain it, and it has also been dissociated from the text that it accompanies. This separation of text and design has precipitated a second event. Publishers, insensitive to any connections between text and design, even those which some distinguished artists have tried to preserve, have transformed what was once a vehicle for highly imaginative, often innovative, observation into a "corporate editorial image" (Robert Weaver, "The Future of Illustration," *The Illustrator in America,* ed. Walt Reed [1967], p. 268).

With these two circumstances, a whole tradition of art that extends back to the Egyptians has been subverted. Now, instead of asking about the quality of observation made by an illustration, we treat it as nonart and as noncriticism; and those who have attempted to rescue illustration from its demise expect us to see in illustration a private statement by an artist who believes in the primacy of design and who militantly asserts its independence from the text it accompanies. Milton's illustrators postulated a different set of premises: they assumed an interdependence of text and design; their objective in illustrating a poem was to illuminate it; their designs, therefore, attempted a crystallization of the Miltonic vision, which the artist then criticized and might even try to correct. Milton illustration, with very few exceptions, is a form of nonverbal criticism.

The history of Milton's illustrators is, as C. H. Collins Baker acknowledges, a "many-sided" subject. It reveals much about the history of painting, both the development of its techniques and the

evolution of its genres; it charts the fluctuations in taste and attitude to which Milton has always been subject. In its grandest moments, it is a record of expanding appreciation and deepening understanding of Milton's poetry. Occasionally an illustration is no more than a pictorialization of Milton's narrative or a visualization of a Miltonic image, but more usually an illustration imposes an interpretation upon a text that it accompanies. In the hands of a highly imaginative illustrator, an illustration may create a whole new perspective from which to view a poem.

The tendency of the twentieth century to confuse illustration and decoration, to regard illustration as merely an ornament, has generated an enmity between illustration and decoration. While illustration may be of the twentieth century, it illumination and elucidation, decoration is generally relegated to a position of insignificance: "ornamental borders, initials, headpieces and tailpieces are not illustrations but decorations," we are told; "like the type and the cover, they belong to the production of the book rather than to the amplification of the author's text" (James Thorpe, *English Illustration* [1935], p. 247). However true such a statement may be of the twentieth century, it ignores the fact that illustration and decoration originally enjoyed a complementary relationship, each reinforcing the other. If the illustration was used to pictorialize a poem's narrative, the decoration, invested with iconographic significance, articulated the poem's principal themes and recurring motifs. Both illustration and decoration, then, are bound inextricably to the text they adorn; however, once this relationship is acknowledged, it is necessary to recognize that various kinds of relationships may exist between illustrations and texts.

Appropriating a technique common to biblical illustrators and also to illustrators of epic poetry during the Renaissance, the eighteenth-century book designer often made a synoptic design, representing a whole structure of events within a single depiction while focusing on one of them. However, this technique was often accompanied by another, which enabled the illustrator to assign gradations of importance to narrative events. He could depart from the synoptic design, on occasion depicting only one episode, and could thereby assign to that episode a prominence, an importance, not possessed by those treated synoptically. Those illustrators who were less concerned with narrative line than with crucial episodes could rely exclusively upon this latter technique. Instead of depicting a cluster of episodes, they could focus on two or three and represent their various stages; they could, for instance, depict the Fall* in various stages, representing Eve's unpleasant dream, Adam's arrogant questioning, Eve's temptation* by Satan, and Adam's temptation by Eve. Still other illustrators preferred to visualize themes, and even others aimed at representing the continuities that joined one book of Milton's epic to another, or even one poem in his canon to some other poem he had written. During the eighteenth century, then, Milton's illustrators, working with an evolving pictorial vocabulary and an array of different artistic techniques, moved in various directions as they sought to achieve different objectives.

This period of experimentation is followed by a period of consolidation. The nineteenth century, which began with a revolution in all the arts, was "in every way the most formative period in the history of book illustration" (Philip James, *English Book Illustration* [1947], p. 14). The nineteenth century—at least the first thirty-five years of it—was also the great period in the history of Milton illustration. A new understanding of Milton began to prevail, and illustration was one important instrument for asserting that understanding. No longer were illustrators moving in different directions; the period of experiment was over, and the Milton iconography had been formed. Every conceivable technique was now being utilized by any given artist; the full Milton iconography was brought into play: an individual illustration was likely to possess a variety of relationships with the poem it accompanied. The great illustrators of this period employed the whole tradition of Milton illustration, but they did so by way of defining their own originality. The early nineteenth-century illustrators continued to render the narrative line of Milton's poetry, but they were concerned primarily with elucidating Milton's vision and with defining the essential qualities of his art. Henry Fuseli* captured Milton's sublimity, John Martin his vast spatial dimensions, and J. M. W. Turner the softness encompassed within the hard lines of Milton's verse. To William Blake* we must credit the fullest exploration and the deepest comprehension of the Miltonic vision. And to give credit where credit is due, we should acknowledge that Blake not only made old techniques serve new ends so as to anticipate the conditions of twentieth-century art, but he raised many of the critical issues with which we continue to grapple, and forged many insights to which we still are strangers.

Since illustration is perhaps the most dependent of all art forms—the art form most completely bound to its own traditions—it is necessary to explore Milton illustration within the context of those traditions. A convenient starting point is David Bland's *A History of Book Illustration* (1969), which complements the studies by Ralph Cohen, *The Art of Discrimination* (1964), and by Philip James, *English Book Illustration* (1947). It is also valuable to look directly at the traditions of classical and biblical illustration (Milton's illustrators are heavily indebted to both) as they are elucidated by Kurt Weitzmann, *Ancient Book Illustration* (1959), and by J. B. Trapp, *Approaches to Paradise Lost*, ed. C. A. Patrides (1968). The essay by Kester Svendsen, *Studies in English Literature*, 1 : 63–73, and that by Merritt Y. Hughes, *Journal of English and Germanic Philology* 60 (1961) : 670–79, discuss various illustrators of Milton. Other essays deal with individual illustrators : Helen Gardner, *English Studies* 9 : 27–38 and Morse

Peckham, *Princeton University Chronicle*
11 : 107–26. A bibliographical guide to dis-
cussions of Blake's Milton illustrations is
provided by J. A. Wittreich in *Calm of
Mind* (1971), p. 126 n21; but this list should
be supplemented by several recent studies:
John E. Grant, *Blake Newsletter* 4:
117–34, and 5 : 190–202; and Irene Tay-
ler, *Blake's Sublime Allegory,* ed. S. Cur-
ran and J. A. Wittreich (1973), pp.
233–58. There are various extra-illustrated
editions of Milton, some of which are
cited in the catalogue below; but a
particularly useful source for the study of
Milton's illustrators is the sixty-volume,
extra-illustrated *Kitto Bible* in the Henry
E. Huntington Library. This Bible con-
tains numerous Milton illustrations; but
what is more important, it presents them
in a setting of hundreds of biblical illus-
trations, which greatly facilitates the study
of their iconography.

Several previous attempts besides the
present have been made to catalogue Mil-
ton's illustrators: C. H. Collins Baker,
Library, 5th ser., 3 : 1–21, 101–19; Marcia
R. Pointon, *Milton and English Art* (1970);
and J. A. Wittreich, *Angel of the Apoc-
alypse* (1973), especially chapter 3.

The catalogue printed below is deeply
indebted to these earlier efforts, but
it also includes illustrators previously
ignored. When a new illustrator is
added to the list, an asterisk (*) has been
added at the beginning of the entry. No
attempt has been made to cite every ap-
pearance of an illustrator's designs. Only
the first occasion of publication has been
indicated, unless an illustrator's work has
been significantly altered by an engraver
or unless an illustrator has made new
designs, or reconceived old ones, for a
subsequent edition. [JAW]

*Marshall's Design, 1645

Poems of Mr. John Milton. London: Printed
for Humphrey Moseley, 1645. The frontis-
piece portrait, designed and engraved by
William Marshall, depicts in its background
a scene from *L'Al.* The entire composition

seems to be inspired by the contrast between
the piper of innocence and the bard of
experience who has achieved the prophetic
strain. Frontispiece portrait (background):
Shepherds dancing in the shade.

Medina, Lens, Aldrich Designs, 1688

Paradise Lost, 4th ed. London: Printed for
Richard Bentley and/or Jacob Tonson,
1688. Of the twelve illustrations (one for
each book of *PL*), all but the fourth, signed
by Bernard Lens and Peter Paul Bouche,
have been attributed to John Baptist
Medina. Of these eleven illustrations, all
except the eighth, which carries no sig-
natures, are engraved by Michael Burgesse
(or Burghers), and all these designs are
attributed to Medina, even though the
ones for Books 1, 2, and 12 are unsigned by
him. However, the New York Public
Library copy of this edition carries a note,
purportedly by Horace Walpole, attributing
the twelfth illustration to "Dr. [Henry]
Aldrich." If this illustration is by Aldrich,
the one for Book 2 also is probably by him.
PL 1: Satan rousing his legions (fore-
ground), Satan and Beelzebub sitting in
council (background); 2: Satan, Sin, and
Death; 3: Heavenly choirs praising the
redeemer (upper half), Satan and Uriel,
Satan on Mount Niphates, Adam and Eve
in their bower (middle ground); Satan
lighting upon this world (lower half); 4:
Uriel descending (foreground), The scales
of justice, Satan leaving Eden, Adam and
Eve in the garden, The animals gamboling,
Evening worship, Adam and Eve sleep-
ing (background); 5: Raphael descending,
Morning hymn (foreground), Adam goes
forth to meet Raphael, Adam and Eve
dining with Raphael (background); 6: The
fall of the rebel angels; 7: Adam and Eve
conversing with Raphael (foreground), Four
scenes of creation (in ovals at top of
design); 8: Adam alone with the birds and
beasts of Eden (foreground), Adam discours-
ing with Raphael, Adam meeting Eve
(background); 9: Satan and the sleeping
serpent (foreground), Adam and Eve con-
versing, The division of labor, The tempta-
tion of Eve, The temptation of Adam,
Adam and Eve sorrowing (background);
10: Guardian angels leaving Paradise
(upper half), The tree of knowledge raped
by serpents, Satan with his assemblage,
The bridging of chaos, Satan, Sin, and
Death (lower half); 11: Michael comes to
Adam and Eve (foreground), Adam and
Michael atop the mountain, Eve sleeping,
The contention of the animals (background);
12: The expulsion.

Gweree's Design, 1705

Paradise Lost, 7st ed. London: Printed for Jacob Tonson, 1705. All these illustrations, except the fourth, are signed by Henrik Elandt; but with the exception of the fourth design, these illustrations are copies of those by Medina (or others). The fourth illustration, signed by J. Gweree, is an adaptation of the Lens design, but it departs from the synoptic character of its original by eliminating all episodes but that of Ithuriel and Zephon discovering Satan, who sits squat like a toad inspiring Eve's dream. The Gweree design is engraved by Elandt.

Pigne's Designs, 1713

Paradise Regain'd, 5th ed. London: Printed for J. Tonson, 1713. These illustrations, previously attributed to Medina, are probably by Nicholas Pigné (see the barely legible signature on the illustration to Book 1 of *PR* and the signature on the design for *L'Al*), Frontispiece, *PR*: Christ's triumph over Satan; 1: The Baptism of Jesus; 2: Jesus in the temple; 3: Jesus conversing with Satan; 4: The ministry of angels. *SA*: Samson pulling down the pillars. *L'Al*: The poet embracing the world. *IlP*: The poet rejecting the world. *Shak*: Portrait. *Carrier* 1: Old man riding a horse behind a wagon.

Cheron, Thornhill Designs, 1720

The Poetical Works of Mr. John Milton, 2 vols. London: Printed for Jacob Tonson, 1720. The first volume contains the Lovis Chéron–James Thornhill illustrations to *PL,* and the second contains the Chéron designs for *PR, SA,* and *Lyc.* The illustrations in the second volume are engraved by Gerard Van der Gucht and Samuel Gribelin, and those for the first are engraved by the same artists and also C. du Bosc. Each book of Milton's epics is accompanied by a headpice, a letter ornament, and a tailpiece. Frontispiece to volume 1: Milton with his muse (*PL*1); 1: Satan calling up his legions (headpiece by Thornhill), Ouroborus (letter ornament), Armor heaped in a pile (tailpiece); 2: Satan, Sin, and Death (headpiece by Chéron), Satan enthroned (letter ornament), Medusa with hell-hounds and serpents (tailpiece); 3: Two angels adoring God (headpiece by Chéron), God's Son in the sun (letter ornament), Satan and Uriel (tailpiece by Chéron), 4: Adam and Eve with the beasts of Eden (headpiece), Bird perched on the branch of a tree (letter ornament), Satan disputing with the angelic guard (tailpiece); 5: Adam and Eve dining with Raphael (headpiece), Tree of knowledge (letter ornament), Bundle of fruit wreathed by flowers (tailpiece); 6: War in heaven (headpiece by Chéron), City of God (letter ornament), Christ on his chariot (tailpiece by Chéron); 7: The creation (headpiece by Chéron), Urania descending (letter ornament), Angels praising God's creation (tailpiece by Chéron); 8: Adam and Eve conversing with Raphael (headpiece by Chéron)), A globe (letter ornament), Raphael departing from Eden (tailpiece by Chéron); 9: The temptation of Adam and Eve (headpiece by Chéron), Harmony disrupted (letter ornament), The expulsion (tailpiece); 10: Adam and Eve led away by Sin and Death (headpiece by Chéron), Sunburst (letter ornament), Adam lying prostrate (tailpiece by Chéron); 11: Michael foretells the future (headpiece by Chéron), Heart pierced by arrows (letter ornament), Animals in contention (tailpiece by Chéron); 12: The expulsion (headpiece by Chéron), Flaming swords (letter ornament), The resurrection of Christ (tailpiece). Frontispiece to volume 2: The baptism (*PR* 1); 1: The first temptation (headpiece), The nativity (letter ornament), Satan departing from Jesus (tailpiece); 2: The banquet temptation (headpiece), Satan bearing the fruits of the earth (letter ornament), The temptation to wealth and riches (tailpiece); 3: The temptation of Parthia (headpiece), Crowns and scepters (letter ornament), The temptation of Rome (tailpiece); 4: Satan inspiring Jesus' ugly dream (headpiece), Crown of thorns (letter ornament), The temptation on the pinnacle (tailpiece). *SA*: Samson eyeless in Gaza (headpiece), Samson spurning Dalila (letter ornament), Samson pulling down the pillars (tailpiece). *Lyc*: Milton accepting his garland from Apollo (headpiece), Shipwreck (letter ornament).

*Medina, Fourdrinier Designs, 1725

Paradise Lost, 12th ed. London: Printed for Jacob Tonson, 1725. Medina's (and others') illustrations are generally praised for maintaining fidelity to Milton's text, especially because they chart pictorially the downward course of Milton's Satan. This set of Medina designs, engraved by Pierre Fourdrinier, deserves special notice inasmuch as the engraver intrudes far enough into two designs that he alters their original conception. In the design for Book 1, the guards on the roof of Pandemonium have disappeared, and the faces of the fallen angels have acquired a grotesque quality wholly lacking in the Medina original. In the design for Book 2, the Rubenesque depiction of Sin disappears as the figure takes on the features of a witch; Satan, who in the original has one angel wing and one bat wing, presumably to mark the beginning of his degeneration, now has two bat wings, one light and the other dark; finally, the tyre that Satan carries in the Medina illustration has been transformed into an ouroborus by Fourdrinier. These two illustrations, then, are better studied as new conceptions than as inept renderings.

Hogarth's Designs, ca. 1725

It has been suggested that William Hogarth's depictions of the council in hell and of the council in heaven are "contemplated or rejected illustrations" for Tonson's 12th edition of *PL* (see Ronald Paulson, *Hogarth's Graphic Works* [1965], 2:113). These designs were later engraved by J. Ireland and reproduced in Samuel Ireland's *Graphic Illustrations of Hogarth*, 2 vols. (1794), 1: opp. pp. 79 and 82.

*Anonymous Designs, 1736

Del Paradiso Perduto. London: Printed by Carlo Bennet, 1736. These woodcuts are, for the most part, purely decorative; however, several of them merit attention either because they articulate Miltonic motifs or, as is the case with the headpiece to Book 7, because they reveal an impulse among illustrators to appropriate biblical illustrations as ornaments for Milton's epic. Most of these woodcuts are reproduced in George Smith Green's *The State of Innocence, and Fall of Man* (London: Printed for T. Osborne, 1745). *PL* 1: Eve with a serpent coiled around her arm (headpiece); 2 and 9: Animals gamboling in Eden (headpiece); 7: Man contemplating God's heaven (headpiece signed by F. Hoffman, dated 1720, and intended as an illustration for Ps. 8:3).

*Balestra, Piati, Crozati, Piazzetta, Zignaroli, Tiepolo, Belij, Bigeri Designs, 1740

Il Paradiso Perduto, 2 vols., with all illustrations in vol. 1. Paris: Giovanni Alberto Tumermani, 1740. This volume contains headpieces to each book, decorative tailpieces to seven of the twelve books, and a frontispiece, depicting Milton's apotheosis, by A. Balestra. The illustrations, previously attributed to Balestra and assigned to 1758, are engraved by Zucchi. Balestra's frontispiece was first published apart from these illustrations in *Il Paradiso Perduto* (Verona: Alberto Tumermani, 1730), where it was engraved by Hylbrouck. *PL* 1: Adam and Eve in the garden; 2: Satan with all his accouterments (by S. Piati); 3: Christ offers himself as redeemer (by G. B.

Crozati; 4: Satan chased from Eden (by G. B. Piazzetta); 5: Adam and Eve watching an angel who stands on the head of Satan; 6: Christ and the evil angels in combat (by G. B. Zignaroli); 7: God vaulting over the universe; 8: Creation of Eve; 9: Temptation of Eve; 10: Sin and Death (by G. B. Tiepolo); 11: Michael descending (by N. Belij); 12: The expulsion (by V. Bigeri).

*Piazzetta, Picart, Chasteau, Tiepolo Designs, 1742

Il Paradiso Perduto, 2 vols., with all illustrations in vol. 1. Paris: Printed by Giannalberto Tumermani, 1742. The decorative tailpieces in the 1740 edition are replaced with interpretive ones, and the frontispiece by A. Balestra is replaced with one by G. B. Piazzetta. Frontispiece to volume 1: God talking with Adam. Tailpiece to *PL* 1: Head of Satan (foreground) and Satan tempting Eve (background; by B. Picart); 2: Angel driving two horses (by B. Picart); 3: Piper with his sheep (by N. Chasteau); 4: Flames and torches; 5: Spears and helmet; 6: Musical instruments; 7: Shepherd with his flock; 8: Two putti; 9: Eve in the wilderness (by N. Ch[asteau?]); 10: Woman and courtier (by G. B. Tiepolo). There are no tailpieces for Books 11 and 12.

Anonymous Designs, 1743

Le Paradis Perdu, 3 vols. Paris: Chez Ganeau, 1743. This edition is decorated with headpieces and tailpieces, which have no apparent interpretive significance.

*Anonymous Designs, 1747

Paradise Lost. Dublin: Printed for John Hawkey, 1747. These headpieces, described on the title page as "brilliant engravings," are purely decorative.

Hayman's Designs, 1749

Paradise Lost, ed. Thomas Newton, 2 vols. London: Printed for J. and R. Tonson and S. Draper, 1749. These frontispiece-illustrations for each book of Milton's epic are designed by Francis Hayman and engraved by Ravenet and Grignion. Volume 1, *PL* 1: Satan calling up his legions; 2: Satan, Sin, and Death; 3: Satan and Uriel; 4: Adam and Eve watched by Satan; 5: Adam and Eve in their bower; 6: The fall of the rebel angels. Volume 2, 7: Adam and Eve conversing with Raphael; 8: Raphael's departure from Eden; 9: The temptation of Adam; 10: Christ descending into Eden; 11: Adam's vision of Cain murdering Abel; 12: The expulsion.

Hayman's Designs, 1752

Paradise Regain'd, ed. Thomas Newton. London: Printed for J. and R. Tonson and S. Draper, 1752. These Francis Hayman illustrations are engraved by J. S. Müller [or Miller], Grignion, and Ravenet; the original designs are in the Houghton Library, Harvard University. *PR*: The first temptation. *SA*: Samson and Dalila. *L'Al*: Poet led by Mirth into a pastoral landscape. *IlP*: Poet and Melancholy contemplating the heavens. *Mask*: The Lady in Comus's chair.

Müller [or Miller], Hayman Designs, 1756

Paradise Regain'd. London: Printed for J. and R. Tonson and for C. Hitch, etc., 1756. This volume contains not only the Hayman illustrations cited above but also a new frontispiece designed and engraved by Johann S. Müller. The design is clearly an adaptation of the Pigné illustration of the same subject, but it is also sufficiently different to require separate notice. Frontispiece, *PR*: Christ's triumph over Satan.

Hogarth's Design, ca. 1764

William Hogarth's Satan, Sin, and Death, engraved by S. Ireland, is reproduced in Ireland's *Graphic Illustrations of Hogarth,* 2 vols. (1794), opp. 1: 179.

Romney's Design, 1770

During this year, George Romney exhibited a painting entitled "L'Allegro and Il Penseroso" at the Society of Artists. The design was engraved by J. Jones in 1778.

Barry's Designs, ca. 1771

James Barry made his début at the Royal Academy with a depiction of Eve tempting Adam, which is now in the National Gallery of Ireland. Probably at this same time Barry was at work on his other designs for *PL,* which survive in the British Museum and the Soane Musuem. *PL* 1: Satan falling, Satan rousing his legions; 2: Satan, Sin, and Death; 4: Satan startled by Ithuriel's spear; 10: Adam and Eve hiding.

Runciman's Designs, 1773

Alexander Runciman did a painting, now lost, entitled "Il Penseroso" and also a companion piece for it called "A Landscape for Milton's L'Allegro," now in the collection of Sir Steven Runciman.

*Anonymous Design, 1776

Paradise Lost. Glasgow: Robert and Andrew Foulis, 1776. The Henry E. Huntington Library copy of this edition has a fore-edge painting that depicts Satan rising from the burning lake (*PL* 1).

Mortimer's Designs, 1776–1779

The Poetical Works of John Milton, 4 vols. Bell's Edition of the Poets of Great Britain. Edinburgh: Apollo Press, 1776–1779. Each of the volumes carries a frontispiece designed by John H. Mortimer and engraved by Hall and Grignion. Volume 1, *PL* 2: Satan flying through air. Volume 2, *PL* 5: Adam and Raphael conversing. Volume 3, *SA*: Samson feeling the breath of heaven blowing. Volume 4, *Passion*: Milton with his muse. Besides these illustrations, Mortimer did a wash drawing of Satan and Death that he intended to exhibit at the Royal Academy in 1779.

Anonymous Design, 1777

Paradise Regain'd. London: Sold by J. Banners, etc., 1777. *PR* 1: The first temptation.

*Dighton's Design, 1777

Comus. London: Printed for J. Wenman, 1777. Frontispiece: Miss Catley as Euphrosyne, with two lines of text beneath. Engraved by Walker.

Anonymous Design, 1779

Paradise Regain'd. London: Printed for Toplis and Bunney and J. Mozley, 1779. Frontispiece to *PR*: Christ's triumph.

*Stothard's Design, ca. 1779

Thomas Stothard made a drawing of Milton's Satan that was engraved by William Blake. For a reproduction, see A. G. B. Russell, *The Engravings of William Blake* (1912), pl. 52.

Malpas's Design, 1780

The Poetical Works of Mr. John Milton, 4 vols. London: Printed for A. Millar and J. Hodges, 1780. Frontispiece to volume 3: Christ's resurrection (*PR*).

*Cipriani Design, 1780

Memoirs of Thomas Hollis. London; 1780. This illustration for *1Def*, designed and engraved by Giovanni B. Cipriani, was initially intended as a frontispiece for Hollis's projected edition of Milton's prose. When that project did not materialize, the depiction of Milton triumphing over Salmasius was included in Hollis's *Memoirs.*

Smirke's Design, ca. 1780

Robert Smirke did two drawings for *L'Al*—"Dancing in the shade" and "Walking in the woods"—that are in the British Museum—and two others—the Lady and Sabrina for *Mask* and Eve looking at her reflection for *PL*—that are in the Victoria and Albert Museum.

Dodd's Designs, 1781

Paradise Lost, 3 vols. London: Printed for Joseph Wenman, 1781. These three volumes, each with a frontispiece, are part of *The Poetical Magazine, or Parnassian* vols. 19–21. [Daniel] Dodd's designs are engraved by Birrell. Volume 1: Satan enthroned (*PL* 2). Volume 2: Adam awaking Eve (*PL* 5). Volume 3: Eve dropping her garland (*PL* 9).

West's Designs, 1782

Robert West exhibited two drawings for *PL* at the Royal Academy. *PL* 1: The fallen Satan; 6: Michael and Satan in combat.

De Loutherbourg's Design, 1782

Philip De Loutherbourg exhibited a drawing of Milton's hell that was destroyed by fire but that has been vividly described by W. H. Pyne, *Wine and Walnuts* (1824), pp. 265–66.

*Gillray's Designs, 1782

James Gillray based two of his published drawings on subjects from Book 4 of *PL*: The devil addressing the sun, Satan observing the couple in the garden.

Freeman's Designs, 1784

T. Freeman exhibited two subjects from Milton at the Royal Academy. *PL* 2: Satan in chaos; 5: Eve and Raphael.

Wright's Design, 1785

Joseph Wright of Derby exhibited a painting called "The Lady in *Comus*," which survives in the Walker Art Library.

*Gillray's Design, 1787

James Gillray published a design inspired by Book 4 of *PL,* carrying the passage ending ". . . love waves his purple wings."

Martin, Peters Designs, 1788

In the Poets' Gallery, Thomas Macklin exhibited a painting by a Mr. [Elias?] Martin called "Comus and the Lady" and another by the Rev. Mr. Matthew W. Peters called "Adam's first sight of Eve" (*PL* 8).

Romney's Designs, 1788–1796

During these years George Romney made a number of sketches for *PL* and one sketch for *PR*. *PL* 1: Satan calling up his legions; 2: Satan, Sin, and Death; 5: Satan startled by Ithuriel's spear; 6: The fall of the rebel angels; 11: Adam's vision of the flood; 12: The expulsion. *PR* 4: Jesus' ugly dream.

*Gillray's Designs, 1790–1792

During this period, James Gillray made three illustrations inspired by Book 2 of *PL*: The birth of Sin, Sin and Death, Satan, Sin, and Death. Another design was inspired by Book 4: Uriel riding a sunbeam.

*Blake's Designs, 1790–1795

William Blake made three major separate designs inspired by Milton's poetry during this period. "The Ancient of Days" (*PL* 7) is reproduced in *Engravings of William Blake,* comp. Geoffrey Keynes (1956), pl. 16; "The House of Death" (*PL* 11) is reproduced by Darrell Figgis, *The Paintings of William Blake* (1925), pl. 26; and "Glad Day," which carries the inscription that begins "Albion rose . . . ," echoing *SA* and thereby suggesting that the design may bear an interpretive relationship to Milton's poem, is also reproduced by Figgis, pl. 69. For other designs by Blake that date from the 1790s, see J. A. Wittreich, "Appendix B," in *Calm of Mind* (1971), pp. 334–35.

Flaxman Designs, ca. 1790

John Flaxman did seven designs for *PL* that survive in the British Museum and in the Slade College of Art. *PL* 1: Satan and Beelzebub; 5: Satan's flight from Paradise; 6: five different scenes.

*Fuseli's Design, ca. 1790

Henry Fuseli drew a head of Satan that was engraved by William Blake. For a reproduction, see *Engravings by William Blake,* comp. Geoffrey Keynes (1956), pl. 42.

*Burney, De Wilde Designs, 1791

Comus. Bell's British Theatre. London: Printed for the Proprietors, 1791. Edward Burney's design, engraved by Bartolozzi, depicts Comus offering his cup to the Lady. Samuel De Wilde's design, engraved by Thornwaite, depicts a lady with a cup in her hand and bears the title, "Miss Storace in Euphrosyne."

Metz's Designs, 1791–1792

Conrad Metz exhibited three Milton subjects at the Royal Academy: "The Lady in *Comus*" and "Samson and Dalila" in 1791 and "The Contest between Sin and Death" (*PL* 2) in 1792.

Schall's Designs, 1792

Le Paradis Perdu, 2 vols. Paris: Chez Defer de Maisonneuve, 1792. Frédéric-Jean Schall's designs, in color, were engraved by Demonchy, Colibert, Bonneyfoy, Gauthier, and Clement. Volume 1, *PL* 1: Satan calling up his legions; 2: Satan, Sin, and Death; 3: Satan and Uriel; 4: Satan watching Adam and Eve; 5: Morning hymn; 6: The fall of the rebel angels. Volume 2, 7: Adam conversing with Raphael; 8: Adam and Eve praying; 9: Eve tempting Adam; 10: Judgment of Adam and Eve; 11: Adam's vision of Cain murdering Abel; 12: The expulsion.

Stothard's Designs, 1792–1793

During this period Jeffryes published a number of Thomas Stothard's designs for Milton's epic. *PL* 1: Satan rising from the burning lake, Faery Elves, Satan rousing his legions; 2: The Council in Pandemonium, Sin and Death; 4: The gate of Heaven; 9: The temptation of Eve.

Braine's Design, 1793

T. Braine is known to have exhibited a picture of Satan during 1793.

*Designs Engraved by Malpas and Wilson, 1794

The Poetical Works of John Milton, 2 vols. Wilkins's Edition of the British Poets. London: Printed by T. Wilkins, 1794. This edition contains five illustrations, all of them in the first volume, and only two of them are signed—the illustration for Book 1 of *PL* is engraved by E. Malpas, and the design for Book 5 is engraved by W. C. Wilson. *PL* 1: Satan calling up his legions; 2: Satan, Sin, and Death; 3: Satan and Uriel; 4: Adam and Eve watched by Satan; 5: Adam and Eve reclining on the bank. The designs for Books 3 and 4 are faithful copies of Hayman's earlier designs, but there are significant alterations of detail in the designs for Books 1 and 5, and the illustration for Book 2 represents a whole new conception of the meeting of Satan, Sin, and Death.

Richter's Designs, 1794

Paradise Lost, 2 vols. London: Printed for J. and H. Richter, 1794. Henry Richter's twenty-four illustrations are engraved by F., J., and C. Richter. Volume 1, *PL* 1: Satan calling up his legions, Fallen angels watching the victorious ones return to heaven; 2: Satan enthroned; 3: God enthroned; 4: Angels guarding Eden, Eve observing her reflection; 5: Eve awaking from her dream, Adam and Eve leaving their bower; 6: Adam and Raphael conversing. Volume 2, 7: Urania descending; 8: Raphael departing from Eden, Adam contemplating, Adam and Eve returning to their bower; 9: Adam and Eve sorrowing, Satan hiding, The temptation of Eve, The temptation of Adam; 10: An angel forsaking Paradise, Adam and Eve listening to the voice of God, Sin and Death; 11: Adam and Michael, Adam's vision of the flood; 12: Christ's nativity, The expulsion.

Westall's Designs, 1794–1797

The Poetical Works of John Milton, with a Life of the Author, ed. William Hayley, 3 vols. London: Printed for John and Josiah Boydell and George Nicol, 1794–1797. Richard Westall's designs are engraved by Simon, Earlom, Schiavonetti, Kirk, Ogborne, Smith, Adel, Leney, and Bestland. Volume 1, *PL* 1: Satan and Beelzebub; 2: Sin springing from the head of Satan; 3: Christ's offer to redeem man; 4: Satan with his crest; 5: Adam and Eve in their bower; 6: Christ grasping ten thousand thunders. Volume 2, 7: Adam and Eve conversing with Raphael; 8: Eve among the fruits and flowers; 9: Eve tempting Adam; 10: Sin and Death; 11: Adam's vision of the cruel tournament; 12: The expulsion. *PR* 1: Jesus hungering; 2: Mary meditating; 3: Jesus rejecting the temptation to glory; 4: The temptation on the pinnacle. Volume 3, *Lyc*: A Shepherd with his flock. *SA*: Samson meditating, Messenger reporting the catastrophe. *FInf*: God calling from a whirlwind. *Nat*: The rout of the pagan deities. *L'Al*: Mirth. *IlP*: Melancholy. *Mask*: The Lady and Comus, Comus giving the Lady his cup, Sabrina releasing the Lady. *Sonn* 23: Milton's apparition. *El* 5: Sylvanus and the violence in the night.

Anonymous Design, 1795

Paradise Regained, ed. Charles Dunster. London: Printed for T. Cadell and W. Davies, 1795. This contemporary design for Milton's brief epic, painted on the fore-edge of Dunster's edition, is somewhat faded though the coloring was originally probably no brighter. This presentation copy from the editor to Dr. W. Falconer is in the Lilly Library, Indiana University. *PR* 4: Great and glorious Rome.

*Burney's Design, 1795

The Works of the British Poets, with Prefaces, Biographical and Critical, by Robert Anderson, 5th vol. London: Printed for John and Arthur Arch, etc., 1795. Edward Burney's design is engraved by Chesham. *PL* 6: Christ expelling Satan.

Kirk, Brown Designs, 1795–1796

The Poetical Works of John Milton, 2 vols. Cooke's edition. London: Printed for C. Cooke [1795–96]. Five of the six illustrations that accompany *PL,* all of them in volume 1, are by Thomas Kirk; one, the illustration to Book 4, is by W. H. Brown. These illustrations are engraved by Nutter, Ridley, Strange, and Neagle. *PL* 1: Satan with expanded wings; 2: Satan, Sin, and Death; 4: Eve observes her reflection, Satan watching Adam and Eve; 8: Adam's dream; 9: Eve confesses.

*Gillray's Designs, 1795–1798

James Gillray published a number of designs inspired by Milton during this period. *Mask*: Virtue driving off Sin and Guilt (1795). *PL* 6: Christ on his chariot, Christ driving out the rebel angels (1795). *PR* 4: The temptation on the pinnacle (1796). *PL* 8: Adam and Eve in their nuptial bower (1797); 9: The temptation of Adam 1798).

Burney's Designs, 1796

Milton's Paradise Regained. London: Printed for T. Longman, etc., 1796. Edward Burney's two frontispiece designs are engraved by Fittler. *PR* 1: The baptism of Jesus. *SA*: Samson and Dalila.

*Stothard's and Graham's Designs, 1796

Samson Agonistes. British Library. London: Printed for George Cawthorn, 1796. Thomas Stothard's "Samson and Dalila," engraved by Heath, serves as frontispiece. [John?] Graham's design, facing p. 13, is engraved by Audinet and depicts Samson meditating.

Corbould, Singleton Designs, 1796

Paradise Lost, 2 vols. London: Printed for J. Parsons, 1796. Richard Corbould provides the designs for all but Books 3, 6, and 11, which are illustrated by Henry Singleton. The illustrations are engraved by White, Saunders, and Heath. Volume 1, *PL* 1: Satan rising from the burning lake; 2: Satan, Sin, and Death; 3: Satan and Uriel; 4: Eve observes her reflection; 5: Morning hymn; 6: Zophiel summons the angelic host. Volume 2, 7: Adam and Eve conversing with Raphael; 8: Creation of Eve; 9: The Fall; 10: Christ with Adam and Eve, Satan's return to hell; 12: Adam and Eve mourning their expulsion.

Lawrence's Design, 1797

Thomas Lawrence exhibited a painting of Satan calling up his legions (*PL* 1) at the Royal Academy.

Burney's Designs, 1799

Milton's Paradise Lost. London: Printed for T. Heptinstall, 1799. Edward Burney's designs are engraved by Landseer, Neagle, Rothwell, Bromley, Blackberd, and Milton. Title-page design, *PL* 10: Adam cursing his creation; 1: Satan calling up his legions; 2: Satan, Sin, and Death; 3: Satan and Uriel; 4: Satan discovered by Ithuriel and Zephon; 5: Raphael descending; 6: The fall of the rebel angels; 7: Adam and Eve conversing with Raphael; 8: Creation of Eve; 9: The temptation of Eve; 10: Satan listening to the sad discourse between Adam and Eve; 11: Christ's intercession for man; 12: The expulsion. About this same time, Burney made a drawing of Adam and Eve walking in the garden, which was engraved by Dadley but not included in this edition. Burney's original drawings are in the Princeton University Library and in the Henry E. Huntington Library and Art Gallery.

Fuseli's Designs, 1799–1800

Henry Fuseli's Milton Gallery, with forty different illustrations, opened on May 20, 1799. *PL* 1: Satan and Beelzebub rising from the burning lake, Satan rousing his legions, Satan with his host, Faery elves; 2: Satan, Sin, and Death, The birth of Sin, Sin pursued by Death, Lapland orgies, Satan's ascent from hell, A gryphon pursuing an arimaspion, Satan flying out of chaos, Ulysses between Scylla and Charybdis; 4: Adam and Eve watched by Satan, Satan startled by Ithuriel and Zephon, Satan discovering his fate; 5: Eve's dream; 8: Creation of Eve, Eve led to Adam; 9: The temptation of Eve, Adam resolving to share Eve's fate; 10: Eve despairing, Sin and Death bridging chaos, Satan enthroned; 11: Adam's vision of the lazar house, Adam's vision of the flood, Adam's vision of Noah; 12: The expulsion. *PR* 4: The temptation on the pinnacle. *Nat*: The ruin of paganism. *L'Al*: Faery Mab, Friar's Lantern, Lubbar fiend. *IlP*: Silence, Cremhild meditating revenge. *Mask*: The Rout of Comus, Orgies of Cotytto. *Lyc*: Solitude (plus three biographical scenes). When Fuseli's Milton Gallery reopened on March 21, 1800, seven new subjects were added. *PL* 2: Sin receiving the key to hell; 9: Satan's first address to Eve, Adam and Eve sorrowing. A design for *FInf*. *L'Al*: Mirth. *IlP*: Melancholy. A design for *Sonn* 3. For locations and reproductions of Fuseli's surviving Milton illustrations, see Gert Schiff, *Johann Heinrich Füsslis Milton-Galerie* (1963).

Rosa's Design, 1800

Paradised Regained, ed. Charles Dunster, 2nd ed. London: Printed by George Stafford, [1800]. The frontispiece illustration, a biblical design by Salvatore Rosa (1615–1673), was engraved by Thomas Phillips and was regarded by Dunster as a source for Milton's brief epic. *PR* 1: The first temptation.

*Rigaud's Designs, 1801

The Poetical Works of John Milton, with a Critical Essay by J. Aikin. 4 vols. London: Printed for J. Johnson, etc., 1801. Stephen F. Rigaud's illustrations are engraved by Neagle, Cooke, Smith, Walker, and Stow. Volume 1, *PL* 1: Satan falling headlong; 2: Sin and Death; 3: Angelic choir praising the Son; 4: Adam and Eve in Eden; 5: Satan discovered; 6: Abdiel returning to the side of God. Volume 2, 7: Raphael discoursing; 8: Adam led to a mountain top; 9: The temptation of Eve; 10: Adam and Eve hiding; 11: Adam and Michael on the mount of vision; 12: The expulsion. Volume 3, *PR* 1: Jesus meditating; 2: Jesus alone in the desert; 3: Jesus rejecting the temptation to glory; 4: The ministry of angels. *SA*: Samson pulling down the pillars. *Mask*: Sabrina rising. Volume 4, *L'Al*: Mirth. *IlP*: Melancholy. In this same year Rigaud exhibited six Milton subjects. Four of Rigaud's drawings are in the British Museum, and sixteen others (all of them for *PL* and *PR*) are in the collection of Walter Brandt.

Taylor's Design, 1801

John Taylor exhibited a drawing for *L'Al*.

Blake's Designs, 1801

William Blake did a set of eight water-color illustrations for *Mask* that is now in the Henry E. Huntington Library and Art Gallery. The subjects illustrated are: Comus and his revelers, Comus disguised, The brothers picking grapes, Two brothers in the woods, Comus with the Lady in his chair, Two brothers with swords raised, Sabrina descending to the Lady, The Lady restored to her parents. For other Milton designs by Blake belonging to the first years of the nineteenth century, see J. A. Wittreich, "Appendix B," in *Calm of Mind* (1971), p. 336. This Huntington set is reproduced in color by Angus Fletcher, *The Transcendental Masque* (1971).

*Burney, Fuseli, Hamilton Designs, 1802

Milton's Paradise Lost, 2 vols. London: Printed for F. J. Du Roveray, 1802. The frontispiece portrait, engraved by Cipriani, contains a new Milton subject by Edward Burney. The designs for Books 1–4, 6, and 12 are by Henry Fuseli, and the others are by William Hamilton; the Fuseli-Hamilton designs are engraved by Bromley, Neagle, Smith, Bartolozzi, Warren, Fittler, and Rhodes. Frontispiece to volume 1: Eve tempting Adam (*PL* 9); 1: Satan calling up his legions; 2: Satan, Sin, and Death; 3: Satan flying through air; 4: Satan startled by Ithuriel's spear; 5: Adam watching unawakened Eve; 6: The fall of the rebel angels. Volume 2, 7: Adam and Eve conversing with Raphael; 8: Creation of Eve; 9: The temptation of Eve; 10: Adam and Eve lying prostrate; 11: Michael descending; 12: The expulsion.

*Opie's Design, ca. 1802

John Opie supposedly painted John Wolcot (Peter Pinder) as a fallen angel in a scene from *PL*; but, according to Ada Earland, the joke missed fire because Milton was so little read (*John Opie and His Circle* [1911], p. 59).

Weinrauch's Designs, 1803

Paradise Lost, translated from the French of R. de St. Maur, 3 vols. Vienna: Printed for R. Sammer, 1803. J. C. Weinrauch's frontispieces, one for each volume, do not carry the name of an engraver. *PL* 1: Satan declaring war; 6: War in Heaven; 12: The expulsion.

*Gillray's Designs, 1803–1805

James Gillray published several more illustrations inspired by *PL*. Beelzebub (*PL* 2; 1803); War in heaven (*PL* 6; 1804); Paradise of Fools (*PL* 3; 1805).

*Chapman, Craig Designs, 1804

Paradise Lost, with a Life of the Author by John Evans, 2 vols. London: Albion Press, 1804. John Chapman designed and engraved the frontispiece, and the twelve illustrations by William M. Craig were engraved by Mackenzie. Frontispiece to volume 1: Milton inspired (*PL* 1); 1: Satan calling up his legions (frontispiece), Broken armor; 2: Satan, Sin, and Death (frontispiece), serpent and skeleton (tailpiece); 3: Satan and Uriel (frontispiece), prayer book, key, crown, and rosary (tailpiece); 4: Adam and Eve praying (frontispiece), Scales of Justice (tailpiece); 5: Adam and Eve dining with Raphael (frontispiece), Coiled serpent (tailpiece). Frontispiece to volume 2: War in heaven (6); 6: canon (tailpiece); 7: Christ in his chariot, receiving the praises of the angels (frontispiece), A globe (tailpiece); 8: Creation of Eve (frontispiece), flames (tailpiece); 9: The temptation of Eve (frontispiece), Serpent slithering through the grass (tailpiece); 10: Christ coming to Paradise (frontispiece), Christ bruising the head of the serpent (tailpiece); 11: Adam's vision of Cain murdering Abel (frontispiece), Noah's ark and the flood (tailpiece); 12: The expulsion (frontispiece), Flaming sword (tailpiece).

Craig's Design, 1805

Poetical Works of John Milton. London: Published by W. Suttaby and C. Corrall, 1805. William M. Craig's new illustration is engraved by Pye. *PR* 1: The Baptism of Jesus.

Designs Engraved by Akin and Harris, 1805

The Poetical Works of John Milton, 2 vols. Charleston: Printed by S. Etheridge and C. Stebbins, 1805. The frontispiece illustration for volume 1 is engraved by James Akin and the one for volume 2 is engraved by S. Harris. *PR* 2: Christ walking alone in the desert; *PL* 9: The temptation of Eve.

*Monsiau, Lebarbier Designs, 1805

Paradis Perdu, translated by Jacques Delille, 3 vols. Paris: Chez Giguet et Michard, 1805. The first frontispiece illustration, designed by Nicholas Monsiau, is engraved by Baquoy; and the other two, designed by Jean Jacques Lebarbier, are engraved by Triere and Thomas. *PL* 6: The routing of the rebel angels; 4: Adam and Eve in Eden; 12: The expulsion.

Thurston, Howard Designs, 1805

Paradise Lost. London: J. Johnson, C. and J. Rivington, etc., 1805. Four of these illustrations are by John Thurston, and the other (the design for Book 5) is by Henry Howard. The designs were engraved by Cromek, Scott, Neagle, and Warren. *PL* 2:

Devils singing; 4: Satan looking toward Eden; 5: Morning hymn; 6: Rallying the heavenly host; 10: Adam cursing his creation. Between 1795 and 1846 Howard exhibited twenty-four mythological subjects for Milton's poetry at the Royal Academy and British Institution; for example, The gardens of Hesperus, Circe, Sabrina, and Proserpina.

Gandy's Design, 1805

J. M. Gandy exhibited "Pandemonium: or Part of the High Capital of Satan and his Peers."

Thurston's Designs, 1805–1806

The Poetical Works of John Milton, 4 vols. Aikin's English Poets (vols. 12–15). London: Printed by J. Heath and G. Kearsley, 1805–6. John Thurston's designs are engraved by Heath, with three new designs appearing in volume 1 and one new design appearing in volume 3. *PL* 2: Satan enthroned, The birth of Sin; 3: Satan and Uriel. *PR* 1: The first temptation.

Fuseli, Westall Designs, 1805–1808

The Works of British Poets, ed. T. Park. London: Printed by J. Sharpe, 1805–8. These new designs by Henry Fuseli and Richard Westall are engraved by Tomkins. The illustrations to Books 1 and 9 of Milton's epic are by Fuseli; the illustration to Book 4 is by Westall. *PL* 1: Satan calling up his legions; 4: Satan, Ithuriel, and Zephon; 9: The temptation of Eve.

Blake's Designs, 1805–1809

During this period, William Blake made a second set of designs for Milton's *Mask,* which is now in the Museum of Fine Arts, Boston. Blake also did a set of twelve illustrations for *PL,* now in the Henry E. Huntington Library and Art Gallery, and a second set of designs for the same poem, this one composed of only nine designs, now in the Museum of Fine Arts, Boston. Finally, Blake painted two sets of illustrations for *Nat,* each with six designs. One of these sets is in the Whitworth Institute Gallery, Manchester, and the other is in the Henry E. Huntington Library and Art Gallery. The subjects for the second set of *Mask* designs are identical with the first (see above). The 1807 illustrations for *PL* 1: Satan calling up his legions; 2: Satan, Sin, and Death; 3: Christ offers himself as redeemer; 4: Satan's and Raphael's entries into Paradise, Satan watching Adam and Eve; 6: Raphael warning Adam and Eve; 6: The rout of the rebel angels; 8: Creation of Eve; 9: Temptation of Eve; 10: The judgment of Adam and Eve: 12: Michael foretells the crucifixion, The expulsion. The 1808 illustrations for *PL* 3: Christ offers himself as redeemer; 4: Satan watching Adam and Eve, Adam and Eve sleeping; 5: Raphael warning Adam and Eve; 6: The rout of the rebel angels; 8: Creation of Eve; 9: The temptation of Eve; 12: Michael foretells the crucifixion, The expulsion. It has been conjectured that the illustration of Satan calling up his legions in the Victoria and Albert Museum, the second depiction of Satan, Sin, and Death in the Henry E. Huntington Library and Art Gallery, and the painting of the Judgment of Adam and Eve in the Houghton Library, Harvard University, belong to this second set, which was at some time broken apart. There is, however, no convincing evidence for supporting such a conclusion. *Nat* (the subjects are the same in both sets): The descent of peace, The night of peace, Shepherds and the heavenly choir, The old dragon, The overthrow of Apollo, The flight of Moloch. The Boston set of *Mask* designs is reproduced in color by William Griggs, *Illustrations of Milton's Comus* (1890) and also by Angus Fletcher, *The Transcendental Masque* (1971), where the Boston and Huntington sets are reproduced side by side. The Huntington set of *PL* designs is reproduced in color by the Lyceum Press, *Paradise Lost* (1906), and by the Heritage Press, *Paradise Lost* (1940); the Boston set of *PL* is reproduced in color by Studio Publications, *Paradise Lost* (1947). Blake's designs for *Nat* have never been reproduced in color, but they are available in fine black and white reproductions: the Whitworth set is reproduced by Geoffrey Keynes, *On the Morning of Christ's Nativity* (1923), and the Huntington set is also reproduced by Keynes in the Nonesuch Milton (1926). For other reproductions of these designs, see J. A. Wittreich, "Appendix B," in *Calm of Mind* (1971), p. 332.

Craig's Designs, 1806

Paradise Regain'd. Albion Press. London: Printed by James Cundee, 1806. The name of the engraver for these new designs by William M. Craig is not given on the plates. Frontispiece, *PR* 1: The first temptation; 2: The banquet temptation; 3: Jesus on the mountain with Satan; 4: The Ministry of Angels.

Fuseli's Design, 1806

Paradise Lost. London: W. Suttaby, B. Crosby, and C. Corrall, 1806. Henry Fuseli's design for Book 2 of *PL,* The birth of sin, is engraved by Raimbach.

Thurston's Design, 1806

Paradist Lost (another edition). London: W. Suttaby, B. Crosby, and C. Corrall, 1806. John Thurston's new design is engraved by Mitan. *PL* 6: A voice is heard from a golden cloud.

Design Engraved by Tiebout, 1808

Paradise Lost. Philadelphia: Published by Johnson and Warner, 1808. This anonymous design for Book 10 of *PL,* Adam and Eve hiding, is engraved by C. Tiebout.

Flaxman's Designs, 1808

Latin and Italian Poems of Milton, trans. William Cowper and ed. William Hayley. Chichester: Printed for J. Johnson and R. H. Evans, 1808. John Flaxman's illustrations are engraved by Raimbach, and the originals are in the Henry E. Huntington Library and Art Gallery. Frontispiece: Milton's apotheosis (to the poet's right is a female figure with a serpent over her head [*PL*], and to his left is the same figure bruising the head of the serpent [*PR*]); *El* 3: The Bishop of Winchester standing before Milton; 4: Doris and her nymphs delivering Milton's epistle. About this time, Flaxman was preparing a set of illustrations for *PL.* The depiction of Satan and Beelzebub is for Book 1, and the drawings of the war in heaven, the atheist crew, and the fall of the rebel angels are for Book 6. These *PL* illustrations are reproduced as pls. xx and xxi by Sidney Colvin, *The Drawings of Flaxman in the University College* (1876).

West's Design, 1809

Benjamin West exhibited a drawing of Milton's Messiah (*PL* 6).

*Gillray's Design, 1810

James Gillray published a design inspired by Milton, depicting Satan with expanded wings (*PL* 1).

*Uwins's Designs, 1811

The Poetical Works of John Milton. London: Published by J. Walker and J. Harris, [1811]. Thomas Uwins's designs are engraved by Rhodes. Frontispiece: Michael descending (*PL* 11). Title-page: Christ's nativity (*PR* 2).

*Designs Engraved by Massard, 1812

Paradiso Perdido, 3 vols. Bourges: J. B. C. Souchois, 1812. These anonymous frontispiece-designs, one for each volume, are engraved by J. Massard. *PL* 1: Satan calling up his legions; 5: Morning hymn; 12: The expulsion.

Design Engraved by Springsguth, 1813

Paradise Lost. London: T. Tegg, 1813. This anonymous design, a frontispiece for the volume, is engraved by S. Springsguth. *PL* 9: Adam tempted.

Metz's Designs, 1814–1816

Three illustrations for *PL* by Conrad Metz are in the collection of Walter Brandt. Two of the designs depict Eve tempting Adam (9) and one depicts Satan meeting with Chaos (2).

Westall's Designs, 1816

Paradise Regained, etc. London: Printed for John Sharpe, 1816. These new Richard Westall designs are engraved by Finden. *PR* 2: Christ's dream of Elijah. *Lyc*: Phoebus speaking to the uncouth swain. *L'Al*: Zephyr with Aurora playing. *IlP*: Gorgeous tragedy. *Sonn* 10: The death of Isocrates. *Nat*: Star-led wizards.

Westall's Designs, 1816

Paradise Lost, 2 vols. London: Printed for John Sharpe, 1816. These designs by Richard Westall, decidedly different from those published in the Hayley edition of 1794–1797, are engraved by Heath, Corbould, Finden, Pye, and Eagleheart. Volume 1, *PL* 1: Satan flying through air; 2: Birth of Sin; 3: Satan and Uriel; 4: Satan startled by Ithuriel's spear; 5: Morning hymn; 6: Christ on his chariot. Volume 2, 7: Adam and Eve dining with Raphael; 8: Creation of Eve; 9: Eve tempted; 10: Adam and Eve repenting; 11: Adam and Eve witnessing the contention among the animals; 12: The expulsion.

Blake's Designs, 1816

William Blake did sets of twelve water-color designs both for *L'Al* and *IlP,* and for *PR.* The designs for Milton's twin lyrics are in the Pierpont Morgan Library and those for *PR* are in the Fitzwilliam Museum. *L'Al*: Mirth and her companions, Night startled by the lark, The great sun, The sunshine holiday, The stories of Corydon and Thyrsis, The poet's dream. *IlP*: Melancholy and her companions, The vision of the moon, Milton and the spirit of Plato, Milton led by Melancholy, The poet's dream, The peaceful hermitage. *PR* 1: The Baptism of Jesus, The first temptation; 2: Andrew and Simon Peter, Mary meditating, Satan in council, The banquet temptation; 3: The second temptation; 4: Jesus' ugly dream, Morning chasing away the spectres of the night, The temptation on the pinnacle, The ministry of angels, Jesus returning to Mary. The

illustrations for *L'Al* and *IlP* are reproduced in color by Adrian Van Sinderen, *The Mystic Genius* (1949) and those for *PR* are reproduced in black and white by J. A. Wittreich, *Calm of Mind* (1971).

Corbould's Design, 1817

Paradise Lost. London: F., C. and J. Rivington, etc., 1817. This illustration by Henry Corbould, which accompanies two previously published designs by Burney, is engraved by Heath. *PL* 4: Adam and Eve in the garden.

*Uwins's Designs, 1818

The Poetical Works of John Milton. London: Printed for J. Walker, F., C. and J. Rivington, etc., 1818. These Thomas Uwins designs are engraved by Corbould. *IlP*: Milton hiding from the day's garish eye. *Mask*: The Lady and Comus.

*Stothard's Designs, 1818

A Series of Magnificent Engravings to Illustrate the Various Folio and Quarto Editions of the Works of Shakespeare and Milton. London: Printed for H. Mc Lean, 1818. This volume supplements Thomas Stothard's previous efforts at illustrating Milton. The designs are engraved by Bartolozzi. *PL* 3: Uriel and Satan, Satan flying through air; 4: Adam and Eve reclining, Eve observing her reflection, Uriel gliding on a sunbeam; 5: Adam with unawakened Eve, Morning Hymn. The New York Public Library has an extra-illustrated copy of William Hayley's *The Poetical Works of John Milton* (1794–1797), which conveniently assembles Stothard's illustrations to *PL,* both in black and white and in color.

*Flaxman's Designs, ca. 1819

The Henry E. Huntington Library and Art Gallery has an illustration by John Flaxman that depicts Adam and Eve sleeping (*PL* 4). The design, on Whatman paper with an 1810 watermark, is reproduced as pl. 19 by Robert R. Wark, *Drawings by John Flaxman in the Huntington Collection* (1970).

Howard's Designs, 1821

Poetical Works of Milton. London: Suttaby, Evance, and Fox, etc., 1821. These new illustrations by Henry Howard are engraved by Portbury. *PL* 2: Moloch. *PR* 4: The temptation on the pinnacle.

Blake's Designs, 1822

Blake began a third set of illustrations to *PL* for John Linnell but completed only three designs: The creation of Eve (8), which is now in the National Gallery, Melbourne; Satan watching Adam and Eve (4), which is also in the National Gallery; and Michael foretelling the crucifixion (12), which is in the Fitzwilliam Museum. All three illustrations are reproduced by Geoffrey Keynes in the Nonesuch Milton (1926).

Hilton's Designs, 1823

William Hilton exhibited "Comus with the Lady: the Enchanted Chair" at the Royal Academy. At about this same time he did a series of illustrations for *PL*: Adam and Eve conversing with Raphael (5), Creation of Eve (8), and The expulsion (12).

Haydon's Design, 1823

Benjamin R. Haydon wrote a letter, dated December 10, 1823, explaining that he had completed a sketch of "Satan alighting" (*PL* 3).

*Stothard's Design, 1823

Thomas Stothard's illustration for Book 4 of *PR* is lost—a depiction of Christ on the pinnacle; but it was reportedly published in an 1823 edition of *PL* and *PR* by Tegg. A. C. Coxhead observes, however, that "In 'Paradise Regained' we have the Temptation, and see Satan cast down from the highest pinnacle of the temple, while angels come to minister to our Lord" (*Thomas Stothard, R.A.: An Illustrated Monograph* [1906], p. 105).

*Anonymous Design, [1824–1827]

The London Stage, 4 vols. London: Published for the Proprietors, [1824–27] (*Mask* appears as no. 23 in vol. 2). This unsigned illustration depicts the Lady in Comus's chair, and it appears as a headpiece for this adaptation of Milton's poem.

*Stothard's Design, 1826

The extra-illustrated edition of Todd's *The Poetical Works of John Milton*, 6 vols. (1826) in the Henry E. Huntington Library and Art Gallery contains an illustration for *Lyc* (the uncouth swain), designed by Thomas Stothard and engraved by Angus. The illustration appears in vol. 5, opp. p. 14.

Martin's Designs, 1826

The Paradise Lost of Milton, 2 vols. London: Septimus Prowett, 1826. John Martin both designed and engraved these illustrations. It should be observed, however, that these small plates, published with the text of the poem, differ markedly from the large plates issued without text. The large plates were also published by Prowett, but they were professionally printed by Messrs. Chatfield and Coleman and J. Lahee. Volume 1, *PL* 1: The fall of Satan, Satan on the burning lake, Satan rousing his legions, Pandemonium; 2: Satan enthroned, Satan, Sin, and Death; 3: Satan flying through air, City of God; 4: Eve observing her reflection, Satan watching Adam and Eve, Satan startled by Ithuriel and Zephon, Angels guarding Eden; 5: Morning hymn, Raphael coming to Eden, Raphael conversing with Adam and Eve; 7: Christ's descent into chaos; 9: The temptation of Eve, The temptation of Adam; 10: Adam and Eve sorrowing, The bridging of chaos, Adam and Eve quarreling; 11: Angelic song, Michael descending; 12: The expulsion.

Corbould's Design, 1829

Paradise Lost. London: Printed for the Booksellers, 1829. This design by Richard Corbould, different from any previously published, carries no signatures. *PL* 4: Adam and Eve in the garden.

Anonymous Design, 1829

Paradise Lost. Chiswick: C. Whittingham, 1829. This wood engraving carries no signatures. *PL* 12: The expulsion.

*Burford's Design, 1829

Description of an Attempt to illustrate Milton's Pandemonium, Now Exhibiting in the Panorama, Leicester Square. London: Printed by J. and C. Adlard, 1829. This volume contains an elaborate series of notes on the design by Robert Burford, which is here printed as a fold-out illustration. *PL* 1: Pandemonium.

*Anonymous Design, 1831

Paradise Lost. New York: S. King, 1831. This title-page design carries no signatures. *PL* 1: Satan flying with expanded wings.

*Design Engraved by Prudhomme, 1831

Paradise Regained and Other Poems. New York: Solomon King, 1831. This volume carries a double frontispiece. The first, engraved by E. Prudhomme, depicts Christ bruising the head of the serpent; the second, unsigned, portrays the crucifixion. Both designs are intended for *PR*.

Gandy's Design, 1831–1832

J. M. Gandy exhibited "The Hall of Pandemonium" and "The Gates of Heaven."

*Cruikshank's Design, 1833

Comus, a Masque in Two Acts. London: John Cumberland, [1833]. Robert Cruikshank's illustration is engraved by Bonner. *Mask*: Comus and his revelers.

*Anonymous, Fuseli Designs, 1833

The Gallery of Portraits, with Memoirs. London: Charles Knight, 1833. The first publication of Thomas De Quincey's "Milton" is accompanied by an anonymous headpiece depicting Adam and Eve with the beasts of Eden (*PL* 4) and by a tailpiece after Henry Fuseli's "Solitude"—a design for *Lyc*. Both illustrations are engraved by [Samuel] Jackson.

Turner's Designs, 1835

The Poetical Works of John Milton, ed. Egerton Brydges, 6 vols. London: John Macrone, 1835. J. M. W. Turner's illustrations are engraved by Brandard, Goodall, Graves, Cousen, Bacon, and Miller. Frontispiece to volume 1: Mustering of the warrior angels (*PL* 6). Frontispiece to volume 2: The expulsion (*PL* 12). Double frontispiece to volume 3: Satan on Mount Niphates (*PL* 4) and The fall of the rebel angels (*PL* 6). Frontispiece to volume 4: The temptation on the mountain (*PR* 3). Double frontispiece to volume 5: The happy man (*L'Al*), The rising of the water nymphs (*Mask*). Double frontispiece to volume 6: The temptation on the pinnacle (*PR* 4), St. Michael's Mount (*Lyc*).

*Richmond's Design, ca. 1835

George Richmond did a water color, recently acquired by the Henry E. Huntington Library, depicting the Lady in *Mask*.

Anonymous Design, 1839

The Poetical Works of John Milton. Edinburgh: Thomas Nelson, 1839. Frontispiece: The expulsion (*PL* 12).

Uwins's Designs, 1839

Paradise Lost. London: English Classics, 1839. Thomas Uwins's new design is engraved by Ransom. Title-page illustration: Satan, Sin, and Death (*PL* 2).

Haydon's Designs, 1840

Benjamin R. Haydon exhibited "Samson and the Philistines" at the Society of British Artists. At about the same time, he was working on a depiction of Adam and Eve, which was exhibited in 1842, and on a painting of Satan and Uriel, which was exhibited at the Royal Academy in 1845.

*Anonymous Design, 1840

Milton's Poetical Works. London: Charles Daly, 1840. This title-page design is unsigned. *PL* 1: Satan calling up his legions.

Harvey's Designs, 1843

The Poetical Works of John Milton, with a Memoir and Critical Remarks by James Montgomery, 2 vols. London: Tilt and Bogue, 1843. William Harvey's illustrations are engraved by Thompson, Smith, Williams, Green, Evans, and Gray. There are, besides the designs catalogued below, numerous decorations, many of them with particular iconographic and interpretive significance. For instance, the *PL* decorations depict a serpent slithering through the grass, a serpent with his head being crushed by a stone, a serpent twined around a cross; and *Nat* is adorned with a cross. Volume 1, *PL* 1: The fall of the rebel angels, Satan and Beelzebub, Satan and the fallen angels, The serpent encircled by a crown; 2: Satan enthroned, The rebel angels falling on their heads, The fallen angels contemplating foreknowledge, free will, and fate, Satan, Sin, and Death, Satan flying upward; 3: Satan flying through air, Angels in adoration, Satan as a stripling cherub, Satan lighting on Mount Niphates; 4: Satan observing Eden, Adam and Eve with animals of Eden, Satan startled by Ithuriel and Zephon, Satan fleeing Eden; 5: Adam and Eve in their bower, Adam and Eve dining with Raphael, Satan awakening Beelzebub; 6: Light and darkness in Heaven, Wounded Angels, The routing of the rebel angels, Eve listening to Raphael; 7: Urania descending, Christ entering chaos, Creation of the animals, Angelic choir; 8: Eve with the animals of Eden, Adam naming the animals, Raphael departing; 9: Satan returning to Eden, The serpent luring Eve, The temptation of Eve, Adam and Eve sorrowing; 10: Adam and Eve hiding, Sin and Death, Discord among the animals, Eve humbling herself at Adam's feet, Adam and Eve in an attitude of humiliation; 11: Adam and Eve observing the contention among the animals, Adam and Michael on the mount of vision, Adam's vision of Cain murdering Abel, Adam's vision of women roving in wanton dress, The covenant; 12: Adam and Michael atop the mountain, Moses with his rod extended, Christ's nativity, The expulsion. Volume 2, *PR* 1: The baptism of Jesus, Jesus going into the wilderness, The wild beasts coming forth to roam; 2: Jesus sleeping, Jesus entering the woody scene at noon; 3: Satan taking Jesus to the mountain top, The second temptation, Jesus beholding the idolaters; 4: The temptation on the pinnacle, Jesus' ugly dream, Jesus returning home. *SA*: Samson eyeless in Gaza, Samson meditating, Dalila shearing Samson's locks, Samson spurning Dalila, The officer unchaining Samson, Samson pulling down the pillars. *Mask*: Comus and the revelers, The Lady lost in the woods, One brother, Comus offering the Lady his cup, Sabrina and her nymphs. *Arc*: Fame descending. *Lyc*: Two shepherds with their flocks, The guarded mount. *L'Al*: Banishing loathed Melancholy, The poet with Mirth, *IlP*: Banishing vain, deluding Joy, Melancholy, The poet in his tower, The poet in the woods, The storied windows, *Sonn* 1: Nightingale. *Sonn* 23: Milton's apparition. *Nat*: The manger scene. *May*: May throwing cowslips and primroses.

*Fuseli's Design, 1844

The Poetical Works of John Milton. London: J. J. Chidley, 1844. Besides the designs by Westall and Martin, there is one previously unpublished design by Henry Fuseli, which is engraved by Rogers. *IlP*: Silence.

*Giraud's Designs, 1846

The Flowers of Milton [1846]. Jane Giraud's illustrations, reproduced in color, contain motifs with important iconographic significance. The lithographers are Day and Haghe. *PL* 4: Serpent slithering through the grass, Serpent coiled around a lily and a rose; 9: Fallen nature, The temptation of Eve, The serpent in a flower. *PR* 1: Crown of thorns; 2: A tree and a cross; 3: Jesus' dream of Elijah; 4: A cross and a tree embracing. *Mask*: Sabrina fair, Comus with his rod and cup, Children blowing a horn, Adonis sleeping in a rose. *L'Al*: Mirth, Poet's window, Shepherd telling his tale, Children carrying a basket of flowers. *Lyc*: Poet weeping, Shepherd with his staff, Shipwreck, Angel weeping. There are also many purely decorative designs, all of them depicting the flowers in Milton's poetry.

G. Scharf, H. O'Neil, W. E. Frost, R. Huskisson, J. Absolon, W. L. Leitch, J. Franklin, F W. Topham, F. Goodall, E. H. Corbould, H. C. Selous, J. Tenniel, K. Meadows, H. K. Browne, E. Armitage, T. F. Marshall, W. C. Thomas, E. H. Webnert, G. Dodgson, H. Warren, J. Phillip, J. Gilbert, J. E. Lauder, F. R. Pickersgill, E. Duncan, F. W. Hulme, E. M. Ward, D. Roberts, H. Vizetelly Designs, 1848

L'Allegro and Il Penseroso. London: Art-Union, 1848. These designs are engraved variously by the Williamses, Cooper, the Thompsons, Measom, Bartin, Nicholls, Green, the Masons, the Dalziels, Jackson, Linton, and Harding. *L'Al*: The poet greeting Mirth and banishing Melancholy, Mirth with sweet Liberty and other companions, Mirth at the poet's window, Shepherd under the hawthorn, Poet viewing the landscape, Towers and battlements, Corydon and Thyrsis, The young and old coming forth to play, Alehouse, Triumph of a knight, Hymen, Comedy, Orpheus, The delights of Mirth. *IlP*: The poet greeting Melancholy and banishing vain, deluding Joys, Melancholy in her bower, Pensive nun, Melancholy with Peace and Quiet, Trim gardens, Poet watching the wandering moon, Poet in his chamber, Poet in his tower watching the stars, Gorgeous tragedy, Orpheus drawing tears from Pluto, Dawn, The poet walking in the twilight groves, Poet lying on the bank, Cathedral, Poet as a priestly prophet.

C. W. Cope, T. Creswick, J. C. Horsley, F. Taylor, H. J. Townsend, C. Stonhouse, R. Redgrave Designs, 1849

L'Allegro, Illustrated by the Etching Club. London: Joseph Cundall, 1849. The plates carry no indication of who engraved them. *L'Al*: Mirth banishing Melancholy, Mirth and the sister graces, Mirth with Jest and Jollity, Dawn, The poet's window, Hound and horn, The eastern gate, The plowman, The milkmaid and mowers, Shepherd under the hawthorn, Shepherd surveying the landscape, Mountains and laboring clouds, Meadows, brooks, and rivers, Towers and battlements, Lady in the tower, Cottage between two aged oaks, Phillis leaving her cottage in haste, Phillis and Thestylis, The young and old coming forth to play, Alehouse, Faery Mab, The lady dreamer, The goblin, Threshing corn, The lubbar fiend, To bed they creep, Towered cities, Knights and barons, Knight in battle, The poet's dream, Orpheus in golden slumber.

Etty's Designs, ca. 1850

William Etty did one depiction for *L'Al* and two for *IlP*; he painted Circe and the three sirens, Sabrina and her nymphs, and the Hesperides for *Mask*, and also the morning hymn for Book 5 of *PL* and Adam's vision of the flood for Book 11; finally Etty did a drawing of Samson and Dalila.

*Designs Engraved by T. Brown, ca. 1850

The Complete Poetical Works of John Milton. Edinburgh: Gall and Inglis, [1850].

Designs 5, 6, and 7 are signed by their engraver T. Brown. Frontispiece: The expulsion (*PL* 12); title-page design: Eve relating her dream to Adam (*PL* 5); *PL* 2: Fallen angels singing of their doom: 7: Adam and Eve conversing with Raphael; 9: Satan entering the serpent; 12: The Nativity. *PR* 4: Satan inspires Jesus' ugly dreams. *L'Al*: Dancing in the checkered shade.

*Harvey's Designs, 1853

The Poetical Works of John Milton. London: George Routledge and Sons, 1853. William Harvey's new designs are engraved by E. Dalziel. Even when an old subject is depicted, that subject is newly conceptualized. Frontispiece: Milton inspired (lower half) and Satan calling up his legions (upper half; *PL* 1); 1: The fall of Satan; 10: Adam forgiving Eve; 11: Adam and Eve watching the contention between the wild animals as Sin and Death look on. *PR* 1: Jesus sleeping among the wild beasts as Satan approaches; 4: The ministry of angels. *SA*: Samson spurning Dalila. *Mask*: Comus giving the Lady his cup.

Foster's Designs, 1855

Milton's L'Allegro and Il Penseroso. London: David Bogue, 1855. These engravings on steel are designed and engraved by Birkett Foster. *L'Al*: Loathed Melancholy, Mirth with her companions, Poet listening to the lark, Poet at his window, Hounds and horn, Poet walking through elms and hillocks, The Plowman, The milkmaid, Shepherd with his flock, Poet beholding the landscape, Towers and battlements, Poet playing his lyre, Corydon and Thyrsis, Binding the sheaves, The young and old come forth to play, Alehouse, Knights and ladies, Orpheus. *IlP*: Divinest Melancholy, Melancholy and Saturn, Trim gardens, Poet listening to the nightingale, Poet beholding the moon, Poet hearing curfew sound, Poet in his tower, Rustling leaves, Poet reclining on the bank, Poet walking the cloister, Poet in peaceful hermitage.

F. R. Pickersgill, E. H. Corbould, B. Foster, H. Weir Designs, 1858

Comus. London: George Routledge, 1858. The thirty illustrations are engraved by the Dalziels. Frontispiece: Comus and the Lady in the enchanted palace; Lady in the wood; Three semi-nudes and child with glass; Comus and the revelers; Elves, fairies, and the sea; The measure; Lady lost in the wood; River scene; Lady with three figures; Oxen and herder; Landscape; Two brothers; Rooster and hens; Sheepfold at night; Two angels with the Lady,

Thyrsis led away, and a monster defeated; Thyrsis calling the two brothers; Young kid; Wolf; Two tigers; Sheepfold; Shepherds, sheep, dog, and river; Landscape with sheep; Lady in her chair, with Comus and his crew being attacked; Lady in her chair with Thyrsis and her two brothers looking on; Misled night wanderer; Two sea nymphs; Sea nymphs; Final dance before the seat of state; Presentation to the father and mother; Three Hesperides and the tree.

*Rossiter's Designs, 1865

A Description of Several Pictures Illustrating Milton's Paradise Lost. New York: Sanford and Harroun, 1865. This volume contains descriptions of five illustrations and identifies the texts being illustrated; however, it does not reproduce any of Thomas Rossiter's designs. *PL* 4–5: Eve, Morning, Noon, Evening, Adam.

*Doré's Designs, [1866]

Milton's Paradise Lost, with Notes and a Life by Robert Vaughan. London: Cassell, Petter, and Galpin, [1866]. Gustave Doré's illustrations are engraved by Tonnard, Laplante, Hotelin, Gusmand, Pannemaker, Jonnard, Coffon, Gauchard, Monvorson, Hurot, Demarle, Piaud, Ligny, Smelton, Hildebrand, Goebel, Gruchard, Baunier, Dumont, Hoyot, and Deschamp. *PL* 1: The fall of the rebel angels, Satan rising from the burning lake, Satan rousing his legions, Fallen angels hovering on wing, Summoning the devils; 2: Satan enthroned, Gorgons, hydras, and chimeras, Satan, Sin and Death, Satan's perilous journey; 3: God and the Son being praised by the angels, Paradise of fools, Satan flying through air; 4: Satan on Mount Niphates, Satan on the savage hill, The happy rural seat, Adam and Eve by the stream, Uriel returning to his charge, Ithuriel and Zephon going to the bower of Adam and Eve, Satan fleeing Eden; 5: Adam and Eve in their bower, The arrival of Raphael, Adam and Eve conversing with Raphael; 6: War in Heaven, The peak of battle, Satan wounded, Nightfall, Michael and his angels standing guard, Routing the rebel angels, Hell receiving the fallen angels; 7: Wave rolling upon wave, Water spawning reptiles, A whale, Fowl, The seventh night in Eden; 8: Raphael departing, Satan rising from the river; 9: Satan contemplating, Satan observing the serpent, Serpent approaching Adam and Eve, Serpent leaving Adam and Eve after the Fall, Adam and Eve sorrowing; 10: Christ's arrival in Eden, The devils awaiting Satan's return, Satan greeted by hissing serpents, Michael with his sword; 11: Heavenly bands arriving in

Eden, Building the ark, The flood; 12: Moses returning with his tablets, The expulsion.

*Small's Design, 1867

Milton's Hymn on Christ's Nativity. London and New York: Frederick Warne, 1867. William Small contributed a single design to this edition, entitled "The Dismal Dance about the Furnace Blue."

*E. M. Wimperis, W. Small, C. J. Durham, A. Moore, L. Frolich, J. Jackson, C. E. Hullah Designs, 1868

Milton's Ode on the Morning of Christ's Nativity. London: James Nisbet, 1868. Frontispiece: The happy morn; Holy sages once did sing; Star-led wizards. Frontispiece to *Hymn*: Emblematic cross; Manger scene; Emblematic letter ornament; Nature doffing her gaudy trim; Bethelehem; Descent of Peace; Mars with his arms laid aside; Hanging up the shield and spears; Neptune calming the ocean; Christ walking the waves; Seascape; Apollo checking his steeds; The morning of the Nativity; Adoration of Pan; The infant good shepherd; Shepherds keeping watch; Cynthia; Moonlight; Angelic choir; The weltering waves; The muses; Iris descending to earth; Mercy, Truth, and Justice; The child Jesus with visions of future suffering and triumph; Mount Sinai; The heathen oracle superseded; The shrine of Apollo; The nymphs mourning; Flamen pouring a libation; Ruined temple: Maids lamenting; The dismal dance; Memphion Grove; Hercules strangling the snake; Jesus triumphing over the pagan deities; Sun and Moon with their steeds; Manger scene.

*Anonymous Design, 187[2?]

The Poetical Works of John Milton. London and New York: Frederick Warne, [1872]. The illustration carries no signatures. Title-page design: Osiris (*Nat*).

*Anonymous Design, 1874

A Library of Poetry and Song, with an Introduction by William Cullen Bryant. New York: J. B. Ford, 1874. The illustration carries no signatures. *Sonn* 19: They also serve who only stand and wait.

*Thrupp Designs, 1879

Paradise Lost. London: Hardwick and Bogue, 1879. Frederick Thrupp's designs are not accompanied by a text of the poem. The designs in outline, unless otherwise indicated, are engraved by Thrupp. *PL* 1: The muse inspires (engraved by Joubert),

Moses inspired, The fallen angels, Satan's possession of hell, Satan calling up his legions; 2: Satan in council, Fallen angels contemplating foreknowledge, free-will, and fate, The birth of Sin, Satan, Sin, and Death; 3: Christ offers himself as redeemer, The humiliation, The triumph of Death, The triumph of Christ, Angelic choirs, Uriel and Satan; 4: Satan in Eden, Martial games, Night in Eden, Eve's dream, Zephon and Ithuriel; 5: Morning hymn, Adam entertaining Raphael, Satan reproved by Abdiel; 6: Michael calling up his legions, Abdiel encounters Satan, Christ's triumph, The fall of the rebel angels, Christ returning from conquest; 7: Grace descending; 8: Creation of Eve (engraved by Joubert), Adam forewarned; 9: Satan watching Adam and Eve, Satan discovering the serpent, Adam warning Eve (engraved by Joubert), The temptation of Eve; 10: Eve humbling herself before Adam; 11: Prevenient grace descending, Adam's vision of the Sons of God and Daughters of Men; 12: The expulsion (engraved by Joubert).

*Anonymous Design, ca. 1880

The Poetical Works of John Milton. Excelsior edition. New York: American News, [1880]. The illustrations carry no signatures. *PL* 4: Eve relates her dream; 7: Christ returning to heaven after the creation; 12: Michael with brandished sword. *PR* 1: Jesus wandering in the wilderness; 4: The temptation on the pinnacle, The ministry of angels.

*Beardsley's Design, 1888

Aubrey Beardsley depicted Milton's "happy man" and "contemplative man" in a single design for *L'Al* and *IlP,* which was first published as pl. 89 in *The Uncollected Work of Aubrey Beardsley* (1925).

Palmer's Designs, 1889

The Shorter Poems of John Milton. London: Seeley, 1889. Samuel Palmer designed and engraved these twelve illustrations. *Lyc*: Shepherds with their flocks. *L'Al*: The eastern gate, The prospect, A towered city. *IlP*: The curfew, The bellman, The lonely tower, Morning, The waters murmuring. *Mask*: Two Brothers, The dell of Comus, The brothers guided by the Attendant Spirit.

*Richomme, Flatters, Lemercier, Melin Bernouville Designs, 1891

Le Paradis Perdu. Paris: Gustave Guérin, 1891. The illustrations are engraved by S. and C. Lalaisse, Darodes, Celee, Pelee, Bein, Dien, Caron, Conquy, St. Eve, Migneret, Geille, Jouannin, Moret, Delaistre, Goulu, Rensonette, Nyon, Le Roux, Audebrand, and Allais. Besides these illustrations, there are various headpiece and tailpiece decorations, which develop the serpent motif by depicting such subjects as Satan meditating, the bat-winged serpent, a coiled serpent. Unless otherwise indicated, the illustrations listed below are by Flatters. *PL* 1: The fall of the rebel angels, The fallen angels on the burning lake, Satan and Beelzebub, Satan rousing his legions; 2: Council in Hell, Satan and Beelzebub, Satan struggling out of hell, Satan in chaos, Satan flying through air, Satan, Sin, and Death; 4: Eve observing her reflection (by Richomme), Eve smelling the roses, Adam and Eve kissing, Eve's dream (by Lemercier); 5: Raphael descending, Morning Hymn (by Lemercier), War in Heaven; 6: Routing the rebel angels, Satan plunging into the burning lake; 9: The temptation of Eve (by Melin), Eve eating the apple, Eve tempting Adam (by Melin); 10: Adam sorrowing, Adam forgiving Eve (by Melin); 11: Adam and Michael on the Mount of Vision, Adam's vision of Jubal and Tubal-Cain; 12: The expulsion (by Bernouville).

*Hornby's Designs, 1896

Three Poems of John Milton. Hertfordshire: Ashendene Press, 1896. These purely decorative designs are by C. H. St. John Hornby.

*Strang's Designs, 1896

Paradise Lost. London: John C. Nimmo, 1796. This is the first appearance of William Strang's designs. Each illustration is accompanied by the argument appended to the appropriate book of Milton's epic and by the text appropriate to the illustration. *PL* 1: Satan rising from the burning lake; 2: Satan, Sin, and Death; 4: Adam and Eve in the garden; 5: Adam and Eve dining with Raphael; 7: Creation of the world; 8: Creation of Eve; 9: The temptation of Eve; 10: Adam spurning Eve; 11: Adam's vision of Cain murdering Abel; 12: The expulsion.

Rickett's Designs, 1896

Early Poems of John Milton. London: Ballantyne Press, [1896]. The woodcut decorations are by Charles Ricketts.

*Bell's Design, 1898

English Lyrics from Spenser to Milton. London and New York: George Bell and Sons, 1898. The design by Robert Anning Bell is hand-colored by Gloria Cardew. *Mask*: Sweet Echo.

*Jones's Designs, 1898

The Minor Poems of John Milton. London: George Bell and Sons, 1898. Though this edition contains some purely decorative designs, most of the designs by A. Garth Jones are illustrative of the poems they accompany. The original pen-and-ink drawings are in the collection of J. A. Wittreich. *L'Al*: Mirth, Zephyr with Aurora playing, Laughter holding both his sides, The poet and the lark, The poet at his window, Shepherd under the hawthorn, Friar's lantern, The well-trod stage, The poet's dream, Orpheus. *IlP*: The poet contemplating, Melancholy, Pensive nun, The poet and the nightingale, The poet in his lonely tower, Orpheus with his lyre, Morn kerchiefed in a cloud, The poet by the stream, The poet in a cloister, The poet in old age. *Nat*: The nativity scene, Peace descending, The star with deep amaze, The parting genius. *FInf*: Weeping poet. *Carrier* 1: Death taking away the light. *Time*: Father Time. *SolMus*: Voice, verse, and music harmonized. *Lyc*: Mourning shepherd, Where were ye nymphs, Sporting with Amaryllis, Weep no more, He rose and twitched his mantle blue. *Arc*: Countess Dowager, Genius of the wood, The dance. *Mask*: The attendant spirit, Comus, Comus and his revelers, Echo, Stars, Attendant Spirit reclining on a bank, Lady bound to Comus's chair, Sabrina fair, Cupid and Psyche. *SA*: Samson meditating, Samson, Dalila, Manoa, Herapha, Samson and Officer, Manoa and Chorus, Samson pulling down the pillars, Samson mourned by the Chorus.

*Savage's Designs, 1901

Comus. The Essex House Press. London: Edward Arnold, and New York: Samuel Buckly, 1901. The wood-block design by Reginald Savage is in color. Frontispiece: Comus and his revelers.

*Anonymous Designs, 1901

On the Morning of Christ's Nativity in *The Critic*, Christmas no., 1901. Title-page design: Two angels in adoration; letter ornament: Two angels singing. Headpiece to *Hymn*: Peace descending; letter ornament: Nature doffing her gaudy trim; Three shepherds on the lawn; Apollo; Angels at the courtly stable; Jesus standing, wrapped in swaddling clothes; ornamental tailpiece.

*O'Kane's Designs, 1902

Comus. New Rochelle, N.Y.: Elston Press, 1902. This edition contains decorations by H. M. O'Kane.

*Townsend's Designs, 1902

L'Allegro and Il Penseroso. Chicago: The Blue Sky Press, 1902. The two illustrations are designed and engraved by Harry Everett Townsend. Frontispiece to *L'Al*: The happy man. Frontispiece to *IlP*: The contemplative man.

*O'Kane's Designs, 1903

L'Allegro and Il Penseroso. New Rochelle, N.Y.: Elston Press, 1903. The woodcuts are by H. M. O'Kane, whose color illuminations are accompanied by border decorations and letter designs. *L'Al*: Zephyr with Aurora playing, Haystacks and the barn door, The eastern gate, Towers and battlements, Cottage between two aged oaks, Youth dancing in the shade, Towered cities, Masque and antique pageantry, The world of Mirth. *IlP*: Sea nymphs, Trim gardens, Cynthia checking her dragon yoke, Som still place, Gorgeous tragedy, Forests and enchantments, Som brook, The world of Melancholy.

*Brodie's Designs, 1903

Lycidas. London and New York: John Lane, 1903. Gertrude Brodie provides eight designs for Milton's pastoral elegy. Frontispiece: Rough satyrs dancing; Headpiece: grim reaper touching the back of Lycidas; With forced fingers rude; The heavy change, now thou art gone; The blind Fury with the abhorred shears; The shearers' feast; The still morn; Tailpiece: The mourning shepherd with his lyre.

Bell's Designs, 1903

Lycidas and Other Odes. Carillon Series. London: George Bell and Sons, 1903. This volume, printed at the Chiswick Press, is illustrated by Robert Anning Bell. A few of the illustrations are only decorative, but most of them are designs depicting scenes from Milton's poetry. Prefatory designs: A garlanded figure, A woman meditating. Frontispiece to *Lyc*: Garlanded Poet; headpiece to *Lyc*: two figures sorrowing; Pan, Satyr, and two shepherds; Pan piping. Headpiece to *L'Al*: Mirth; Mirth with the poet who is banishing loathed Melancholy; Landscape. Frontispiece to *IlP*: Two figures in contemplation; headpiece to *IlP*: Landscape: Three figures in an attitude of contemplation; Poet burning the midnight lamp. Frontispiece to *Nat*: Manger scene; headpiece to *Nat*: The wise men; Two angels; Three angels singing; tailpiece to *Nat*: The poet receiving a wreath of laurel.

Hyde's Designs, 1904

The Poetical Works of John Milton. London: Astolat Press, 1904. William Hyde's illustrations are composed of etchings, mezzotints, and copper engravings. *L'Al*: The poet under the elms and hillocks, The eastern gate. *IlP*: Morning kerchiefed in a cloud. *May*: The bright morning star. *Arc*: Nymphs and shepherds dancing. *Lyc*: Shepherds with their flocks, The sinking day-star. *Mask*: Comus and his revelers. *PL* 1: Satan rising from the burning lake; 3: Satan flying through air; 4: Adam and Eve retiring to their bower; 6: The fall of the rebel angels; 9: The temptation of Eve. *PR* 1: Angels coming to the nativity, Satan bowing low his gray dissimulation. *SA*: Samson pulling down the pillars.

Strang's Designs, 1905

Paradise Lost. London: G. Routledge and Sons, and New York: E. P. Dutton, 1905. This volume contains twelve photogravures after the designs of William Strang (two portraits and ten illustrations). *PL* 1: Satan rising from the burning lake; 2: Satan, Sin, and Death; 4: Adam and Eve in the garden; 5: Adam and Eve dining with Raphael; 7: Creation of the world; 8: Creation of Eve; 9: The temptation of Eve; 10: Adam spurning Eve; 11: Adam's vision of Cain murdering Abel; 12: The expulsion.

King's Designs, 1906

Comus. Photogravure Series. London: George Routledge and Sons, and New York: E. P. Dutton, 1906. The twelve designs are by Jessie M. King. Frontispiece: The soothest shepherd; title-page design: A charmer with two pipes; dramatis personae page: Comus with his cup and wand and two children (upper border), Two charmers with pipes (lower border); Attendant Spirit; No goblin or swart faery; Thyrsis; Comus offers the Lady his cup; The Lady in the enchanted chair; Carol her goodness; The flight of Sabrina; The Lady with a cross and halo.

Harding, Robinson Designs, 1907

Milton's Hymn on the Morning of Christ's Nativity. London: George Allen, 1907. The illustrations are by Emily I. Harding and T. H. Robinson. Frontispiece: Virgin putting her babe to rest; Mary, Jesus, and two angels; Say, heavenly muse; Star-led wizards; Descent of Peace; The stars with deep amaze; Three shepherds on the lawn; Three shepherds beneath a tree; Angelic choir; Truth, Justice, and Mercy; Nymphs mourning; Lars and Lemures moaning;

Mooned Ashtaroth; Christ triumphing over the pagan deities; Three angels sitting in order serviceable.

*Anonymous Designs, 1908

The Poetical Works of John Milton, 4 vols. Boston: R. H. Hinkley, 1908. The illustrations that accompany this edition carry no signatures. Volume 1, *SA*: Samson meditating, Samson pulling down the pillars. Volume 2, *PL* 1: Satan and Beelzebub; 2: Satan, Sin, and Death; 5: Adam and Eve in the garden; 6: The fall of the rebel angels; 7: Adam and Eve conversing with Raphael. Volume 3, 9: The temptation of Eve; 12: The expulsion. *PR* 2: Mary meditating. Volume 4, *Mask*: The Lady and Comus. *Nat*: Christ routing the pagan deities. *L'Al*: Mirth. *Sonn* 23: Milton's apparition.

*Anonymous Design, 1912

The Henry E. Huntington Library and Art Gallery has an unsigned illustration, reminiscent of those by James Gilray, which depicts loathed Melancholy and which is entitled "Il Penserosevelt."

Rackham's Designs, 1921

Comus. London: William Heinemann, and New York: Doubleday Page, 1921. A separate edition was published during the same year in Paris by Librairie Hachette. Some of Arthur Rackham's illustrations are in color, and others are in black and white. Though there are a few decorative pieces, most of the designs are illuminations. *Mask*: Comus and his revelers, Attendant Spirit descending, Revelers headed like wild beasts, Neptune, Circe, Human countenances changed into brutish forms, Revelers carrying the head of a beast, Revelers making riotous and unruly noise, Pert faeries and dapper elves, Wood nymphs decked with daisies, A reveler, Two revelers dancing (the same motif governs the next two designs), Three revelers dancing, The head of a reveler, Comus as a harmless villager, The Lady entering the woods, The lonely traveler, A thousand fantasies, The Lady calling her brothers, Sweet Echo, Comus with his rod and cup, Three sirens in a bed of flowers, Two brothers, Snaky-headed Gorgon, Hag walking by night, Goblin, Faery and Virgin in the Forest, The huntress Dian, Revelers filling the air with barbarous dissonance, A stately palace, Daphne turning into a laurel tree, Ugly-headed monsters, Two brothers raising swords, Two revelers dancing, Sabrina and water nymphs, Water nymphs, Sabrina sitting under a translucent wave, Fair Legia's golden comb, Nymphs dancing, Sabrina rising, Water nymph, Sabrina attended by her nymphs, Sabrina rising again, Sabrina descending, Dancing at the end of the masque, Ludlow castle, Country dancers, Dancing lords and ladies, Iris with her arc.

Lowinsky's Designs, 1924

Paradise Regained. London: The Fleuron, 1924. *PR* 1: The infernal crew; 2: The banquet temptation; 4: The temptation on the pinnacle. Tailpiece to 4: Crown of thorns. Besides these illustrations there are a number of decorative headpieces and tailpieces also by Thomas Lowinsky.

*Russell's Designs, 1926

The English Sonnets of Mr. John Milton. Chelsea: Swan Press, 1926. The designs by Rachael Russell that accompany the poems are decorative.

*Bacheler's Designs, 1929

Early Poems of John Milton, ed. Mercy A. Brann. New York: Henry Holt, 1929. The illustrations are by Isabel Bacheler. Title-page design for *L'Al*: Mirth with two companions; By hedgerow elms, The nibbling flocks, Towers and battlements. Title-page design for *IlP*: Female votary and cloister; The studious cloister's pale. Title-page design for *Mask*: Comus, the Lady, and three revelers; Offering the orient liquor; Soon as the potion works; On the tawny sands and shelves; The flowery kirtled Naiades; Retaining her maiden gentleness; Ludlow Castle. Title-page design for *Lyc*: Flowers and butterflies; Ye valleys low; The guarded mount.

*Evergood's Designs, 1929

Lycidas. New York: H. L. Biness, 1929. This volume contains four original etchings by Philip Evergood. Female figure, surrounded by many others, preparing to bestow a garland; Two shepherds; The dead Lycidas; Alpheus and Arethuse.

*Brodovitch's Designs, 1929

A Brief History of Moscovia and Less-known Countries. London: Blackamore Press, 1929. This volume contains seven ornamental designs, including a frontispiece, by A. Brodovitch.

*Thompson's Designs, 1930

On the Morning of Christ's Nativity. Sussex: Pear Tree Press, 1930. The designs are by S. M. Thompson. End-papers: Mary and child. Frontispiece: Peace descending and pagan deities fleeing.

Hughes-Stanton's Designs, 1931

Comus. Newtown: Gregynog Press, 1931. These designs are by Blair Hughes-Stanton. Frontispiece: Attendant Spirit descending. Title-page design: The Lady. Comus with his rod and cup, The Lady, Two brothers with swords drawn, Thyrsis, Sabrina, Virtue.

Galanis's Designs, 1931

Paradise Lost. London: Cresset Press, 1931. These woodcut illustrations are by D. Galanis. Frontispiece to the volume: Satan rising from the burning lake (*PL* 1). Frontispiece to *PL* 1: The expulsion. 2: Satan flying through chaos; 3: The crucifixion; 4: Satan despairing; 5: Eve's dream; 6: The fall of the rebel angels; 7: Creation of Man; 8: Adam and Eve in their nuptial bower; 9: Eve tempting Adam; 10: Satan transformed into a hissing serpent; 11: The rainbow and a dove; 12: Death expelling Adam and Eve from Eden. Tailpiece to the volume: A coiled serpent.

Galanis's Designs, 1931

Paradise Regained. London: Cresset Press, 1931. These woodcut illustrations are by D. Galanis. *PR* 1: The Baptism, Adam and Eve in the happy garden; 2: The banquet temptation; 4: Great and glorious Rome, Satan falling from the pinnacle. The volume also contains a tailpiece decoration.

*Ruzicka's Design, 1932

Milton's L'Allegro. Stamford, Conn.: Ashlar Press, 1932. The woodcut is by Rudolph Ruzicka. Title-page design: Loathed Melancholy.

Hughes-Stanton's Designs, 1933

Four Poems by John Milton. Newtown: Gregynog Press, 1933. The designs are by Blair Hughes-Stanton. Half-title-page design for *L'Al*: Mirth with a companion; Girl and nude, male archer; Tailpiece: Girl and nude, male archer. Half-title-page design for *IlP*: Girl and nude, male archer separated and walking away from each other; Man, woman, and child. Half-title-page design for *Arc*: Two figures; Countess Dowager. Half-title-page for *Lyc*: Lycidas in the sea, ministered to by two mermaids; Black Proteus; Tailpiece: A shepherd piping.

*O'Kane's Designs, 1934

Samson Agonistes. New Rochelle, N.Y.: Elston Press, 1934. The woodcuts by H. M. O'Kane are decorative.

*Petrina's Designs, 1936

Paradise Lost and Paradise Regained, with an Introduction by William Rose Benét. San Francisco: Limited Editions Club, 1936. These illustrations are designed by Carlotta Petrina. *PL* 1: Satan plunging into the burning lake; 2: Sin and Death; 3: The Father and Son; 4: Adam and Eve with the animals of Eden; 5: Adam and Eve dining with Raphael; 6: War in heaven; 7: The creation; 8: God creating Eve; 9: Fallen Eve; 10: The hissing serpents and Adam and Eve repentent; 11: Adam's vision of the future with three crosses in the distance; 12: The expulsion. *PR* 1: The baptism; 2: The banquet temptation; 3: The Kingdoms temptation; 4: The temptation on the pinnacle.

*Groom's Designs, 1937

Paradise Lost. London: Golden Cockerel Press, 1937. The illustrations by Mary Groom accompany a ten-book version of *PL*. Besides the illustrations, there are decorations at the beginning of each book of Milton's epic. *PL* 1: Milton inspired, Satan calling up his legions, Pandemonium; 2: The infernal trinity, Satan addressing the council; 3: God and the Son contemplating the fate of man, Christ offers himself as redeemer, The angels adoring the redeemer; 4: Satan entering Eden, Adam and Eve reclining by the stream; 5: Adam awakening Eve, Adam and Eve sleeping, Adam and Eve dining with Raphael; 6: War in heaven, Good and bad angels, Satan with his host; 7: Adam and Eve conversing with Raphael, The tawny lion; 8: Creation of Eve; 9: Milton beginning to soar, The temptation of Eve, The temptation of Adam; 10: Angels leaving Eden, Satan, Sin, and Death, Adam and Eve sorrowing; 11: Adam and Eve praying, Adam's vision of biblical history; 12: The expulsion.

*Mc Kenzie's Design, 1937

On the Morning of Christ's Nativity. Newtown: Gregynog Press, 1937. The woodcut engraving is by Alison McKenzie. *Nat*: Jesus in his manger.

Farrar's Designs, 1937

The Mask of Comus, ed. E. H. Visiak. Bloomsbury: Nonesuch Press, 1937. The illustrations are by M. R. H. Farrar. *Mask*: Comus and the Lady, The Attendant Spirit descending, Sweet Echo, The rabble, Sabrina.

*Anonymous Designs, 1947

John Milton Poems. Mount Vernon, N.Y.: Peter Pauper Press, [1947]. These anonymous designs are decorative.

Dulac's Designs, 1954

The Masque of Comus. Cambridge: Printed for the Limited Editions Club at the University Press, 1954. Edmund Dulac's designs are printed in color. *Mask*: The huntress Dian, Circe, Comus and his revelers, Comus and the Lady, Nude Lady with a tree and dragon. The Lady in Comus's chair.

IL PENSEROSO: *see* L'ALLEGRO AND IL PENSEROSO.

IMAGERY, VISUAL AND AUDITORY. *Imagery* is used by literary critics in two general senses. One meaning is "figures of speech, mainly similes and metaphors." *Milton's Imagery,* by Theodore H. Banks (1950) construes the term in this way. Study of the areas of experience to which a poet instinctively turns in search of analogies can lead to interesting conclusions about his mind and character; and the tracing of filiations may often reveal elaborate, although not necessarily intended, structural patterns in his writing. The other meaning has to do with the "literal and concrete representation of a sensory experience" (William Flint Thrall and Addison Hibbard, *A Handbook to Literature* [1960], "Image"). The second meaning will be adopted here. What is of concern to the present discussion is not figures of speech that can be given rhetorical names but what the attentive reader of Milton's poetry sees and hears as his eyes follow the lines. Thus the sentence "The grass is green" contains a visual image because greenness is a visual sensation, and "He spoke loudly" contains an auditory image because loudness is appreciated only by the ear. The test is whether anything in the poetry might be represented by a musical analogue, as by a roar of drums or singing strings, or might be painted, if only by a slash of color. Because the major poems—*Mask, PL, PR,* and *SA*—resist synoptic treatment, half the space will be

given to shorter works, and Latin, Italian, and Greek poems will not be discussed at all. A review of earlier scholarship is prevented by its richness. Nearly all searching discussion of Milton's artistry has necessarily paid some attention to imagery, but aside from Banks's study no essay or book is "classic."

Apart from the translations of some psalms, Milton's earliest surviving English poem is *FInf* (1628). The experiment was by no means an altogether happy one, and the visual imagery is sometimes awkward. The baby girl is at first a "fairest flower" whose blossom has been dried by "Bleak winters force"; the flower's color then becomes "that lovely die / That did thy cheek envermeil," and Winter's amorous kiss results in the child's death. If the image contains an implicit shiver, the effect is weakened by the fancy that Winter had felt himself diminished by the North Wind's "boisterous rape" of Orithyia and therefore had determined "to wipe away th'infamous blot, / Of long-uncoupled bed, and childless eld." The two-year-old girl—an "infant"—is a ludicrously inappropriate object for the god's purpose, so that we must choose between thinking Winter very stupid and suddenly metamorphosing the baby into a ripe maiden. A recovery is made in the third stanza, where the god's "ycie-pearled carr" and "freezing aire" are satisfyingly frigid. His descent from "his Snow-soft chaire" to give the girl a "cold-kind embrace" that unhouses her virgin soul develops still further a conceit that must have had its origin in a personification of "cold" or "chill." From this point the images appear mostly in brief phrases and flash across the reader's consciousness almost too quickly to be sensed: for example, the transformation of Hyacinth to a purple flower, a corpse corrupting "in earths dark wombe," a "low delved tombe," a face that shines divinely, a bright spirit hovering "above that high first-moving Spheare / Or in the Elisian fields," a star falling "from the ruin'd roofe / Of shak't Olympus," "the wall / Of sheenie Heav'n," a "nectar'd head," "white-robed truth" in the guise of a crowned matron, and Satan or his works as "Swift-rushing black perdition." The final stanza sinks to quiet acceptance but is marred by a promise the young poet had no right to make. Yet despite flaws the poem's imagery shows both visual energy and an ability, whether native or acquired by practice in writing Latin verse, to offer rapid but meaningful glimpses of objects that would suffer from elaborate description.

Vac (1628) begins with a description of childish speech, full of "tripps, / Half unpronounc't," which "slide through . . . infant-lipps"; but the verse itself does not trip. Milton was never to seek the cheap victories of blatant onomatopoeia. The "first endeavouring tongue" thus drove "dum silence from the portal dore [the mouth], / Where he had mutely sate two years before." If, as W. R. Parker has noted, the phrase contains a double tautology, it also suggests a taste for personification derived, possibly, from Latin poetry and Milton's favorite English poet, Spenser*. In the crisper couplets that follow, the English interpolated in a Latin exercise is described as the daintier dishes that follow a substantial feast, and the "wardrope" or poetic vesture of the thought is desired to be not fantastic, as—probably—in metaphysical verse*, but rich and gay, as is suitable for deep spirit and choice wit. The thoughts that cram the poet's head and "knock to have their passage out" are as yet "naked." The "graver subject" that is to follow (a description of *Ens* or Being and the ten Aristotelian* "predicaments") is presented vividly as seeking the "fit sound" that marked a song sung by Apollo about "secret things that came to pass / When Beldam Nature in her cradle was" and "Kings and Queens and *Hero's* old"—as in that other song sung by Demodocus at the feast of King Alcinous, "While sad *Ulisses* soul and all the rest / Are held with his melodious harmonie / In willing chains and sweet captivitie." In the meantime we have heard of the necessity of English speech to search among its

coffers, of a "deep transported mind" soaring "Above the wheeling poles" and looking in "at Heav'ns dore" to "see each blissful Deitie / How he before the thunderous throne doth lie," of Hebe bringing "Immortal Nectar to her Kingly Sire," of "Spheres of watchful fire," of "mistie Regions of wide air," of "hills of Snow and lofts of piled Thunder," and of "green-ey'd *Neptune*" raving while he musters his waves in defiance of Heaven. In what remains the sharpest visual shock is extra-literary : when a fellow student named Rivers "rose" through a trapdoor or from behind some stage property in response to the command "RIVERS arise," the hall must have rocked with laughter, and the din must have increased as the poet speculated with mock seriousness about what river he might be. The young writer has made progress. Already his verse is visually rich, and the *Exercise* contains no sensory anomaly like that of the infant maiden in the earlier work. At most, an exceptionally eye-minded critic might object that dumb Silence is not "driven" instantaneously from a child's lips but retreats slowly as syllables become words and these, in turn, phrases, and finally sentences.

Nat (1629) although still youthfully exuberant, is more mature. As Arthur Barker observed (*University of Toronto Quarterly* 10 : 167–81), the scene is elaborately cleared for Christ's birth. Nature wears no gawdy trim, does not wanton with the sun; the sinful landscape is covered with "innocent Snow." There is universal peace : spear and shield hang on the wall, the hookèd war-chariot stands motionless unstained with blood, the trumpet is silent, kings sit quietly and look awe-inspiring. The winds are "whist"; halcyons sit brooding on charmed waves; the stars are "fixt in stedfast gaze"; the sun hesitates to rise; the shepherds sit "simply chatting in a rustick row." We are thus made expectant; and when the "Divinely-warbl'd voice" and a "stringed noise" or group of instruments break the hush, they are at the focus of our attention and relieve a strain.

Elsewhere the imagery is also striking. Mercy is described, in a future time, as wearing "Celestial sheen" and "With radiant feet the tissued clouds down stearing." We perceive brightness and glory ("radiant") and are startled by the spectacle of a goddess "stearing" with her feet as she descends, rudder foremost, as it were, pushing billowy clouds aside, or making for cleavages between them as if they were a real obstacle. A moment later we glimpse as a smiling and passive infant the Christ who "on the bitter cross / Must redeem our loss." The implicit contrast of comfortable lying with painful hanging, of helpless infancy with helpless adulthood, and of smiling with an inferred expression of agony, is very sharp. When mention is made of "The wakeful trump of doom" clamor breaks out: thunder, clang, ringing. The appropriate response is to become, like the earth, "agast" with terror.

So much, and more, even before we come to the celebrated stanzas that describe the flight of pagan gods from their oracles (19–25). Here the auditory imagery is especially powerful: "shreik," "resounding," "weeping," "loud lament," "sighing," mourning, moaning, "A drear and dying sound," ringing cymbals, and "lowings loud," all specified in verse that unobtrusively imitates the sounds by its sonority and movement. Last of all, quiet returns, again suddenly. Before we realize what is happening the rising sun is in bed, lolling indolently behind red curtains (the clouds) with his chin on a pillow (the ocean). The shadows "Troop to the'infernal Jail"; the ghosts, dragging fetters —which do not, however, sensibly rattle— "slip" to their graves; the fairies fly away "after the Night-steeds," and we see the "Babe" again at rest. The cessation of movement extends to the new star, which, like the stars at the beginning, has "fixt" its polished car to attend its lord like a handmaiden with a lamp, and about the manger "Bright-harnest Angels sit in order serviceable." It is a bravura performance by a poet as yet barely twenty-one-years old.

Passion, written almost certainly in March 1630, was an unsuccessful attempt to do for Good Friday what had successfully been done for Christmas. It is a textbook example of dogged determination unbrightened by any spark of inspiration. When Christ, the "sov'ran Priest," accepts human form He stoops "his regal head / That dropt with odorous oil down his fair eyes." The reader may sense, incorrectly, that the purpose of the stooping was to deflect the oil from his eyes. In entering a "Poor fleshly Tabernacle" the Son bows "His starry front low-rooft beneath the skies." Although the image to some tastes may seem to verge on grotesquerie, it carries surprise; we watch stars, usually high in the heavens, move down to earth at the same time we try to see them as constituting or decorating a forehead, and then both stars and forehead disappear within a vaguely perceived body that, because it now contains the Godhead, is also a tabernacle. At the very end of the poem the tears of grief shed over the crucifixion engrave lines of verse (the poem itself) as they fall on the "sad Sepulchral rock" that seals Christ's tomb. Milton is trying hard, but nothing works. Elsewhere the imagery—for example, of night in the fifth stanza and of Ezekiel's chariot in the sixth—is, for Milton, undistinguished. The young poet was right in being "nothing satisfi'd with what was begun" and in leaving the poem unfinished.

Although almost certainly not written next, *Circum* (1631–1633) belongs with *Nat* and *Passion* as one of three occasional poems written for Christian holy days. In its latter half the poem is basically conceptual. The earlier section, however, begins with the "flaming Powers, and winged Warriours bright" who, "with Musick, and triumphant song," sang their joys to the shepherds on Christmas Eve. It then moves to grief and begs the angels, who because their essence is fire cannot weep, to borrow "Seas wept from our deep sorrow" to bewail the fact that "He who with all Heav'ns heraldry whilear / Enter'd the world, now bleeds to give us ease." The whole poem is thus focused on Christ's bleeding both when circumcised and when crucified and derives from a perception of sameness in wounds from which blood spurts.

EpWin (1631) attracts attention to its sound-patterns through the avoidance of mechanical movement by exactly the margin necessary to reveal deftness. No poet of Milton's aural sensitivity could have rhymed on "WINchesTER" without awareness that he was skillfully distorting normal pronunciation. Evidently he obtained pleasure also from cramming the lines with precise data, as in "A Vicounts daughter, an Earls heir" and "Summers three times eight save one / She had told, alas too soon." The impression given is that precisely the firmness that had been lacking in the strung-out sentences of *Passion* has been achieved, and with masterly ease. Similarly, the comfort offered at the end lacks the brash presumption of the promise in *FInf*.

Visual quality is subsumed within ordered sound without the sacrifice of its proper interest. The "honour'd Wife" now interred by the marble has had only a "short time of breath" (the motor image of breathing substituted for "life") before housing "with darkness, and with death." The darkness is succeeded by fancies about the Marchioness's wedding: a god sitting at the marriage feast holding "a scarce-wel-lighted flame" and wearing a garland that included a half-hidden cypress bud emblematic of early demise. The "early Matrons" had once "run / To greet her of a lovely son," and now she "goes" to childbed again, to be met there, instead of by Lucina, by Atropos, who spoils both "fruit and tree" (son and mother) and causes the child to be buried while still in the womb, as a carefully cultivated carnation may be "Pluck't up by som unheedy swain" who at the same time destroys the plant. The poet himself brings "tears of perfect moan / Weept for thee in Helicon, / And som Flowers, and some Bays" to strew the roads before the hearse. The dead mother, now a saint, sits high in glory like Rachel, who had

died in giving birth to Benjamin and, like the Marchioness, is "clad in radiant sheen." Again the characteristically strong forward movement has prevented the leisurely development of images. For the poet and his expected reader, hints are enough. The success of the epitaph indicates that at this stage Jonson's* poetic mode was still well within Milton's scope and that he might have followed a path from which he turned away.

Several shorter poems written at various dates may be considered together. *Time* (1633?), possibly written for inscription on a clock case, personifies its subject as a runner who urges on "lazy leaden-stepping hours," glutting himself meanwhile on what is destroyed by time ("what thy womb devours"). No loss results, since Time can eat up only "what is false and vain, / And meerly mortal dross"; and in the end he must devour himself and give way to eternity, at whose kiss "Joy shall overtake us as a flood." The dominant images are of running and devouring. *SolMus* (1630–1633?) is concerned with "concent" or harmony, especially that of "Voice, and Vers," or poetry and music. If voice and verse are indeed "Sphear-born harmonious Sisters," they resist visualization, and the wedding of their "divine sounds" has no pictorial aspect. The "undisturbed Song" that results is sung before "the saphire-colour'd throne" of God. At this point the imagery becomes prevailingly auditory: we hear shouts and "solemn Jubily," listen to angels blowing uplifted trumpets and playing thousands of harps, and are told of—though we do not hear—hymns and psalms. Again outright onomatopoeia is avoided, and the most remarkable auditory quality of the poem is the necessity of marking vocally the syntactical relationships of a sentence prolonged through twenty-four lines. *May* (1629–30?) pictures briefly "The Flowry *May,* who from her green lap throws / The yellow Cowslip, and the pale Primrose." The verse is auditorily pleasant, but from the special point of view adopted here is unremarkable. *Shak* (1630) is based on the conceit that Shakespeare does not need a visual monument like a bust over his tomb because he has built himself "a live-long Monument" in our wonderment at his genius. Indeed, we ourselves are made "Marble with too much conceaving," so that as we sit immobile with the plays in our hands we might be mistaken for effigies. Finally—since space is lacking for a one-by-one consideration of the English sonnets—the two *Carrier* poems (1631) are exercises in wit and consist largely of grotesque metaphors. Sensory response is sometimes invited but is rarely vivid. When we read that "Here lies old *Hobson,* / Death hath broke his girt, / And here alas, hath laid him in the dirt," we may, if we like, see a dangling saddle and a rider lying on a dusty or muddy road. Alternatively, Hobson may be "stuck in a slough, and overthrown." Finally we see Death showing old Hobson "his room where he must lodge that night," pulling off his boots, and departing with the candle. The second of the companion-pieces is given over almost entirely to paradoxes and need not concern us.

L'Al and *IlP* (1631?) show in a different way the Jonsonian* influence apparent in the *EpWin*. The pace of the firm tetrameter couplets varies between the speed of "Com, and trip it as you go / On the light fantastick toe" and the agreeable retardation of "And joyn with thee calm Peace, and Quiet, / Spare Fast, that oft with gods doth diet." (Ten consecutive readings of the first couplet by the present writer took thirty-three seconds, ten readings of the second sixty seconds.) The reason why a jog trot is avoided is partly this variation and partly the density of the imaginal content.

Auditory imagery, although subsidiary to visual, is plentiful. In *L'Al* we hear shrieks in the Stygian cave, the faint crackle of quips and cranks, laughter, the lark's singing, the cock's crow, the clatter of hounds and horn, the whistling of the plowman, the milkmaid's songs, the whetting of the mower's scythe, the murmur of shepherds' voices, the music of merry bells and jocund rebecks, the whisper of winds, contentions of wit or arms, and, finally, the "soft *Lydian* Aires" that contain "many a winding bout / Of lincked sweetness long drawn out, / With wanton heed, and giddy cunning," so that the "melting voice through mazes running" untwists "The hidden soul of harmony" from its chains. *IlP*, although more contemplative, also contains sounds: the Muses singing about Jove's altar, the nightingale—if it deigns a song—"Smoothing the rugged brow of night" with its melody, the evensong of Melancholy herself, the "far-off *Curfeu*" sounding "Over some wide-water'd shoar, / Swinging slow with sullen roar," the cricket on the hearth, the drowsy charm of the bellman, the imagined song of Musaeus or Orpheus, fit to draw "Iron tears down *Pluto's* cheek," the loud piping of "rocking Winds," a quiet shower that causes "minute drops" to fall from the eaves, the *silence* of "the rude Ax with heaved stroke," the bee's hum, the water's murmur, the "sweet musick" breathed by "som spirit," and, last of all, the pealing organ and "full voic'd Quire," so sweet that they can dissolve the hearer into ecstasies. The writer of the poems keeps his ears wide open and registers faithfully some of the auditory qualities of his real and imagined experiences.

The visual energy of the twin pieces is even greater, although its demands on the reader are sometimes extreme. For example, "Sport that wrincled Care derides" may to many readers appear not essentially different from "playfulness that makes fun of seriousness." Yet Wrinkled Care is both concept and image: image because, like the Black Care in Horace's* *Post equitem sedet atra Cura* (*Carmina* 3. i. 40), he is given a visual trait, wrinkles, which in turn require the sensing of a forehead. It would be a mistake to suppose either that a wrinkled forehead cannot be imagined alone or that, once seen, it must be fleshed out with the rest of a face and a whole body. "Laughter holding both his sides" is a comparable image in which the stress falls on posture. "The Mountain Nymph, sweet Liberty," is, in contrast, more concept than girl, whereas the scattering of "the rear of darknes thin" by the cock's crow evokes the disruption of a marching column with sufficient vividness almost to smother the concept. At places we see clearly but without detail, as when we come to "Towers, and Battlements . . . / Boosom'd high in tufted Trees." Again, the situation is clearer than the spatial arrangement, as when we meet Corydon and Thyrsis "at their savory dinner set / Of Hearbs, and other Country Messes, / Which the neat-handed *Phillis* dresses." The sitting suggests relaxation after toil, but unless "dresses" is borrowed from a peripheral glimpse of Phyllis's costume, what we perceive is chiefly neat hands arranging dishes. When the "Lubbar Fend," Puck, "lies him down" and stretches out "all the Chimney's length" after drinking the cream set out for him, we are made aware of spatial arrangements but see dimly, or not at all, the body of the recumbent goblin. Once more, Orpheus* heaves his head from "golden slumber" on a bed piled with Elysian flowers. The impression is of a reluctant awakening amid softness and a riot of color. In both pieces the evocation of attitudinal biases is accomplished by the happy union of cortical and sensory activity that marks Milton's poetry from the beginning.

Arc, an entertainment written between 1630 and 1634, is the last of the poems we can look at synoptically. The first "song" is dominated by light imagery and the admiration its source evokes. (Brilliance regularly suggests goodness in Milton. Where it does not, we are warned.) The Dowager Countess blazes with majesty, spreads radiant state "In circle round her shining throne," and shoots forth "beams like silver threds" as she sits, goddesslike, "In the center of her light." Unless we wish to perceive the circle and threads as equivalent to voluminous skirts spread carefully over flagstones or grass, little can be sensed but brightness; but light can easily be seen simply as light. The Genius's speech, which follows, picks up brilliance by referring at once to "bright honour" sparkling in the swains'—really *"Noble Persons'"*—eyes, then moves through a subdued glimpse of rivers to "the breathing Roses of the Wood." These are at once identified as "Fair silver-buskin'd Nymphs" who have also come to show honor and devotion to "the great Mistres of yon princely shrine," toward whom the reader's eyes revert for a split second. Next comes the Genius's description of his care for the wood, which includes his "Oak'n bowr," saplings, a "grove / With Ringlets quaint," plants, dew-covered boughs, a "hurtfull Worm with canker'd venom," slumbering leaves, the tasseled horn of a deer that "Shakes the high thicket," and sprouts. As often, a basic question arises : does a word like *Saplings,* even when qualified by *tall,* or better still, the unqualified and generalized *Plants* produce an image? Or do images result only when the generic term is sharply qualified, as when the boughs are said to be covered with "evil dew" that the Genius must brush off? Or are even these too little specific? To such questions each reader must give his own answer.

At this point the imagery becomes predominantly auditory as the poet speaks of "the celestial *Sirens* harmony" produced by beings that "sit upon the nine enfolded Sphears" of the celestial universe as they sing to the Fates, who "hold the vital shears, / And turn the Adamantine spindle round." Such music as this has "sweet compulsion . . . / To lull the daughters of *Necessity,* / And keep unsteddy Nature to her law," so that the lower world is drawn "in measur'd motion" after the "heavenly tune." Only such music is fit to "blaze" ("emblazon," with a suggestion of brightness) the Countess. The Genius is unable to "hit / Inimitable sounds" adequate to his purpose but will do the best he can as the nymphs and swains "Approach, and kiss her sacred vestures hemm." Here follows the song that caused A. E. Housman to cut himself because of the rising of goosepimples if he happened to think of it while shaving: "O're the smooth enamel'd green . . ." The piece concludes with a second song filled with sonorous proper names. We need not wonder that the author was invited later to write the complete—or longer—work that we know as *Mask*.

Like the other poems remaining to be discussed, *Mask* (1634) is much too complex to be done justice in a few paragraphs. The major settings are the "perplex't paths" of a "drear Wood," the "stately Palace" of Comus, and "*Ludlow Town and the Presidents Castle*." Of these, the first is Dante's *selva oscura*, a part of "the smoak and stirr of this dim spot, / Which men call Earth," but it is not at first elaborately described. When we meet the Lady, we learn that it has "blind mazes" and is "tangl'd," includes pines and thickets, and is not at the moment lighted by the stars, which are closed up in Night's dark lantern. In consequence the wood consists, visually, of "nought but single darknes." We recognize threat in it—density, opaqueness, crowding branches and leaves—but cannot distinguish its forms clearly.

After the Lady has been persuaded to go off with Comus we hear more details from the brothers. The wood is "*Chaos, that raigns here / In double night* of darkness, and of shades," and is affected by "black usurping mists." Chill dew, "rude burrs and thistles," a cold bank, and "the rugged bark of som broad Elm" are mentioned. If we elect to do so, we can ascribe to it the desolation of the "grots, and caverns shag'd with horrid shades" within which the chaste Lady may "pass on with unblench't majesty." Still later the wood is a "dark sequester'd nook." For Thyrsis, who comes next upon the scene, it is "hideous" and within its navel contains "cypress shades" that "immure" Comus's dwelling. At night the wolvish or tigerish howls of Comus and his "monstrous rout" are heard. It is bordered, however, by the pleasant meadows in which Thyrsis's pretended flocks took their supper "on the savoury Herb / Of Knot-grass dew-besprent" before being folded for the night. There,

before he was aroused by the Lady's song, Thyrsis had sat "upon a bank / With Ivy canopied, and interwove / With flaunting Hony-suckle." Evidently the wood is not the whole world but only a dangerous part of it. Beyond the edges lie order and peace. The wood itself, however, has "paths, and turnings oft'n trod by day." Within it, presumably, are at least some of the virtuous plants, healing herbs, and "simples of a thousand names" known intimately to the "Shepherd Lad" of Thyrsis's acquaintance. The present danger, we understand without conscious inference, results not from the wood's intrinsic evil but from darkness and the malignant sorcerer. That the Lady is lost in the wood offers cause for alarm, but Thyrsis and the brothers appear to feel no concern for themselves.

The character of the two other settings is different. The palace, described only in a stage direction, besides being stately is "set out with all manner of deliciousness: soft Musick, Tables spred with all dainties." It contains an enchanted chair, and in it Comus offers the Lady a "cordial Julep . . . / That flames, and dances in his crystal bounds / With spirits of balm, and fragrant Syrops mixt." Few as they are, the details are enough to suggest the luxury to which the Lady is invited, at her peril, to yield. As for Ludlow Town and the Earl's castle, they are not described at all. The "Countrey-Dancers" who appear with them belong properly to neither and do not affect whatever walls, roofs, and streets we may sense as background. The ambience is Civilization: comfort and safety as contrasting with the wild forest in which we have been imaginatively plunged. We emerge from real or imagined dimness into light and are appropriately reassured.

Aside from the Lady, the personages who move within these settings, although adequately known to us from the speeches, are physically almost blank. The Guardian Spirit wears "pure Ambrosial weeds" in his proper home "Before the starry threshold of *Joves* Court" and in his first appearance. Later he is disguised as a shepherd. The only visible properties of the brothers are their rainbow-colored clothing (298–99) and the "iron stakes" of their swords when they are alarmed by Thyrsis's approach. Comus, we know, possesses a wand. The Lady is beautiful and white-skinned ("Your nerves are all chain'd up in Alablaster"), has "dainty limms," possesses the beauty that "is natures brag, and must be shown," not hoarded, and is not like homely-featured girls who have "course complexions / And cheeks of sorry grain." Instead, she has "a vermeil-tinctur'd lip . . . / Love-darting eyes," and "tresses like the Morn." Economical as the suggestions are, they are enough. She is the archetypal Beautiful and Virtuous Virgin, and we accept her as the fit object of an attempt at seduction.

Of course the masque is full of images that do not relate either to settings or to personages, and a few of these may be noticed. We read of a "Golden Key / That ope's the Palace of Eternity" (13–14); of "Sea-girt Iles" that, like rich gems, "inlay / The unadorned boosom of the Deep" (21–23); of Thyrsis shooting helpfully from Heaven "Swift as the Sparkle of a glancing Star" (80); of sounds and seas, with their "finny drove," moving to the moon "in wavering Morrice" (115–16); of dazzling spells hurled "into the spungy ayr" (153–54), so that perhaps some kind of harmless blue fire sends curls of smoke over the stage; of gray-hooded evening rising "from the hindmost wheels of *Phoebus* wain" (187–89); of an "unblemish't form of Chastity" that the Lady sees visibly but we cannot (214–15); of "flowry-kirtl'd *Naiades* / Culling their potent hearbs, and balefull drugs" (253–54); of evening as the time when "the labour'd Oxe / In his loose traces from the furrow came, / And the swink't hedger at his Supper sate" (290–92); of a hermit's weeds, books, beads, maple dish, and gray hairs (389–91); of a watching dragon "with uninchanted eye" (394); and of much else. The most famous image of all, perhaps, appears in a visually opulent speech of Comus to the Lady. Nature has "set to work millions of spinning Worms, / That in their green shops weave the smooth-hair'd silk" (714–15), a figure that combines in two lines busy activity, visual and tactile richness, and an awareness of King James's abortive effort to encourage sericulture in England. Like the late Shakespeare*, Milton does not require much visual stimulation. He alludes to a pregnant detail or two and passes on. The verse, too, both in diction and movement has a fastidious delicacy like that of the Lady's moral scrupulosity. Whatever scorn may be felt by "liberated" modern readers for the Puritanical ethic, the work is sensorily luxurious.

Lyc is not only an exceptionally rich poem but has been so much written about, especially in recent decades, that a brief description is difficult. Like others of Milton's poems, it is verbal music—so much so that at first reading an aurally sensitive person may be unable to attend to the meanings. It also presents itself as song ("Monody"). The mourner will sing: Lycidas was skilled at singing; the entire elegy is tearful melody ("som melodious tear"). The Muses are asked to "sweep the string." The speech by Phoebus is a musical "strain," after which the poet resumes his "Oat." If Camus and St. Peter speak ("quoth he," "bespake"), they do so within a "*Dorick*" lay." Moreover, within the song singing is often mentioned. The gray-fly "winds her sultry horn." The dance of satyrs and fauns is "Temper'd to th'Oaten Flute," which makes a glad sound that old Damoetus loved to hear. Lycidas himself has been accustomed to make willows and hazels fan their leaves to his soft lays. The River Mincio is "crown'd with vocal reeds." Even the bad shepherds denounced by St. Peter produce "lean and flashy songs" as their sermons; and the saints who welcome Lycidas to Heaven "sing, and singing in their glory move." The sounds that are not explicitly called song are absorbed into the song, so that when we hear of "the rout that made the hideous roar" at the dismembering of Orpheus, or of the *pronouncing* of Jove on each deed, or of the *asking* of Triton, or, most strikingly of all, of the "sounding Seas" that wash the drowned shepherd's body "far away," we instinctively modulate the sounds to musical rhythms and absorb them into our awareness as altering tonalities and not as breaks in the song.

The visual imagery is correspondingly rich but comes so fast and thick that, lulled or stunned as the reader's mind may be by the music, appreciation of it may come slowly. We begin with glimpses of laurels, withered myrtles, and ivy disturbed by a clumsy hand plucking unripened berries, and from that point on we are seeing, although sometimes vaguely, at the same time we are bombarded with sounds. When we read that Lycidas knew how to "build the lofty rhyme," we sense the energetic upward thrust of a growing monument. We see the dead poet floating upon his watery bier and weltering to a wind that paradoxically desiccates the wave-tossed body. We watch "some gentle Muse" pass a black-shrouded urn, turn, and wish it peace. We see morning coming like eyelids opening, perceive Venus sloping toward the western horizon, glimpse the roughness of dancing satyrs and the cloven heels of fauns, perceive wild thyme and gadding vines spreading in mournful abandon, observe as motionless leaves that formerly had fanned. There is, however, no space to expand the catalogue, which every reader must fill out for himself. The essential problem is not *what* the reader may sense, if he enjoys visual awareness, but *whether* he will sense, or with what limitations. The opposite faults are dullness (an inability to register) and overexuberance (a reluctance to trust the poet, to see only the details he presents, without expanding the images to include what has been left outside the pictorial frame). Taken on its own terms, the visual imagery swells, recedes, returns, and alters in such a way as to form a pattern appropriate to the changing moods. The imagery of blasted or uncontrolled vegetation in the early lines, for example, bursts into the brilliant color of the catalogue of flowers (139ff.) as if to say, "The pathetic

fallacy adopted earlier was a fiction. *Of course* nature, which is insensible to human grief, continued really to flourish."

PL is too huge to permit more than a few highly selective comments. Color, about which little has hitherto been said, is especially noteworthy in the early books, each of which has a dominant and a subdominant hue : in 1 and 2, black with a subdominant of red; in 3, blazing light with a subdominant of gold; in 4, green with a subdominant of gold. In later books the scheme is less orderly; but the contrasts of Hell*, Heaven*, and earthly Paradise* are unforgettable. In the last eight books, except for the War in Heaven* and a return to Heaven, Chaos, and Hell in Book 10, the physical setting is Paradise, which in 10–12 begins to change into the less idyllic world we know. The change is announced in terms of cold and heat, blustering winds, the war of beast with beast, fowl with fowl, and fish with fish, and, finally, the diseases and man-produced horrors shown or told to Adam by Michael in 11 and 12.

Within this framework it is possible to talk about the images of settings (Heaven, Hell, Chaos, the Garden) or of representation of abstract qualities (good, evil*, obedience*, love*, etc.) or even of such transient states as confusion, disorder, and shame. With relation to the representation of goodness and evil, for example, the epic* might easily be divided into sections. In 1 and 2, we see—and hear—evil in Hell; in 3, goodness, including justice and mercy, in Heaven; in 4 and most of 5, goodness in earthly Paradise and its two obedient and loving inhabitants; in the rest of 5 and in 6, evil combating goodness in Heaven; in 7, goodness engaged in creating a perfect universe; in 8, the goodness of angel in converse with the goodness of unfallen man; in 9 and 10, the change of good into evil by the Fall; in 11 and 12, evil in times to come and divine goodness taking countermeasures against it.

How this works out can be suggested only by two sets of details. The prelapsarian Adam is an image of goodness. He is "erect and tall, / Godlike erect, . . . / In naked Majestie." In his appearance —and Eve's as well—"The image of thir glorious Maker shon, / Truth, wisdome, Sanctitude severe and pure." He is formed for contemplation and valor, has a broad forehead and "Eye sublime." "Hyacinthin Locks / Round from his parted forelock manly hung / Clustring, but not beneath his shoulders broad"; and he is "the goodliest man of men since borne / His Sons" (4. 288–324). This is an initial impression that is developed but not contradicted until the Fall*. In the interval we glimpse him embracing Eve, worshipping in front of the "shadie Lodge" (4. 720), "Leaning half-rais'd, with looks of cordial Love" (5. 12) over the sleeping Eve, checking the "Fruitless imbraces" of "pamperd boughes" (5. 214–15) as he gardens, advancing "with submiss approach and reverence meek" (5. 359) to greet the visiting Raphael, playing the host at a vegetarian dinner, and so on. The picture is self-consistent. We add detail to detail but do not find it necessary to go back and correct misapprehensions. Unless the reader is determined to impose his own values upon the perceptions, what comes through to him is the Adam Milton imagined as appropriate to his epic scheme.

So with the image of evil, which one also sees and hears: in Satan's thunder-scarred face (1. 601); in the voluntary self-diminution of the devils in order to congregate in a hall for the plotting of further mischief (1. 777–80); in the speeches at the "great consult" (1. 798); in Satan's haughty defiance of the allegorized* Death; in his steeling of himself on Mount Niphates against a resurgence of good impulses (4. 32–123); in the biased and self-serving oratory by which he seduces all his heavenly followers but Abdiel; in the War in Heaven; in the Fall of Adam and Eve; in the whole elaborate panorama of Book 11 and the described miseries of Book 12. This is to say that the sensory content of the concept *evil* is unfolded and made to impinge on our nerve-endings. We hear the disguised

insincerity, perceive—and, if we read aloud, ourselves produce—the fluctuating tonalities, watch the changing expressions, feel the internal writhings. If the epic sometimes required rational explication, it also sometimes required this; and imagery has been provided abundantly by a poet who must have been constitutionally driven to sense as well as to think. When sensory data are deliberately excluded, as in God's speeches in Book 3, it is evident that the exclusion has been contrived for a special purpose (here, the demonstration of Pure Reason exercised by a loving but rigorously logical Deity).

Since most published discussion of imagery in *PL* has had to do with specific passages, let us look briefly at a few, omitting, however, as too familiar and too intricately beautiful the celebrated epic similes. One of the most admired images appears in a description of Eve at a point where the ostensible subject is Paradise:

> Not that faire field
> Of *Enna,* where *Proserpin* gathering flours
> Her self a fairer Floure by gloomie *Dis*
> Was gatherd, which cost *Ceres* all that pain
> To seek her through the world.
> (4. 268–72)

The fair field compared with Paradise has in it a flowerlike young woman who is gathering flowers. Into this scene erupts a "gloomie" underworld god who "gathers" the woman by sweeping her off underground, so that Ceres, her mother, must seek her painfully throughout the whole world. Except for the two words designating flowers, the passage is empty of explicit sensory content. "Gloomie" might as well refer to Dis's mood as to the darkness in which he habitually lived. Yet the cooperating reader has no trouble "seeing" the action, and we may pause to inquire why.

One reason is the vivid contrast between "faire field" and what follows. We need not know what the flowers in the field were (though in fact we have just heard that they are "worthy of Paradise," are "profuse on Hill and Dale and Plaine," are "of all hue," and include "without Thorn the Rose," 4. 241–43, 256) to have a generalized vision of brilliant colors against a background of greenery. Into this image we introduce a girl, whom because of our acquaintance with Proserpine we know to have been young, stooping to pluck blossoms and add them to a cluster she already holds. Gloomy Dis now intrudes—surely with a rush—to "gather" her by a rapacious sweep. The violent movement contrasts with the placidity of the girl's earlier motions. Finally, after the quickest of transitions, we see a worried and grieving Ceres engaged in a distressed search which, because it took her "through the world," we understand was protracted. That she became fatigued and walked drearily is implied by the dragging pace of "all that pain / To seek her. . . ." Inevitably, we associate the melancholy event with an incursion of Satan, which we know is impending. Because the poet himself has sensed powerfully, he has not loaded his lines with descriptive adjectives and adverbs but has relied on us to provide what the stripped-down narrative requires for its sensory completion.

So the poet's mind worked habitually, not regularly separating vision, hearing, and concept but often giving us all three nearly simultaneously. In consequence, only by analysis can sensory activity be isolated from intellectual and emotional meanings. An associated quality of the passage deserves comment. Because Milton knew Greek and Roman literature intimately, he often puts immediate settings and events side by side with classical ones that give them added reverberation. The result is that sensory richness is enhanced at the same time that a kernel of similarity is found between scriptural truth, as imaginatively expanded by a Christian poet, and pagan fictions that tended to corroborate Scripture by suggesting that something like what was revealed by God to His people was intuited by fantasizing pagans.

Some of the sensory associations lie beneath the poetic surface and may easily escape detection. At the end of Book 10,

Adam understands that the best way to respond to his altered situation is by confession to God. Let us, he says to Eve, "prostrate fall / Before him reverent" and "pardon beg, with tears / Watering the ground." Accordingly, the couple

> forthwith to the place
> Repairing where he judg'd them prostrate fell
> Before him reverent, and both confess'd
> Humbly thir faults, and pardon beg'd, with
>   tears
> Watering the ground.
> (10. 1087–1102)

At the beginning of 11 the twice-mentioned watering of the ground provides a transition to the image of Deucalion and Pyrrha, who after the destruction of the world by flood "before the Shrine / Of *Themis* stood devout" (11. 8–14). The fall of flowing tears upon the earth has generated a perception of the mud-befouled ground upon which the mythical petitioners stood at Themis; and there is further relevance in the fact that both pairs survived a catastrophe that marked the end of an age. A visual detail has exfoliated into a meaningful parallel. The grotesquerie of the parallel (tears water the ground, watery ground suggests a receding flood) does not impair the effectiveness of the comparison because the peripheral glimpse of water remains beneath the threshold of awareness while producing a continuity that is sensed as smooth.

Innumerable such complexities are present in the imagery. Davis P. Harding, in *The Club of Hercules* (1962), has urged that recognition of a classical parallel should lead the reader to remember not only the original passage but also its context. When we read that Eve, as she parted from Adam before the Fall, "*Delia's* self / In gate surpass'd and Goddess-like deport" (9. 388–89), we are to recall not only Virgil's* description of Diana (born on Delos) leading a train of dancers (*exercet Diana choros, quam mille secutae / hinc atque hinc glomerantur Oreades—Aeneid* 1. 499–500) but also a phrase further down the page,

"Such was Dido" (*talis erat Dido*). As a result our awareness that Dido will try to deflect Aeneas from his mission warns us that Adam will be swayed from his duty by Eve (*ibid.*, pp. 87–88). If Harding is right, we must add to the immediate sensory richness of derivative passages that of the entire context at which they glance referentially. Here, besides Dido—not mentioned by Milton—we are also, presumably, to imagine the thousand *dancing* followers of "*Delia's* Traine" (9. 387).

Whether Milton had any such intention, or at this point remembered more of the Virgilian passage than is reflected in his own lines, is doubtful. The chances, indeed, are about even that the intended parallel is with an earlier line of *Aeneid* 1. If we emphasize the second part of the phrase "*Delia's* self / In gate surpass'd" instead of the first, the Virgilian echo is from line 405 : after Venus had spoken to Aeneas in disguise, as she turned away she revealed her identity by her gait (*et vera incessu patuit dea*). Nevertheless it is true that the classical scholar may add to the images arising directly from Milton's text others present in the classical passages to which he alludes. The relevance of each such addition must be judged separately.

Besides developed images are others that flash so quickly across the retina of imagination that entertainment of them may remain subconscious. When Eve separates from Adam to work alone on the morning of the Fall, "from her Husbands hand her hand / Soft she withdrew" (9. 385–86). The gesture, which includes tactile and motor elements, is emblematic of a spiritual rupture that will not be healed until, in the final lines of Book 12, we learn that the two, "hand in hand with wandring steps and slow, / Through *Eden* took thir solitarie way." In the interval their only physical contact was motivated by "Carnal desire," not love (9. 1013); but now a second emblem shows us that the broken spiritual union has been restored.

Before passing on from *PL* to the later works one may notice a few characteristics of the auditory imagery. Milton seldom attempts outright onomatopoeia but instead is content to modulate the sound of his verse suggestively. When he mentions the nightingale's song he does not imitate it but describes its quality in lines that focus on warbling and softness : "nor then the solemn Nightingal / Ceas'd warbling, but all night tun'd her soft layes" (7. 435–36). If the last clause is itself soft, the effect may be the result less of the poet's attempt to write onomatopoeically than of his instinctive and sensitive response to subject matter.

To be sure, Milton had early sought to clothe his fancy "in fit sound" (*Vac* 32), and the judgment of particular instances must draw careful dinstinctions.

> Heav'n op'nd wide
> Her ever during Gates, Harmonious sound
> On golden Hinges moving.
>
> (7. 205–7)

Here the last phrase might be thought a textbook example of onomatopoeia, and an undergraduate student might hail appreciatively the concentration of low back vowel sounds as appropriate to the mention of gold. Yet one rather feels than can demonstrate the appropriateness, and the sounds can more safely be described as suitable than as imitative. Sometimes the effect depends more on movement than on the sonority of vowels and consonants. When Satan was flung from Heaven,

> from Morn
> To Noon he fell, from Noon to dewy Eve,
> A Summers day; and with the setting Sun
> Dropt from the Zenith like a falling Star,
> On *Lemnos* th'*Aegaean* Ile.
>
> (1. 742–46)

Satan is "with" the sun syntactically as well as physically. He "dropt" on an island in the northern Aegaean at a time when the sun was setting—a relationship that the phrasing preserves. The dropping comes fast and abruptly in a line that moves rapidly because the first foot is reversed and the idea of dropping invites, and the arrangement of sounds permits, speed. Once more, when, in 8. 271–77, Adam describes his first efforts to speak, the lines move jerkily, as if he were making an initial effort to use a foreign language. He progresses only slowly from naming to predication, so that the lines are filled with an extraordinary number of caesuras.

Such effects can be found in *PL* by the scores or hundreds. Nothing more can be done with them here than to assert their presence and to urge readers to be constantly on the lookout for them. Milton would not be well served, however, by a practice of valuing them more than the meanings that they were meant to enrich and subtilize but for which they do not substitute.

We move to the last major poems, *PR* and *SA*. At an initial reading the former, especially, seems poetically sparse; but judgment is altered by greater familiarity. That Milton was still capable of bombarding his readers with sensory impressions appears, for example, from the brilliant descriptions of imperial Rome in *PR* 4. 25ff., of Athens in 4. 236ff., and of the storm sent by Satan in 4. 409ff. The lower key of both poems was dictated not by flagging poetic energy but by subject matter and purpose. In the storm scene the tumult about Christ is opposed by the phrase "only stoodst / Unshaken," which reveals His utter indifference to Satan's malignity. The violence is ended with almost comical ease when morning "with her radiant finger still'd the roar / Of thunder, chas'd the clouds, and laid the winds, / And grisly Spectres" (4. 420–21, 428–30). Predominantly, however, the spareness conceals a sensory content adequate for the fit audience to whom alone Milton—having abandoned the hope of wide popularity—now wrote.

How the spareness works can be illustrated by examples. When Christ has entered the wilderness to meditate, his disciples miss him and are concerned.

Then on the bank of *Jordan*, by a Creek:
Where winds with Reeds, and Osiers whis-
    pring play

Plain Fishermen, no greater men them call,
Close in a Cottage low together got
Thir unexpected loss and plaints out breath'd.
        (*PR* 2. 25–29)

The setting is the junction of a creek with the Jordan, where winds create a rustle among reeds and osiers. The "breathing" of complaints by Christ's followers echoes this "whisp'ring" of vegetation. The closeness of the little band suggests their spiritual unity, the lowness of the cottage in which they have gathered their humble station: "Plain Fishermen, no greater men them call." Their subdued speech implies that as yet the new faith has an almost conspiratorial quality, a meaning strengthened by a second meaning of *Close*, "secretive." The colloquial diction and idiomatic syntax of "in a Cottage low together got" is appropriate to the mention of uneducated persons. Yet what is accomplished is done wholly without fuss, as if by now the poet could get things right without conscious effort.

Effortlessness is one of the work's dominant traits. When the subject demands that a transition be made to Heaven from Satan, now directing "His easie steps; girded with snaky wiles" (*PR* 1. 119–20) by the Jordan, the shift is accomplished within the limits of a relative clause. Unknowingly, Satan fulfilled

The purpos'd Counsel pre-ordain'd and fixt
Of the most High, who in full frequence
    bright
Of Angels, thus to *Gabriel* smiling spake.
        (*PR* 1. 127–29)

Of the assembly we are given only a sense of crowding ("full frequence") and of brightness; of God we learn only that He spoke smiling.

A final example is taken from the poem's climax, where some stylistic fireworks might be thought pardonable. Milton rejects them so utterly that full appreciation of what has happened requires a double-take. Having placed Christ on the pinnacle of the temple—not flat, as in most Renaissance drawings, but pointed—Satan taunts him with the Scripture that God has charged His angels to uplift the one for whom He is a refuge lest he should dash his foot against a stone. Nowhere is Milton more laconic than in what follows:

> To whom thus Jesus: also it is written,
> Tempt not the Lord thy God, he said and
>   stood.
> But Satan smitten with amazement fell.
> (PR 4. 560–62)

A moment passes before we realize what has happened. Jesus stands on the spire, quite against Satan's expectation, and the latter's surprise has caused him to fall instead of his victim. If we like, we can entertain the image demanded by the context and see both the balancing and the fall, but Milton's words are as simply denotative as possible. It is left to the reader to comprehend what is not said, that to the end Jesus persevered in relying on his merely human resources in order not to grant Satan the miraculous demonstration of divine power that he has tried consistently to evoke.

Since *SA* is as yet not conclusively dated, we can never be sure that the economy shown in such passages represents the latest development of Milton's poetic style. Progress can be traced from the imagistic exuberance of the early poems, through the clatter and roar of *PL* 1, to the quiet density of *PL* 11 and 12, and, finally, to the self-effacing lack of emphasis in *PR*. On this hypothesis it would be correct to say that images, as the term is often understood, ceased to be necessary for Milton because his acuteness had become almost preternatural.

The hypothesis is not sharply contradicted by the possibility that his last poem was *SA,* for this, too, although full of dramatic tension is imagistically spare. In part the tension derives from the humanity of the dramatic personages. In the opening lines Samson speaks to someone who is leading him.

> A little onward lend thy guiding hand
> To these dark steps, a little further on;
> For yonder bank hath choice of Sun or shade,
> There I am wont to sit. . . .

The protagonist's eyes cannot see the bank, which is therefore described merely as containing both sunny and shady spots, which the body can differentiate in terms of warmth. The prison mentioned immediately (6–9) is characterized as having "air imprison'd . . . close and damp, / Unwholsom draught." At the moment Samson feels instead "The breath of Heav'n fresh-blowing, pure and sweet, / With day-spring born" (10–11). Visual imagery has disappeared because Samson can see nothing, and the only sounds are those of his spoken words.

In a moment the subject of the words amid the blaze of noon . . ." (70–72, 80). becomes precisely the deprivation of sight: "Light the prime work of God to me is extinct, / And all her various objects of delight / Annull'd . . . O dark, dark, dark, amid the blaze of noon . . ." (70–72, 80). In the famous lament what Samson remembers is not so much the objects revealed by light as light itself. The key terms are "light" and "dark," so that unless brightness by itself is "seen" (and therefore an image) the passage is visually nearly blank. When Samson complains about the vulnerability of the eye ("why was the sight / To such a tender ball as th'eye confin'd? / So obvious and so easie to be quench't"—93–95), the reader may sense sphericity and tenderness, but whether he *perceives* them is problematical. "My self, my Sepulcher, a moving Grave" (102) may induce peripheral images of stone tombs and grass-covered mounds, or it may not. Although Samson may perhaps recall things seen before his eyes were destroyed, his perceptions of the present must exclude sight.

When the Chorus enters the language changes at once:

> See how he lies at random, carelessly diffus'd,
> With languish't head unprop,
> As one past hope, abandon'd,
> And by himself given over;
> In slavish habit, ill-fitted weeds
> O're worn and soild.
> (118–23)

Since the tragedy "never was intended" for the stage, we must be told what Samson would look like if it were. The brief set-piece, however, is followed by lines that have minimal sensory content. Formerly Samson

> tore the Lion, as the Lion tears the Kid,
> Ran on embattelld Armies clad in Iron,
> And weaponless himself,
> Made Arms ridiculous.
>
> (128–31)

We may, or may not, glimpse the lion as we feel the tearing, sense a weaponless figure rushing upon ironclad soldiers, and watch sword and spear flash uselessly against air. Again, do we, or do we not, see anything when we read "A thousand fore-skins fell, the flower of *Palestin*"? (144). Every reader must make up his own mind. What is clear is that the poet is not going to paint elaborately filled-in canvases but will make a few bold sweeps to indicate movement, or contour, or color, or whichever of these is appropriate. The rest is up to the reader, whose responses might perhaps be predicted from his reaction to the line "When insupportably his foot advanc't" (136). Although the image is predominantly motor, the strongest single impression being that of ruthless and irresistible advance, it can include the sense of an archetypal foot —not detailed, not bare or clad in a specific type of footgear, but none the less rich in *foothood*. For most readers, perhaps, it will not.

That the imagery should generally be of this kind is not surprising in view of the tragedy's subject. Much of the talk is about God's purposes for Samson and Samson's betrayal of them. Accordingly the language is often abstract: "Just are the ways of God, / And justifiable to Men; / Unless there be who think not God at all" (293–95); "Appoint not heavenly disposition, Father, / Nothing of all these evils hath befall'n me / But justly" (373–74); "I cannot praise thy Marriage choises, Son, / Rather approv'd them not" (420–21); and "He all thir Ammunition / And feats of War defeats /

With plain Heroic magnitude of mind" (1277–79). The issues are cosmic: were God's predictions a mockery? Can human unworthiness frustrate divine plans? The replies can hardly be found in sensory images but must be threshed out by mental struggle. Until the end, when the Officer's description will necessarily focus upon a visible event, we must expect more soul-searching than sensory stimulation.

Of course the approach of new personages motivates some description. Manoa comes as a "reverend Sire / With careful step, Locks white as doune" (326–27). Harapha draws near like a storm, has "no inchanting voice," offers no "bait of honied words"; he strides on "Haughty as is his pile high-built and proud" (1065–69). The Officer bears "A Scepter or quaint staff" and "Comes on amain, speed in his look" (1303–4). The richest details are offered when we meet Dalila, and they are sufficiently connotative to persuade us that Milton had lost none of his descriptive power. She approaches

> Like a stately Ship
> Of *Tarsus,* bound for th'Isles
> Of *Javan* or *Gadier*
> With all her bravery on, and tackle trim,
> Sails fill'd, and streamers waving.
>
> (714–18)

She is hesitant:

> now stands & eies thee fixt,
> About t'have spoke, but now, with head declin'd
> Like a fair flower surcharg'd with dew, she weeps
> And words addrest seem into tears dissolv'd,
> Wetting the borders of her silk'n veil.
>
> (726–30)

When she speaks, the movement of the verse is beautifully appropriate to her divided mind:

> With doubtful feet and wavering resolution
> I came, still dreading thy displeasure, Samson.
>
> (732–33)

The poet senses as keenly as ever. It is because his dramatic subject is a remorse leading to despair (649–51) and the gradual rise from despair to a psychological state that permits heroic action that the sensory imagery is more sparse even than in *PL*. [WS]

IMITATIONS. Imitations may be a form of flattery, a sure sign of awareness and a probable sign of understanding, and a key to influence* and reputation*. Imitations of Milton's poetry begin around 1646 and have continued to the present. They may be close, partial, "translations," or parodic*; to be labeled "imitation," however, they should follow the style*, language, metric and form, or treatment of subject matter closely and with intention. They do not merely quote lines or make allusions, as does, for example, Edward Young's *The Complaint; or, Night-Thoughts* (1743), 6. 435–44 :

Like Milton's Eve, when gazing on the lake,
Man makes the matchless image, man admires:
Say then, shall man, his thoughts all sent abroad,
Superior wonders in himself forgot,
His admiration waste on objects round,
When heaven makes him the soul of all he sees
Absurd : not rare! so great, so mean, is man.

Despite the references, the diction*, the language, and the blank verse*, this is not an imitation of Milton; it shows, instead, influence from *PL*. On the other hand, a close and intended imitation of the epic* is the section inserted by Wentworth Dillon, Earl of Roscommon (1633?–1685), into the second edition (1685) of *An Essay on Translated Verse*, lines 377–403. This "Essay on blanc verse out of the 6th Book of *Paradise Lost*," as a marginal note calls it, begins :

Have we forgot how *Raphaels* Num'rous Prose
Led out exalted souls through heavenly camps,
And mark'd the ground where proud Apostate Thrones
Defy'd *Jehovah*? . . .

The poem into which it was inserted is in heroic couplets. Here the imitation lies in all the things noted before : style, language, metric and form, treatment of subject matter, and intention.

Frequently the relationship of a poem is explicitly stated, such as Anne Finch, Countess of Winchilsea's "Fanscomb Barn. In Imitation of Milton" (*Miscellany Poems, on Several Occasions* [1713], pp. 58–65), or Abel Evans's *Prae-Existence. A Poem, In Imitation of Milton* (1714), pp. 1–12. Frequently the point of imitation for the author is choice of meter; for example, Catherine Jemmat's "A Paraphrase on the 104th Psalm, in Imitation of Milton's Style," in *Miscellanies, in Prose and Verse* (1771), pp. 227–30. Frequently it is a specific poem, although as in the following example the meter is in "Miltonicks" (blank verse) : William Bowman's "Night. An Imitation of Milton," in *The Altar of Love*, 3d ed. (1731), pp. 32–70, an imitation of *IlP*. Frequently it is choice of genre and its treatment; for example, the anonymous *A Monody to the memory of the Late Mr. Cholwell, Rector of Stevenage, and the Archdeacon of Huntingdon. In Imitation of Milton's Lycidas* (1774). Frequently it involves the kind of subject matter as well as meter (usually blank verse, but at times iambic tetrameters), genre, and treatment; for example, *Joshua: A Poem in Imitation of Milton: Humbly Inscrib'd to the Duke of Marlborough* (1706).

At times a poem is even assigned to Milton, such as the anonymous "An Extempore upon a Fagot, by Milton" in *Oxford and Cambridge Miscellany Poems* (1709), pp. 286–87. Alexander Pope* and Philip Dormer Stanhope, Lord Chesterfield, tried to pass off a "Sonnet : Found in a Glass Window at Chalfont St. Giles" as Milton's to fool Jonathan Richardson* in July 1737. It was published in Thomas Birch's* edition of the prose works in 1738 (1 : xxxviii). The influence of *PL* is seen in the two anonymous imitations "A Divine Rhapsody : or, Morning Hymn" and "An Evening Hymn" in *A Miscellany of Poems by Several Hands*, ed. J. Husbands (1731), pp. 255–62, 266–70. As companion poems, they also reflect influence from *L'Al* and *IlP*. This pattern is at times repeated; for example, see the two poems "A Hymn to Morning, A Hymn to

Night," "Attempted in Miltonic Verse" (that is, in blank verse) in *Universal Magazine* (November 19, 1737). John Pomfret's "The Choice" (1700) is in imitation of *L'Al*, and the anonymous "Il Penseroso" (with an epigraph from *PL* 9. 249), pp. 161–69 of Husband's collection, reflects its namesake. There are also sonnets that show their line of descent, such as the anonymous "Sonnet. In Imitation of Milton's Sonnets," in *London Magazine* 7 (July 1738):356. Some interesting imitations are Johann Jacob Bodmer's *Noah,* which was translated into English prose by Joseph Collyer (1779) with comment on the Miltonic origins in the preface; the anonymous *Milton's Sublimity Asserted: In a poem. Occasion'd by a Late Celebrated Piece, Entituled, Cyder, a Poem; in Blank Verse, by Philo-Milton* (1709); Friedrich Gottlieb Klopstock's* *Der Messias* (1748); William Shenstone's "Eve's Speech in Milton, upon her Expulsion out of Paradise," pp. 40–41, of *Poems upon Various Occasions* (1737); Nathaniel Evans's "To Melancholy," a fragment, in *Poems on Several Occasions* (Philadelphia, 1772), p. 135; *Die Schöpfung der hölle nebst einigen andern gedichten* (Altenburg, 1760) by Friedrich Wilhelm Zachariä, who also translated *PL*; and Robert Alves's "Malevolence : An Ode, an Imitation of Il Penseroso," in *Odes, on Several Subjects* (Edinburgh, 1778).

Poetical imitations exist when sections of a poem rather than the whole poem employ style, diction, language, subject matter, or treatment with direct intention. Joseph Trapp's *Thoughts Upon the Four Last Things : Death; Judgement; Heaven; Hell. A Poem in Four Parts* (4 vols., 1734–35) and William H. Roberts's *A Poetical Essay, on the Existence of God. Part I; on the Attributes of God. Part II; on the Providence of God. Part III* (3 vols., 1771) illustrate partial imitation well. Perhaps to be noticed also are centos like Robert Lloyd's *Arcadia; or, The Shepherd's Wedding. A Dramatic Pastoral* (1761), which is derived from *L'Al, Arc,* and *Mask.* With this might be compared

Samuel Boyse's *The Tears of the Muses: A Poem, Sacred to the Memory of the Right Honourable, Anne Late Viscountess of Stormont* (Edinburgh, 1736), which shows influence from *PL* and *Lyc* throughout though it is not an imitation.

"Translations*" present Milton's work in a different form, so different a form that the work is no longer truly Milton's. In 1699 John Hopkins produced a rhymed version of two books of *PL* "for the ladies" who found the original too difficult to understand. In 1760 Madame Marie-Anne du Boccage published *Le Paradis Terrestre, Poëme imité de Milton,* in six books (chants), clearly not a translation though at times it has been so treated. Another type of translation is the prose paraphrase of the War in Heaven* that Samuel Johnson (not, of course, Milton's biographer) inserted into his play *The Blazing Comet: The Mad Lovers; or, The Beauties of the Poets* (1732), Act 4, Scene 1, p. 35.

John Philips's* "In Imitation of Milton" appeared in two poetical collections in 1701 : *A Collection of Poems . . . With Several Original Poems, Never Before Printed,* pp. 393–400, and *A New Miscellany of Original Poems, on Several Occasions,* ed. Charles Gildon, pp. 212–21. This is "The Splendid Shilling," finally published under the author's name and its new title in 1705. The poem is a parody of style, diction, language, and was followed by numerous imitations such as James Bramston's *The Crooked Six-Pence* (1743), which is as much a parody of Philips as it is of Milton. It also spawned works like *Bartholomew-fair: or, a Ramble to Smithfield. A Poem in Imitation of Milton* (1729); *Lucifer's Defeat: or, The Mantle-Chimney. A Miltonic* (1729); Alexander Blunt's *Freedom: a Poem written in Time of Recess from the Rapacious Claws of Bailiffs, and Devouring Fangs of Gaolers* (Exeter, 1730);) and E. C.'s *Gin, a Poem, in Miltonick Verse* (John Gay had published in 1708 *Wine*; a poem in parody of Milton's style) in *London Magazine* 3 (December 1734) : 663. *A Pipe of Tobacco*

(1736) by Isaac Hawkins Browne consists of six poems "In Imitation of Six Several Authors." Imitation III, pp. 13–15, has been considered both a parodic imitation of Milton and of James Thomson in *The Seasons*, which is strongly influenced by Milton's poetry; Browne was really poking fun at Thomson. But *PL* and blank verse are not the only subjects of parodic imitation. There are also *L'Allegro ed il Penseroso in Sonno: or, The Power of Sleep. An Ode* (1742) and William Mason's "Il Bellicoso," which parodies "Il Penseroso," in John Almon's *The Fugitive Miscellany. Part the Second* (1775), among many others.

Almost all the examples given have been from the eighteenth century, but they could be amplified greatly. Philips, for example, also wrote *Cyder* and *Cerelia*, both style parodies, and Richard Alsop's *Aristocracy. An epic poem* (Philadelphia, 1795) is typical of the serious imitative and otherwise influenced verse produced on themes of freedom in America at the end of the century. For the eighteenth century was notable in its elevation of Milton as the touchstone of literary taste and achievement. It was *PL* that predominated, with major influence also coming from the companion poems and *Lyc*. Imitations were begun in the seventeenth century and were continued to some extent through the nineteenth and twentieth centuries. John Keats's* imitation of Stanza XIX of *Nat* in "Ode to Psyche" is often cited as an example. But for the most part, though influence continued strongly in the last two centuries, imitations themselves decline.

Imitations, or in some cases appropriations, which give evidence of what will turn into imitative approaches, during the seventeenth century are the following, in chronological order (omitting only those already cited):

Robert Baron, *Erotopaignion or the Cyprian Academy* (1647); numerous imitations and appropriations from the 1645 *Poems;* 2d ed., 1648.
Robert Baron, *Pocula Castalia* (1650), in "Tuchesphaira: or, Fortunes Tennis Ball."

Edward Benlowes, *Theophila, or Loves Sacrifice* (1652); imitations of *Nat, L'Al, IlP, Mask,* and *Lyc;* parts were written as early as 1646.
Andrew Marvell, *The First Anniversary of the Government under His Highness the Lord Protector* (1655), lines 151–52, 218, 358 (from *Nat* and *Lyc*).
Joshua Poole, *The English Parnassus: or, A Helpe to English Poesie* (1657); appropriations rather than imitations; 2d ed., 1677; 3d ed. 1678.
Thomas Flatman, *Poems and Songs* (1674); further editions in 1676, 1682, 1686.
John Dryden*, *Aureng-Zebe* (1676); imitation of *SA* in Act 1, p. 8; numerous other editions.
Urian Oakes, *An Elegie upon the Death of the Reverend Mr. Thomas Shepard* (1677); drawn from *SA*.
Nathaniel Lee, *The Rival Queens* (1677); imitation of *PL* in Act 4, p. 44; numerous other editions.
Edward Ecclestone, *Noah's Flood; or, The Destruction of the World* (1679); 2d ed., *The Cataclysm* (1685); *Order and Disorder: or, The World Made and Undone* (1679); imitation of *PL* (?).
Nathaniel Lee, *Caesar Borgia* (1680); imitation in Act 5, Scene 2, p. 69; numerous other editions.
John Dryden, *Absalom and Achitophel* (1681); numerous other editions.
Andrew Marvell*, *Miscellaneous Poems* (1681); "The Garden," lines 53–56 (from *IlP*); "Fleckno, an English Priest at Rome," line 28 (from *Lyc*); "Upon Appleton House," passim (various poems); "The First Anniversary," see before; written earlier in late 1640s and early 1650s.
J. S., Gent, *The Visions of Don Francisco de Quevedo Veilegass: The Second Part* (1682); echoes from *PL*.
Richard Steere, *The Daniel Catcher* (written 1682), first edition nonextant, published in New York, 1713; and "Earth Felicities, Heavens Allowances. A Blank Poem"; imitations of *PL*.
John Dryden, *MacFlecknoe* (1682); parody of *PL* 6. 719–22 in line 135–38; numerous other editions.
John Dryden and Nathaniel Lee, *The Duke of Guise* (1683); see especially Act 4, Scene [1], pp. 43–44; numerous other editions.
John Shirley, *The Complete Courtier: or, Cupid's Academy* (1683); echoes of *L'Al* pp. 20, 35.
Thomas Brown (?) or Samuel Wesley (?), *Maggots: or, Poems on Several Subjects, Never Before Handled* (1685); see "Out of Lucian's true History, Part the First," p. 119 (from *Nat*).

Robert Gould, *Love Given Over* (1686); imitation, p. 2; 2d ed., 1690.

S. F., *Female Advocate* (1686); influence from *PL* in the first part; 2d ed., 1687.

M(atthew?) S(tevens?), *The Great Birth of Man* (1686); imitations of *PL*.

"Lord Lucas His Ghost" (1687?); imitation of the Attendant Spirit's opening and final speeches in *Mask;* various manuscripts and first printed in *A Third Collection of the Newest and Most Ingenious Poems, Satyrs, Songs, &c. against Popery and Tyranny* (1689) as "The E. of Essex's Ghost. 1687," p. 22; numerous other printings.

Thomas D'Urfey, *New Poems* (1690), "An Ode to the Queen," pp. 20–21; echo of *PL*.

Thomas Yalden, "A Hymn to the Morning. In Praise of Light. An Ode," in *Examen Poeticum*, ed. John Dryden (1693), pp. 127–31; "A Hymn to Darkness," ibid., pp. 132–37.

"On Rebellious Spirits," in *Gentleman's Journal* 2 (ed. Peter Motteux) (February 1693): 44–45.

Thomas D'Urfey, *A Funeral Pindarique Poem* (1695); imitations of *PL* throughout; see, for example, Stanza 7 and compare 3. 645–653.

Sir Richard Blackmore, *Prince Arthur* (1695); 2d ed., 1695; 3d ed. (1696).

Sir Richard Blackmore, *King Arthur* (1697).

Samuel Wesley*, *The Life of Our Blessed Lord and Savior Jesus Christ* (1693); imitations from *PL* and *IlP;* 2d ed., 1697.

Anna Bullen (undated), a play known only in manuscripts. [JTS]

IMPRISONMENT, MILTON'S. The events attendant on the disruption of the Interregum included the apprehension of regicides, other enemies of the monarchy, and seditious material. The House of Commons resolved on June 16, 1660, that Milton should "be forthwith sent for, in Custody, by the Sergeant at Arms attending this House" (*Journals of the House of Commons,* 8 : 65–66). A few weeks before this, it appears, probably aware that the action was imminent, Milton went into hiding. The Anonymous Biographer recalls this, and Phillips says his uncle went to stay with a friend (still unidentified) in Bartholomew-Close. The king's proclamation* of August 13 notes that Milton has fled or so obscured himself that he can not be brought to legal trial. The Act of Free and General Pardon, Indemnity, and Oblivion was promulgated on August 29, and Milton, not excepted from the amnesty, came out of hiding and moved to Red Lion Fields in Holborn. But for reasons that are unclear, James Norfolk, Serjeant-at-Arms to the House of Commons, arrested Milton and took him to prison, presumably the Tower. The date of arrest is uncertain. It was probably not before the Act of Oblivion, since Milton would still have been in hiding; it may have been during September 13–November 6 when the House was adjourned. The *Hollandsche Mercurius* for December 1660, pp. 163–64, reported that Milton had "lain thus long in the Tower," but the Anonymous Biographer says Milton "was quickly set at liberty." It has been suggested that Norfolk acted under the earlier resolution of June 16, without considering the Act of Oblivion. On the other hand Godfrey Davies argued that the arrest was a deliberate attempt on the part of Milton's friends in government to protect him from other kinds of punishment through double jeopardy; Milton's high fine of £150 is explained as a diversionary tactic (see *Huntington Library Quarterly* 18: 351–63).

Upon payment of his fine, Milton was released on December 15, 1660. There are records of this release in the *Journals of the House of Commons,* 8 : 208; in the Public Record Office, Index to Warrant Books, 1660–1722, A–P, Index 8911, p. 201; and in the PRO, Dockers Signet Office, Index 6812. According to Phillips, the release came about through Andrew Marvell's* help, and Jacob Tonson* and Jonathan Richardson* both report it was through Sir William Davenant*. On December 17, in any case, Marvell complained that the fine was excessive (*Journals of the House of Commons,* 8 : 209) and the matter was referred to a committee (William Cobbett, *Parliamentary History of England,* 4 [1808], col. 162). No action by the committee is recorded. [JTS]

IN EFFIGIEI EIUS SCULPTOREM. This four-line Greek epigram appeared beneath the portrait-engraving of Milton in the 1645 edition* of his poems and was reprinted in the 1673 edition with the above Latin title. The engraving, done by William Marshall, was not to Milton's taste. Rather than make a fuss over it, however, he had Marshall, who apparently knew no Greek, inscribe these most unflattering lines beneath his work.

The cream of Milton's jest, according to Thomas O. Mabbott, lies in the ambiguity of the fourth line, best translated perhaps as "Laugh at the bad picture of a worthless engraver"; for the word meaning engraver is in the genitive case and can be translated equally well as *by* or *of* the engraver. Mabbott believed that the ambiguity was intentional: "the idea is that the picture represents the man who made it, not the supposed subject" (*Explicator* 8, item 58).

Milton tells us in *3Def* that he submitted "at the instance and from the importunity of the bookseller [Humphrey Moseley], to employ an unskilful engraver, because at that period of the war there was no other to be found in the city . . ." (9 : 125). How unskillful Marshall was may be gauged by comparing his work with the so-called Onslow portrait of Milton at age twenty-one. The comparison is a fair one since Marshall labeled his engraving as Milton at that age. This fact suggests that Milton, tired of sitting for the engraver, may have referred him to the earlier portrait, hoping perhaps that he would catch some of its attractive nature. If so, his hope was in vain, for Marshall's work is the likeness of an ugly old man. It is not surprising that Milton disliked it.

Posterity has shared Milton's poor opinion of Marshall's work. The assessment in *DNB* is representative: "Some of Marshall's plates are engraved with miniature-like delicacy and finish, and have a pleasing effect; but the majority, probably on account of the low rate of remuneration at which he was compelled to work, are coarse and unsatisfactory. . . ." [ERG]

IN OBITUM PRAESULIS ELIENSIS. This Latin poem memorializes Nicholas Felton*, Bishop of Ely (1556–1626). It appeared in the 1645 and 1673 editions* of Milton's poetry with his notation that it was composed at age seventeen and is thus one of four poems that Milton wrote commemorating persons important to the Cambridge community who died in the autumn of 1626.

Two of these persons—Felton and his distinguished colleague, Lancelot Andrewes*—had been Anglican bishops. The poems in which Milton mourns them —like the other poems in the group—are conventional rather than personal in their expression. Since the Milton family lived near the church of St. Mary-le-Bow in London, where Felton was rector for some years, Milton may have heard him preach; but no real evidence suggests that the poet was personally acquainted either with him or with Andrewes. On the other hand, Milton was probably sincere enough in regretting their deaths. His disenchantment with episcopacy lay some years in the future, and both men had been exemplary clergymen.

Of Felton, Thomas Fuller*, the seventeenth-century church historian, observed that he "had a sound head and a sanctified heart, beloved of God, and all good men, very hospitable to all, and charitable to the poor." Fuller also noted marked similarities in the lives of Felton and Andrewes: "Both being sons of seafaring men, who . . . attained comfortable estates; both Scholars, Fellows, and Masters of Pembroke Hall [at Cambridge]; both great scholars . . . preachers in London for many years . . . ; both successively bishops of Ely" (*Church History of Britain* [1837], 3 : 359). Appropriately, then, the poems in which Milton mourns them are much alike. *El3*, which is dedicated to Andrewes's memory, is written in elegiac meter; "In Obitum Praesulis Eliensis" with a reference to meters and dimeters. Both poems, however, have sixty-eight lines; both make extensive use of classical allusion; and both move from despair to acceptance of the subject's death. Milton further links them together by opening "In Obitum Praesulis Eliensis" with a reference to *El3* : he was still grieving over Andrewes's death, he writes, when he heard of Felton's.

Most of the poem is an oration that Felton speaks from his grave. Seeking to allay the poet's anger at Death, Felton defends her as the harvester of God and declares that virtuous souls like his are happy indeed to answer her call. In the concluding lines, he describes his sensations as he journeyed through the stars to Paradise, where he now anticipates eternal happiness. Some critics have felt that these concluding lines foreshadow the mature Milton's ability to suggest the vastness of cosmic space. If they do, the foreshadowing is at best a faint one. At seventeen, Milton had not yet learned—as he later did—to transcend the conventions that he employed; and the dominant impression that the poem leaves is that it has as much in common with the many other funerary poems of its age as it does with Milton's own later works. [ERG]

IN OBITUM PROCANCELLARII MEDICI. Dr. John Gostlin*, 1566?–1626, whose death is mourned in this poem, was a vice-chancellor at Cambridge during Milton's undergraduate days there. The poem appeared in both the 1645 and 1673 editions of Milton's minor poems with the notation that it was composed at age sixteen; but since Dr. Gostlin died in October 1626, when Milton was seventeen, this clearly is a mistake. Milton's notation, however, may be of some assistance; for William Riley Parker has observed that "since in assigning dates to eight of his Latin poems (probably in 1645, while preparing them for publication) Milton gave the verses on Gostlin an earlier date than any of the others, we may infer that it was written *first* of the four poems commemorating persons who died in the autumn of 1626 . . ." (*A Tribute to George Coffin Taylor,* p. 121).

All the persons commemorated were important to the Cambridge community, and none more so than Dr. Gostlin, who as vice-chancellor held the second-highest office in the university administration. A physician, Dr. Gostlin had become Master of Caius College in 1619, had been appointed Professor of Physic in 1623, and had served as vice-chancellor once before in 1618, the office being an annually elective one. It has sometimes been speculated that Dr. Gostlin may have taken a personal interest in Milton, particularly in connection with his rustication* in 1626. But Gostlin's position as a high university official most likely precluded close friendship with a young undergraduate like Milton, and Milton's tribute to him is on the whole a conventional poem of its type. Its basic thought—the paradox that the skilled physician could not save himself—is embellished with numerous classical allusions. Some of these same allusions, Donald C. Dorian points out, appear in an elegy that Milton's friend Charles Diodati* wrote on the death of the noted antiquarian William Camden*—a fact that underscores their commonplace nature as well as Milton's indebtedness to his friend (*The English Diodatis,* pp. 107–9).

As with most of Milton's juvenilia, the commentary has emphasized autobiographical* rather than aesthetic matters. Walter MacKellar, however, has praised the poem for both its construction and its imagery* (*The Latin Poems of John Milton,* p. 45); and one should note too the interesting albeit undeveloped observation of Mario Praz that lines 41–44 reveal "the same kind of chastened sensuality" to be found in Poussin's "Metamorphosis of the Plants" (*Seventeenth-Century Studies Presented to Sir Herbert Grierson,* p. 201). [ERG]

IN QUINTUM NOVEMBRIS. This 226-line Latin poem—quite the longest of five that Milton composed on the Gunpowder Plot* of Guy Fawkes—appeared in both the 1645 and 1673 editions* of Milton's work with a note indicating composition at age seventeen. It was thus composed around the autumn of 1626, a period of great poetic activity for Milton. Now in his second full year at Cambridge, he produced within a few months four poems on the deaths of prominent Cantabrigians, QNov, and, possibly, the shorter poems on the Gunpowder Plot.

In all these poems, Milton was intent on displaying his Latin style and learning; in none of them did he reveal much personal involvement with his subject. Certainly the vehement anti-Catholicism of QNov reveals more about the holiday for which it was composed than it does about Milton's own outlook. Hatred of Roman Catholicism—always a familiar sentiment in seventeenth-century England—reached its yearly peak of intensity in those events celebrating the discovery of Fawkes's plot in 1605; and a poet like Milton—hoping perhaps that he would be asked to read his work in a university assembly—would have been expected to share that intensity. If, besides, he impressed his auditors with his erudition, so much the better.

He probably succeeded, too, in impressing them, for at seventeen Milton was remarkably erudite. The list of authors whom critics have cited as sources for QNov attests to this. Some figures in the list—like Nicolaus Perottus, Bernardino Ochino*, and George Buchanan*—can be dismissed as having perhaps supplied Milton with a detail or two; others, however, require some discussion.

Ovid* and Virgil* are two such figures. Since they were both staples in the educational curriculum of his day, Milton assumed a wide familiarity with their works. When, for example, he blended materials from both writers in creating his own allegorical* figure of Fame, he could assume that his audience had read the relevant passages in the *Metamorphoses* (12. 39–63) and the *Aeneid* (4. 173–97). Ovid's work, which was a compendium of classical mythology*, provided him with a store of allusions to gods and goddesses; Virgil's may have provided even more. At least Macon Cheek, who has written the most sub-

stantial study of *QNov,* believes that it did : "in over-all conception and technique, in its larger movements and in its smaller details alike, . . . the 'In Quintum Novembris' is modeled very closely on Virgil, and affords striking evidence . . . that Virgil was Milton's first master in his epic apprenticeship" (*Studies in Philology* 54 : 179).

Phineas Fletcher* is another figure whose influence—a conjectured one—requires comment. He wrote two Fifth of November poems—a Latin one, *Locustae,* and an Englishing of it, *The Apollyonists.* These have often been mentioned as sources for *QNov;* but although they are valuable as analogues to Milton's work, their date of publication, 1627, indicates that they are not sources. The possibilities exist, of course, that Milton may have misdated his poem when he published it, or even that he may have seen copies of Fletcher's poems in manuscript. Neither possibility is very convincing, however, nor is either one necessary when we consider that Milton's work resembles Fletcher's only in a general way. As Herbert E. Cory observed in his study of *Spenser, the School of the Fletchers, and Milton* (p. 347) : "Both [Fletcher and Milton] used popular contemporary ideas. Both treated a popular superstition in a vein of classical and Spenserian allegory."

The vein of classical and Spenserian* allegory dictated that the characters in *QNov* be either pure abstractions like Murder and Treason or near-abstractions like Satan and the Pope, who are the principal figures. The Satan of *QNov* has aroused interest because of his more famous counterpart in *PL.* Each, Cheek observes, is the eternal wanderer and exile from heaven; each, the eternal envier and willful destroyer; each, the wily plotter (pp. 180–81). Two further observations of Cheek's are also worth noting, however : (1) in *QNov* Milton is not entirely successful in combining these elements into a viable dramatic character; (2) the elements themselves are highly traditional in portrayals of Satan. No less traditional is the Pope in *QNov.* He has nothing in common with the historical figure, Paul V, who was pontiff in 1605. Rather, he is the conventional monster of Protestant propaganda—a lascivious hypocrite who keeps a whore in his bedchamber.

Such dated parochialism should not be allowed to obscure the occasional vigor in Milton's satiric portrayal of Roman Catholicism. His method is that of the mock-heroic, which insists on a discrepancy between the importance of the matter and the manner in which it is presented. Because of God's Providence*, the Plot will fail—as Milton's readers well knew. Hence the machinations of Satan and the Pope are ultimately of little consequence; but Milton's manner of presenting them—at first glance—suggests that matters of grave concern are involved. Closer inspection reveals a variety of images that suggest that Roman Catholicism is not only evil but absurd as well: the Eucharist is merely the Pope's "gods of bread"; the mendicant friars in a papal procession carry candles in their hands, yet ironically live their lives in Cimmerian darkness; the worshipers in St. Peter's try to sing a chant but succeed only in sounding like Bacchus and his followers having an orgy.

The images above all occur in a lively passage of fourteen lines (lines 54–67). Elsewhere, Milton's inventiveness flags. In *QNov* he has created a work that is episodic in structure and only intermittently successful as poetry. The opening discovers Satan embarked on an aerial survey of Europe that reveals to him that only in England is his will thwarted. Determined to punish that happy, God-fearing land, he voyages to Rome, arriving at dusk in time to witness a papal procession as it winds through the streets to mass at St. Peter's. Night falls, and the Pope retires for an evening of dalliance with his secret mistress. After he is asleep, Satan appears to him in a dream disguised as a Franciscan friar and incites him to destroy the English king and Parliament with gunpowder so that papal supremacy will be restored in the island. Morning

comes, and the Pope, awakening, summons from their cave those old retainers of the Roman Church—Murder and Treason—and instructs them in the Plot. The scene shifts abruptly to the tower of Fame, the many-tongued monstress who spreads rumors across the earth. God, who has been amused by the actions of Satan and the Pope, instructs her to publish tidings of the Plot, which she does, thus thwarting it. The conclusion is huddled; the tower of Fame episode, poorly integrated and out of proportion (23 lines), given the length of the poem.

In short, Milton did not succeed in shaping his materials into a well-proportioned whole or in writing equally well in each section of the poem. Nevertheless, *QNov* deserves study. In his edition of Milton's *Poems upon Several Occasions,* the eighteenth-century poet-critic Thomas Warton* observed that "this little poem, as containing a council, conspiracy, and expedition of Satan, may be considered as an early and promising prolusion of Milton's genius to the *Paradise Lost*" ([1791], p. 497). Quite apart from its foreshadowing Milton's later work, however, the little poem has qualities to recommend it, for Latinists like Edward Kenner Rand have given it high marks as poetry (*Studies in Philology* 19: 121–22). Ironically, its very language is increasingly a barrier, even to serious students of Milton. The nineteenth-century Miltonist David Masson might comment in his *Life* that *QNov* is "one of the cleverest and most poetical of all Milton's youthful productions, and certainly one of the most characteristic" (1 : 174), but twentieth-century Miltonists, including the biographers, have added remarkably little to the commentary. [ERG]

INCARNATION is the Christian belief that the Son of God* at a point in time joined with flesh from his human mother Mary to become the historical Jesus, who was and still is fully God and fully man. The dogma was promulgated in 451 at the Council of Chalcedon, though many of the details of the union remained for later theology to refine. The subject is central to Christianity because it defines the very being of its founder.

For Milton's mature understanding of this dogma, the major statement is *CD,* as for all of his mature theological views. There he recognizes the divine and human distinction of Christ's nature (15 : 259) but argues at least the possibility that two persons rather than two natures were joined (pp. 264–66), a belief identified with the Nestorian heresy*. Milton's error—if that is what it is—seems to come from his interesting conception of individuality, whereby the individuality of any being is identified with his essence, neither of which can be shared with another being. Using an argument similar to that whereby he distinguished the being of the Son from that of the Father* (with consequent charges of Arianism*), Milton insists that the two different natures in Christ are really two essences and thus two persons. Orthodoxy had postulated one person (the divine) and two natures (the divine and the human).

But before complete committal to Nestorianism Milton refuses further argument : "The mode of union is unknown to us" and we should "be contented with remaining wisely ignorant" (pp. 271, 273). He is unsure whether the two persons in this one being have two wills and two understandings, one divine and the other human (p. 275). It seems clear, however, that he did not accept the traditional "two natures in one person." The two entities remain for him somewhat separable. It is striking that the conception of such a union has been applied to the relationship of Christ with the members of his church; some groups like the Calvinists* believe that such salvation enjoyed by the Elect cannot be severed. For Milton, as for the Arminians*, this relationship could be dissolved by the human member's falling away—regaining, so to speak, his individuality apart from the unity of all in Christ. Satan's fall can be viewed in this light. The same concept of potential divisibility appears in Milton's concept of

divorce*. Marriage* had been viewed by some as being indissoluble. It signifies "unto us the mystical union that is between Christ and his church," the *Prayer Book* states in the marriage service. But the individual in Milton's eyes may assert his individuality to break up that union too, though the union of divine and human persons for him was an eternal one. In comparison, Satan incarnates himself with the serpent in *PL* 9, a union that concludes like a bad marriage as soon as circumstances no longer demand it.

Milton's understanding of the life of Jesus is presented most fully in *PR,* where Jesus is tempted, but only in his human nature (he "was in all points tempted like as we are, yet without sin," observes the author of Hebrews 4:15, and the divine cannot be tempted).) To achieve this conception Milton assumes the doctrine of kenosis*, derived from Philemon 2 : 7–8, whereby the Son at the Incarnation "emptied himself" of his divinity and "took upon him the form of a servant, and was made in the likeness of men." The temptations* depicted in *PR* are thus real ones, directed to the human nature. But Milton even goes so far as to argue that the divine suffers and dies with the human at the crucifixion (15 : 307)—an argument limited, however, to *CD*. The Incarnation continues after the Resurrection; as the Father proclaims, the Son will

Thir Nature also to thy Nature joyn;
And be thy self Man among men on Earth,
Made flesh, when time shall be . . .
Nor shalt thou by descending to assume
Mans Nature, Less'n or degrade thine owne.

Finally

    thy Humiliation shall exalt
With thee thy Manhood also to this Throne;
Here shalt thou sit incarnate.
           (*PL* 3. 282ff.)
           [WBH]

INDEPENDENTS should take that name, said Milton—a sometime Independent himself, "from the true freedom of Christian doctrin and church-discipline subject to no superior judge but God only" (6 : 96). They believed that Christ is the only head of the Church, the Bible its only rule for faith* and practice, willing covenant its only requirement for membership—with doctrinal differences left to individual conscience. They believed that each congregation should be self-governing in secular as in religious affairs, with any coordinating agency serving in a merely advisory or service capacity, and with no state support or control at all. Their original aim was a new form of organization that would allow for widest toleration of any Christian church, and their first congregation, led by Henry Jacobs in 1616, achieved a fine compromise among Separatists, who wanted no external ties at all; Presbyterians*, who wanted to impose their own rigid structure as a hedge against heretical* sects; and supporters of the national church as it was. Jacobs introduced congregational autonomy in the Separatist mode while providing a form of decentralized Calvinism* as a doctrinal sop to Presbyterians and still retaining communion with the Church of England, taking the Oath of Supremacy and even paying tithes.

By 1644 when he wrote *Areop*, Milton was moving toward Independency. The essence of the movement was independence from state control, but by this time Independents were quickly becoming the State itself. Their emphasis on the sanctity of conscience and concomitant defense of the sectaries attracted their strong support, creating thereby a political movement that culminated in the Commonwealth. In 1651 Milton saw a flaw in "the Good Old Cause." His sonnet to Cromwell warned against certain Independent ministers who were then petitioning for a state-supported and -controlled clergy: "Threat'ning to bind our souls with secular chains" (line 12). This premonition proved prophecy.

Seven years later the Savoy Conference issued, along with a doctrinal statement that differed very little from the Presbyterian's *Westminster Confession of Faith*, a strong Erastian* recommendation to the Protector that churches be regulated by the civil magistrate. In 1659 Milton recognized that Independent ministers had become a hireling crew. Instead of Independents, he said, they should be called rather Dependents, since they will be "Dependents on the magistrate for thir maintenance," and Magistrates "will pay none but such whom . . . they find conformable to their interest and opinions" (6 : 96). Thus, disgusted with Independency, Milton took his solitary way on a natural progression "from negative Puritanism" to affirmation of Presbyterianism to Independency and then pure individualism itself (Parker, *Milton*, p. 216). [PMZ]

INDEX LIBRORUM PROHIBITORUM, the Roman Catholic index of books that Catholics were forbidden to read except with special dispensation. It listed three of Milton's publications during the eighteenth century: *Literae, 1Def,* and *PL* in an Italian translation*. Although listed under Milton, *Literae* was placed on the index because it printed letters by Cromwell*, Puritan leader. It first appears in *Index Librorum Prohibitorum Innoc. XI. P. M. Jussu Editus Usque Ad Annum 1681. Einem Accedit in Fine Appendix usque ad Mensem Junij 1704* (Rome: Camerae Apostolicae, 1704), specifically in *Appendix ad Indicem*, pp. 347 and 361, where we learn that it was placed on the index on December 22, 1700. However, Parker (*Milton*, 2 : 1185) says the work was cited on November 22, 1694. The listing is continued throughout the eighteenth century. *1Def* was placed on the Spanish provincial index of prohibited books, before 1707: see *Novissimus Librorum Prohibitorum et Expurgandorum Index pro Catholicis Hispaniarum Regnis, Philippi V. Reg. Cath.* ([n.p.], 1707), 1 : 660, and *Index Librorum Prohibitorum, ac Expurgandorum Novissimus Pro Universis Hispaniarum Regnis Serenissimi Ferdinandi VI. Regis Catholici, hac Ultima Editione* (Matritia: Emmanuelis Fernandez (1747), 2:686. Paolo Rolli's* translation of *PL* was placed on the index in *Appendix Novissimae Appendici ad Indicem Librorum Prohibitorum a Mense Maii MDCCXVIII. Usque ad totum Mensem Julii MDCCXXXIX* (Rome: Camerae Apostolicae, 1739), p. 506; it was prohibited on January 21, 1732. Rolli had published Books 1–6 in London in 1729, and the full poem in London and Verona in 1730; the last was the edition to be banned. [JTS]

INDEX THEOLOGICUS. In *CB* Milton refers a dozen times, in entries made after 1639, to a companion collection, now lost, which he once labels his "Index Theologicus." As it survives, *CB* consists of "Ethical," "Economic," and "Political" indexes. Presumably the lost theological section was to be a compilation like the rest of *CB,* its subjects related to theology. *CB* cross-refers a number of them: "Of Church Property" (several times), "Of Idolatry" (twice), "Of not Forcing Religion," "Of the Pope," "Of the Church," and "Of Councils."

It has been assumed that the posthumous *CD* ultimately resulted from this collection, but this can hardly be true. None of the subjects cross-referred become chapters in *CD,* and indeed they have relatively little status there. The overall organization of the treatise follows that of contemporary Calvinists* like Ames* and Wolleb*. Indeed, rather than a florilegium of biblical texts, as so much of *CD* is, the lost notebook must have been a collection of nonbiblical texts (like the rest of *CB*) on religious subjects. One may surmise that a heading like "Church Property" would refer to examples of church corruption by largess such as the supposed Donation of Constantine*. Under it Milton would have entered from John Gower's* *Confessio Amantis,* "This day is poison poured into the church," and from St. John Chrysostom*, "Religion brought forth wealth, and the daughter devourd the mother," which he would cite in arguments as widely separated in time as *Apol* (1642), *Eikon* (1649), and *Hire* (1659), a fact suggesting his reliance upon a single collection of notes associated with theology as he similarly employed the collections of *CB.* [WBH]

INFLUENCE ON AMERICAN LITERATURE, MILTON'S. John Milton appeared to early Americans as a poet of titanic stature. From colonial days through the early years of the republic his shadow often eclipsed Homer* and Virgil*, and occasionally he stood side by side with scriptural prophets and singers like Isaiah and David. William Livingston declared in *Philosophic Solitude: A Poem* (1747) that he was divinely inspired, and Benjamin Church, in *The Choice* (1757), presented an image of greatness that reflected American sentiments for nearly a century:

HAIL Briton's Genius, *Milton*! deathless
    Name!
Blest with a full Satiety of Fame:
Who durst attempt Impertinence of Praise?
Or sap insidious thy eternal Bays?
For greater Song, or more exalted Fame,
Exceeds Humanity to make, or claim.
These to peruse, I'd oft forget to dine,
And suck Refection from each mighty Line.
               (p. 8)

Early Americans indeed nourished their hearts, minds, and souls on the poetic bounty Milton supplied. Schoolmasters quoted his words to illustrate points of grammar* and rhetoric*, and recommended his diction* and style*. Moralists presented his Eve as an ideal of womanly virtue and found in his picture of prelapsarian bliss a design for nuptial love. Ministers transposed his lines into rubrics of worship, cited him to support their positions, and so absorbed his vast images that their congregations envisioned the Christian story not so much as depicted in Scripture as described in *PL.* Politicians applauded his stand on civil and ecclesiastical liberty*, and, after his epic had become a common possession, turned his portraits of evil* and of good into propagandist devices to fight party disputes of the day. Even more significantly, poets called on him to pattern their language, imagery, syntax, and verse forms. Had T. S. Eliot* known the story of

Milton in early America, he might never have recanted his position on the singular dangers to poetic creation he found in Miltonic verse.

Colonial poets, far from perceiving such dangers, invoked Milton often and faithfully in their attempts to create a new literature on American shores. As early as 1682 William Steere sought to enhance several lines in his *Daniel Catcher* with Miltonic diction, and in the 1713 edition of this collection of poems he copied Milton's verse paragraph and presented a picture of earthly bliss similar to Milton's depiction of Eden. But his clearest attempt to achieve a Miltonic style may be seen in his ode *Upon the Coelestial Embassy Perform'd by Angels,* a poem that follows the imagery and verse form of *Nat,* and even catches something of its spirit and tone. Steere indeed turned to Milton not only for poetic but also for moral and religious instruction; he set a pattern of discipleship that ran through American poetry for a hundred or more years.

As the eighteenth century unrolled, poets embroidered this pattern and consciously sought in Milton ways to refine their sentiments and elevate their style. Not all admirers of Milton, of course, could be considered disciples. Samuel Davies, for example, simply incorporated into *A Poem Wrote by a Clergyman in Virginia* (1750) a few Miltonic phrases. James Bowdoin translated the hymn to nuptial love in Book 4 of *PL* into clanging heroic couplets (*Pietas et Gratulatio* . . . [1761], pp. 102–3) to celebrate the marriage of George III to Charlotte Sophia of Mecklenburg-Strelitz. Thomas Godfrey, best known for his tragedy *The Prince of Parthia* (in *Juvenile Poems* [1765], echoed *Lyc* in his elegy on General Wolfe and copied the syntax of the famous image of Satan presiding over the Infernal Council (pp. 34, 52, 88). But James Ralph and Mather Byles—the first only a quasi-American, the second a product of New England—felt Milton's attraction, openly admired his grand style, and guided a considerable amount of their

verse in accordance with Miltonic models. Even more than Steere, they could be called Milton disciples.

As a critic, James Ralph deplored imitations of Milton. Milton's numbers, he said, were so majestical that no one could follow them and write in "good grace," in illustration of which he cited John Philips*, who would have "succeeded better if he had not paid so strict a deference to *Milton's* manner, and thereby neglected his own." But Ralph promptly forgot his critical stance when he himself sat down to write *Night: A Poem* (1728) —a piece in which he asked for illumination, called on light to guide him through darkness, and invoked a power to lift him to adventurous and daring heights of poetic creation. He failed to reach the heights he yearned to ascend, but he did manage to present a creditable picture of evening, an achievement due mainly to Milton's description of the arrival of night in Book 4 of *PL.* Even more consciously than Ralph, Mather Byles made Milton his model. Witty, urbane, and inordinately ambitious for literary fame, he published in 1744 *Poems on Several Occasions* and in 1745 *Poems by Several Hands,* both of which proved to be literary events of the day. Echoes of Milton sound in both volumes, but the first shows the imprint of Milton more clearly. Here Byles included "Written in Milton's *Paradise Lost,*" a poem of earlier date imitating Milton's imagery and style. What impressed Byles most was Milton's power of description, a combination of harmony and force that could set forth equally the sublimities of the spiritual world or the beauties of nature. Somewhat timidly, but with more boldness as he progressed, Byles imitated both powers, revealing, as he did so, a growing tendency among American poets to turn to Milton for special pictorial effects. In the great battles on the plains of Heaven, Milton had pointed the way to sublimity; in the picture of Adam and Eve in the Garden of Eden, he had presented a model of charm and delight (*Poems on Several Occasions,* pp. 26f., 33). Byles could do no better than to aspire to such excellence.

So successful was Byles in his aspirations that the poet John Adams proclaimed that Byles had reached Milton's "godlike heights." Such a claim may be attributed more to friendship than to sound critical judgment, yet Adams's praise is significant. He too believed that through Milton American poets could achieve greatness, in witness whereof he himself turned to *PL* to enliven his longest and most ambitious poem, *The Revelation of St. John the Divine*, printed in *Poems on Several Occasions* (1745). In this translation and paraphrase of Scripture, Adams disclosed a habit of mind becoming widespread in both the religious and poetic communities: the incorporation of Miltonic imagery into native poems for the express purpose of achieving special pictorial and dramatic effects. To St. John's cryptic story of the War in Heaven*, telling of Michael's fight against that old Serpent called the Devil and Satan, Adams added, though in greatly condensed form, details from the more dramatic account of this action in *PL*:

Now War upon the Heav'nly Plain began,
The Host with *Michael* blazing at their Van;
While the fierce Dragon led his Angels on,
Whose Rebel-Pow'rs at once were overthrown:
Eras'd from Heav'n, their shining Place was
    lost,
Headlong he fell, and all his fainting Host:
That ancient Serpent, who deceives the World,
Was on the Earth in flaming Ruin hurl'd.
                              (pp. 138–39))

Milton had already given to the Christian story a pictorial dimension, a dramatic urgency only suggested in Scripture; Adams now incorporated this dimension into his own poem, hoping thereby to make his account more graphic and moving. Before the end of the century images from *PL* would become an orthodox part of the Christian tale of sin and redemption: where Holy Writ left off and Milton began could no longer be clearly distinguished.

Nowhere is this welding more evident than in William Livingston's *Philosophic Solitude*, a meditative poem about half of which stemmed from *PL*. Like Adams and Byles, Livingston drew from Milton's scenes of celestial warfare to picture Satan's defeat on the plains of Heaven. His narrative showing Michael in angelic conflict with Satan, the appearance of the Messiah, and the final doom of the rebels follows almost precisely Milton's account, though in truncated form; and for his philosophic meditations on the nature of God and the wonders of creation he turned to Adam and Eve's morning hymn in Book 5. In such scenes he sought, with the help of Milton, to achieve sublimity; through the image of Adam and Eve in the Garden of Eden expressing their prelapsarian love, he sought to move tender affections. Livingston reproduced a good part of this charming scene in Book 4, which Milton had crowned with his moving hymn to wedded love; but in his attempt to capture the spirit of the hymn itself he dismally failed:

By love directed, I wou'd chuse a wife,
T' improve my bliss, and ease the load of life.
Hail *Wedlock*! hail, inviolable tye!
Perpetual fountain of domestic joy!
Love, friendship, honour, truth, and pure
    delight
Harmonious mingle in the nuptial rite.
                      (pp. 32–33, 24–26, 38)

Such unimaginative couplets do violence to Milton's sentiments on wedded love; but Livingston's poetic instinct was sound. This hymn, as well as the hymn to the Creator, became stock in trade for imitation among American poets, and in their original form, excerpted from context, they soon became popular and served as rubrics of lay worship to celebrate the glory of God and His manifest design for the increase of mankind.

The last disciple of Milton in colonial America was Francis Hopkinson. Statesman, musician, and political satirist, Hopkinson was more strictly a Revolutionary than a colonial figure, for he achieved his considerable reputation after the break with England and became widely known for his popular *The Battle of the Kegs*. But in his youth he admired Milton, and, what was important for American poetry, his interest lay not so much in the grand style of *PL* as in the lilting verse of *L'Al* and *IlP*. In his *Ode to Music,* a short poem inspired by the notes of a harpsichord, Hopkinson obviously had Milton's companion poems in mind, as evidenced in both his language and verse form; and one month after the appearance of this poem he published in *The American Magazine* (Oct. and Nov. 1757) direct imitations of *L'Al* and *IlP*. Hopkinson began his own *L'Allegro* with the familiar injunction, "HENCE *Melancholy,*" and then proceeded, after a description of Mirth, to trace a fancied journey through a summer's day and a winter's night, seeing sights and hearing sounds similar to those Milton had earlier presented. Such joys so entranced Hopkinson that he, like Milton, could live forever with Mirth:

> If such thy pleasures, *smiling Joy!*
> Oh may'st thou e'er my mind employ;
> Dawn in my breast continual day,
> And chace dull sorrows far away.
> (Nov. 1757, pp. 84–86)

Hopkinson followed an identical procedure in his *Il Penseroso,* reproducing even more faithfully Milton's language and structure. Yet neither of his verses possesses a tithe of the charm or shows a semblance of the seriousness of its original. As early attempts at mood poetry, however, they merit some praise, particularly when compared with most magazine verse of the time. They have a lilt and an ease seldom found in that early day, and they spurred a movement—in fact, set a vogue—that shaped American poetry into the early years of the republic. Imitation of Milton indeed revealed a twin impulse in the literary community, a reaching for greatness and a reaching for charm: *PL* could point the way to the first, *L'Al* and *IlP* to the second.

Attempts to achieve greatness through imitation of Milton characterized most epic* poetry of the Revolution, with the result that the first great surge to celebrate New World experience produced some of the most artificial verse of the century.

Patterns of Miltonic language and forms established during colonial days now merged with an urgent national desire to create a distinctly American literature. So strong was this urge that a patriot proposed that Congress establish an American poet laureateship, an office that would allow some ambitious poet to "raise a new Parnassus on the Allegany mountains, and open a second Helicon at the source of the Potowmack." Congressmen apparently looked at this proposal with skeptical eyes, but unquestionably the Revolution spurred a deep-seated desire to "rehearse" in "glorious numbers" the "rise and progress of the American Millennium" (*The New Haven Gazette and the Connecticut Magazine* 1, no. 10 [April 20, 1786]: 79–80). So noble an aim and so monumental a task asked for inspiration from the highest possible source, asked for practical help from such a poet as the great Milton himself, who could point the way to sublimity.

Among the first to invoke Milton as visions of an American millennium took form was Hugh Henry Brackenridge, who with Philip Freneau composed *The Rising Glory of America,* a commencement poem envisioning, among other things, a Homer and a Milton arising on the American strand. The part Brackenridge played in this joint effort was small; but it is important to note that three years after the appearance of this work, when he composed *A Poem on Divine Revelation,* he contended that Milton was the source of his style. In a prefatory notice to this latter verse he confessed that imitation of Milton could be traced through the entire argument. Such a confession, he implied, would serve a dual purpose: it would clarify his position that imitation of great originals could produce excellent writing —a principle, he said, that he had found in Longinus*; and it would forestall objections as to the source of his poem. Consciousness of Milton and admiration for his style clung to Brackenridge through the early years of his life. In a sermon preached before the American Army a few days prior to the Battle of Brandywine he quoted from Milton and divulged that he had been touched by the "magic sound" of his "harp"; and somewhat later, as he viewed an island from the banks of the Allegheny, he envisioned a poet pouring his "magic numbers on this scene," a poet comparable to Homer or Milton, whom he considered the father of modern bards. Such admiration led him to attempt the roll of Milton's blank verse in *A Poem on Divine Revelation* (1774), and loosely follow the structure of *Mask* in his own *Masque* honoring George Washington's visit to Warm Springs, Virginia. But clearly the grand style attracted him most. "Miss Urany," he once said, was his "flame"; and not until late maturity could he say that Milton's muse* no longer inspired him. In the meanwhile, however, "prospect" poetry flourished. What Brackenridge had hoped to accomplish through imitation of Milton, more talented pens attempted in more ambitious effusions. Failing to find expression for his particular genius in verse, he sensibly left prophetic visions to others and later sought fame in *Modern Chivalry*.

But not so Philip Freneau, who possessed a much greater poetic talent and who still holds an important place in the annals of American literature. Freneau had composed most of *The Rising Glory of America,* a poem that opened with the discovery of the New World, inquired into the origin of American Indians, sketched the early struggles of immigrants, and concluded with a vision of the present condition and future prospects of the land. So grand a sweep asked for a grand style, for a flexible blank verse* ornamented with proper names freighted with memories and often mellifluous in sound. Such Miltonic characteristics, Freneau thought, would lift his vision above commonplace poems and invest it with dignity and high purpose. At any rate, when Freneau pictured the landing of Columbus, he widened his panorama to include the story of Cortez and

> the story old in fame,
> Of Atabilipa, by thirst of gold
> Depriv'd of life: which not Peru's rich ore,
> Nor Mexico's vast mines cou'd then redeem.
> (*Poems,* ed. F. L. Pattee [1902], 1:52)

Freneau found Milton so useful that, to fashion America's glorious future, he turned to the vision the Angel Michael had vouchsafed Adam in the latter books of *PL.* The view of eternal bliss that Adam had glimpsed, Freneau turned into a historical paradise, a time when joy would cover the earth, when men would see from a "fairer Pisgah" a new Canaan, of whose happiness Americans would be the first to partake. Such a millennium* would bring a new Eden, happier far than the one Adam had lost. No dangerous tree or deathful fruit would grow; no "fierce disease," no "direful" plagues would afflict mankind. After so fair a sight the step to *The Conquest of Canaan* could not be postponed very much longer.

But Freneau was not at his best in attempting the grand style. His bent was more toward light, lyric verse, and for help in this mode he followed the lead of Francis Hopkinson and turned to *L'Al* and *IlP.* The result was *The Power of Fancy,* one of the most derivative yet one of the happiest poems of Freneau's youth. The poem opens with a direct address to Fancy, after which Freneau presented her lineage and a series of images to enliven her character. The lineage and nature of Fancy once established, Freneau was ready to demonstrate her power, which he revealed in a journey with her through a night and a day. The first scene to come into view recalls the dim religious light and the sound of the organ in *IlP*:

> Lo! she walks upon the moon,
> Listens to the chimy tune
> . . . .
> Leads me to some lonely dome,
> Where Religion loves to come,
> Where the bride of Jesus dwells,
> And the deep ton'd organ swells
> In notes with lofty anthems join'd,
> Notes that half distract the mind
> (1:35f.)

Toward the end of the poem, Freneau and Fancy encounter Day; and, after presenting such pleasures as light could provide, Freneau implored Fancy to pursue with him a solitary way:

Come, O come—perceived by none,
You and I will walk alone.
(1:39)

The similarities between Milton's twin poems and *The Power of Fancy,* however, end here. Milton made his two journeys to evaluate two significant modes of experience; Freneau traveled with Fancy to show the transitory nature of the human condition. If *The Power of Fancy* cannot be included among his best lyrics, it can be listed as one of the most skillfully executed poems of his youth, an achievement directly attributable to the excellence of the models he followed.

Both *The Rising Glory of America* and *The Power of Fancy* strengthened tendencies in American poetry already present. Great subjects demanded the style of *PL;* shifting moods asked for the lilting couplets of *L'Al* and *IlP.* As the Revolution moved inexorably toward open hostilities, Freneau perceived that Milton's grand style could become an instrument of satire. In *A Voyage to Boston,* he presented General Gage in a midnight consultation with Admiral Greaves, Lord Percy, General Burgoyne, and other enemies of American freedom—a consultation cast in the image of the Infernal Council in Book 2 of *PL*:

High in the dome a dire assembly sat,
A stupid council on affairs of state;
· · · · · · · · · · · · · · · · ·
First, Gage was there—a mimic chair of state,
Gage starts, rebounding from his ample seat,
Swears thrice, and cries—"Ye furies, are we beat?
· · · · · · · · · · · · · · · · ·
He ceas'd, the anger flash'd from both his eyes,
While Percy to his query thus replies
(1:167f.)

Following Lord Percy's speech, Admiral Greaves and General Burgoyne arose to deliver their views, a scene suggesting immediately the speeches of Mammon, Moloch, and Belial; and as the scene unrolled Freneau's mock-epic intention became clear. He needed only to cast his lines into Miltonic constructions and to use some of the imagery of *PL* to convey the combined futility and evil of plotting against a land blessed by the prospect of an imminent millennium. The Party of Satan and the Party of God faced each other across clear Manichaean lines.

Brackenridge and Freneau thus channeled a Miltonic course in American poetry as the nation moved into its most intense period of literary activity prior to the Romantic movement. Augustan standards still demanded heroic couplets; Alexander Pope*, Hugh Blair, and Edward Young still stood as models for hundreds of American poems. Furthermore, Brackenridge and Freneau soon dropped Milton from the forefront of their poetry and sought individual styles. But during the ferment of the time Milton dominated their millennium verse, and this pointed straight to the epic poems of the Connecticut Wits. Only Miltonic language and imagery appeared to be sufficiently grand to envision the great American dream.

Yet only Joel Barlow and Timothy Dwight produced serious imitations* of *PL.* John Trumbull, rather than celebrating New World experience in the grand style, chose to follow Freneau's lead and assess current events through the fable and imagery of Milton's poem. The result was *M'Fingal.* Trumbull initially conceived of his poem as a simple satire on Whig and Tory positions, but as the fable grew in his mind it turned into a mock-epic, with all the machinery of battles and visions. Samuel Butler's *Hudibras* was his main inspiration; Homer and Virgil stood in the wings; but Milton was present on the stage from beginning to end. Sometimes Milton spoke through single words or phrases, sometimes through imagery that illuminated whole scenes of mock-heroic adventure. The skirmish between Whig and M'Fingal, for example, achieved a particular mock-heroic effect by being described in terms of the great duel between Michael and Satan in *PL.* Michael's finely tempered sword, which had caused Satan pain, became, in Whig's hands, a ridiculous spade that sent M'Fingal on a flight so precipitous that he appeared like "Old Satan struggling on through chaos." As Trumbull admitted, readers only "slightly versed in epic poem" would immediately recognize Milton's phrases, images, and heroic actions. The picture of Whig and M'Fingal grappling in battle would, when envisioned against the titanic struggles and cosmic vistas of *PL,* belittle the Tory position by rendering its adherents ridiculous and ineffective. In Trumbull's hands, Milton's transcendent scenes became devices of satire*.

But in the last part of *M'Fingal* Trumbull dropped the mock-heroic mask and presented a serious view of America's future. Even as Adam had ascended a high hill with Michael to view the future history of mankind, so M'Fingal and his Tory friend Malcolm, as M'Fingal reported in an address to his Tory companions, had climbed a ladder from whose height they could see events leading up to the end of the War. After a parade of famine, plague, and bloodshed, a fair vista began to unfold :

And see, (sight hateful and tormenting!)
This Rebel Empire, proud and vaunting,
From anarchy shall change her crasis,
And fix her pow'r on firmer basis;
To glory, wealth and fame ascend,
Her commerce wake, her realms extend;
. . . .
Gay cities, tow'rs and columns rise,
And dazzling temples meet the skies.
(*Poetical Works* [1820], 1 :106ff., 174)

Here Trumbull presented the same eighteenth-century vision of progress that had fascinated Brackenridge and Freneau, a vision consonant with the hopes of Revolutionary America. Perhaps on this virgin land, in this New World, the Utopian dreams of mankind could at long last come true. Such a heady vision could not be denied, even in a mock-heroic poem.

In *The Conquest of Canaan* (1785)

Timothy Dwight embraced it and made it central to his typological fable. Incredibly serious and theologically minded, Dwight saw in the story of Joshua leading the Children of Israel into the land of Canaan an allegory* of American experience; and he set about to find a form suitable to tell so important a tale. Virgil he knew in the original, and the *Iliad* and *Odyssey* in Pope's handy translations. *PL* was his constant companion. Why not, then, draw from all four; why not, since Milton had presented a great vision, follow the structure of *PL*? The problems Dwight encountered in telling the Old Testament story in Miltonic style with typological significance in terms of American experience overwhelmed him. No one now turns to *The Conquest of Canaan* for insights into the human condition, or for fresh views on New World experience. Dwight's epic indeed is an amorphous *tour de force,* a prime example of the disjuncture of matter and form. But it is significant in that it reveals the derivative nature of early American poetry, and more particularly in that it shows the shaping force of Milton's hand.

Even a cursory reading of *The Conquest of Canaan* reveals a surprising number of Miltonic phrases. Milton was fond, for example, of saying *amaze* for *amazement,* and so also was Dwight. Milton's distinctive syntax in the opening scene of the Infernal Council, by now etched on the American mind, so fascinated Dwight that he could scarcely begin a graphic description without following the word order of that famous image, as evident, for example, in "High in the van exalted Irad strode," or "High on her ramparts Gibeon's children rose." Even more noticeable is Dwight's use of Milton's narrative techniques. Milton often pictured morning and evening to indicate the passage of time, sometimes lingering with such sensitivity on the scenes he presented that schoolmasters made them a part of their repertory for classroom recitation. The smell of morn was sweet in his nostrils, and eventide possessed special charms. Dwight indicated the passage of time in the same way, pausing even more often than Milton had paused to describe morning and evening, sometimes in Milton's own words. So close is his description of evening in Book 9 of *The Conquest of Canaan* to that in Book 4 of *Paradise Lost* that it is hard not to believe that Dwight had Milton before him as he sketched his own scene. The clothes metaphor, the spangled sky, the planets, the clouded moon, the silence, the retiring tribes—all are there, almost in the order of Milton's original (p. 227).

Milton's images so impressed Dwight that he incorporated many of the most famous into his own unfolding story. In his account of the Creation*, Milton had achieved some of his most happy pictorial effects. The creeks began to swarm with fry innumerable, and shoals of fish glided "under the green Wave," or through groves of coral strayed, showing "to the Sun thir wav'd coats dropt with Gold." Meanwhile, the sky filled with fowls : the eagle, the stork, and the solemn nightingale, and unnamed smaller birds spread their painted wings in flight. Dwight condensed Milton's description but nevertheless rendered a faithful account of his original :

He spoke; and fishes fill'd the watry rounds,
Swarm'd in the streams, and swam the
    Ocean's bounds;
The green sea sparkled with unnumber'd dies,
And varying beauty wav'd upon the skies.
                                          (p. 38)

Even the order of description is the same in both accounts.

In a similar fashion Dwight copied Milton's morning hymn, Adam and Eve's first appearance in Eden, and selected images from the Infernal Council (pp. 30, 38f., 6. 16). As he came to the end of his story, he presented, as Milton had done, a vision of things to come, a picture of the New Canaan in the New World. The precedent of Brackenridge, Freneau, and Trumbull compelled him to do so. Even as Milton had allowed Michael to unfold the future to Adam, so Dwight had an angel* instruct Joshua. Like Adam,

Joshua expressed discouragement and bewailed his fate. Like Adam, Joshua was taken to a high hill to see the future unroll so that he could come into an understanding of the providence* of God. Like Adam, Joshua was informed of biblical history, and, as the story pictured the entrance of Israel into the land of Canaan and the coming of the Messiah, it moved to the New Canaan, the *"Glory of the Western Millennium"* :

Far o'er yon azure main thy view extend,
Where seas, and skies, in blue confusion blend,
Lo, there a mighty realm, by heaven design'd
The last retreat for poor, oppres'd mankind!
. . . .
No dangers fright; no ills the course delay;
'Tis virtue prompts, and GOD directs the way.
                                      (pp. 253–54)

Sustained by this vision, Joshua now turned to the immediate task before him, the conquest of old Canaan; and with this final action ended one of the most promising, yet one of the most unfortunate imitations of Milton in early America. Dwight's taste for the sweeping and grand simply outran his talent, however much he was praised in his own day as a second Homer or Milton. *The Conquest of Canaan* stands as a monument to confused means and aims.

Yet so intense was literary ferment during this period that no one seemed aware of the problems Dwight encountered, least of all Joel Barlow, whose ambition to write an American epic haunted him for more than two decades. His *Vision of Columbus* (1787), a long philosophical poem on the discovery of America, followed in the path of earlier "prospect" poetry, and exhibited nearly all the difficulties of adapting the grand style to the ideals of the Enlightenment. Like many American poets before him, Barlow copied Milton's syntax and imagery to delineate throne scenes or other royal occasions. Whether he envisioned Old World dynasties or the metallic opulence of the New mattered little : the famous picture of Satan presiding over Pandemonium furnished a structure and form :

Fair on her throne, revolving distant fate,
Imperial Katharine majestic sate,
. . . .
There, robed in state, high on a golden
   throne,
Mid suppliant kings, dread Montezuma shone.
                              (pp. 182; 59)

Barlow evidently believed that Milton's syntax possessed a poetic magic, that its use would automatically lift his poem from the commonplace to the grandeur of *PL.* Such a hope indeed impelled him to pattern not only individual scenes but whole epic battles in the Miltonic manner. Barlow himself recognized how closely he had followed Milton when he likened the clash of arms on the American shore to the conflicts between Satan and Michael on the ramparts of Heaven. As "on the plains of light," he wrote, "when Michael strove, / And swords of Cherubim to combat move," so unrolled the struggle for the New World. All was grand, all was general:

They tread the shore, the arduous conflict
   claim,
Rise the tall mountains, like a rolling flame,
Stretch their wide wings in circling onset far,
And move to fight, as clouds of heaven at war.
                              (pp. 160–61)

Most of the campaigns of the New World, including the capture of General Burgoyne and the progress of General Greene, present gigantic figures wielding massy weapons in an ethereal setting. Raphael's story of warfare in Heaven had so crystallized Barlow's battle imagination that even skirmishes took on the appearance of titanic encounters.

Raphael's voice, in a sense, informed the whole structure of *The Vision of Columbus.* The action opened with the appearance of a Raphael-like angel attempting to comfort Columbus, who, lying in prison, regretted the day he had discovered the New World. But if the visiting angel looked like Raphael, he performed the commission of Michael; and Columbus responded to the unfolding story of carnage and bloodshed that followed his discovery precisely as Adam had responded in *PL.* "O visions ill foreseen," Adam had lamented, after viewing the destruction of man in the Flood; better had he lived "ignorant" of the future than by his foreknowledge be tormented with visions of things to come. "O! hapless day," cried Columbus in anguish, as he viewed the savagery of heathen and Christian alike in the conquests that followed in the wake of his voyage. "Oh, hide me in the tomb," he implored, after seeing the destruction of Peru. To check growing despair, the angel informed Columbus that fairer days lay ahead and for a while he was comforted; but his happiness, like Adam's at the appearance of the Rainbow, was illusory. Even the Enlightenment, which witnessed a bold race growing up in America, brought conflict and suffering. To "thee 'tis given," the angel informed Columbus, "To hold high converse, and enquire of heaven"; but it was not in man's province to encompass truth at one sweep. Man must move to perfection through gradual steps and slow.

Loosely stated, this was the eighteenth-century idea of progress, the idea of man's perfectibility through a historical process. The Nativity and Passion of Christ, which brought hope to Adam, faded before the clear light of reason; and as the narrative picked up in Book 9 an enlightened world came into view. Disease had been conquered; commerce had united the world; universal harmony prevailed. The Angel denied to Columbus the actual sight of such a millennium; Heaven neither permitted, nor could the Angel show, "The unborn glories of that blissful day." All that could be revealed was the parliament of man, the federation of the world, with "One centred system, one all-ruling soul" (pp. 63, 130, 216, 244, 253ff.). Columbus had to be satisfied with that. Combining the concept of benevolence with observed cruelty in man, the love of God with faith in science, the idea of progress with man's limited knowledge, Barlow presented a vision so confused that even years of revision failed to sharpen its focus. The old heroic picture of man and his destiny could not be accommodated to the ideals of the Enlightenment.

After the ferment of the Revolution and the literary activity it engendered Milton moved into the broad stream of American culture. Reiteration of his greatness and widespread reference to his works so exalted his name that he became a popular idol and a symbol of authority throughout the land. As *The Monthly Anthology* (4 [Sept. 1807] : 489–92) observed : "So delicate were his perceptions of taste, so exuberant was his fertility of fancy, so enlarged were the faculties of his mind, and so extensive the range of his erudition," that it would be "hazardous to deny" what his "sentiment" established. Far from hazarding a denial, Americans invoked his authority in textbooks of grammar and rhetoric, in sermons and theological tracts, in journals of manners and morals, and in political disputes of the day. Milton *dixit* was enough to establish the truth of almost any proposition, on any subject, on any occasion. For a moment in history he ranged more variously over the moral, spiritual, and intellectual life of the country than any one man. The very weight of his name indeed overwhelmed verse of the time, whether it appeared anonymously in weekly and monthly journals, or in slender volumes emblazoned with authors now unknown or forgotten. Nathaniel L. Frothingham, for example, incorporated the last lines of *PL* into a song celebrating the departure of the senior class on July 31, 1811, from Harvard University ! Richard H. Townsend turned *L'Al* and *IlP* into a barren and hackneyed adventure with Mirth (*Original Poems* (1809), pp. 124f.). Charles Love wrote *A Poem on the Death of General George Washington* (1800) which included an invocation, a request for spiritual aid, and an assertion that the argument would justify the ways of God to man. Thomas Brockway presented to the world *The Gospel Tragedy* (1795), a brief epic of incredible dullness stamped with language and images from *PL* and *PR*. Poet after

poet forced on his verse an idiom suited neither to his time nor his talent, stiffening his language and syntax, congealing his imagery and verse forms. The appearance of *Smoking a Segar in the Manner of Milton* penetrated the stale literary atmosphere of the day with a refreshingly pungent aroma (*The Port Folio* 2, no. 5 [Feb. 6. 1802] : 40, under "Original Poetry").

So dismal a record of Miltonic poetry in the early Republic lends at first glance some credence to T. S. Eliot's twentieth-century injunction that young authors should eschew a study of Milton lest he affect their own style. For if *L'Al* and *IlP* had earlier sinewed American verse, giving it a toughness of texture seldom seen at that time, by the end of the century these twin pieces had frozen mood poems into artificial and meaningless postures, even as *PL* had forced serious poetry into dull and predictable patterns of thought and expression. Ironically, the more forcefully Milton spoke to the moral, religious, and intellectual life of the day, the more he overpowered poetry, to its distinct disadvantage. As a result, a schism arose among critics : the majority sustained the image of greatness inherited from an earlier day, but some began to question his manner and matter, foreshadowing the very views later expressed by Eliot and other Milton detractors. Yet Eliot's position, translated to the early Republic, would hardly explain the desert of verse at that time. The same warning could be uttered for Dryden* or Pope, or for Thomson or Young, or Gray. Milton's more distinctive style simply revealed with a special clarity and force the derivative nature of early American poetry. Milton *could* stir the imagination, *could* furnish an imagery and thought to create a very high form of art; but before such could happen Americans had to break the mold of neoclassic imitation and fashion a fresh idiom to accommodate their heritage of spiritual greatness. A Romantic movement had to sweep aside husks that had been gathering for decades. [GFS]

Studies and articles investigating the influence of Milton on nineteenth- and twentieth-century American literature are amazingly few and what has been published is generally superficial. The present remarks are accordingly inadequate to the subject and aim at indicating a major area in Milton studies needing research and publication.

The epic tradition that the American Revolution inspired, as in Philip Freneau and Hugh Henry Brackenridge's *The Rising Glory of America* (1772), Richard Alsop's *Aristocracy: An Epic Poem* (1795), or the anonymous *Demos in Council: or 'Bijah in Pandemonium. Being a Sweep of the Lyre, in Close Imitation of Milton* (1799), continued through the first two decades of the new century. The most important of these epic poems, which often employed the suffix *-iad* as clear indication of their genre (or mock genre), was *The Columbiad* (1807) by Joel Barlow (1754–1812), a revision of his great American epic first called *The Vision of Columbus* (1787). It was written in heroic couplets, as a great many of these works were, and falls under the classification of prophetic poem in its genealogy from *PL*. Columbus, dying in prison, has a vision revealed by a "radiant seraph," as Adam sees the future through Michael's guidance, but unlike Adam's frequently distressing view of man's corruption, the vision is one of future glories for America and ultimately of a league of nations established to achieve political harmony for all mankind. Barlow's purpose comes straight out of Miltonic thought: "to inculcate the love of national liberty, and to discountenance the deleterious passion for violence and war; to show that on the basis of republican principles all good morals, as well as good government and hopes of permanent peace, must be founded." Usually, though, the influence emerged in a confusion between a romantic view of the revolutionary against tyranny and a casting of an opponent as a Satanic figure, as in *The Fredoniad*, which is concerned with the march and defeat of General John Burgoyne.

Yamoyden by James W. Eastburn (1797–1819) and Robert C. Sands (1790–1832), published in 1820, shows a similar reading of *PL*, for King Philip (that is, Metacamet, chief of the Wampanoag Indians) and the various Indian nations he led in raids on the New England Puritans are cast as heroic figures. The Puritans, as usurpers of land, are cast as totally wrong. It was written in six cantos. All of these works reject Milton's prosody, his involved epic "plot," and his characterizations in *PL*, and replace them with a rather straightforward narrative, drawn for the most part on the surface, but with language, allusions, and style commonly labeled "Miltonic."

The kind of influence that one finds indicated here and there in print is imitative, such as William Cullen Bryant's "The Massacre of Scio," which derives from Milton's Piedmont sonnet (no. 18), or verbal, such as Lizette Reese's "Tears," which echoes Milton's so-called blindness sonnet (no. 19), or ideological, though often disagreeing with Milton's alleged ideology, such as Karl Shapiro's "Adam and Eve." The sonnet particularly was influential as form and in its political and nonamorous subject matter, although no adequate study exists. One finds verbal echoes and phonic echoes in Edgar Allen Poe's poems, yet his poetic principles were quite opposed to Milton's practice. One wonders whether this does not say something about Poe's understanding (or misunderstanding) of poetry that has yet to be vocalized by Poe scholars. There has been no investigation by Miltonians, either, of the poetry (1901) of William Vaughan Moody (1869–1910) later in the century, for example, despite the fact that he was the editor of the popular first Cambridge Edition of Milton's Collected Poetry. Moody's poems have been characterized, however, as recognizing that confused desires plague and possess man; still the poet is spiritually convinced that man will eventually reach his high destiny. The influence of *PL*, at least, was surely not absent. And what of T. S. Eliot* (1888–1965)? His note to *The Waste Land*

(1922) has its satiric humor, but the Miltonic voice (to distinguish it from the imitated voice) is truly heard behind that poem, the Mariana poems, the "Four Quartets," and such plays as *The Cocktail Party* (1950) and *The Confidential Clerk* (1954). This in spite of Eliot's disavowal of Milton, or did the disavowal involve a psychological denial of self?

It has been suggested that Nathaniel Hawthorne's "Young Goodman Brown" (1846) is a reversal of the rebirth theme of *PL* 9–10, and the investigation of the nature of evil in "Rappacini's Daughter" (1846) has patent ties to the epic. Yet Hawthorne's debt to Milton remains un-stated : what of the divorce tracts? what of the ministerial actions of the Son in *PR*? what of Milton's iconoclasm? The only book devoted to Milton and an American literary figure is *Milton and Melville* by Henry F. Pommer (1950). Its stress is upon *Moby-Dick* (1851) and Ahab's quest as reflections of Milton's anatomy of evil; but the popular reading of Satan as hero seems to color much that Pommer discusses. The good-evil ambiv-alence of Ahab and of Moby-Dick shows that Melville entertained the idea that Satan was justified in his actions. And the evil of whiteness, which is so detailed in the novel, may find part of its source in a remark in *Areop* ("excremental white-ness," Milton calls it), which served as scenario for the epic (to use the term given it by Edward Le Comte). Such detail suggests a pervasive influence. Yet, al-though Pommer looked at other works by Melville (*Redburn*, 1849; *Billy Budd*, 1891), a few years after publication rela-tionships between *Typee* (1846) and the epic were pointed out. Chapter 3 of *Three Children of the Universe: Emer-son's View of Shakespeare, Bacon, and Milton* by William Wynkoop (1966) is devoted to "Milton as the sayer." Emer-son's* view and use of Renaissance thought, according to Wynkop, comes from these three authors, and it is Milton who articulated in person, deed, and writing the Renaissance ideal. In the twentieth century Saul Bellow's *Herzog's*

identification of himself with Milton (1964), John Steinbeck's employment of *In Dubious Battle* (1936) for the title of a novel dealing with the rise of unionism, and Clifford Odets's *Paradise Lost* (1935), a play that deals with domestic and financial ills, imply a deeper understand-ing of Milton and his works than mere imitation* does. For Herzog as psycholog-ical and sexual being makes clear that Bellow understands Milton as person better than many a Milton scholar. And the double meaning in Satan's calling his challenge to God a dubious battle —dubious, he thinks, because its outcome is unknown, but dubious, God and we know, because the outcome of any battle with God is clear—subtly places Stein-beck's estimate of the strength of the masses against management (and govern-ment) into the existential world that *PL* portrays. And surely the struggles of Odets's depressed middle Americans are the clear inheritance of Adam and Eve's Fall while at the same time it is their reactions to the forces creating those struggles that loses what Paradise they can ever have.

The real influence of an author lies in this kind of deeper, pervasive under-standing rather than in direct quotation and imitation, and in affinities that the creative spirit identifies. In "Walking on Water : Milton, Stevens, and Contem-porary American Poetry" (in *Milton and the Line of Vision*, ed. Joseph A. Witt-reich [1975], pp. 231–68), Joan Webber looks at those who, like Milton, have the power to create themselves in their work: Walt Whitman, Wallace Stevens, Gregory Corso, Allen Ginsberg, Adrienne Rich, Robert Bly, Randall Jarrell, among many others. "The fulfillment of their vocation is the capacity to find in their own expe-rience the universal element and to speak out as prophets even when they know they cannot succeed in changing the world." While the influence of Milton may not be direct on all these poets, they prove R. W. Griswold's observation that "Milton is more emphatically *American* than any author who has lived in the• United States." [JTS]

INFLUENCE ON THE LITERATURE OF THE SEVENTENTH AND EIGHTEENTH CENTURIES, MILTON'S. Most of the story of Milton's influence on these centuries has been told in adaptations*, allusions*, controversy over blank verse*, poetry editions*, prose editions*, imitations*, influence on American literature*, reputation*, translations*, and Milton's influence on the Whigs*. Here that influence can be summarized and other authors or thinkers not previously cited can be detailed.

For the most part the influence of Milton's prose works is limited to his arguments for republicanism in *Tenure, 1Def,* and *CivP;* his evidence against tithing in *Hirelings;* his demolition of licensing and certain forms of censorship in *Areop;* his position on divorce*, particularly in *DDD,* 2d ed.; his authority in *Brit;* and his views on education in *Educ.* The antiprelatical tracts were generally ignored; *Eikon* became notorious and was often quoted; the second and third *Defenses* were referred to from time to time; the important *Way* had a short and ineffectual life, as did the other lesser pamphlets of 1660; and *TR* had a small audience in nineteenth-century America. The period of the Succession Controversy, late 1670s and 1680s, and of the Protestant Settlement, late 1680s and 1690s, saw a resurgence of the works listed before : *Tenure, 1Def, CivP, Hirelings,* and *Areop.* They were adapted to complete, partial, and paraphrased forms; they were quoted or alluded to by both proponents and antagonists. Probably Milton's works themselves were also read by the politically interested, and in any case That Grand Whig, Milton, was a major shaping force in governmental thinking (including censorship) during this period. With republican principles in hand, eighteenth-century England could ignore all of these except *Areop,* since forms of censorship still arose and copyright laws, first passed in 1709, with the influence of

Areop being felt in the arguments for its passage, had to be revised in 1842 after much intervening agitation, and except *Hirelings,* since tithing continued to exist. The tract reappeared in 1717, 1723, and 1743; it was the first American publication of a Miltonic book in 1774 and again in 1777. *Areop* was reprinted in England in 1738 (with a Preface by James Thomson, whose "Seasons" became embroiled in a copyright suit in 1766–69), 1772, 1789, 1791, and 1793. In France Count Mirabeau* called his version *Sur la liberté de la presse* in 1788, 1789 (twice) and 1792. Catherine Mauculay [Graham] discussed Milton's ideas in *A Modest Plea for the Property of Copy Right* (1774). Milton thus contributed to alterations of policies toward tithing and censorship and copyright during the eighteenth and early nineteenth centuries in England, America, and France. For the Irish Movement against British control *Tenure* was republished in Dublin 1784; and J. B. Salaville produced a French *1Def* with *Theorie de la Royauté d'après la doctrine de Milton* in 1789 (twice), with a preface perhaps by Mirabeau, and 1791 and 1792. *Tenure* thus aided in bringing off the Irish uprisings of the 1790s under Wolf Tone, and *1Def* aided in justifying the French Revolution and its aftermath as it had the British rejection of monarchy.

Divorce controversies in which Milton's work figured as a collaborative view flourished on the Continent at the end of the seventeenth and beginning of the eighteenth centuries; see Leo Miller, *John Milton Among the Polygamophiles* (1974). And with the rise of historiography* just prior to Milton's death, his analysis of the fabulous in early histories and his knowledge of names and places were commonly used to correct errors of the past; see Thomas Blount's *Animadversions upon Sir Richard Baker's Chronicle, and its continuation, Wherein many errors are discover'd, and some truths advanced* (Oxford, 1672), pp. 20, 58, 98–99; Aylett Sammes's *Britannia Antiqua Illustrata* (1676), pp. 48, 50, 83, 387, 476–77, and 559; James Tyrell's *The General History*

of England (1697), 1 : vi, viii, 17, 20, 136;
(second pagination), 17, 116. The State
of Church-Affairs (1687) draws from Brit
repeatedly. Milton's position as historian
is seen from Aaron Thompson's com-
ments in The British History (1718),
Laurence Eachard's The History of Eng-
land (1707–1718), John Oldmixon's The
Critical History of England (1724–1726)
and Clarendon and Whitlock Compar'd
(1727), and Zachary Grey's A Defence of
our Ancient and Modern Historians
(1725) and An Appendix to the Defence
(1725). His status is firm through the rest
of the century and the next. The influence
of Educ was not felt until the eighteenth
century, when Tannequi Lefevre's A
Compendious Way to Teaching Ancient
and Modern Languages (1723) appeared.
John Jebb's Remarks Upon the Present
Mode of Education in the University of
Cambridge: To which is added, A Pro-
posal for Its Improvement (Cambridge,
1773), George Colman's "Orthopaedia: or,
Thoughts on Publick Education, " Prose
on Several Occasions (1787), and Jean-
Jacques Rousseau's very important and
influentially longlasting Emilius and
Sophia: or, A New System of Education
indicate its theoretic importance. It was
frequently reprinted in editions of the
minor poems as well as separately;
there were also a Dutch and a French
translation.

The most extensive and continuing
influence of Milton lies in his poetry. It
begins early with Richard Baron's imita-
tions in 1647 and it notable in the poems
of Andrew Marvell* and John Dryden*.
Influence in the seventeenth century is
first in an appropriation of lines, or
images, which then transcends with Dry-
den into adaptation (in The State of
Innocence), parodic* use (in MacFleck-
noe), and characterization and meaningful
allusion (in Absalom and Achitophel).
After his death and particularly after the
1688 fourth edition of PL, poetry began
to reflect the epic genre as altered by
Milton, at times the blank verse* in which
it was cast, the biblical subject matter,
the characterization (but primarily that of

Satan), the language and style*, and the
"sublime" ideas. The two different poems
of Sir Richard Blackmore, Prince Arthur
(1695) and King Arthur (1697) illustrate
this influence on secular themes, and
Edward Ecclestone's Noah's Flood, or the
Destruction of the World (1679) or
Samuel Wesley's* The Life of Our Blessed
Lord and Saviour Jesus Christ (1694) the
employment of other "Miltonic" elements
in the religious poem.

But it was the eighteenth century that
picked up and extended these leads of
influence. John Philips* gave us the par-
ody The Splendid Shilling in 1701, the
language, meter, and style being at issue,
as they were in the numerous parodies
that followed Philips. Appropriations,
allusions, and some ideas—all still from
PL—dominate in the poems of Alexander
Pope*, Matthew Prior, Anne Finch,
Mark Akenside (particularly "The Pleas-
ures of Imagination"), James Thomson
(particularly "The Seasons"), Walter
Harte, William Somervile (especially "The
Chace"), David Mallet, James Ralph,
Robert Blair ("The Grave"), John Dyer,
William King ("Milton's Epistle to Pollio,
from the Latin"), Edward Young (notably
"Night-Thoughts" , Joseph Warton, and
Thomas Warton* (both the older and the
younger). This list cites only well-known
poets writing (and publishing) before
1750. But during this same period, prob-
ably led by the reputation of PL, other
poems of Milton's became influential also:
the companion poems L'Al and IlP for
their meter (octosyllabic couplets), images
and language, and general setting and
theme; Lyc for its genre, language, and
poetic stance; the sonnets for their form
and subject matter (nonamorous situations
and political or philosophic import); Mil-
ton's translation of Horace's Fifth Ode
for prosody (that is, in stresses and syn-
tax), and Nat for odic form; and Mask
for its language and style.

Joseph Addison's* "An Ode for St.
Cecilia's Day" (1699) seems to usher in
the significance of the twin poems for the
next century in the work of John Hughes,
Thomas Parnell, John Dyer (especially

"Grongar Hill"), William Collins, Thomas Gray, William Mason, William Cowper*, and Joseph Warton. Pastoral* elegies emerge from Moses Browne ("Colin's Despair," Eclogue 5, 1729), Richard West ("Monody on Queen Caroline," 1737), William Mason ("Musaeus," on Pope's death, 1747), and George, Lord Lyttelton ("To the Memory of a Lady Lately Deceased," 1747). Various sonnets showing Milton's influence were produced from around 1701 onward, despite the inaccurate generality that the form died out after Milton and before Wordsworth*, Shelley*, and Keats*. Important writers of sonnets during this period were Thomas Gray, Thomas Edwards, William Mason, and Thomas Warton. Aside from Dalton's* version of Comus, Gilbert West wrote "Instruction of the Order of the Garter, a Dramatick Poem" during the first half of the century in 1742 and Thomas Warton, the elder, composed "Invocation to a Water-Nymph," around 1745. Samuel Say did a translation of Horace's Ode 16, from Book 3, and "To His Harp, from Casimir," around 1701–1720; and there are Thomas Warton, the elder's "Ode to Taste" (1744–45), William Collins's "Ode to Evening" (1746), and Joseph Warton's Odes, nos. 8 and 13. Again, Samuel Say reflects Nat in "Psalm xcvii, in Paraphrastic Verse" (ca. 1730), as Collins does in "Ode to Simplicity" and Joseph Warton in Odes, nos. 4 and 5.

The influence did not abate in the second half of the century; to the contrary, the position of Milton had risen so high that his work became the touchstone of excellence. Accordingly, parodies declined, blank verse increased somewhat, and the elements of imitation noted before flourished. Particularly noteworthy are Christopher Smart's work (especially "The Hop-Garden," 1752), John Dyer's "The Fleece" (1757), William Shenstone's poems, and John Ogilvie's (particularly "Providence, An Allegorical Poem," 1764), Richard Jago's "Edge-Hill" (1767), William Mason's "The English Garden" (1772–1782), George Crabbe's "Midnight" (ca. 1779), William Cowper's translations

of Homer (1784–1791), James Hurdis's "The Village Curate" (1788), Richard Cumberland's "Calvary, or the Death of Christ" (1792), and the earlier poems of such Romantics as Robert Southey and Walter Savage Landor, and of such translations as H. F. Cary's Dante—all descending from PL. L'Al and IlP continue to be discerned in the work of Smart, Thomas Warton, James Grainger, Sir James Marriott, John Langhorne, Robert Lloyd (especially "Arcadia," 1761), William Dodd, Charles Churchill, Ogilvie, Hugh Downman, Tobias Smollett, Catherine Jemmat, and Anna Seward. Lyc reappears in James Scott's "The Redemption" (1763) and "The Vanity of Human Life" (1767), Samuel Taylor Coleridge's* "Monody on Chatterton" (1790), and William Lisle Bowles's "Monody, Written at Matlock" (1791). Sonnets are numerous; e.g., those of Anna Seward, George Hardinge, William Hayley, William Lisle Bowles, William Cowper, and H. F. Cary. A few more excursions derived from Mask appear, like William Mason's "Sappho, a Drama" (1778), but the frequent performances and publications of the Milton-Dalton-Colman texts seem to have a negative influential effect along with the decline in new dramatic presentations one finds toward the end of the century. The influence from the two odes continues either in direct translations (like Thomas Warton, the younger's) or in original work (like Gray's "Ode for Music," 1769).

On the Continent and in the American colonies the influence also flourished; the effects on music and "Observations on the Correspondence Between Poetry and Music," as Daniel Webb (1719?–1798) called one of his works in 1768, define another area of impact. The interpretation of PL and the evaluations of the literary achievement of the work led to long (sometimes bitter) debate. Translations became so frequent that by 1800 PL had appeared in the most likely languages of Europe, and other poems as well. Milton moved into encyclopedias and language or poetic dictionaries. By the end of the eighteenth century, he was more en-trenched in the position in which he was held at its beginning : the exemplar of sublime thought and expression, the source of imitation and quotation, and the authority for ideas and language and form (and for poetic license). While *PR* was to have some consideration during the century, for example by Richard Meadow-court in 1732 and Goronwy Owen, the important but not well-known Welsh poet; and *SA* primarily in rebuttals of Johnson's* criticism (1751), for example, by Richard Cumberland in 1785 and William Mickle in 1788, these major poems had only limited reputation and influence. The Romantics picked up and praised and extensively imitated *PR* as prophetic poem and in its four-book struc-ture, language, and style, but *SA* con-tinued to be generally ignored. Perhaps we can see in the importance of *PL,* the twin poems, the odes, and *Lyc* the reaction of a basically classically oriented reading and writing public. For primarily it is such "classical" (or better, traditional) elements that appear in those works that serve the eighteenth-century poet. The innovations seem often misunderstood and certainly unmined. The more artistically subversive elements of the sonnets and *PR* become important to a later "romantic" age, which moved well away from the rather slavish imitation of some of its predecessors. [JTS]

INFLUENCE ON THE LITERATURE OF NINETEENTH-CENTURY ENG-LAND, MILTON'S.

It would be difficult, indeed, to overstate the influence of John Milton on nineteenth-century England. In an age given to hero worship and a deep and abiding reverence for men of genius, Milton was literally worshipped by many who in an age of revolution found in him the embodiment of all those positive qualities of mind of which the times seemed so utterly bereft. "Milton! thou shouldst be living at this hour : / England hath need of thee," wrote William Words-worth* at a time when, according to Moorman's biography, he was much troubled about the state of England's "soul." Returning from France in Septem-ber 1802, Wordsworth was offended by the vanity and ostentation of a nation prospering in a time of war. Compared with the plain living and high thinking of the Puritan heroic age, England was, indeed, "a fen / Of stagnant waters," a nation of "selfish men." In his country's hour of need, Wordsworth unhesitatingly called forth Milton :

Oh! raise us up, return to us again;
And give us manners, virtue, freedom, power.
Thy soul was like a Star, and dwelt apart;
Thou hadst a voice whose sound was like the
  sea:
Pure as the naked heavens, majestic, free,
So didst thou travel on life's common way,
In cheerful godliness; and yet thy heart
The lowliest duties on herself did lay.

At precisely the same time and largely from the same impulse, William Blake* invoked Milton in his great poem of that title. Like Shelley*, who later in song commanded the West Wind : "Be thou, Spirit fierce, / My spirit !", Blake in the somber harmonies of *Milton* becomes one with the prophetic spirit of his hero who descends from heaven to save the nation and arouse the people once more to the sacred task of recreating "Jerusalem, / In England's green & pleasant Land."

To those like Wordsworth and Coleridge* whose faith in the French Revolution and hope of freedom had been replaced by a sense of frustration and at times despair, those of the seventeenth century whom Wordsworth celebrates in his sonnet, "Great men have been among us"—"The later Sidney, Marvel, Harring-ton, / Young Vane, and others who called Milton friend"—served increasingly as an inspiration. And as J. B. Beer has pointed out in *Blake's Humanism,* "one particular figure of that century," Milton, stood out "as offering the union of liberty, godliness and poetic inspiration by which England might still regain her true stature in the world."

For instance, Byron, whose vision of England was as somber as was Words-worth's, looked upon Milton as an image of intellectual courage, strength of will, and steadfast freedom of mind that made time-servers and turncoat poets like Robert Southey "shabby fellows" indeed.

Think'st thou, could he—the blind Old Man—
    arise,
    Like Samuel from the grave, to freeze
    once more
The blood of monarchs with his prophecies,
    Or be alive again—again all hoar
With time and trials, and those helpless eyes,
    And heartless daughters—worn—and pale—
    and poor;
Would *he* adore a sultan? *he* obey
The intellectual eunuch Castlereagh?
                        (*Don Juan* 1. 11)

This image of Milton the tyrant-hater was especially appealing to the Romantic poets who like Shelley in "Mont Blanc" saw England the victim of "Large codes of fraud and woe," and who in "The Hymn to Intellectual Beauty" bemoaned a world in the throes of "a dark slavery" from which it must be freed. When in a dream Milton's spirit rose up before the sleeping Shelley and touched "his Uranian lute,"

. . . sweet thunder flowed, and shook
All human things built in contempt of man,—
And sanguine thrones and impious altars
    quaked,
Prisons and citadels.
                        ("Milton's Spirit")

This concept of Milton as shaker of thrones and altars grew, of course, out of his strong and uncompromising stand against the tyranny of church and state under Charles I* expressed in such prose works as *Tenure* and *2Def.* Yet neither of these appealed so strongly to the Romantics as did *Areop.* Milton's eloquent defense of liberty* and free speech moved Blake and Shelley not because, in the words of Northrop Frye, it was "the plea of a nervous intellectual who hopes that a brutal majority will at least leave him alone," but because it was "a demand for the release of creative power and a vision of an imaginative culture in which the genius is not an intellectual so much as a prophet and seer." (*Fearful Symmetry* [1947], pp. 159–60.)

Milton's vision of England as "a noble and puissant Nation rousing herself like a strong man after sleep, and shaking her invincible locks" (*Areop* 4 : 344) prefigures those moments in the writings of Blake when he sees through the eyes of prophecy humanity shaking off the Urizenic sleep of death and, like Orc, the embodiment of divine energy and creative desire, rising to greet the dawn of Everlasting Day. To Blake, whose artistic endeavors were a relentless struggle against tyranny both physical and spiritual, the Milton of *Areop* was a prophet and seer of the highest order, purged of all his selfhood and freed from any taint of single vision.

It is as a prophetic poet, the Greek *vates,* that Milton perhaps most powerfully appealed to the Romantic poets, who sought to reestablish the notion of the divine inspiration of poetry. Unlike the Augustans, they conceived of the poet as in large measure a visionary in the tradition of the Hebrew prophets, Homer*, Shakespeare*, and Milton. Blake and Coleridge as we know were visionaries, and Wordsworth thought of the poet as a seer, the prophetic voice of moral grandeur and religious truth. Moreover, Shelley in his *A Defence of Poetry* identified poetry with prophecy. Therefore one can readily understand the significant role that Milton, the last great prophetic poet in the English literary tradition, played in their art. His belief that the epic poet's "abilities, wheresoever they be found, are the inspired gift of God rarely bestow'd" (*RCG* 4 : 238) was shared by all of his great Romantic disciples who cherished him as the primary model of poetry and along with Homer and Shakespeare a divinity. "The divine Milton" is ever on Wordsworth's lips, and the prophetic strain flowing from Milton is ever present in the poems of Blake and Shelley.

Harold Bloom sees "the prophetic Protestant and radical vision of Milton revived in English poetry" in the later poems of Blake's first book, *Poetical Sketches,* and his *Milton* begins with the famous lyric "And did those feet in ancient time" in which, as Bloom has said, "Blake sees himself as inheriting the Miltonic chariot of fire, the prophetic vehicle that first appears in Ezekiel's vision" (*The Visionary Company* [1961], p. 94). This prophetic strain continues in Wordsworth, who believed that Milton's mind fed on the writings of the Hebrew prophets. And from him and Coleridge it flows onward into the mind and art of Keats* and Shelley, who in their rather different ways demonstrate the vitality of such a vision as late as 1819, when both *The Fall of Hyperion: A Dream* and *Prometheus Unbound* were composed. While Keats's fragmentary *Fall* marks a new phase, in which his concept of poet as visionary deepens into a fervent religion, Shelley's fully matured, lyrically exuberant *Prometheus* climaxes the sustained and ever more ethereal prophetic voice of his brief but brilliant career.

Milton was not only the last great prophetic poet, but he was also the last great epic* poet in the English literary tradition. And as such, he was of enormous significance to the Romantics. Whether or not one is willing to agree that such works as Blake's *Milton* and *Jerusalem,* Wordsworth's *The Prelude,* Byron's *Don Juan,* and Keats's *Hyperion* are epics, there can be little doubt that these poets had the epic tradition in mind and were, however heterodoxically, striving toward epic statement in their works.

Doubtless the epic impulse was deeply embedded in the Romantic mind, aware as it was that an orthodox world or, as Arnold was later to express it, an epoch of concentration was passing away and a strange new world, an epoch of expansion, was at hand. Milton's epic task had been "to justify the ways of God to man," and this, too, was the supreme task the Romantic poets hoped to repeat for their own time. "Indeed," as J. B. Beer has written, "the dead hand which science seemed to be laying on the world rendered the task more urgent than in Milton's day" (*Coleridge the Visionary* [1959], p. 50).

Although Milton's means of justifying the ways of God to man and his method were not to the Romantics sufficient for the epic demands of a radically different age, as epic poet his presence was strongly if variously felt. For instance, *PL* was a major concern to Blake throughout his career as poet and artist, and, despite the rather audacious liberties Blake took in reinterpreting the epic to suit his own needs, it formed the basis of his four "levels of vision" that were objectified in his prophetic books.

Blake, as is well-known, rejected Milton's God because to Blake he was the embodiment of a stultifying reason, and as such, he was assigned to the hell into which he had cast Satan. Thus, the hell of *PL* became the prototype of Blake's Ulro, the realm of single vision in which benighted reason reigns. Around the aspiring Satan, whose energies enabled him to escape from hell, Blake built a higher sphere in which passion, desire, and energy are freely exercised—the realm he later called Generation. Above these two, according to Beer's reading of Blake's development, "he placed two more. Superior to both was the state of Milton's Paradise, the state of wedded happiness; and superior to all three was the world of Milton's Heaven, the world where music and light, love and life, conspiring, render unnecessary anything so mean as self-assertion and self-love" (*Blake's Humanism* [1968], p. 30).

Although Blake through his visionary conversations with Milton—". . . I saw Milton in imagination and he told me to beware of being misled by his *Paradise Lost*"—and his epic poem *Milton* was able to correct his master's errors by "rewriting" *PL,* other Romantic poets albeit in less dramatic ways also rewrote Milton's epic while, like Blake, assimilating his influence and diffusing it in significant ways throughout their work.

In the lines prefaced to *The Excursion,* which express his epic intentions and aspirations, Wordsworth in blank verse* reminiscent of Milton in its imagery*, allusions, and technique invokes in traditional epic fashion the Muse* of *PL,* Urania. But in expressing his need for guidance and in reviewing the ardors of his proposed task, Wordsworth thinks, perhaps, that he will need yet "a greater Muse, if such / Descend to earth or dwell in highest heaven! / For I must tread on shadowy ground, must sink / Deep—and, aloft ascending, breathe in worlds / To which the heaven of heavens is but a veil."

However, in such lines Wordsworth, in the very act of implying that his theme surpasses that of Milton, is following his master (and other Renaissance poets) in claiming greater loftiness of theme than that of his predecessors. Again, further on in these lines, Wordsworth implies a criticism of *PL* when he writes :

> . . . Paradise, and groves
> Elysian, Fortunate Fields—like those of old
> Sought in the Atlantic Main—why should they be
> A history only of departed things,
> Or a mere fiction of what never was?

Yet the very fabric of the verse itself, as well as the imagery, reflects the powerful impact of Milton's work on Wordsworth's thought and art.

Just how pervasive and various Milton's influence was on the Romantic epic poets is exemplified in the case of Wordsworth as he approached the great task. When in the autumn of 1795 he wrote the introductory sections of *The Prelude,* he believed himself to be a poet set apart by the Divine Power in the universe to write a great poem which, like Milton's epic, would be "doctrinal and exemplary to a Nation" (*RCG* 3 : 237). As he walked joyously across the countryside toward his future habitation, "to the open fields," he "told / A prophecy: poetic numbers came / Spontaneously to clothe in priestly robe / A renovated spirit singled out, / Such hope was mine, for holy services." And although his earnest desire was to "grapple with some noble theme," the young poet found that the right subject eluded him.

Both the sense of dedication and the desire to write an epic, as well as his initial problem concerning the choice of theme, are, as Wordsworth was well aware, paralleled in Milton's own literary autobiography*. One need only recall that the young Milton, too, felt himself singled out for holy services and destined to write an epic poem. Moreover, Milton's problem in choosing a fit subject for his supreme work is well known.

Just as Milton often pondered the question : "What K[ing] or knight before the conquest might be chosen in whom to lay the pattern of a Christian Heroe" (*RCG* 3 : 237), so too did Wordsworth in his mind debate whether to "settle on some British theme, some old / Romantic tale by Milton left unsung," or to choose a chivalrous adventure in the manner of Spencer's*Faerie Queene.*

In deciding that the "haunt, and the main region" of his song would be "the Mind of Man," and that he himself, the poet, would be the hero, Wordsworth, according to Brian Wilkie, by rejecting "the purely martial idea of a hero" was following Milton's example. Moreover, in "making the heroic ideal an interior one," Wordsworth again had Milton for a precedent. "Milton in particular," as Wilkie goes on, "had pointed the way for Wordsworth by making the essential heroic attribute not deeds but a state of mind. The deepest hell is within Satan, and to Adam is revealed a 'paradise within thee, happier farr'" (*Romantic Poets and Epic Tradition* [1965], p. 70).

Milton's influence on Keats's attempt at epic, *Hyperion: A Fragment,* is equally instructive. In addition to the Miltonic diction* and rhetorical* devices, Milton's presence in the first two books is felt in various scenes, including the initial one that discovers the fallen Titans benumbed and desolate, who like Satan and his fallen angels lie thunder-struck in a region remote from heaven. Keats's council scene in Book 2 is reminiscent of the "great consult" held in Pandemonium*. Just as Satan, overcome by defeat and the appalling sight about him, essayed again and again to control his misery and to speak, so Saturn

as he walk'd into the midst,
Felt faint, and would have sunk among the
      rest,
But that he met Enceladus's eye,
Whose mightiness, and awe of him, at once
Came like an inspiration; and he shouted,
"Titans, behold your God!" at which some
      groan'd;
Some started on their feet; some also shouted;
Some wept, some wail'd, all bow'd with
      reverence.
                    (*Hyperion* 2. 105–12)

Furthermore, Keats's essential theme, the deification of a true poet through his imaginative apprehension of the pain and mystery of life, recalls the traditional pattern of a great poet's development given, for the Romantics, consummate expression in Milton's own life and work. And Keats's comment on "The Genius of Milton," which he penned in his copy of *PL,* suggests how Milton's example fortified Keats to leave the realm of Flora and old Pan and seek the terrible wisdom that led to the agonizing metamorphosis objectified in his Apollo.

> The Genius of Milton, more particularly in respect to its span in immensity, calculated him, by a sort of birthright, for such an "argument" as the paradise lost. he had an exquisite passion for what is properly in the sense of ease and pleasure, poetical Luxury—and with that it appears to me he would fain have been content if he could so doing have preserved his self-respect and feel of duty perform'd—but there was working in him as it were that same sort of thing as operates in the great world to the end of a Prophecy's being accomplish'd—therefore he devoted himself rather to the Ardours than the pleasures of Song, solacing himself at intervals with cups of old wine—and those are with some exceptions the finest parts of the Poem. [In some par(ts)] With some exceptions—for the spirit of mounting and adventure can never be unfruitful or unrewarded—had he not broken through the clouds which envellope [*sic*] so deliciously the Elysian fields of Verse, and committed himself to the Extreme we never should have seen Satan as described
>   But his face
> Deep Scars of thunder had entrench'd &c.
>   (transcribed in *The Romantics on Milton,* ed. Joseph A. Wittreich [1970], p. 553)

The thunder-scarred Satan to whom Keats refers was, indeed, to the Romantics a symbol of experience in a fallen world. To them Satan, Milton's "archangel ruin'd," was a superb image of how the human mind had perverted itself and brought about its fall. And although they often praised Satan as a projection of Milton's aspiration and creative energy and, like Shelley in his Preface to *Prometheus Unbound,* admired his "courage, and majesty, and firm and patient opposition to omnipotent force," the Romantic poets were fully aware of Satan's moral deficiencies.

As Shelley went on to point out in his Preface, Satan, despite some admirable elements of character, is ultimately unsatisfactory and as an "imaginary being " falls below the figure of Prometheus, who besides embodying all his positive traits is exempt "from the taints of ambition, envy, revenge, and a desire for personal aggrandisement, which, in the Hero of *Paradise Lost,* interfere with the interest. The character of Satan," continued Shelley,

> engenders in the mind a pernicious casuistry which leads us to weigh his faults with his wrongs, and to excuse the former because the latter exceed all measure. In the minds of those who consider that magnificent fiction with a religious feeling it engenders something worse.

Blake's famous criticism of *PL* voiced by "The Devil" in the youthful and ironic *The Marriage of Heaven and Hell* centers on the contraries Reason and Energy. Milton's Satan or the Devil of *PL* again is, in this context, an emblem of energy, desire, unrestrained freedom—all that his contrary, Milton's Messiah, as Reason, militates against. According to "The Devil," therefore,

> Those who restrain desire, do so because theirs is weak enough to be restrained; and the restrainer or reason usurps its place & governs the unwilling.
>   And being restrain'd, it by degrees becomes passive till it is only the shadow of desire.
>   The history of this is written in Paradise Lost, & the Governor or Reason is call'd Messiah,

As a climax to these provocative assertions on the part of "The Devil," Blake appended the famous ironic *Note* that has led to so much confusion:

> The reason Milton wrote in fetters when he wrote of Angels & God, and at liberty when of Devils & Hell, is because he was a true Poet and of the Devil's party without knowing it.

As Harold Bloom has pointed out in his Commentary in David Erdman's edition of *The Poetry and Prose of William Blake,* Blake here

> offers an aesthetic criticism of *Paradise Lost,* not a reading of Milton's intentions. . . . What Blake traces is the declining movement of creative energy in *Paradise Lost* from the active of the early books to the passive of the poem's conclusion, where all initiatives not . . . God's own are implicitly condemned. More simply, Blake posits a split in Milton between the moral philosopher or theologian and the poet. From this split ensues what Blake claims is a falsification *in the poem* of the relation between human desire and the idea of holiness. Milton's Satan overly embodies human desire, and Milton's Messiah is too exclusively the representation of a minimal and contrasting kind of reason.

That Blake was fully aware of the Father of Evil's shortcomings is abundantly demonstrated in *Milton,* an epic work of his maturity, which depicts Satan as the embodiment of Selfhood, the creator of the fallen universe. In a grand parody of the procession of the Son in *PL,* Blake represents Satan

> Coming in a cloud, with trumpets & flaming fire,
> Saying: "I am God the judge of all, the living & the dead.
> "Fall therefore down & worship me, submit thy supreme
> "Dictate to my eternal Will, & to my dictate bow.
> "I hold the Balances of Right & Just & mine the Sword.
> "Seven Angels bear my Name & in those Seven I appear,
> "But I alone am God & I alone in Heav'n & Earth
> "Of all that live dare utter this, others tremble & bow. . . .

The Romantics were almost to a man opposed—strenuously—to the kind of personality revealed in the Satan of Blake's *Milton* who, "making to himself Laws from his own identity, / Compell'd others to serve him in moral gratitude & submission," etc. Fretful of the fact that "from our birth the faculty divine / Is chain'd and tortured—cabin'd, cribb'd, confined, / And bred in darkness," Blake and Shelley, like Byron, created Promethean-like embodiments of human desire battling to free themselves from the chains forged by diabolical gods who demand obedience.

Such a being is Shelley's Prometheus in *Prometheus Unbound.* Chained to a ravine of icy rock in the Indian Caucasus, Prometheus is an image of the titan in man bound to a cold, inhospitable nature, the emblem of the dead, mechanical universe of Newtonian physics. His adversary, the author of such a universe, is Jupiter, a striking embodiment of qualities derived from both the Satan and God the Father* of *PL*. He is "the supreme tyrant" who is seen seated "on his throne / Of burning gold." How reminiscent Shelley's Jupiter is of Satan can be seen in his address in Heaven which, of course, recalls Satan's speech to the fallen angels in Pandemonium:

> *Jupiter.* Ye congregated powers of heaven, who share
> The glory and the strength of him ye serve,
> Rejoice! henceforth I am omnipotent.
>   (3:1)

It is a speech filled with dramatic irony; for although Jupiter thinks it is the hour of final victory over "the soul of man," it is, in fact, the hour in which he is cast out of heaven into "the bottomless void" of hell. Just as Jupiter's fall prepares the way for a kindlier, more humane god, so will the imminent fall of Keats's Satan-like Hyperion lead to the accession of a more "beautiful" concept of deity embodied in Apollo. "Unsecure," "Blazing Hyperion on his orbed fire" is discovered by Keats filled with omens dire as his Pandemonium-like palace

bright
Bastion'd with pyramids of glowing gold,
And touch'd with shade of bronzed obelisks,
Glar'd a blood-red through all its thousand
    courts,
Arches, and domes, and fiery galleries.
                                    (1 : 176–80)

Such instances as these of the power with which Milton's Satan impressed itself on Romantic literature can be multiplied many times, for his character was so rich and his portrayal so compelling that it gave rise to a various and wide-ranging representation in the poetry of the nineteenth century. Beginning with his manifestation in Blake's works, Satan reappears in such varied guises as the Oswald of Wordsworth's early play *The Borderers,* the Lucifer of Byron's drama *Cain,* and later as such figures as the somewhat Faustian hero in Philip James Bailey's long spasmodic poem of 1829 entitled *Festus,* and in a whole host of Miltonic epics by minor authors that continue deep into the Victorian period.

The Romantic poets' qualified approbation of Satan and their rather splendid portrayals of Satan-like beings at war with restraint and arbitrary law were met with much alarm by the more conservative and orthodox of their contemporaries, men who, like the High Church, Tory, Poet-laureate Robert Southey, accused them unjustly of viewing Satan as a wholly admirable being. The proliferation of satanic figures in the poetry of his day greatly alarmed Southey, who in his famous Preface to *A Vision of Judgement* uncovered what he claimed to be a "Satanic school" of poetry of which Byron was the leader.

Obviously referring to Byron, Southey lashed out against "the men" of the day whom he saw responsible for infecting literature with Satanism :

> Men of diseased hearts and depraved imaginations, who, forming a system of opinions to suit their own unhappy course of conduct, have rebelled against the holiest ordinances of human society, and hating that revealed religion which, with all their efforts and bravadoes, they are unable entirely to disbelieve, labour to make others as miserable as themselves, by infecting them with a moral virus that eats into the soul! The school which they have set up may properly be called the Satanic school; for though their productions breathe the spirit of Belial in their lascivious parts, and the spirit of Moloch in those loathsome images of atrocities and horrors which they delight to represent, they are more especially characterized by a Satanic spirit of pride and audacious impiety, which still betrays the wretched feeling of hopelessness wherewith it is allied.

Byron was outraged by Southey's attack and—besides challenging him to a duel—brilliantly demolished him in *The Vision of Judgment.* Nevertheless, Southey's point of view was shared by many who continued to accuse the Romantics of making common cause with the Father of lies. As a result, there developed over the years a considerable discrepancy between what, for instance, Blake, Shelley, and Byron actually thought about Milton's Satan and what their antagonists supposed they thought. Consequently, a whole host of modern Miltonists have, in the words of Joseph Wittreich, sought "to fortify modern criticism against" the kind of intellectual irresponsibility and moral weakness that so many have attributed to Blake, Shelley, and Byron (*Studies in Philology,* 65 : 829). In actuality, only recently has there come into being a Satanic school, which views Milton's Satan with the wholehearted admiration so long attributed to the Romantics. Whereas the Romantics seldom if ever saw Satan as a morally admirable figure, the modern Satanists do.

If the Romantics often found the energy and aspirations of Satan compelling, the Victorians were more wary. Less prone to indulge an admiration for unrestrained passion and unbounded desire, they tended to see Satan—even aesthetically—as dangerous. Indeed, one suspects that John Henry Newman's preference for Robert Southey's *Thalaba* over *PL* derives, at least in part, from his displeasure with Milton's Satan.

Seriously concerned about the impact of Satan on the minds of the Victorians,

Newman in a lecture, "On the Characteristics of True Poetry," agreed with John Dryden's* conclusion that Satan was the hero of *PL*. Moreover, continued Newman, he "is assigned the most prominent place, and he is also made the most poetical person in the poem." Then he concluded :

> The *poetry* of Milton's mind has made the evil spirits beautiful, and this is wrong, and even dangerous, as wherever evil is poetised, and therefore made beautiful, it is a dangerous departure from truth, not only theological and religious, but even moral. This principle is exemplified in Byron's "Cain," where the character of the first murderer is made a beautiful one; and when Byron was censured for this, he defended himself by the example of Milton, who had made Satan poetical.

This view that in making Satan an aesthetically pleasing and compelling figure Milton added to the pernicious effect of his hero on the minds of his readers was increasingly a matter for debate among the Victorians. Originating in William Hazlitt's* discussion of Satan in his lecture "On Shakespeare and Milton," the argument about the wisdom of Milton's freeing Satan of his horns and hoofs and thereby enhancing his aesthetic appeal enlisted a host of eminent personages. Wordsworth apparently had been the first to remark that the "great merit" of *PL* was Milton's "getting rid of the horns and tail of the Devil"; and Hazlitt, then, repeated this when in his lecture he declared :

> The deformity of Satan is only in the depravity of his will; he has no bodily deformity to excite our loathing or disgust. The horns and tail are not there, poor emblems of the unbending, unconquered spirit, of the writhing agonies within. Milton was too magnanimous and open an antagonist to support his argument by the bye-tricks of a hump and cloven foot; to bring into the fair field of controversy the good old catholic prejudices of which Tasso and Dante have availed themselves, and which the mystic German critics would restore. He relied on the justice of his cause, and did not scruple to give the devil his due. Some persons may think that he has carried his liberality too far, and

injured the cause he professed to espouse by making him the chief person in his poem.

In similar vein, Thomas Babington Macaulay, who believed that "of all the poets who have introduced into their works the agency of supernatural beings, Milton has succeeded best," in his essay on Milton wrote :

> The spirits of Milton are unlike those of almost all other writers. His fiends, in particular, are wonderful creations. They are not metaphysical abstractions. They are not wicked men. They are not ugly beasts. They have no horns, no tails, none of the fee-faw-fum of Tasso and Klopstock. They have just enough in common with human nature to be intelligible to human beings. Their characters are, like their forms, marked by a certain dim resemblance to ·those of men, but exaggerated to gigantic dimensions, and veiled in mysterious gloom.

Unlike Shelley and Blake, Macaulay openly admired Milton's Satan without reservation, and although he noticed the resemblance between Prometheus and Satan, he clearly finds Satan much the more impressive and satisfactory of the two.

However much involved some of the Victorians were in the debate concerning Milton's Satan, the temper of the times was increasingly away from a concern with such questions. Speaking about "Hell" and the "Devil," David Masson* as early as 1844 observed that "the spirit of these words has become obsolete, chased away by the spirit of exposition. . . . The going out of the belief in Satanic agency (for even those who retain it in profession allow it no force in practice), M. Comte would attribute to the progress of the spirit of that philosophy of which he is the apostle." But Masson accounted for it "by the going out, in the progress of civilization, of those sensations which seem naturally fitted to nourish the belief in supernatural beings. The tendency of civilization has been to diminish our opportunities of feeling terror, of feeling strongly at all. The horrific plays a much less important part in human experience than it once did" ("Three Devils," *Essays Biographical and Critical: Chiefly on English Poets* [1856], p. 83).

Walter Raleigh* expressed the sentiments of the late nineteenth century when in his critical study, *John Milton* (1900), he declared: "Satan himself is not what he used to be; he is doubly fallen, in the esteem of his victims as well as of his Maker, and indeed

Comes to the place where he before had sat
Among the Prime in Splendour, now depos'd,
Ejected, emptyed, gaz'd, unpityed, shun'd,
A spectacle of ruin.

> (*PR* 1. 412–15)

Nevertheless, there can be no doubt that the splendid figure of Satan was very appealing to the nineteenth-century imagination. Part of this appeal lay in the fact that the readers of *PL* saw Milton's own life objectified in his characters—especially Satan. For instance, William Hazlitt in his second essay "On Genius and Common Sense" flatly declared that "Milton has by allusion embodied a great part of his political and personal history in the chief characters and incidents of Paradise Lost. He has, no doubt, wonderfully adapted and heightened them, but the elements are the same; you trace the bias and opinions of the man in the creations of the poet."

That such a response was carried on into the Victorian period is illustrated by Walter Bagehot, who believed that

> though the *theme* of *Paradise Lost* obliged Milton to side with the monarchical element in the universe, his old habits are often too much for him; and his real sympathy—the impetus and energy of his nature—side with the rebellious element. . . . Milton's sympathy and his imagination slip back to the Puritan rebels whom he loved, and desert the courtly angels whom he could not love although he praised. There is no wonder that Milton's hell is better than his heaven, for he hated officials and he loved rebels, for he employs his genius below, and accumulates his pedantry above. (*Literary Studies* [n.d.], 2:321.)

This common tendency to read Mil-

ton's life in his literary creations grew out of the Romantic critics' notion that he was, unlike Shakespeare the objective poet, a subjective artist whose life was mirrored in his works. Both Coleridge and Hazlitt in their lectures often compared Milton with Shakespeare in order to suggest that these men were exemplars of two kinds of poetry. For Coleridge as for Hazlitt, Shakespeare was the selfless, impersonal poet who was able to dart himself forth and pass "into all the forms of human character and passion"; he was "the one Proteus of the fire and flood." Milton, on the other hand, was the kind of poet who attracted "all forms and things to himself, into the unity of his own ideal. All things and modes of action shape themselves anew in the being of Milton, while," Coleridge continued, "Shakespeare becomes all things, yet forever remaining himself" (*Biographia Literaria*, chap. 15).)

This view is also present in Hazlitt, especially in those essays in which he describes Shakespeare's sympathetic imagination, a critical commonplace that grew out of the eighteenth-century notion of the imagination as grounded in sympathy. According to Hazlitt, in his essay "On Shakespeare and Milton," there were two types of poetic imagination, one based on sympathy and the other on self-love. Shakespeare, wrote Hazlitt, "was the least of an egotist that it was possible to be." But Milton possessed what Hazlitt called genius in ordinary, which is a more obstinate and less versatile thing. While Shakespeare "is only the vehicle for the sentiments of his characters," Hazlitt concluded, Milton's characters "are only a vehicle for his own."

This view of Milton as a poet who lived in himself and created a universe in the likeness of his own image was generally not regarded necessarily as a flaw; yet it doubtless was the basis for the charge that Milton was haughty, proud, and egotistical. Blake's Milton in the poem of that title recognizes his own selfhood in Satan and returns to the fallen world, in part, in order to subdue this Satanic element and restore to himself his own lost emanation:

"What do I here before the Judgment? without my Emanation?
"With the daughters of memory & not with the daughters of inspiration?
"I in my Selfhood am that Satan: I am that Evil One!
"He is my Spectre! in my obedience to loose him from my Hells,
"To claim the Hells, my Furnaces, I go to Eternal Death."

And although Keats admired Milton beyond almost all else and thought of him as a great philosophic poet—"Chief of organic numbers! / Old Scholar of the Spheres"—he was to the mind of Keats, like Wordsworth, a supreme example of what he referred to in a letter to Richard Woodhouse of October 27, 1818, as the "egotistical sublime." Milton's imagination lacked the ability of a Shakespeare possessed of what Keats in another context called "negative capability" to transform itself at will into all sorts and conditions of men. On the contrary, Milton's imagination assimilated the universe of things into itself and imbued it with the colors of his own mind.

As we have seen, Milton was assiduously read and studied by the major Romantic poets and critics, who found his art and philosophy* of great value to them. Yet it is doubtful that the public at large was so attentive. If Milton was read to any extent by the literate of that day, it was as a religious poet whose *PL* could be perused with edification on a pious Sunday afternoon. And doubtless his poems were bought to grace the parlor table. As early as 1800, Wordsworth, in the Preface to the second edition of *Lyrical Ballads,* had complained about the neglect of Milton by the general reader, and had blamed it on what he described as a plethora of "frantic novels, sickly and stupid German tragedies, and deluges of idle and extravagant stories in verse." And in a letter to Edward Quillinan dated March 9, 1840, he was still of the opinion that *PL* was only "bought because people for their own credit must now have it."

Although he went on to lament the fact that when the all-too-few read the epic "it is almost exclusively not as a poem, but a religious book," one suspects that his view was somewhat uninformed and outdated. For there is evidence to suggest that Milton was being read more widely and for a more varied range of reasons during the 1830s and 40s than during the early decades of the century.

For instance, the restless, often rebellious working-class men and women who in the early Victorian period were learning to read in increasing numbers were turning with enthusiasm to Milton's writings for other than religious reasons. One of the most striking examples of a self-educated laborer who read Milton was Thomas Cooper, the Chartist, the son of a working dyer. In his autobiography, he recalls having read *PL* for the first time at the age of thirteen. And although he found the epic above his "culture and learning," he was by no means discouraged. Having set himself the task of committing the entire *PL* to memory, Cooper spent his Sunday mornings memorizing, and as he repeated the lines of the poem to himself, the "verse seemed to overawe" him. In time, "the perfection of his music, as well as the gigantic stature of the intellect," he wrote of Milton, "were fully perceived by my mind."

Milton, however, was more than just a great religious poet to Cooper and others like him: he was also the patriot, the lover of liberty*, the regicide, and dissenter. Prized for his republican sentiments and his supposedly democratic sympathies, Milton was to many of the laboring classes a revered hero whose life and writings were an inspiration. As a result, the early Victorian era saw a marked revival of interest in Milton's life and his prose works.

In the opinion of those interested in Milton's political views his biography had largely been the exclusive domain of Church of Englanders and Tories. Such was the opinion of Macaulay, whose seminal essay on Milton of 1825 furnished the background for such an argument. "The civil war," Macaulay suggested, had been more discussed, and was less understood, "than any event in English history." Consequently, the motives and actions of Milton and his fellow champions of English liberty had been and still were misrepresented to the public by his biographers*. According to Macaulay, "the friends of liberty" had labored "under the disadvantage of which the lion in the fable complained so bitterly. Though they were the conquerors, their enemies were the painters."

That many shared his opinion is suggested by the fact that numerous authors undertook to set the record straight. An important aspect of this attempt to re-write the life of Milton was a widespread condemnation of Dr. Johnson's* *Life of Milton.* For example, Joseph Ivimey, a Baptist preacher, prefaced his *John Milton: His Life and Times, Religious and Political Opinions* (1833) with "Animadversions on Dr. Johnson's Life of Milton," a diatribe in which he maintained that the critic's "ultra-toryism and bigotry" blinded him to Milton's true character and opinion.

William Carpenter in *The Life and Times of John Milton* (1836) raised another objection to the pre-Victorian biographies of Milton when he wrote that they were too voluminous "for general circulation and too discursive and critical for popular reading." Similarly, Ivimey declared that he undertook to write his biography of the poet because "the Lives of Milton have usually been so large and expensive, that they have been placed out of the reach of the generality of readers." Ivimey, therefore, hoped that his "small volume, comprising everything of importance respecting this noble-minded and gigantic man, will not be unacceptable nor unprofitable to the bulk of his countrymen."

Primarily interested in Milton's life as a republican and advocate of liberty, the early Victorian biographers played down Milton the poet and emphasized Milton the prose writer. As a result, there was a resurgence of interest in Milton's prose, which had as Macaulay asserted in 1825 been long since relegated "to the dust and silence of the upper shelf." For instances, in 1835, Robert Fletcher edited *The Prose Works of John Milton,* and, in his "Introductory Review," he wrote that since "Prelates, and tithes, and kings, were not the burthen of his song," Milton's poetry had often been praised by his Tory biographers who "would fain suppress all other monuments to this Englishman." Consequently, he went on to declare, "it remains for us to appreciate them. Let us never think of John Milton as a poet merely, however in that capacity he may have adorned our language, and benefited, by ennobling, his species. He was a citizen also, with whom patriotism was as heroical a passion, prompting him to do his country service, as was that 'inward prompting' of poesy, by which he did his country honour."

As early as 1833 when he published his *Milton,* Ivimey felt that an era of better feeling toward the prose was opening. "The prejudice," he wrote, "which has existed against Milton's prose works, on account of his republican and dissenting principles, fully accounts for their having been so little known; but it is hoped that such feelings are rapidly subsiding, if they are not yet become quite extinct." To be sure, the prejudice had not disappeared, but Milton's prose was to become rather popular, especially with the Chartists, who sought to establish a government in England similar to the ideal republic outlined by Milton in his prose works. The enthusiasm for Milton's writings can clearly be seen in the epigraphs and extracts from *Tenure, Eikon, Way,* and others that appeared constantly in such publications as *The Chartist Circular.*

Another major factor that added new dimensions to the nineteenth-century attitude to Milton and altered the pattern of response was the rise of the middle class to a position of dominance in the 1820s and 30s. This group, which produced virtually all "the great Victorians," be they poets, novelists, scientists, or statesmen, was on the whole as devoted to John Milton and as ardent in his praise as the other groups here discussed. And perhaps the best means in short compass of indicating the middle-class attitude toward Milton is through a review of Macaulay's famous essay on Milton, which brilliantly captured the middle-class response toward him.

As we know, Macaulay embodied in a quintessential way both the intellectual and moral virtues as well as the limitations of the early Victorian middle-class mind. Moreover, he was almost exclusively interested in his own class and never tired of delineating its characteristics and extolling its virtues. Writing at the moment when at last the middle class in England had inherited the earth, Macaulay in his famous essays on such illustrious men of the past as Francis Bacon and John Milton often found the opportunity of charting the rise of what he with pride referred to as "a new and remarkable species" of men. For instance, Macaulay's interest in Bacon*, as the reader of his essay on the great philosopher and states-man may observe, did not alone reside in his enormous respect and enthusiasm for his "method." Rather, Macaulay saw Bacon's philosophy of "fruit and progress" as a characteristic product of the newly emergent middle-class mind. In Bacon and his father, Sir Nicholas, and others like them, Macaulay recognized "a strong family likeness. The constitution of their minds," he noticed, "was remarkably sound." And his carefully detailed passages of description are strikingly remin-iscent of his lengthy disquisition on Mil-ton's character in his essay on the poet. For Milton, like his great contemporary Bacon, was to Macaulay's mind a splendid specimen of the middle class as it began its rise to prominence in the sixteenth and seventeenth centuries. In both Bacon and Milton, Macaulay recognizes what in the essay on Milton he describes as "a power-ful and independent mind, emancipated from the influence of authority, and devoted to the search of truth."

Likewise, Milton's birth, parentage, religion, university, temper, and cast of mind—all were in keeping with the pattern Macaulay sets forth to such advantage in his essay on Bacon. It was because of the advent of such men as Bacon and Milton that religion was reformed, the nation set on a course toward liberty, science freed from super-stition, and utility and progress secured.

Commencing his essay on Milton, Macaulay dutifully examines Milton's poetry, writing with felicity and due ardor about *L'Al* and *IlP* and *Mask*. Joining in the debate over which was the better, Macaulay gives his vote to *PR* over *SA*, which he accounts a failure. In so doing, and in the style and accent that was to characterize his prose throughout his life, the youthful critic is quick to assure his readers that he is

> by no means insensible to the merits of this celebrated piece, to the severe dignity of the style, the graceful and pathetic solemnity of the opening speech, or the wild and barbaric melody which gives so striking an effect to the choral passages. But we think it, we confess, the least successful effort of the genius of Milton.

In his encomium on the poetry, Macaulay is, on the whole, superficial in his remarks rather than perceptive or illuminating. It is doubtful from what he writes that Milton's poetry had any deeply emotional or intellectually profound sig-nificance for him. To be sure, for one with so marvelously retentive a memory as Macaulay possessed, Milton's richly allu-sive poetic mode was, indeed, a stimulus and a joy. Consequently, he singles out this very aspect as "the most striking characteristic of the poetry of Milton."

For instance, Macaulay, in one of his celebrated passages, observes that

> we often hear of the magical influence of poetry. The expression in general means nothing: but, applied to the writings of Milton, it is most appropriate. His poetry acts like an incantation. Its merit lies less in its obvious meaning than in its occult power. There would seem, at first sight, to be no more in his words than in other

words. But they are words of enchantment. No sooner are they pronounced, than the past is present and the distant near. New forms of beauty start at once into existence, and all the burial-places of the memory give up their dead.

In his essay, *PL* is habitually seen like Kubla Khan's pleasure dome in Xanadu as "a miracle of rare device," a fragile, precariously sustained marvel of art that remains to us a glorious monument of its creator's heroic efforts to overcome seemingly insuperable obstacles. Having informed his readers of the near impossibility of a cultivated, highly educated poet's being able to create a great work of imaginative art in the present advanced state of civilization, Macaulay declares that "no poet has ever triumphed over greater difficulties than Milton." And having further elaborated his idea that in an enlightened and literary society a poet is at a distinct disadvantage, Macaulay reiterates his belief that in the writing of *PL* "the strength of his [Milton's] imagination triumphed over every obstacle. So intense and ardent was the fire of his mind, that it not only was not suffocated beneath the weight of fuel, but penetrated the whole superincumbent mass with its own heat and radiance."

It is with the full realization of this in mind in addition to his knowledge of the difficult conditions under which it was written that Macaulay stands in awe of Milton's greatest achievement:

> Hence it was that, though he wrote the *Paradise Lost* at a time of life when images of beauty and tenderness are in general beginning to fade, even from those minds in which they have not been effaced by anxiety and disappointment, he adorned it with all that is most lovely and delightful in the physical and in the moral world. Neither Theocritus nor Ariosto had a finer or a more healthful sense of the pleasantness of external objects, or loved better to luxuriate amidst sunbeams and flowers, the songs of nightingales, the juice of summer fruits, and the coolness of shady fountains. His conception of love unites all the voluptuousness of the Oriental harem, and all the gallantry of the chivalric tournament, with all the pure and quiet affection of an English fireside.

His poetry reminds us of the miracles of Alpine scenery. Nooks and dells, beautiful as fairyland, are embosomed in its most rugged and gigantic elevations. The roses and myrtles bloom unchilled on the verge of the avalanche.

Doubtless Milton's "strength of mind" in the face of adversity like that of his Satan was in Macaulay's eyes a characteristic preeminent of the model middle-class man whose duty it is to rise above every adversity in this vale of soul-making. Having risen through self-control, strength of purpose, and a sense of right to a place of power, the middle class of Macaulay's day admired the stern-souled person who rejected the blandishments of pleasure as well as the flight of the timid from reality.

The key to Macaulay's admiration of Satan lies in the fact that "the might of his intellectual nature is victorious over the extremity of pain. Amidst agonies which cannot be conceived without horror, he deliberates, resolves, and even exults," Macaulay observes.

> Against the sword of Michael, against the thunder of Jehovah, against the flaming lake, and the marl burning with solid fire, against the prospect of an eternity of unintermitted misery, his spirit bears up unbroken, resting on its own innate energies, requiring no support from anything external, nor even from hope itself.

Such a description calls to mind Macaulay's brilliantly drawn portrait of the lofty-spirited Milton who endured with unbowed head the trials and tribulations of the post-Cromwellian era.

As eloquent and enthusiastic as is his praise of Milton's poetry, Macaulay in his essay is primarly attracted to Milton, the man. The publication of Charles Sumner's translation of the recently discovered *CD* (which is ostensibly the reason for the young reviewer's essay) is clearly an excuse for an opportunity "to commemorate, in all love and reverence, the genius and virtues of John Milton, the poet, the statesman, the philosopher, the glory of English literature, the champion and the martyr of English liberty."

Thus, having discussed the beauties of his poetry and having compared *PL* at some length with "the only poem of modern times which can be compared with [it] . . . , the *Divine Comedy,*" Macaulay proceeds in due course to conclude his remarks on these two poems and lead into an extended treatment of the topic in which he is most interested—Milton's character.

"The poetry of these great men [Milton and Dante]," he writes, "has in a considerable degree taken its character from their moral qualities." Disagreeing with the Romantic poets and critics who found the subjectivity of *PL* less praiseworthy than the objectivity of Shakespeare's plays, Macaulay staunchly maintains that Milton and Dante* "are not egotists. They rarely obtrude their idiosyncracies on their readers." With Byron and Shelley perhaps in mind, Macaulay declares that Milton and Dante

> have nothing in common with those modern beggars for fame, who extort a pittance from the compassion of the inexperienced by exposing the nakedness and sores of their minds. Yet it would be difficult to name two writers whose works have been more completely, though undesignedly, coloured by their personal feelings.

Noticing traces "of the peculiar character of Milton" in all his works, Macaulay finds it "most strongly displayed in the sonnets." In so doing, he was at one with his times. For the Victorians regarded the sonnet primarily as a means of expressing deeply felt personal emotions. Although Dr. Johnson had found the sonnet not very suitable to the English language, poets and critics from Wordsworth to Oscar Wilde gave it serious, synpathetic attention.

The temper of the middle-class mind displays itself in Macaulay's evaluation of Milton's sonnets. They appeal to him because they make no effort at wit, no attempt at artifice. "They have," he observes with approval, "no epigrammatic point. There is," he informs us, "none of the ingenuity of Filicaja in the thought, none of the hard and brilliant enamel of Petrarch in the style." For this reason, he

believes, they have been misunderstood and undervalued by those expecting the highly wrought, self-conscious work of the Italians and Elizabethans. For Macaulay, Milton's sonnets appeal because they reveal "the feelings of the poet" undisguised by false sentiment and a clever style.

As a result, the majesty of Milton, the nobility of his character, the severity of his life-style impress themselves upon the mind of the reader. Although their subject matter varies, "they are, almost without exception, dignified by a sobriety and greatness of mind to which we know not where to look for a parallel."

The wise, generous, independent, scrupulously honest man whom Macaulay observes with admiration in the sonnets is the same man he finds in life. "His public conduct was such as was to be expected from a man of a spirit so high and of an intellect so powerful." With none of the jaundice with which Dr. Johnson had approached Milton's conduct during the course of the Puritan Revolution, Macaulay sees Milton playing an honorable, indeed, admirable role during "one of the most memorable eras in the history of mankind, at the very crisis of the great conflict between Oromasdes and Arimanes, liberty and despotism, reason and prejudice." And "of those principles, then struggling for their infant existence, Milton was the most devoted and eloquent literary champion."

Even more than Bacon, Milton emerges as Macaulay's ideal of the middle-class man. Perhaps this is why he is loath to see Milton as either a Puritan, a freethinker, or a Royalist. Rather, he sees him as the embodiment of

> the noblest qualities of every party . . . combined in harmonious union. From the Parliament and from the Court, from the conventicle and from the Gothic cloister, from the gloomy and sepulchral circles of the Roundheads, and from the Christmas revel of the hospitable Cavalier, his nature selected and drew to itself whatever was great and good, while it rejected all the base and pernicious ingredients by which those finer elements were defiled.

In his perfect hatred of tyranny and his love of literature, chivalry, and "every elegant amusement," Milton combined the best qualities of both Puritan and Royalist. Yet what, for Macaulay, sets Milton apart from all others is "the battle which he fought for the species of freedom which is the most valuable, and which was then the least understood, the freedom of the human mind." Nothing endeared Milton to the hearts of Macaulay and the Victorian middle class more than did this trait. For nothing was more feared by them than the evils of moral and intellectual slavery and nothing more prized than the benefits that the liberty of the press and the unfettered exercise of private judgment bestowed.

Although Macaulay's discussion of the prose writings is brief and restricted for lack of space, his remarks clearly indicate his high regard for them. Regretful that these works "should, in our time, be so little read," Macaulay characterizes them as "a perfect field of cloth-of-gold," rising to one of his most extravagant passages of praise :

> Not even in the earlier books of the *Paradise Lost* has the great poet ever risen higher than in those parts of his controversial works in which his feelings, excited by conflict, find a vent in bursts of devotional and lyric rapture. It is, to borrow his own majestic language, "a sevenfold chorus of hallelujahs and harping symphonies."

Throughout the essay, Macaulay exhibits toward his subject that reverence and love which was to characterize the attitude of many of the great Victorians toward Milton. So completely did he embody their idea of manhood that not infrequently did their praise verge on absolute veneration and worship. "The sight of his books, the sound of his name, are pleasant to us," Macaulay unabashedly writes as he brings his idol before our eyes for the last time.

> His thoughts resemble those celestial fruits and flowers which the Virgin Martyr of Massinger sent down from the gardens of Paradise to the earth, and which were

distinguished from the productions of other soils, not only by superior bloom and sweetness, but by miraculous efficacy to invigorate and to heal. They are powerful, not only to delight, but to elevate and purify. Nor do we envy the man who can study either the life or the writings of the great poet and patriot, without aspiring to emulate, not indeed the sublime works with which his genius has enriched our literature, but the zeal with which he laboured for the public good, the fortitude with which he endured every private calamity, the lofty disdain with which he looked down on temptations and dangers, the deadly hatred which he bore to bigots and tyrants, and the faith which he so sternly kept with his country and with his fame.

If to Macaulay Milton was the model of middle-class independence, virtue, and strength of mind, he was to George Eliot, as U. C. Knoepflmacher has shown, "the great 'philosophic' poet who in *Paradise Lost* had justified man's lot in the temporal world." Like so many of her contemporaries whose post-Romantic belief in the truth of science did not allow them "to create a supernatural world of essences," George Eliot, nevertheless, could share "Milton's purpose." As Knoepflmacher contends, "in its subject matter, its treatment of vision and knowledge, in its temporal ironies and even in the nature of its reconciliation, *Adam Bede* reveals George Eliot's intimate understanding of Milton's great poem" (*ELH, A Journal of English Literary History* 34 : 523–24).

Although it was a joy and an ever more inspiriting experience for a Macaulay to contemplate the rapidly developing Victorian world of fruition and progress, it was a less pleasant and often dispiriting affair to others. Too secular-minded to question, much less lose, the evangelical faith in which he had been reared, Macaulay found little trouble in accepting Newton's dead mechanical universe. Yet for George Eliot, "acceptance of an existence darkened by the materialism of Victorian science," in the words of Knoepflmacher, was not so easy (p. 527). Finding in *PL* a paradigm of man's coming to terms with the temporal world by creating "a paradise within," the novelist was encouraged in her endeavors to impress upon her readers the wisdom of Adam's words to Eve :

"That which before us lies in daily life,
Is the prime Wisdom, what is more, is fume,
Or emptiness, or fond impertinence. . . ."
(*PL* 8. 193–95)

Unlike Macaulay and many of Milton's lower-and middle-class devotees in her involvement with Milton's immensely significant articulation of his aim to justify man's lot in the fallen world, she, like them, was aware of the value of Milton's prose. As her two reviews of Thomas Keightley's *An Account of the Life, Opinions, and Writings of John Milton* (1855) show, the novelist found Milton's tractate on education of great interest and his tracts on divorce of moment for the contemporary scene. George Eliot praises Keightley for providing not only "an account of the views contained in" Milton's prose works, but "well-chosen extracts as specimens of their style" (*Westminster Review* 64 [1855]: 601–4). Whereas Macaulay was primarily engaged with Milton's personality in his art, George Eliot was ultimately concerned with the ideas in his art. The influence of Milton on this great novelist is revealed in the very fabric of her vision of experience objectified in her novels.

Such also is the case with Alfred, Lord Tennyson, who found the philosophic content of Milton's poetry expressive of some of his most characteristic and deeply held views. Although in his early volumes of poetry Tennyson imitated Milton's blank verse, his diction, and subject matter, the attraction was of a more subtle and fundamental kind; it was the attraction that one congenial mind has for another—a meeting of two minds that considered the true poet to be both artist and seer.

Tennyson like Milton was fully aware that his talents were of an "ethereal origin and celestial descent" (*AdP*) and of God rarely bestow'd" (*RCG* 3 : 238). that his abilities were "the inspired gift

And, needless to say, Tennyson agreed with Milton's claim that the poet rivaled the power of the pulpit "to imbreed and cherish in a great people the seeds of vertu, and publick civility, to allay the perturbations of the mind, and set the affections in right tune, . . . to deplore the general relapses of Kingdoms and State from justice and Gods true worship" (*RCG* 3 : 238).

Although Tennyson seems to have had little interest in Milton's religious and political ideas *per se,* his attitude toward fate* and free will*, passion and reason, and poetic fame were strikingly similar to that of Milton. Although free will was absolutely essential to their idea of man, Milton and Tennyson did not reject without considerable thought the possibility that the course of man and nature was purely a matter of chance. The emotional tension in *Lyc* is due in part to the young poet's fear that a life of ostensible promise and purpose might be cut short by "the blind *Fury* with th' abhorred shears," and the tense drama of *In Memoriam* is again supported by the fact that science suggests that "the stars . . . blindly run" (3) and that Time is merely "a maniac scattering dust, / And Life a Fury slinging flame" (1).

But perhaps more than any other, the problem of reason versus passion is the most real and perilous problem in the poetry of Milton and Tennyson. Although Raphael tells Adam and Eve to "take heed least Passion sway / Thy Judgement to do aught, which else free Will / Would not admit" (*PL* 8. 635–37) our first parents succumbed to temptation. Similarly the reason of Paris in Tennyson's "Oenone" is swayed despite the fact that he also is aware of the true path : "Self-reverence, self-knowledge, self-control," Pallas reminds the young shepherd, "These three alone lead life to sovereign power."

Nowhere in Tennyson's poetry is the war between passion and reason more powerfully depicted than in the *Idylls of the King,* where Arthur's splendid city built to music is broken and destroyed by bestial lusts and the failure of man to distinguish between the true and the false. The tangled forest encroaches upon the city, the animal subdues the human, and "the darkness of that battle in the West / Where all of high and holy dies away" hangs over the world because man has lost his reason. The *Idylls* is an excellent exposition of Milton's realization in *Areop* that "good and evill . . . in the field of this World grow up together almost inseparably" and the rather pessimistic comment the later books of *PL* provide.

Of ultimate importance to Tennyson, however, was Milton the artist. In his sonnet on Milton, Tennyson extols him as the "mighty-mouth'd inventor of harmonies," the "God-gifted organ-voice of England"; and in his many references to Milton recorded in *Alfred Lord Tennyson, A Memoir by His Son,* the Laureate speaks of him as the most sublime of all poets, the supreme exponent of the "grand style" of poetic diction. *Lyc* was for Tennyson what it was for Matthew Arnold, a touchstone of poetic taste.

Nursing no illusions about "unpremeditated art," Tennyson found Milton's conscious artistry an ever-present inspiration in his endeavors to create his own consummate art. As the Victorian critic Frederic Harrison once wrote: "In the whole range of English poetry, Milton alone can be held to show an equal or even greater uniformity of polish than Tennyson." The stanzas of *In Memoriam* are "after Milton's the most faultlessly chiseled verse in our language."

In his high regard for Milton's art, the major poet of the Victorian period was in complete agreement with the major critic of the day, Matthew Arnold*. Basing his criticism of Milton on his assessment of the nation's frame of mind, Arnold rejected those aspects of Milton's life and writings which, in his opinion, appealed to the excessively Hebraic temper dominant in nineteenth-century England, and he praised those qualities which reinforced what he thought of as the Hellenistic element.

In Arnold's view, the Reformation and the subsequent Puritan Revolution had been for England a most untimely event. A product of a resurgence of Hebraism with its emphasis on conduct and obedience, these events had brought about an eclipse of Hellenism, which with its bent toward the free play of the intellect had produced "such wonderful fruits" in the reign of Elizabeth. As a result, "for more than two hundred years the main stream of man's advance has moved towards knowing himself and the world, seeing things as they are, spontaneity of consciousness"; yet, Arnold laments, "the main impulse of a great part, and that the strongest part, of our nation has been towards strictness of conscience. They have made the secondary the principal at the wrong moment, and the principal they have at the wrong moment treated as secondary." ("Hebraism and Hellenism," *Culture and Anarchy.*) Since to Arnold's mind Milton had played a not inconsiderable role in the resurgence of Puritanism and was himself a product of it, Arnold, in his major statement on the poet, "A French Critic on Milton," disparages Milton's Hebraic frame of mind and reserves his praise for the Hellenistic character of his art.

In his condemnation of Milton's puritanical characteristics Arnold in his essay is, indeed, relentless. "In kindness, and in all which that word conveys or suggests, Milton does not shine," Arnold declares.

> He had the temper of his Puritan party. We often hear the boast, on behalf of the Puritans, that they produced "our great epic poet." Alas! one might not unjustly retort that they spoiled him. However, let Milton bear his own burden; in his temper he had natural affinities with the Puritans. He has paid for it by limitations as a poet.

Milton, in Arnold's view, shares with all too many Victorians a defective attitude of mind that is in its narrowness and contentiousness the antithesis of the Hellenistic temper with its emphasis on "seeing things in their essence and beauty." Because the Puritanical temper of the Victorian mind finds its image in Milton and his writings, it welcomes such opportunities as Macaulay's essay on Milton provides to glory in the splendor of such an illustrious embodiment of the Hebraic frame of mind. To such essays, Arnold observes, many readers repair "with their minds full of zeal for the Puritan cause, and for Milton as one of the glories of Puritanism." But as Arnold proceeds to point out, "a disinterested reader," one whose Hebraic temper of mind has been modified by a proper infusion of the Hellenistic desire for sweetness and light, will be dissatisfied with the reckless adulation and biased views of a Macaulay.

Incensed and exasperated by Macaulay's panegyric on Milton's personality, Arnold exclaims:

> And Milton's temper! His "sedate and majestic patience"; his freedom from "asperity!" If there is a defect which, above all others, is signal in Milton, which injures him even intellectually, which limits him as a poet, it is the defect common to him with the whole Puritan party to which he belonged,—the fatal defect of *temper*. He and they may have a thousand merits, but they are *unamiable*. Excuse them how one will, Milton's asperity and acerbity, his want of sweetness of temper, of the Shakspearian largeness and indulgence, are undeniable.

Nowhere is Milton's defective temper more obvious than in his prose which, despite its moments of "mighty eloquence" and its occasional magnificence of style, does not bear out Macaulay's "belief that the total impression to be got from Milton's prose writings is one of enjoyment and admonition." Milton's readers, Arnold maintains, "are misled" and their "time is wasted" if they "are sent to Milton's prose works in the expectation of finding it so. Grand thought and beautiful language do not form the staple of Milton's controversial treatises, though they occur in them not infrequently."

Viewing Milton's prose through the eyes of the French critic Edmond Scherer, in his greatest effort at being disinterested, Arnold concludes:

No doubt there is, as M. Scherer says, "something indescribably heroical and magnificent which overflows from Milton, even when he is engaged in the most miserable discussions." Still, for the mass of his prose treatises, "miserable discussions" is the final and right word.

Since the contents of Milton's *PL* are, as Scherer contends, "given by Puritanism," Arnold is in strong agreement with the French critic's rather severe indictment of the epic. With obvious approval, Arnold quotes Scherer's opinion that

> *Paradise Lost* is a false poem, a grotesque poem, a tiresome poem; there is not one reader out of a hundred who can read the ninth and tenth books without smiling, or the eleventh and twelfth without yawning. The whole thing is without solidity; it is a pyramid resting on its apex, the most solemn of problems resolved by the most puerile of means.

In such a passage the main lines of the criticism of Milton to the close of the Victorian period begin to emerge —points of view that through Arnold are transmitted to Walter Pater and thence to Walter Raleigh* at the close of the century. Milton's epical matter is first dismissed as a patchwork of favorite Puritan dogmas—"The Fall, justification, God's sovereign decrees—" a didactic work vitiated "by the conjoint necessity and impossibility of taking its contents literally."

Yet, with Scherer, Arnold maintains that the work is immortal. And why is it immortal? Because of its artistry. Like a gorgeous brooch, *PL* is in the eyes of Scherer and Arnold studded with incomparable beauties—dazzling lines, splendid passages. But "lastly, and above all," Scherer informs us, Milton "has a something indescribably serene and victorious, an unfailing level of style, power indomitable," a quality Arnold and his followers seize upon as "what is undoubtedly Milton's true distinction as a poet, his 'unfailing level of style.'" On this note Arnold rises to sing Milton's praises with full-throated ease. And in so doing he sounds the keynote of the late nineteenth-century criticism of Milton. "Milton has always the sure, strong touch of the master," Arnold declares.

> His power both of diction and of rhythm is unsurpassable, and it is characterised by being always present—not depending on an access of emotion, not intermittent, but, like the grace of Raphael, working in its possessor as a constant gift of nature.

Always prone to value a classic writer's art in accordance with its suitability to the needs of a particular time, Arnold in turning his gaze upon the literature of his day finds it "full of vigour and genius" but "peculiarly impaired by gropings and inadequacies in form." At such a time, "the study of Milton," Arnold writes, "may well have an indescribable attraction"—not through its subject matter nor through its ability to convey the Puritanical temper of its creator, but through its style.

> Shakespeare himself, divine as are his gifts, has not, of the marks of the master, this one: perfect sureness of hand in his style. Alone of English poets, alone in English art, Milton has it; he is our great artist in style, our one first-rate master in the grand style. He is as truly a master in this style as the great Greeks are, or Virgil, or Dante. The number of such masters is so limited that a man acquires a world-rank in poetry and art, instead of a mere local rank, by being counted among them. But Milton's importance to us Englishmen, by virtue of this distinction of his, is incalculable.

As impressed with the importance of style as was his contemporary Walter Pater, Arnold, in his last extended statement on Milton before his death in 1888, returned to Milton's preeminence in style. "The mighty power of poetry and art is generally admitted," Arnold told his audience at the unveiling of a window in memory of Milton's "late espoused saint" in St. Margaret's church, Westminster, "but where the soul of this power, of this power at its best, chiefly resides, very many of us fail to see. It resides chiefly," Arnold went on to observe,

in the refining and elevation wrought in us by the high and rare excellence of the great style. We may feel the effect without being able to give ourselves clear account of its cause, but the thing is so. Now, no race needs the influences mentioned, the influences of refining and elevation, more than ours [the Anglo-Saxon]; and in poetry and art our grand source for them is Milton. ("Milton," *Essays in Criticism, Second Series.*) [JGN]

INFLUENCE ON TWENTIETH-CENTURY LITERATURE, MILTON'S. To the question "What influence has Milton had on twentieth-century literature?" the immediate answer of academic English Literature specialists is frequently "None." False as the answer may be, the fact that it can be voiced thus, and with confidence, is symptomatic. Unless we take account of the prevailing but superficial view that Milton has not been influencing writers of late, we shall fail to do justice to a complex yet crucial literary development that will be seen in the future as a mark of our times, whether or not we ourselves bring it into the open. If the overt influence of Milton on twentieth-century poetry has been slight, compared to that of Donne, say, this does not mean that, at a deeper level than that at which verbal and stylistic indebtedness is immediately apparent, there has not been a perhaps more decisive and fundamental shift in literary attitudes under a Miltonic impulse than has occurred under the more obvious impact of other seventeenth-century writers.

The underestimation of Miltonic influence must be accounted for before exploring the influence itself. It may in part be due to the historic accident that Milton was more slowly released from the grip of nineteenth-century humanistic psychological criticism than was Shakespeare*, for instance. Critics began to look at Shakespeare as a poet and not a misplaced Victorian psychological novelist, as an Elizabethan and not "a Bernard Shaw from Nature's womb untimely ripped" over thirty years ago (E. E. Stoll, *Art and Artifice in Shakespeare* [1933], p. 111). It is only in the last decade that the corresponding lesson has fully sunk home with Milton's critics. In the same book, writing of *Othello,* Stoll says, "All art aspires to the condition of music . . . ," a point we must return to later, while a footnote quotes Bonamy Dobrée's *Restoration Tragedy*: "The conception of character being the playwright's object has vitiated, not only criticism, but also playwriting, for longer than it is agreeable to think." A reaction against the critical obsession with "character," and a full recognition of the poet's pursuit of thematic order and harmony ("the condition of music") were changes necessary to Miltonic as well as to Shakespearean criticism before the true quality of *PL* could be appreciated.

Some thirty years after Stoll, B. A. Wright protests that "Helen Darbishire* overlooked the fact that Milton's mind is not only acutely logical but nicely theological" (*Milton's Paradise Lost* [1962], p. 141), and rebukes A. J. A. Waldock* for his "suppressed assumption . . . that we need take no account of differences in conventions of thought and feeling between the seventeenth century and our own." The argument here is that the rejection of the post-Romantic attitude to *PL,* an attitude that tried to rob the poem of its intellectual and imaginative coherence and its essential *religiousness,* came too late for it to be generally digested in educational culture by recent writers brought up in that culture. Since *PL* was for so long read as a psychological narrative, readily digestible by anti-theological nineteenth-century minds, and with an apologetic or scornful neglect of those parts of the poem which obdurately defied treatment within the categories congenial to the *Zeitgeist,* it could not possibly be a generally accepted and recognized literary influence. What it was praised for doing, or criticized for not doing, was not all that different from what George Eliot and others like her had done with greater frankness and consistency. The *PL* of late nineteenth-century and early twentieth-century psychological criticism was neither a rational, a coherent, nor a balanced work of art. It could not be expected to influence the minds of young writers unless they were big enough to see through the current critical misunderstanding. Some of them were.

Of course individual voices have been raised intermittently against misinterpretation of Milton well before the general critical mood changed. C. S. Lewis* in *A Preface to Paradise Lost* stressed the theological orthodoxy and consistency of the poem and gave a fatal wound to the romantic, heroic Satan; but he did much less than justice to the style of the poem, and it was perhaps Charles Williams in his edition of the English *Poems* who was the first notable twentieth-century critic to grasp the wholeness of the poem imaginatively as well as intellectually, to see it as "concerned with a contrast and a conflict between two states of being," to define those states of being, to make clear that they are not only mythological, but "human and contemporary," and to specify the human universality of the poem's crucial moments. "There are no linked lovers in our streets who are not more beautiful and more unfortuante because of those last lines," he says of the closing couplet (Introduction).

The issue of changing critical attitudes is relevant only insofar as it sheds light on Milton's influence, or lack of influence, on twentieth-century literature. But if the climate of Miltonic criticism is now much healthier, as a delayed result of the work of critics such as Lewis and Williams, the general change is too recent to have had an educational effect comparable to its significance. The argument here is that sensitive appreciation of Milton's distinctive qualities has been confined to a few. But perhaps the few include the greatest writers of the century, and that would make Milton's influence a most important one. It could not in the circumstances be an overt influence, readily recognizable, for the reasons already implicit in this argument. That is to say, so long as the Milton of nineteenth-century critical mythology dominated the academies and journals, the real influence of *PL,* where it did occur, would naturally not be detected and, through sheer prudence, not be advertised. For to claim discipleship of Milton would have been a foolish thing for a writer to do if he understood that the name *Milton* in common parlance denoted a mythical figure with qualities dominant in his work quite other than those the writer admired.

There is a converse to this argument. Just as a writer deeply influenced by Milton might have little to say on the matter, and might readily be assumed by others to be well outside the range of the Miltonic spell, so too writers actually making great claims to be disciples of Milton might in fact turn out, on examination, to be alien in thought and imagination to the Milton presented by Charles Williams.

Such is perhaps the case with Robert Bridges*, though here one must distinguish between Bridges the critic and Bridges the poet. Bridges's critical articles on Milton reflected a detailed study of the prosody, which was influential in changing the academic view of *SA* when its verse had come to be regarded as clumsy and insensitive, but whether this technical interest spilled over fruitfully into Bridges's poetry is another matter. Much is heard about "Bridges's master John Milton" in Edward Thompson's study of Bridges (1944), yet even Thompson admits that Bridges's blank verse at first owed more to Tennyson's *Idylls of the King,* for which Bridges professed no admiration, than to Milton. Indeed the Miltonic element in Bridges seems to be chiefly located in lists of proper names and certain prosodic principles derived from his study of Milton's prosody. When Thompson argues of *The Testament of Beauty* that "its closest kinship is with the two greatest works of Bridges's master John Milton," one must surely register a protest, the real connection being that the poems in question are big and, though in vastly different ways, "philosophical." The Milton we have come to know since

Charles Williams was not a living influence on the subject matter of Bridges's poetry. This admission does not, however, underrate Bridges's valid contribution to the appreciation of Milton's versification in *SA.*

One of the difficulties of tracing literary influences is that a strong bond of similarity may tie together writers whose lives were far from contemporaneous, and yet that bond may mark a shared allegiance rather than an influence. This is perhaps especially the case with Christian writers whose minds are attuned to common beliefs and common modes of symbolization. This must be said because a case might be made for a strong Miltonic influence on the work of Charles Williams, though, oddly enough, rather on his work as a novelist than on his work as a poet. Certainly Williams's reiterated insistence that *"Paradise Lost* then is chiefly concerned with the choice between . . . two states of being" reflects the dominating concern of his own work. Writing of the eternal City, the City of Love, in her detailed study of Charles Williams's work *The Theology of Romantic Love,* Mary Shideler says, "The opposite to the City is the Infamy, which repudiates the co-inherence" and "there is, in the end, no compromise between the two; there is only choice" (p. 183). "The infamy," she continues, again quoting Williams's own words, "denies inclusion." That the contrast between the City and its diabolical perversion (like the correspondence between the City and its earthly image) is fundamental to *PL* and to Williams's work does not necessarily constitute an influence. The two writers are indebted to the same tradition. Again, the close connection between the Satanic persona and the Satanic method in *PL* and the studies of evil in Williams's work is such that the word *influence* would spring immediately to one's lips did one not suspect that, Williams's spiritual history being what it was, his imaginative work as a poet and a novelist would not have been different had Milton never lived. Nevertheless, when there is loose talk of discipleship, one may justly point out that there is a Miltonic flavor to many a passage in Williams's novels such as one would certainly not find in the *Testament of Beauty.*

Of course, once one has committed oneself to this kind of comparison, many others leap to mind. Most of them would probably represent subjective associations only. It would be difficult for the Milton enthusiast not to have *PL* brought to mind when reading novelists who explore the diabolical on a fantastic scale with real potency in their imagery and vitality in their characterisation. Mervyn Peake's *Gormenghast* trilogy and indeed Muriel Spark's novels, like *The Ballad of Peckham Rye,* are cases in point. But the significance of such parallels does not lie, one may guess, in the fact that *PL* has been a school textbook throughout our universal educational system; rather, it lies in the fact that while God is one and indivisible, Satan is one and indefinitely divisible. It is a fact of theology not an event of literary history.

It would be unjust to imply that the Miltonic spell operates only on writers who have deep sympathy with Milton's Christian profession, though indeed it is perhaps the case that Milton's minor poetry, *Lyc* especially, tends to be cited with especial approval by writers (and by critics) whose thinking rejects the religion of *PL.* Blind Milton seems to be present in Dylan Thomas's mind in "Do not go gentle into that good night" and Thomas allegorically personifies Sin in "Ballad of the Long-legged Bait" : ("Sin who had a woman's shape"), but generally it is the Milton of *Lyc* that Thomas's critics cite as an influence. Where Thomas is most closely indebted to Milton (e.g., the meter of *Nat* in "There was a Saviour"), the aim is to parody*. And indeed the name of Milton does not appear in the index to Thomas's Notebooks.

The paucity of meaningful references to Milton in criticism of twentieth-century poets is precisely the issue engaging us —that and the inadequate notion of Milton revealed in some of the parenthetic throwaways in which he is actually named. Monroe K. Spears tells us in *The Poetry of W. H. Auden* (1936), p. 168, that "Auden parallels to a limited extent in his later poetry the Gravesian contrast between the true Muse (the 'White Goddess') and the false Muse (Apollo) who inspired Virgil and Milton." This may not tell us much about Auden, but it tells us something about our century's failure hitherto to do justice to Milton. Surely no one for whom the Muses of Virgil* and Milton are identical is at grips with the real Milton.

Even about Auden Stephen Spender in *World within World* (1928, p. 57), has voiced again the old comparison over the use of proper names in Milton, saying that Auden uses technical words as "Milton uses names of heathen gods, with an intellectual awareness of what they signify and yet like a kind of abracadabra." The Milton of organ music and versified telephone directory dies hard. But it should be noted that Auden is little touched by Milton, though Milton is our greatest Christian poet. Auden is not one of those who feel it necessary to make their bows to Milton whether or not he has influenced them. Not that such gestures are to be disparaged. They do not necessarily reflect pretentiousness or affectation. Rather, they reflect the peculiar status of Milton as one of the few English poets who cannot be attacked with genuine inner confidence by anyone. His past dominance, carrying with it the weight of classical scholarship and culture united to prophetic Christian integrity, is something more than the dominance of a man : it is the dominance of a religious and cultural tradition. In *W. B. Yeats* (1962 : p. 237), Joseph Hone tells us of Yeats, working on his essay "Synge and Ireland" while staying at Maud Gonne's, and "reading a little of Milton's prose every morning before he began to work." That puts the point in a nutshell. The daily duty done to Milton is solemn cultural preparation for the day's work. One guesses that Yeats would feel positively virtuous over the performance of this rite, as one might over keeping the regular offices of the Church. We may assume that Yeats would be especially sensitive to the vigor of Milton's prose style and sympathetically responsive to the lone poet's prophetic stance and revolutionary ardour. Probably too the imagery of such early poems as *IlP* fed something into Yeats's vein.

Milton's influence was crucial upon James Joyce. If one accepts the status accorded to Joyce by T. S. Eliot*—that of the major imaginative writer of the age— and then accepts a very significant Miltonic influence upon him, Milton is indeed established as a most important influence on the literature of this century, perhaps even *the* most important influence by an English poet, Donne and the metaphysicals* notwithstanding. The influence is neither obvious nor as yet generally recognized. Perhaps nothing that matters in Joyce's work is obvious. Perhaps his most important literary qualities are still far from widely recognized. If that is so, the failure to bring to light the Miltonic vein and the Miltonic influence, in respect of *Ulysses* and *Finnegans Wake,* is neither surprising nor exceptional. But Joyce gave readers guidance within his work and without.

In Thomas McGreevy's essay, "The Catholic Element in *Work in Progress*," published in 1929 (p. 120 in *Our Exagmination Round His Factification*), we find the following :

> But every chapter and passage [of *Finnegans Wake*] that has appeared is so admirably realised and so related to every other chapter and passage that one has no doubts that when the end does come the author of *Ulysses* will have justified himself again as a prose writer who combines a wellnigh flawless sense of the significance of words with a power to construct on a scale scarcely equalled in English literature since the Renaissance, not even by the author of *Paradise Lost.* The splendour of order, to use Saint Thomas's phrase, has not been the dominating characteristic of modern English prose and it is partly because the quality was demonstrated on a vast scale in *Ulysses* that the book marked a literary revolution.

In examining this crucial statement one should recall that, in a letter to Valery Larbaud in July 1929, written from the Imperial Hotel, Torquay, Joyce accepted responsibility for inspiring the lines of thought pursued by his disciples in the *Exagmination* from which McGreevy's essay is taken. "What you say about the Exag is right enough. I did stand behind those twelve Marshals more or less directing them what lines of research to follow" (*Letters* [1957], p. 283).

Now we are in a position to understand why Milton's influence on twentieth-century literature has gone unrecognized. In the phrase *the splendour of order* lies the key to that influence. But Joyce's *Ulysses* was for long regarded as a disorderly work, and its fine and complex organization has only slowly come to be appreciated. Moreover, at the time in question, as has been observed, *PL* did not generally receive acclaim as a masterpiece of organization but as a work fundamentally disordered by romantic transmutation of villain into hero and accidental vitiation of explicit Christian judgments by implicit humanistic values. Since neither *PL* nor *Ulysses* was seen as possessing those qualities which to a high degree linked them as comparable artistic achievements, it is scarcely surprising that the Miltonic influence on this century has been underrated. The *PL* of humanistic critical mythology was perhaps not quite so false as the *Ulysses* of popular conception, but there could be no recognition of indebtedness between works comparably misunderstood.

T. S. Eliot was unwavering from the start in his recognition of what Joyce was about and how important it was. So it is interesting to note the paragraphs in his first essay on Milton, printed in *Essays and Studies* (1936), in which he makes a direct comparison between Milton and Joyce.

> The initial similarities are musical taste and abilities, followed by musical training, wide and curious knowledge, gift for acquiring languages, and remarkable powers of memory perhaps fortified by defective vision.

Now the emphasis on musical ability and training, coming from the author of *Four Quartets,* is significant. The organization of that poem, in detail and in large design, is musical; so is the organization of *Ulysses*; so is the organization of *PL.* An emphasis upon the musical character of these writers' gifts is an emphasis upon their way of achieving "the splendour of order." And Eliot adds, in this essay, that "both Milton and Joyce are so exalted in their own kinds, in the whole of literature, that the only writers with whom to compare them are writers who have attempted something very different."

One of the difficulties of dealing with James Joyce critically is his Protean versatility and multifariousness. Scarcely has one detected a Homeric element in the structuring and content of a given episode in *Ulysses* before a Dantean element or a Miltonic element comes uppermost to mind. This multifariousness does not get out of control because the skeletal framework that undergirds the structure of *Ulysses* as a whole is itself an intertwined articulation indebted to Homer*, Dante*, Shakespeare, Milton, and others. Thus, to isolate the Homeric structure with its climax in the homecoming of Bloom, the drawing of the bow, and the reunion with his Penelope, is valid, but artificial and misleading if one does not also attend to the Dantean structure by which the reader goes spiraling down through the various circles of unreality ("modern subjectivity" is McGreevy's phrase) to the depths of the modern Inferno in the brothels of Dublin.

The underlying Miltonic structure is less extensive but intensely significant. A thought-out balance is maintained between the *Telemachiad,* the first three episodes of *Ulysses,* and the twelve episodes of Book 2 that constitute the central body of the work. In Book 1 (the *Telemachiad*) one shares the movements of Stephen Dedalus's mind and his day: in Book 2 one largely shares in the movements of Leopold Bloom's mind and his day. In the first book one finds a highly intellectualized and spiritualized treatment of issues appropriate to Stephen Dedalus. In the second book one shares a far more fleshly, sensuous, physically rooted and emotionally active experience characteristic of Bloom, the everyman. Similarly, in *PL,* all the questions and issues of good and evil*, obedience* and rebellion, are thrashed out at the intellectual and spiritual level in the opening books (the scenes in Hell* and the scenes in Heaven*). The reader is in a kind of pre-human, pre-carnate world before the Word has been made flesh, just as he is in the opening episodes of *Ulysses.* Then he comes down to earth, into the presence of the flesh-and-blood Adam and Eve, to find the same issues of good and evil, obedience and rebellion, worked out in an environment as richly packed, in terms of sensation and emotion, as that of Joyce's *Calypso* episode that opens Book 2. Coming down from the intellectualized world of Stephen Dedalus to Bloom's world of potent smell and touch and taste and sound is a parallel movement to the Miltonic one. Moreover, as in *PL,* it is the same issues that are worked over on the two balancing planes, intellectual and mundane. In the great scenes in the Garden of Eden there is much that illustrates and develops the theme of the corruption of good by evil, and that corruption is presented in terms of God's bounty and man's gifts betrayed and abused: moreover, it is presented on a level of rich sensuous awareness of the natural world and the physical responsiveness of the human being. In balanced anticipation of those scenes are the scenes in Hell and in Heaven where one sees, in the first place, the corruption of the good in terms of reason and intellect abused and eroded, and in the second place, the corresponding beauty of good in terms of intellect and reason fruitfully exercised. The Joycean balance between intellectualism and earthiness, on which the whole patterning of the Dedalus-Bloom relationship depends, reflects the Miltonic shaping of material. And of course the coming together of artistic and intellectual Dedalus and earthy, emotional Bloom represents a synthesis needed to make our civilization healthy and balanced—and it is to be related to a balance between the Hellenic and the Hebraic that the reader of Milton is bound to find especially interesting.

Milton's correspondences between the heavenly City, the earthly city that is (or should be) its image, and the hell that is its perversion have already been mentioned. By echoes of Revelation and the Song of Solomon, the New Jerusalem and the mystical Bride are paralleled with the idealized human femininity of Eve, as they are grotesquely parodied and perverted in the figure of Sin. An important link in the chain of correspondences is the parallel between the heavenly City, the human feminine ideal, and the Promised Land of man's earthly pilgrimage. There can be little doubt that Joyce was indebted to Milton in his handling of comparable themes, and attention may be drawn to two distinct strands in this indebtedness.

The first is that, though Joyce sends one spiraling down in Dantean fashion to the depths of his twentieth-century hell, when one gets there, the conception of hell realized is Miltonic as well as Dantean. It is essentially a parodic hell in which Zoe, the potential heavenly Bride turned harlot, is dressed in a sapphire slip with a bronze clasp in perverse imitation of the pure white "womancity" with its imagery of sapphire and bronze (*Ulysses*, 1961 ed., p. 477). It is likewise a parodic hell, a mock-up of the New Jerusalem, that is brought into being in the mind of Bloom-Everyman as he gives rein to his twentieth-century materialist-humanist daydreams in the depths of Nighttown. Bloom's mental entry into the *false* Promised Land (p. 483) (as distinct from his later Pisgah glimpse of the real one) is marked by the construction of the New Bloomusalem, the *Urbs Beata*'s parodic antithesis, in which there are electric dishwashers for all. "Tuberculosis, lunacy, war and mendicancy must now cease. General amnesty, weekly carnival, with masked licence, bonuses for all,

esperanto, the universal brotherhood. . . . Free money, free love, and a free lay church in a free lay state" (pp. 489–90).

This mock heaven, which is really hell, shows us the dreams of Milton's Mammon realized in a twentieth-century context. "For *Ulysses* is an inferno," McGreevy says, and he relates the wanderings of Ulysses, Aeneas, and Dante himself to Leopold Bloom's—"Mr. Joyce sent his hero through the inferno of modern subjectivity." The vision of the New Bloomusalem represents a peak point of that subjectivity.

The second strand in this particular indebtedness concerns the figure of Molly Bloom. Bloom's hunger for his wife is an aspect of Everyman's hunger for his earth-goddess, for his mother, for the warmth and security and fulfillment that earth can never permanently provide. Therefore it corresponds with man's idealized seeking for the everlasting Virgin Bride, and with his turning to Church and Madonna, mystical Bride and divine spouse. At one moment Molly corresponds to the mother country, at another to the Mother Church, at another to the Mother of the Son of Man. Similarly her infidelity to her husband may correspond now with Ireland's betrayal of her children, now with Eve's betrayal of Adam, and so—via a symbolic reading of *Hamlet*—with the betrayal by the frail, erring human flesh of the manhood it has mothered. Molly Bloom's symbolic status as first Eve and second Eve is important throughout. By one or two deft touches Joyce keeps the Miltonic correspondences in the reader's mind. For instance, the Promised Land of the Zionist's dreams and of Everyman's dreams is equated with the Ithacan homeland whose soil the returning Ulysses kissed with passion. It is equated with Molly's buttocks, the very basis of that earthy femininity, messy but fertile and abundant, whose demands the partly living everyman is evading. The imagery linking the melons of the Promised Land to the cheeks of Molly's buttocks is complex but persistent; and when the climax comes and Bloom gets a glimpse of the fruition he has sought, "the land of promise . . . posterior female hemispheres, redolent of milk and honey" (p. 734), and he kisses "each plump melonous hemisphere," the repeated emphasis on the word *hemisphere,* taken in the context of other allusions to Milton, suggests the related vision of ultimate fulfillment granted to Adam when Michael leads him up the Hill of Paradise

> from whose top
> The Hemisphere of Earth in cleerest Ken
> Stretcht out to the amplest reach of prospect lay.
> (*PL* 11. 378–80)

The correspondence becomes clearer and more significant when one appreciates Joyce's use of Milton's key phrase *hand in hand,* which in *PL* is charged with the full weight of universal associations—paradisal love and harmony, severance and disobedience and betrayal, repentance and redemption. No phrase crystallizes more of the poem's essence as a human story. And in *Ulysses* Joyce makes the phrase the concluding words of *Matcham's Masterstroke* (the divine Match-maker's Masterpiece), the prize-winning (Eve-winning) story from *Tit-Bits* (the collection of nourishing fragments, miniature baby food, in fact). The whole epic of human loss, betrayal, frustration, and recovery is summed up in some of Joyce's characteristically laden words. *"Matcham often thinks of the masterstroke by which he won the laughing witch who now, Begins and ends morally. Hand in Hand"* (p. 69).

It will be observed that Joyce's indebtedness to Milton is indicated frequently by nothing more than a single word or a brief phrase. Thus, for instance, the "blind stripling" of *Ulysses* is first seen as an apparently innocent and pathetic figure whom Bloom takes pity on and helps across the road through the traffic (pp. 180–181). Then Bloom directs him on his way. The stripling's mission is to tune up the piano, a symbol of betrayal in *Ulysses,* betrayal of reality to sentimentality, of real fulfillment to

pseudo-fillment in the *Sirens* episode, and associated at Bloom's home with the more active adulterous betrayal of man's household by the wife who fails to stay at her husband's side. *Stripling* is the only word in the text at the points in question that directs the mind to the complex correspondence with *PL.* Satan assumes the shape of a "stripling Cherub," and thus temporarily deceives Uriel, who directs him on his way (*PL* 3. 634ff.). It is some time later that Uriel notes the stripling's facial contortions, expressive of his real character as he ponders his vile plan (*PL* 4. 114ff.). Uriel's moment of realization is paralleled by the shock administered to the reader of *Ulysses* when the blind stripling first utters a sentence, after brushing against someone in the street: "God's curse on you, he said sourly, whoever you are. You're blinder nor I am, you bitch's bastard" (*Wandering Rocks,* p. 250).

There are two points to be made about this technique of verbal recall by which a single word or brief phrase can bring into view complex parallel situations from another work of literature. The first point is that it works by accumulation. A single instance, like the above, might be regarded as an interpreter's fanciful daydream, were it not that other comparable correspondences with Milton can be cited. It is the gradual accumulation of such instances that ultimately compels the reader to take the correspondences as part of a complex overall indebtedness.

The second point is even more important. Quite apart from the interest we take in Joyce's recalls of Milton, one should note that the technique of recall is itself a technique practiced by Milton. If Joyce's *hemisphere* or *hand in hand* are slight in themselves as the bases of such wide and profound correspondences with Milton, Milton's own *dense or rare* (2. 948) or his *living Saphire* and *living Saphirs* (*PL* 2. 1050, 4. 605) are slight in themselves as the bases of the profound correspondences they establish with Dante. Likewise Milton's word *adornd* (*PL* 2. 1049; 4. 634, 713) is in itself a slight means of recalling Revelation, but taken alongside many other decisive or less decisive recalls, its purpose in that respect is unmistakable. One might add that Milton's recalls of Virgil's *Aeneid* depend on comparably slight echoes (e.g., his use of *Part* and *contend*, *PL* 2. 528–31, to recall *Aeneid* 6. 642–44). But, as with Joyce, it is the accumulation of related echoes that gradually brings the Virgilian, Dantean, and Spenserian* worlds to bear on the detailed fabric of *PL*. In short, Joyce is indebted to *PL* for the technique he uses in recalling *PL*. The double indebtedness here is of immense significance. Since Joyce has made his technique of recall the prime means of giving universality to his study of twentieth-century life, and an important means of knitting together his material, one should not be surprised if (as seems likely from his admission in the letter quoted above) he directed Thomas McGreevy's attention to *PL* as the major English poetic achievement with which his own epic achievement should be compared. In thus attributing Joyce's technique of recall at least in part to Miltonic influence, one must bear in mind that T. S. Eliot's technique of recall is fundamentally the same. This raises the significance of all that is said about the Joycean indebtedness to a new level.

There is an aspect of Joyce's indebtedness to Milton that must be touched on with especial care because it concerns the parodic element in the work of the two writers, and if anything in literature has been more misunderstood than the parodic element in *PL,* it is that same element in *Ulysses.* The parodic element in *PL* is simply a logical reflection of the parodic element in the universe. If things earthly image things heavenly, things diabolical parody things heavenly. Hell is, of course, a mock heaven. Satan is a mock divinity (see how he goes into battle in parodic imitation of the Son, *PL* 6. 99ff. and 749ff.). All the devils are mock divinities and therefore fitly equated with the idols and false gods of paganism. But if Satan is a mock divinity, a parody of

Father* and Son*, with Sin his daughter, he is also *ipso facto* a mock hero, a parodic hero. He is that essentially by virtue of Milton's theological orthodoxy in this poem. He is not that by artistic blunder or literary neglect, or by inner humanistic or anti-hierarchical leanings on Milton's part. He is the parody of the epic hero by theological necessity and by virtue of the fact that Original Sin makes us all inclined to turn him into our "hero" through our rebellious wilfullness. The failure to discern the parodic aspect of Satan's heroic stance is partly due to moral weakness or ignorance and partly to atrophy of the sense of humor. Nevertheless, it is not difficult to share Milton's chuckles when Satan plays the epic hero, the Great Wanderer Returned, as he comes back to Hell from his adventure on earth and slips onto his throne in the diabolic council unseen (10. 441), or when he enjoys and endures the hero's reunion with long-lost members of his family, Sin and Death, in Book 2. But one needs to reckon with a comparable parodic vein in the descriptions of Satan's gigantic stature and gigantic arms. In the vast inflations that Milton writes here, there is, one may suspect, the source of a parodic vein much exploited in *Ulysses.* For the parodic element in *Ulysses* is as moral and rational as it is in *PL*. Bloom is paralleled with Ulysses, not in order to make Homer look silly, but in order to give Bloom, the twentieth-century everyman, the stature of the epic* hero. This is not parody. Satan is a mock hero to be laughed at, Bloom a genuine hero to be taken very seriously. But Joyce has learned from Milton's parodic treatment of the epic convention of inflation and has pushed the trick to uproarious lengths. One thinks, with a wry smile, of the great armor of Aeneas and Achilles when reading of Satan's moonlike shield and mastlike spear (*PL* 1. 286ff.). One thinks of them with a belly-laugh when reading in *Ulysses* of the Citizen's enormous handkerchief decorated with innumerable pictures, historical and topographical, from the four evangelists to the lakes of Killarney and Guinness's brewery (*Cyclops* episode, pp. 331–32). One must not forget that the gigantic inflations of *Ulysses* (in *Cyclops* especially), with their mammoth catalogues, uproarious in dimension and multifariousness, derive no doubt from Homeric and Irish origins in many cases, but Joyce's use of these devices in severe moral judgment upon the men of violence and hatred, by means of parody, is exactly parallel to Milton's use of them in the representation of devilry. Moreover, Joyce's larger adaptation of the classical structure and style, to a sphere of life superficially alien to the worlds of Homer and Virgil matches Milton's blend of classical and Christian traditions.

In the case of T. S. Eliot it is difficult to distinguish between direct indebtedness to Milton and indirect indebtedness through the influence of Joyce. One might be content to subsume Eliot's indebtedness to Milton wholly under Joyce's influence, were it not that Eliot himself has brought the question into the open by the references quoted above. Aware of the common musical bias revealed in Milton's work and in Joyce's work, the author of *Four Quartets* could scarcely be unaware of his kinship with both of them in this respect. Nothing has been said about Joyce's technique of literary recall and his verbal method of giving order to his vast survey of twentieth-century life that would not apply equally to Eliot. Here is the crucial link between Milton and Eliot, but it would seem impossible to detach Joyce from the connection. There is, however, one device much used by Eliot that makes his reader recall Milton without conjuring up the mediating figure of Joyce; for though the exploitation of heavily charged key words is a characteristic of all three writers, there is a particular habit of reiterating loaded monosyllables with persistent rhythmic emphasis in Eliot that inevitably throws the reader's mind back to Milton. The word *rock* is used five times in eight lines, then three times in six lines, in the first thirty lines of *The Waste Land* 5, and one can match this degree of repeti-

tion many times elsewhere, notably in *Four Quartets* with such words as *time, world, word, light,* and so on; and the practice recalls Milton's way of hammering at key words like *spite, fruit, blithe, mute, woe,* and so on. And there is another device common to Milton and Eliot which, because it is a metrical matter, has little relevance to Joyce. Milton's habit of giving a heavy rhythmic weighting to a key word at the beginning or the end of a line in such a way as to recall contexts elsewhere in *PL* in which the same word is used, thereby sharpening its usage with parallel connotative enrichment or conversely with ironic contrast, is a device familiar to Eliot's readers. The ironic potency of the word *adorned* at the end of *PL* 11. 280 is a case in point.

It is significant that Eliot uses this device in three ways: first, to make connections within a poem (as *Chill, Burnt Norton,* 132, pre-echoes "The chill ascends from feet to knees," *East Coker,* 162); second, to make connections from poem to poem in his own canon (as, for instance, the emphatic *Nothing, Waste Land,* 305, *The Fire Sermon,* recalls not only the *Nothing* of *Waste Land,* 120, 123, and 126, *The Game of Chess,* but also the subtly related "I could see nothing behind that child's eye" of *Rhapsody on a Windy Night*); and third, to make connections with the work of other poets. So, fittingly enough may be cited the emphatic *Homeward of Waste Land,* 221, *The Fire Sermon,* as an apt recall of diabolical stirrings and musterings, with their immense consequences on the human scene, through the emphatic *Homeward* at the beginning of *PL* 5. 688. Similarly the emphatic line-ending *perilously spread,* which follows three lines later, presses the associative link further. It rings a bell that the reader who knows his Milton is not free to ignore, firmly recalling a familiar accent in *PL* (cf. 4. 454; 5. 715, 880; 11. 343). Like Joyce, Eliot recalls Milton and uses Milton's technique of recall to do so.

The cumulative connotative enrichment of key words in Milton, Joyce, and

Eliot is a main means of giving pattern and order to their work. It is a device that can be fully exploited only over a big work, whether big in outward scale, like *PL* and *Ulysses,* or big in range and intensity, like *The Waste Land* and *Four Quartets.* Many distinct repetitions of the word *fruit* in Milton, *horse* in Joyce, or *word* in Eliot, are needed before these words gather to themselves their full connotative or symbolic value. New dimensions of meaning are continually added by cunning linkages formed through internal and external cross reference. Thus the association between these three writers here established is essentially bound up with the inner orderliness of Joyce's work and Eliot's work, with their interest in that character of the poetic art by which "it aspires to the condition of music." But our age has only slowly accepted *Ulysses* as exhibiting the splendor of order; and study of Eliot's key words and key themes is as yet at an early stage of development. These are some of the reasons why the close relationship of Milton, Joyce, and Eliot has not been advertised and why the major Miltonic influence on our time has been too little attended to.

The reader may think that certain obvious indebtednesses to Milton, even in Eliot, have been overlooked, but there are deeper obligations to Milton in twentieth-century literature than have yet been brought to light. No doubt *Murder in the Cathedral* owes much to *Samson Agonistes;* but David E. Jones points out (*The Plays of T. S. Eliot* [1960], p. 52) that the latter is a dramatic poem whereas "Eliot restored the full-throated chorus of Greek tragedy" to the living theater. Jones believes "Milton's adaptation of the Greek form to a Biblical theme" to be a "less radical transformation" than Eliot's fusion of Aeschylean tragedy and Christian theology. Nevertheless, Milton was the man who brought these two traditions together in our literature with supreme artistic effectiveness, and since the synthesis of classical and Christian has been a matter of such deep concern with both Joyce and Eliot, the shadow of Milton hangs large

over both of them. Joyce's own hell, the Nighttown of *Ulysses,* is a blend of the classical and the Christian. It is indebted comparably to Homer and Dante, but yet is reminiscent of *Mask* and *PL,* in which the blend is anticipated. The meeting of Dedalus and Bloom confirms the synthesis. "Jewgreek is greekjew. Extremes meet" (*Ulysses,* p. 504).

The image of the shadow of Milton hanging over Joyce and Eliot is peculiarly appropriate. *Lyc* is a much-quoted poem in *Ulysses,* its imagery of drowning and resurrection providing symbolic enrichment of these themes at many points. And it is the image of Christ as represented in *Lyc*—"Through the dear might of him that walked the waves"—that hangs over Stephen Dedalus's thinking like a shadow.

> Of him that walked the waves. Here also over these craven hearts his shadow lies and on the scoffer's heart and lips and on mine. (*Nestor,* p. 26)

There is a comparable inescapability about the shadow of Milton that hangs over Joyce and Eliot—and if over these two, then perhaps over the most significant literary output of the twentieth century. Eliot repeatedly allows for the overshadowing Miltonic presence, with fitting vagueness and persistence, in *Four Quartets,* and at last, with quiet pathos, leaves Milton and Joyce folded together in a single party as "one who died blind and quiet" (*Little Gidding,* 179). [HB]

INGULF (d. 1109), Abbot of Croyland (or Crowland), and secretary to William the Conqueror. His *Historia,* written to give support to the Abbey's land claims, was accepted as genuine by Milton and most other seventeenth-century scholars, although it since has been shown to have been an early fifteenth-century forgery. Milton used Ingulf's work as one of his sources in *Brit,* probably from the second edition of Sir Henry Savile's* collection *Rerum Anglicarum Scriptores Post Bedam* (Frankfurt, 1601). [WM]

INSPIRATION. The obvious importance of inspiration to Milton may be seen as early as his *El* 5, "On the Coming of Spring." Celebrating the return of spring, he also celebrates the return of his poetic powers, granted to him through the "bounty" of the "spring." The experience, as he describes it, is no less than ecstatic: "my soul is deeply stirred, is all aglow with mysterious impulses, the madness of inspiration and holy sounds stir me to my deeps within. . . . Now my mind is whirled up to the heavenly steeps, and, freed from my body, I move 'mid the roving clouds" (11ff.). Transcendent in nature, inspiration allows the disembodied poet, released from his physical confines, to have knowledge of what is holy to the gods, to envision what is ordinarily hidden from mortal sight. We find a similar idea in *Vac,* wherein the poet, singing of "secret things," will "soar" beyond "the wheeling poles, and at Heav'ns dore / Look in, and see each blissful Deitie / How he before the thunderous throne doth lie" (32–36).

As these lines suggest, inspiration exalts the poet: it provides him with powers that cause him to stand apart from other men. This posture of aloofness is precisely what emerges in Milton's distinction between two kinds of poets in *El* 6, "To Charles Diodati, now staying in the country." Whereas the writer of the "lightfooted Elegy" may allow himself "generous feasts" and frequent potations of "old, old wine" as sources of inspiration, he who would sing of things divine, "the holy counsels of the gods" and the infernal realms, must live sparingly: "let pellucid water stand near him, in a tiny cup of beechen wood, and let him drink only sober draughts from the pure spring" (49–62). In his purity, the poet should be like the priest, when "resplendent with holy vestments and with lustral waters," he arises "to go forth to face the angry gods" (65–66). "For the bard," Milton says, "is sacred to the gods, he is priest to the gods; the secret deeps of his soul, and his very lips alike breathe forth Jove" (76–78). The poet who aspires to wrote of divine things, then, may not allow himself the indulgences of the light-hearted elegist, who has Bacchus, Ceres, Erato, and Venus as his patrons. The priestly poet, on the other hand, must seek his inspiration not from pagan sources but from true celestial power.

That distinction, drawn by such writers as Scaliger* and Minturno*, is basic to Milton's concept of inspiration. Its pervasiveness in his writings may be seen, for instance, in *RCG,* in which Milton further clarifies his views concerning the nature of inspiration. On the one hand, he associates the "vulgar Amorist," the "riming parasite," and the "libidinous and ignorant Poetasters" with the "vapours of wine" and the "heat of youth" (3 : 239–41). On the other hand, he envisions the true poet as one who is inspired as the result of "devout prayer to that eternall Spirit who can enrich with all utterance and knowledge, and sends out his Seraphim, with the hallow'd fire of his Altar, to touch and purify the lips of whom he pleases" (3 : 241). We are, of course, made to think of Isaiah 6 : 6–7: "Then flew one of the seraphims unto me, having a live coal in his hand, which he had taken with the tongs from off the altar: And he laid it upon my mouth, and said, Lo, this hath touched thy lips." (See also *Nat,* 27–28.) As the allusion suggests, the biblical character of the inspiration to which Milton refers places the true poet within a prophetic context. Added to this is the idea, already touched upon in *El* 6, that the poet must live a pure life, tempered by self-discipline, "industrious and select reading, steddy observation, insight into all seemly and generous arts and affaires" (3 : 241).

The importance of such ideas to Milton's view of inspiration and its relation to the poetic process is nowhere more evident than in *PL.* There the various references to inspiration, apparent in the elegies and prose works, are explored in full. For example, the distinction between different kinds of inspiration receives renewed significance. Once again, that form of inspiration associated with the pagan world, especially as it is related to

Bacchus, is called into question. Thus, the poet in *PL* implores his Muse* to save him from the fate of the pagan poet Orpheus*, who was dismembered by the bacchanalian revelers (see Ovid's *Metamorphoses* 11. 1–60, and compare *Lyc* 58–63):

> But drive farr off the barbarous dissonance
> Of *Bacchus* and his revellers, the Race
> Of that wilde Rout that tore the *Thracian Bard*
> . . . nor could the Muse defend
> Her Son. So fail not thou, who thee implores:
> For thou art Heav'nlie, shee an empty dreame.
>   (7 : 32–39)

The Muse is Calliope, the mother of Orpheus and the pagan Muse of epic* poetry. Unable to save her son, she would be equally incapable of aiding the Christian poet, whose source of inspiration must be heavenly. Thus, Milton invokes Urania* (7 : 1), the Muse of astronomy, the meaning of whose name ("heavenly") emphasizes the divine nature of his inspirational source. "Following" her "Voice divine," he is able to "soare" above "th' *Olympian* Hill," above "the flight of *Pegasean* wing" (7 : 2–4). The effect of such inspiration on the poet may be seen if we explore in some detail the proems to Books 1, 3, 7, and 9 of *PL,* where Milton reveals the essential mediatorial roles he assumes as the result of being inspired.

We have already seen how the view of inspiration expressed in *RCG* associates the poet with the role of prophet. Similarly, in *PL*, Milton causes his inspirational source to place him within a prophetic context. To suggest the nature of his prophetic role, the poet associates himself with Moses on Horeb or on Sinai (1 : 7). Like Moses the Shepherd (1 : 8), who received inspiration from the burning bush on Horeb (Exod. 3), the poet is inspired by the divine light of God, invoked in the proem to Book 3. 1–6. Here, the poet in complete humility confronts the absolute center of his creative world, the complete antithesis of the darkness that characterizes the fallen environment. By means of this light, he will be able to transcend the darkness of his fall

and experience the creation of a new nature. From the Mosaic point of view, moreover, the image takes on additional overtones. As the burning bush was unconsumed, so God's light or "bright essence" is "increate," that is, not only eternal but existing totally by and through itself and creating its "bright effluence" out of itself. In that way, it becomes the unceasing and self-perpetuating source not only of wisdom and protection but of eloquence; for as Moses was "slow of speech" and then through God was inspired to speak eloquently (Exod. 4 : 10), so is the poet given the power to voice God's Word in order to deliver man from the bondage of his Fall*.

If Horeb represents the announcement of delivery, Sinai represents the fulfillment of delivery, at least as it typifies the final salvation through Christ. As God on Sinai spoke through Moses to prophesy "by types / And shadows" the coming of the "destind Seed" (12. 232–33), the poet likewise interprets God's will prophetically by revealing through types and shadows the entire course of human history. These are not, however, the only overtones suggested by the allusion to Sinai. Milton, in *CD* (15 : 299), associates the experience on Sinai with the kingly function, and *PL,* with its reference to the ordaining of laws on Sinai (12. 230), implies no less. In his kingly role, the poet acts as earthly guide by instructing man how to prepare himself in this kingdom for his existence in the next (see 12. 582–83). In accordance with that idea, the allusion to Sinai reinforces the allusion to Sion (1. 10). Like David, who wished to construct a temple for God's laws after Nathan was inspired at Sion (2 Sam. 7), the poet wishes his poem to reveal how man should conduct his temporal affairs (cf. Isaiah 2 : 3). The poet's kingly function, then, as it derives from the allusions to Sinai and Sion, is important to our understanding of how Milton places the idea of inspiration within a biblical context.

Of equal importance is the way he characterizes the poet's priestly role by means of his allusions to Siloam. Through the waters of Siloam, the poet will be inspired to sing of re-creation and eternal life. While, on the one hand, the spiritual effluence of God allows the blind poet to be prophetically inspired, the waters of Siloam purify the poet for his sacerdotal office. By associating himself with *"Siloa's Brook"* (1. 11, and 3. 30), the poet deliberately causes his "sacred Song" (3. 29) to suggest the character of one inspired by the "Oracle of God" (1. 12), the place of divine revelation. Despite his blindness, his song concerns renewed sight and the healing of blindness through Christ (1. 11–12). In the same manner that Michael cleansed the vision of fallen Adam so that Adam could experience the rebirth process culminating in the Savior, Jesus' baptismal cleansing of the blind man's eyes with the holy waters of Siloam (John 9 : 7) symbolizes the sacerdotal vision of rebirth that the poet receives. That idea of lustration is likewise implicit in Siloam's "flowrie Brooks" that "wash" the "hallowd feet" of Sion (3. 30–31). Replete with overtones of anointing in order to make sacred, the imagery suggests both the anointing of Christ's feet (Luke 7 : 38) and Christ's anointing of his disciples' feet (John 13 : 15). As we have seen, Milton's attitude toward such lustration is revealed in *El* 6, wherein the poet becomes a "priest" "resplendent with holy vestments and with lustral waters." Culminating in the allusion to Siloam, then, the poet's role has moved from the personal (prophet) to the worldly (king) to the divine (priest). In these three respects, the poet is inspired to carry out God's divine plan.

This, however, is only one means by which inspiration characterizes the poet's role in *PL*. Equally important are the metaphorical overtones that inspiration assumes. One might consider, for example, the sexual connotations implicit in the poet's relationship with his Muse. Their relationship suggests a metaphor of generative union in which the roles of male (poet) and female (Muse) are reversed. As Satan inspired Eve by whispering in her ear while she was asleep (4. 800), the

Muse inspires the poet by bringing her message "nightly" to his "Ear" (9. 47). The pattern of impregnation during sleep is repeated in the figures of Adam and Eve. Adam sleeps and then awakes to find Eve created out of him (8. 452–90); Eve sleeps and then awakes to find a paradise created within her because of the grace* of God (12. 606–14). Paradoxically, however, each figure is "wakeful" while he sleeps (Adam, for instance, visually experiences the creation of Eve despite the fact that he is asleep [8. 458–61]). The poet likewise is "awake," that is, aware of the inspirational process while he is asleep. As a metaphor for the poet, the "wakeful Bird" (3. 38) is always prepared for flight, always ready for inspiration. Within his hidden "Covert" (3. 39), the bird, like God (who in his secrecy never sleeps but is always watchful and who creates in the likeness of a bird) is "wakeful" the night long (4. 602–3).

What the creative process involves manifests itself partly in Milton's reference to the Muse as one who "dictates" to him "slumbring, or inspires / Easie" his "unpremeditated Verse" (9. 22–24). Clearly, these lines imply that man is not the cause of his own inspiration; rather, man (unlike God, who is the source of inspiration rather than the recipient of it) must be inspired from without. We would be mistaken, however, to interpret these lines as an indication that the poet's work is produced effortlessly. That, of course, is not the case at all. We know that Milton expended a great deal of labor and energy in the composition of his poem, and we recall from *El* 6 and *RCG* that Milton viewed the poet as one whose creations were the product of industry and self-discipline. These ideas take on paradoxical significance in *PL*.

There creativity assumes a sense both of effortlessness and of preparation and consideration. Paradoxically, Milton uses two distinct methods of representing the creative process: the spontaneous existence as if by magic with the spoken word and natural evolution through time. Both concepts are implicit in the proem to

Book 1 of *PL*. On the one hand, we see that the "Heav'ns and Earth / Rose out of *Chaos*" (1. 9–10), as if by a power inherent in the words as they are uttered. On the other hand, we discover a few lines later that the heavenly spirit for an indeterminate period "Dove-like satst brooding on the vast Abyss / And mad'st it pregnant" (1. 21–22). The significance of these occurrences for the poet may be seen by the fact that he experiences a similar situation, at once placed in the position of having his work produced effortlessly ("easily") as the result of inspiration, while likewise made to labor industriously to fulfill the exigencies of his craft.

That Milton embraced both aspects of the creative process appears from statements he makes concerning the nature of inspiration in the preface to *Bucer*. Casting himself in both roles, passive and active, he says: *"I could allege many instances, wherin there would appear cause to esteem of me no other then a passive instrument under some power and counsel higher and better then can be human. . . . [H]e who tries the inmost heart, and saw with what severe industry and examination of my self, I set down every period* [in *DDD*], *will be my witnes"* (4 : 11). Both points of view, therefore, were fundamental to his concept of the creative process.

If we explore the second point of view in some detail, we shall discover what thematic significance it has in further describing the poet's role in *PL*. The experience involving industry, labor, and self-discipline at least partly underlies the meaning of Milton's claim to forging for himself and for his poem a "Heroic name" (9. 40–41), one earned as the result of "the better fortitude / Of Patience and Heroic Martyrdom" (9. 31–32). Such are the characteristics of Milton's "adventrous Song" (1. 13), upon which Milton stakes all and through which he "attempts" what has never been attempted (1. 16). For the poet, that "attempting" is represented by his hazardous journey to the nether world, where he risks possible destruction. Nor would he be able to ascend from that world were it not for the aid provided by his Celestial Patroness. He is, then, able to "escape" the *"Stygian* Pool" (3. 14) because he has been "Taught by the heav'nly Muse to venture down / The dark descent, and up to reascend" (3. 19–20). Clearly, that descent has psychological connotations : it suggests the poet's dangerous descent into his own Chaos, into his own fallen nature and subsequent reascent as an aspect of the creative process. One thinks of Milton's description of Jesus' entering the wilderness in *PR*: "with holiest Meditations fed, / [He] into himself descended" (2. 110–11). Similarly, the poet's descent in *PL* suggests a meditative process by which the poet engages in the creative act. Like God, he is "brooding" (in both senses of the term) on the "vast Abyss" and making it "pregnant" (1. 20–21). Out of that pregnancy will arise his offspring, his poem.

But that event will not occur until the full import of the reascent is likewise experienced, for the poet reascends not to the realm of earth but to the realm of Heaven, as equally dangerous a venture as the descent. Thus, he addresses the Muse :

> Up led by thee
> Into the Heav'n of Heav'ns I have presum'd
> An Earthlie Guest, and drawn Empyreal Aire,
> Thy tempring; with like safetie guided down
> Return me to my Native Element.
> (7. 12–16)

In recounting the War in Heaven*, the poet has been permitted to view the timeless workings of a transcendent world, to behold in ecstatic vision the symbolic warring of good and evil* and the overcoming of evil by good. Through his Muse, he has been able to breathe the air of Heaven, that is, be heavenly inspired despite his earthly limitations. After the experience of that vision, he has been able to descend to his own limited environment, because again he has been guided in safety by his Muse. Such an experience brings us full circle to Milton's early ecstatic experiences expressed with genuine excitement in *Vac* and in *El* 5. It also brings us full circle in this treatment of inspiration, expressed here through the pattern of descent and reascent, in *PL*. (*See also* INSPIRATION, SEASONAL.) [ML]

INSPIRATION, SEASONAL. According to Edward Phillips, Milton stated that "his Vein never happily flow'd, but from the *Autumnal Equinoctial* to the *Vernal*," or, as John Aubrey* puts it, Milton's "Invention was much more free and easie in the Aequinoxes than at the Solstices; as he more particularly found in writing his Paradise lost." From such statements derives the tradition that Milton, subscribing to the theory of climatic influence, was most productive between the autumn and spring seasons. (Aubrey sugsuggests May as the time when Milton's creativity abated.) These assumptions were later called into question by John Toland*, who counters Phillips's statement by saying that one of Milton's "more judicious" friends informed him that Milton "could never compose well but in the Spring and Autumn." That assertion, in turn, was questioned by Jonathan Richardson*, who states : "*Toland* says he had been inform'd he wrote only in the Winter, but he does not believe it, for Sure 'twas a Mistake. for My Own Part I cannot comprehend that Either is Exactly True; that a Man with Such a Work [*PL*] in his Head can Suspend it for Six Months together, or but One; though it may go on more Slowly, but it must go On. This laying it Aside is contrary to that Eagerness to Finish what was Begun, which he says was his Temper."

Both Toland and Richardson are in agreement, however, in pointing to *El* 5, "On the Coming of Spring," as an indication that Milton's creativity took fire during the spring months. Their feelings are not unfounded, for in that elegy Milton writes, "Am I beguiling myself? or is strength coming back into my songs also, and have I, thanks to the bounty of spring, inspiration at my call? *Is* inspiration here, by the gift of spring, and is it again winning vigor from the spring —who would think it?—, and demanding now for itself some achievement, some creation?" (5–8). As Richardson says, "that Sweet part of the Year he certainly Lov'd, Everybody does, Those of a Poetical Turn are Remarkable for it, and He in particular . . . ; his Muse was used to Revive as the Vegetable World does at That Season, it did So when he was Young, as well as in his Advanc'd Years." In line with that view, Milton expresses concern over the possible deleterious effects that a cold climate might have on his creativity. Aware, as he says in *Mansus,* that his Muse was "nurtured but hardly 'neath the cold Bear" (28), he is still hopeful, as he wrote in *RCG,* that "there be nothing advers in our climat" to write a great poem (3 : 237).

Milton's sentiments are, at least in part, the product of a seventeenth-century commonplace, ultimately traceable to Aristotle's* *Politics* (7. 7), that cold climates have an adverse influence upon creativity. That the idea received full treatment in the Renaissance is evident in Bodin's *Republique* (5. 1), which contains an entire chapter on the matter, and in Giovanni Botero's *Relations of the Most Famous Kingdomes and Common-wealths throughout the World.* From works like these emerges the Renaissance consensus that the inhabitants of the colder northern countries of Europe tended to be deficient in the arts and learning and in politics. Habitually, the English thought of England as a northern country and of themselves as inhabitants of a cold climate.

Thus Milton states in *PL* :

> higher Argument
> Remaines, sufficient of it self to raise
> That name, unless an age too late, or cold
> Climat, or Years damp my intended wing
> Deprest.
>
> (9. 42–46)

Among the possible reasons why Milton's creativity might be thwarted, the coldness of the climate assumes a prominent position, especially as it is related to the passing of the years. In that relationship, Milton also suggests the association of the theory of climatic influence and the concept of the humours. Assuming that old age will bring "a melancholly damp of cold and dry / To weigh [man's] Spirits down" (*PL* 11. 544–45), Milton is just as afraid of the coming of cold melancholy with old age as he is of England's cold climate. His fears are quelled, however, by his faith in his Muse, the true source of inspiration*, whose permanence transcends limited considerations of seasons, climates, and human frailty. [ML]

IRETON, HENRY: *see* ASSOCIATES, POLITICAL.

IRONY: *see* PROSE STYLE; RHETORIC; SATIRE.

ITALIAN INFLUENCES ON MILTON. Italian literature was of decisive importance to Milton's poetry. It helped to shape his conception of the poet's task, guided him in the construction of his mature poems, and extended its influence to the very fabric of his verse. His relationship to Italian culture is an expression of his debt to Renaissance humanism*, which not only revived the study of Greek and Roman literature, but also made it an intrinsic part of the intellectual life of Christian Europe. The fascination Italy exerted over Milton springs also from his appreciation of the Italian language, and of music* (his lifelong feeling for these may have been given him first by his father, who was an accomplished amateur musician).

The importance Milton attached to his journey to Italy and the confidence he derived from his reception there are evident in the account he gives in *RCG*. His references to Dante*, Petrarch*, and Tasso*, and to Renaissance theory and practice, show that he granted the Italians an artistic authority equal to that of the Greek and Roman classics. This was of course the view of the Italians themselves, but it was accepted generally in Europe

until the nineteenth century. The importance for Milton of his own adherence to it was indicated, though casually, by Dr. Johnson*, and defined by W. P. Ker. But only in the last fifty years has the full extent of Milton's debt begun to be understood.

That Milton had the fondest recollections of Italy (and particularly of Florence) appears not only in his prose, but in the references to Valdarno and Vallombrosa in *PL* (1. 290ff.); in the Sonnets, both English and Italian; and perhaps even in the description of ancient Rome in *PR* (4. 80ff.). One of his personal links was through the Diodati* family, Protestants who had left their native Lucca (see Donald C. Dorian, *The English Diodatis* [1950]). Charles Diodati, the closest friend of Milton's youth, was a descendant of this patrician family. But Milton's Protestantism, though too outspoken to be welcome in Italy, did not prevent him from delighting in the friendship of many Catholic men of letters whom he met in Florence and elsewhere (see his letters to Buonmattei*, Lukas Holste*, and especially Carlo Dati*).

David Masson in 1859 gave a survey of the literary circles where Milton was entertained as a distinguished guest. John Arthos in *Milton and the Italian Cities* (1962) offers a more modern discussion of the culture he would have encountered in Florence, Rome, Naples, and Venice. In Part II, "Milton and Monteverdi," he reminds us that, according to Edward Phillips, the poet shipped from Venice "a Chest or two of choice Musick-books of the best Masters flourishing about the time in *Italy*"; he goes on to summarize theory and practice in the emerging Italian opera, and in Christian tragedy (particularly in Girolamo Bartolommei), arguing that there is a relationship between *SA* and *melodrama*.

It has long been recognized that *PL* is connected with *L'Adamo,* a poetic drama on the Fall* published by Andreini* in 1617 (it was translated in the eighteenth century by William Cowper*). *L'Adamo* retains much of the scope and allegorical* method of the cycles of medieval religious drama, which survived as *sacre rappresentazioni* in seventeenth-century Italy. Milton's first plans for treating the subject of the Fall (preserved in the *TM*) envisaged a drama, *Adam Unparadiz'd*, which would have shared some features with *L'Adamo,* though it would have been simpler and more severe in construction. Arthos has discussed at some length the relationship between *L'Adamo* and *PL,* in both *Milton and the Italian Cities* and in "Milton, Andreini, and Galileo" (in *Approaches to "Paradise Lost,"* ed. C. A. Patrides [1968]. In the latter volume F. T. Prince also considers the two works together, though from a different point of view).

In *Dante and Milton* (1966) Irene Samuel has shown that the *Divina Commedia,* though so completely different from *PL* in design, in style, and in its version of Christian orthodoxy, nevertheless offered Milton what no other poet, Italian, Greek, or Roman, could have done : deep and complex religious vision, projected into countless details of imagery*, action, and comment. For Milton Dante* and Petrarch* were, among other things, witnesses to pre-Reformation antipapal sentiment. The more narrowly "Petrarchan" influence appears in Milton's sonnets in Italian, but nowhere else in the whole body of his poetry (but see the reference to Beatrice and Laura in *Apol*). He draws on Ariosto's* comic and satiric imagination in creating his Paradise of Fools in Book 3 of *PL* and in the invention of gunpowder by the rebel angels in Book 6. He reveals his enjoyment of chivalric romance in allusions to it in both the epics; and admiration of the *Gerusalemme Liberata* may have led him to turn over the notion of an epic on King Arthur* longer than he would otherwise have done. The War in Heaven* has some general resemblances to *L'Angeleida* (1590) by Erasmo da Valvasone, including the use of cannon by the rebels. It was claimed in the nineteenth century, and by Norman Douglas ("On 'Paradise Lost,'" *Life and Letters,* vol. 58, no. 132

[August 1948]) that *PL* was influenced less by *L'Adamo* than by a similar work, Serafino della Salandra's *Adamo Caduto,* published in 1647; the question is unresolved.

Modern studies of Renaissance iconography have brought out a dimension of Milton's thought neglected by earlier scholars—his debt to Florentine Neoplatonism* (for example, in *IlP;* see R. Klibansky and others, *Saturn and Melancholy* [1964]). Milton makes splendid use of the classical mythology* that was exploited by so many Renaissance artists, and he does so in accordance with the tradition of Florentine mythography. But it is noticeable that he has no references to painting or sculpture. Of the visual arts he might have studied in Italy, only architecture seems to have interested him; and his evocations of Roman architecture, in the descriptions of Pandemonium* and of ancient Rome in *PR,* are set firmly in contexts from which he withholds approval.

Far more important than any other connection with Italy is the direct influence Italian poetic techniques had on Milton's verse. Following Spenser*, Milton drew partly on Italian models in his earlier poetry; but the Italian journey may have been the result of his feeling that he had more to learn that would be of use in the major works he aspired to. At any rate, the poetry of his middle and later years is more decisively stamped by Italian ideals of style.

His work as a whole is indebted in style and structure to three Italian verse forms : the *canzone,* the sonnet, and blank verse* (*versi sciolti*). All three, in the sixteenth-century modifications that gave most to Milton, are found in the work of Tasso*; and in the case of epic blank verse, Tasso's precepts and practice are of special importance. It will be convenient to discuss the bearing of the three Italian forms on Milton's work in an order based on the chronology of their first impact, beginning with the *canzone.*

The *canzone,* like the sonnet, was in origin a medieval lyric based on music,

Dante described it at some length in the *De Vulgari Eloquentia*. W. P. Ker (*Form and Style in Poetry* [1928]) pointed out the importance for English poetry of the harmony, praised by Dante, between eleven- and seven-syllabled lines (which become in English ten- and six-syllabled); and demonstrated the relevance of *canzone* form to Spenser's *Epithalamion*, *Lyc*, and later English odes*. The *canzone* can consist of one stanza, but more usually the stanza is repeated to make a poem of some length, which ends with a *commiato* or envoy. Lines of varying length (but limited normally to eleven and seven syllables) are one of the most obvious sources of musical effect. The stanza is made up of two main sections that are linked by a key line (*chiave*); this opens the second part of the stanza, and rhymes with the last line of the first part. Each of the two sections has its own internal symmetry; these subdivisions, and the main divisions of the stanza, were originally a framework into which the sentence structure was fitted, giving a distinctive movement and emphasis to different parts of the stanza. In the sixteenth century the desire for novelty and the influence of Latin poetry led to a greater fluidity of sentence structure, and eventually to stanzas constructed on new principles.

Milton's first major poem, *Nat*, derives from the *canzone* tradition, both as it was adapted by Spenser and as it was handled by Tasso. The first six lines of the stanza of the hymn have a shape favoured by Tasso (for example, in *Parafrasi dell'inno Stabat Mater*). But Milton's stanza recalls Spenser in ending with an alexandrine, and includes a line of eight syllables (alien to the *canzone*); it also allows for "cataleptic" rhythms in the shorter lines. An impulse to vary the line-lengths more widely than in the Italian runs through all Milton's poems that are related to the *canzone*.

However, *Circum* is an isolated attempt to follow Italian practice more closely. Ants Oras noted how near Milton's stanza is to that in Tasso's *canzone* to Our Lady of Loretto (see *Notes and Queries* 197 : 314–15); but Tasso had slightly altered a stanza that Milton followed exactly, that of Petrarch's *Vergine bella, che di Sol vestita*. The last two lines of Milton's stanza (written as one in *TM*) use the Italian device of *rimalmezzo* (see F. T. Prince, *The Italian Element in Milton's Verse*, pp. 61–63).

Circum is a short poem, and it is apparently the last except the songs in *Mask* and the psalm translations that Milton wrote in stanzas. He evidently preferred to develop the freer lyric forms we find in *SolMus* and *Time*. These two pieces recall the Italian practice of writing extended epigrams or inscriptions in the form of madrigals, the madrigal being a short, close-knit verse paragraph related to the *canzone* in its use of longer and shorter lines and interwoven rhymes. Tasso, Marino* (and Drummond of Hawthornden in English) offered Milton many examples. His own two poems are characteristic in varying the line-lengths (there are concluding alexandrines, and lines of seven and eight syllables), and developing a powerful forward movement by means of complex syntax (see J. B. Leishman, *Milton's Minor Poems* [1969], pp. 96–115).

In *Lyc* we see for the first time how Italian experiments could help Milton to re-create Virgil's* art in English. The framework for study of the classical and rich neo-Latin background is still James H. Hanford's study (*Publications of the Modern Language Association* 25 : 403–47). John Crowe Ransom interpreted the metrics of *Lyc* as a willfully broken version of *canzone* form (*American Review* 4 : 179–203). Ants Oras traced the rhyme schemes of the verse paragraphs to the madrigal as used by Bembo and Tasso (*Modern Philology* 52 : 12–22). Prince (pp. 71–88) tried to establish a connection between the technique of *Lyc* and the attempts by Italian sixteenth-century poets to adapt the *canzone* to pastoral* eclogue, elegy*, and drama. In the later sixteenth century the liberation of *canzone* rhythms and rhyme patterns emerges clearly in Tasso's *Aminta* and

Guarini's rival work, *Il Pastor Fido*. But earlier in the century the vernacular eclogues of Sannazaro and Berardino Rota show a stricter emulation of Virgilian effects, which is closer to Milton in spirit. These experiments often play off the sentence structure against the rhyme schemes, among which the *canzone* is prominent.

The metrics of *Lyc* keep closer to the *canzone* tradition than those of *SolMus* and *Time*. In a total of 193 lines there are only 14 shorter lines (usually of six syllables); they are all rhymed with an immediately or closely preceding long line. Six out of ten verse paragraphs conclude with a couplet. Ten lines, scattered throughout, are left unrhymed. The verse paragraphs are closely though irregularly rhymed, and the interweaving of rhyme patterns and sentence structure (that is, the relation of a new rhyme, or series of rhymes, to the beginnings and ends of sentences) strongly recalls *canzone* form. The movement associated with the *stanza divisa* and the *chiave* is felt throughout; yet there is no rigid or systematic application of these principles. If the key line is taken in its strict sense of one that rhymes with at least *two* preceding lines, Prince has overemphasized Milton's use of it (p. 86). But there is undoubtedly a "rhetoric of rhyme" (p. 85) deriving from the *canzone* tradition, where it is inseparable from the use of syntax; and this is the starting-point for the interweaving of sentence structure and rhyme patterns in *Lyc*, which so powerfully dramatizes the movement of thought and feeling. The concluding *ottava rima* is Milton's equivalent of the *commiato* in a *canzone*, as well as of the conclusions of some of Virgil's eclogues.

The lyrical and semi-lyrical parts of *SA*, though metrically more varied than *Lyc* and looking to different classical models, are also related to the sixteenth-century Italian liberated forms deriving from the *canzone*. Following his earlier bent, Milton extends the range of the line-lengths (which run from four syllables to twelve) and introduces an almost be-wildering variety of rhythmic effects, inspired by Greek verse. But the foundation of these structures is still laid with the help of Italian experiments: the dialogue and choruses of *Aminta* and *Il Pastor Fido*, and some versions of the Greek tragic chorus in Trissino's *Sofonisba* and Tasso's *Torrismondo*. Prince has argued (155–56)) that *SA* follows these dramas in distinguishing between speech and chant (but see Arthos, *Milton and the Italian Cities*, pp. 190–91): the Chorus can sometimes use speech (e.g., *SA* 326–29, 710–24), Samson can chant (80–109, 606–51). The use of rhyme is involved in this distinction, and indeed throughout the lyrical and semi-lyrical passages there is an application of that unmistakably Italian "rhetoric of rhyme," which is the clearest evidence that here Milton had not only Greek models in mind. Edward Weismiller in *The Lyric and Dramatic Milton* (ed. Joseph H. Summers [1965], pp. 115–52) has argued for some influence on the Choruses from Cowley's* *Pindarique Odes* (1656); this is the more likely in view of Milton's known esteem for Cowley. However, the Choruses* in *SA* are marked by what Dr. Johnson called Milton's "uniform peculiarity of diction," and this is related directly to Italian verse, as we shall see in examining the Sonnets and the epics.

John S. Smart's edition of *The Sonnets of Milton* (1921) first showed their direct relationship to the evolution of the sonnet in sixteenth-century Italy. Pietro Bembo (1470–1574) had revived the sonnet as a form that could be cultivated with all the refinements of humanist learning, though looking back to Petrarch. The sonnet became a medium for neoclassical experiment, and Giovanni Della Casa* (1503–1556) gave it a Virgilian and Horatian* grandeur of rhythm and diction. (Milton acquired a copy of Della Casa's *Rime e Prose* in 1629.) Tasso became an enthusiast for Della Casa's style, and sought to emulate and exploit it, not only in his Heroic Sonnets, but in the *ottava rima* of the *Gerusalemme Liberata* and the blank verse of his poem on the Creation. In his *Discorsi* Tasso illustrates the "magnificent" style proper to epic by means of many passages from Della Casa's sonnets.

Tasso's theory and practice account for the link between Milton's sonnets and the blank verse of *PL*. Smart pointed out that "As examples of his treatment of verse the sonnets stand midway between the simpler style of *Mask* and that of *PL* with its sentences 'variously drawn out from one verse into another. . . .' In his epic style he gains both beauty of sound and effective emphasis by an unexpected ending at an unusual part of the line, meter and meaning being separated or opposed, instead of being combined with monotonous uniformity" (p. 24). But Smart did not explicitly connect this prosodic development with the new complexity of word order that we find in the sonnets, which alone makes it possible.

The "magnificent" style is most apparent in the sonnets written from 1642 onwards, in which Milton made his own application of Tasso's idea of the Heroic Sonnet to the issues and events of the Puritan Revolution. The sonnets to Fairfax and Cromwell have that rugged grandeur for which Tasso uses the term *asprezza* (see Prince, pp. 39–40). Milton adapts devices common to Della Casa and Tasso : the abrupt opening with the name of the person addressed, extended as an apostrophe by means of long subordinate clauses (four lines for Fairfax, eight and a half for Cromwell); the contrast between long sentences and short, terse phrases; the suspension of the meaning by inversions of the "normal" word order; and the addition of strong pauses within the lines, to the emphasis on line-endings obtained by full-sounding rhymes. The sonnets on the Piedmontese Massacre and "When I consider how my light is spent" show a greater freedom than even Della Casa allowed himself, in the way the sentences run over the subdivisions of the sonnet, and in the frequency of strong pauses within the lines.

The earlier group of sonnets, both in English and in Italian, show Milton's deliberate acquisition of mastery of the form. *Sonn* 1 is dated variously between 1627 and 1629; *Sonn* 7 may now be dated December 1632. Between them, in the poet's own arrangement, are placed the six pieces in Italian. *Sonn* 1 begins with a reminiscence of Bembo (*O rosignuol, che'n queste verdi fronde*); it is not markedly Italianate in diction, but it establishes the pose of Milton as lover and poet that continues in the poems in Italian. Sergio Baldi has studied these minutely (*Poesie italiane di Milton* in *Studi Secenteschi* 7 : 103–30); and he brings together in his commentary numerous verbal parallels from Italian sonnets that Milton might have known. Baldi is inclined to put the date of composition between 1627 and 1630, but suggests that the poems might have been revised and improved after Milton's journey to Italy, and before their publication in 1645; this would account for their "almost unexceptionable" (p. 104) use of the language. Mario Praz had already seen in these poems "a profound knowledge of Bembo's style" (*Rapporti tra la letteratura italiana e la letteratura inglese,* in *Letterature Comparate* [1948], p. 168). Baldi's investigation leads him to conclude that their language is that of "the Petrarchism of the Cinquecento as a whole," running from Bembo's *Rime* to Tasso's; and that Tasso is "the major source of Milton's poetic language" (pp. 112–14). Milton's exercises in this Italian poetic idiom undoubtedly furthered his command of the sonnet. Prince has argued that a new skill appears in the phrasing and syntax of *Sonn* 7 (pp. 91–97).

Milton's epic blank verse which includes that of *SA* differs significantly, not only from his own highly wrought blank verse in *Mask,* but from all previous blank verse in English. His own statement on this "*English* Heroic Verse without Rime," prefixed to the second edition of *PL,* was prompted by the bewilderment of many readers : it refers to the unrhymed verse of Homer and Virgil, but also to the modern example of "some both *Italian* and *Spanish* poets of prime note." Tasso was in fact the Italian poet who contributed most to the verse and diction of *PL*. For Milton, he had the authority of both Renaissance art and Christian aspiration; and he was the nearest in time of the great Italians, a major poet whose former patron, Manso*, Milton could seek out on his Italian travels (see *Mansus,* with its prefatory note referring to Tasso). Yet Milton's debt to Tasso is not to his masterpiece, the *Gerusalemme Liberata,* but to other aspects of his work; and, where blank verse is concerned, to Tasso's theory as much as to his practice. The *Discorsi dell'Arte Poetica* (1587) put forward the epic poem as the highest object of a poet's ambition, and define the "magnificent" style proper to it. The *Discorsi del Poema Eroico* (1594) give long and detailed prescriptions for the attainment of such "magnificence." The style should aim at *asprezza* (difficulty or "roughness") by means of complex diction and slow-moving rhythms. Tasso recommends long-drawn-out sentences, in which the sense is suspended; and for this purpose he says the poet should depart from the word order (and the vocabulary) of common usage. The verses should be "broken up and enter into one another" (i.e., the sentences and phrases should not be in conformity with the beginning and ends of the lines), and their movement should be slowed down by various verbal devices : elision or its opposite (the coming together of open vowels with a hiatus left between them), and the placing of words with heavy consonantal terminations at the line endings. Tasso gives quotations from Dante, Petrarch, and others to exemplify all these devices; many of his illustrations are drawn from Della Casa, whom he regards as the first Italian poet to aim consciously at "magnificence." (It is assumed throughout the *Discorsi* that the ultimate models of epic magnificence are Homer and Virgil.)

According to Praz, the precepts of the *Discorsi,* "which Tasso usually put on one side when inspiration visited him . . . were followed methodically by Milton"

(*Rapporti,* 168–69); and Tasso's influence on the style of *PL* was a matter of "his theories" rather than of "his effective example" (see "Milton and Poussin," in *Seventeenth Century Studies Presented to Sir Herbert Grierson* [1938], pp. 194–97). Certainly the *ottava rima* of the *Gerusalemme Liberata* did not easily accommodate the new "magnificence"; there Tasso's *parlar disgiunto* often seemed contorted and pretentious. Prince has tried to show that the stylistic devices displayed in the *Discorsi* could find their full scope and structural value only in blank verse, not in the rhymed stanza of the Italian romantic epic, which had a valid structure of its own. Tasso's most considerable attempt to write in the epic style is therefore found in the blank verse of his last long poem, *Le Sette Giornate del Mondo Creato* (printed 1607). Here "magnificence" could expand more freely, and justly itself also by functioning as a structural factor in the verse. While the poem is inferior to Tasso's best work, it offers an unmistakable model of Milton's "*English* Heroic Verse without Rime," both in its diction and in its prosody (Prince, pp. 50–57).

If the above account of Milton's blank verse is accepted, it follows that his prosody cannot be understood if it is studied without reference to his diction: both are structural forces, interrelated and interdependent. Such studies as those by Robert Bridges (*Milton's Prosody* [1921]) and S. E. Sprott (*Milton's Art of Prosody* [1953]), admirable as they are, are based on a theoretical abstraction, the single line of verse : they assume that its mechanics can be detected and defined, the scansion measured, by something like a scientific investigation of physical phenomena. But prosodic analysis of this kind has never yet come to grips with quantity in English, and still less with meaning, or syntax, as a force at work both in single lines and in whole series of lines.

Tasso in the *Discorsi* makes no distinction between those features of a poem which Bridges would consider strictly prosodic (elision, or synalaepha) and those which are usually regarded as rhetorical devices (for example, word order, the relation between lines and sentences, or the use of clustered consonants). Milton's own note on "The Verse" of *PL* seems to endorse just such a solidarity as Tasso assumes between verse and diction*. Indeed, Milton's "apt Numbers, fit quantity of Syllables, and the sense variously drawn out from one Verse into another" could cover exactly the same range of devices as Tasso covers.

"Apt Numbers" could mean the decasyllabic line, combining stress and syllable; "fit quantity of Syllables" could mean the weighting of the rhythms by both elision and synalaepha, and the exploitation of quantity (including consonantal effects); and "the sense variously drawn out" naturally covers both syntax and word order, and the use of pauses within the lines. If, as seems likely, there are now to be attempts to analyze Miltonic verse by means of statistical methods, investigators should realize that *all* these aspects and features will have to be taken into account, and related to one another, and to the whole effect. [FTP]

ITALIAN JOURNEY. During most of 1638–39 Milton was traveling on the Continent, for the most part in Italy, accompanied by one manservant. Aside from some few records that have been found, a few personal letters from and to Milton, and poems written during the period or associated with it, information about the journey comes from Milton's biographical account in *2Def.* The early biographers* derived their knowledge of these years from Milton's own summary. Around April 1638 Milton began to prepare for his trip, as we learn in a letter from Sir Henry Wotton*, dated April 13. Wotton had been James I's* ambassador at Venice and was now at Oxford. Milton spoke with Wotton around April 1, and sent him a letter, which is not extant, on April 6. Wotton advised Milton to visit Paris and sent him a letter of introduction to Michael Branthwaite* there. Branthwaite would be able to aid Milton

in further planning his itinerary through Italy. Wotton suggested that Milton proceed through Marseilles, then by sea to Genoa, and then to Tuscany, that is, to Florence and Siena. A postscript implies that Milton's departure from England was imminent; it is therefore dated April or May 1638. (The original letter has disappeared, but an eighteenth-century copy is known, and Milton printed it as an introduction to *Mask* in the 1645 *Poems.*) According to an undated letter from Henry Lawes* to Milton, found with Milton's *CB,* Lawes acquired a passport for Milton.

In Paris Milton met John, Viscount Scudamore*, whose son was being tutored by Branthwaite. Through Scudamore, he met Hugo Grotius* and received letters to English merchants along his route. He proceeded to Nice, then to Genoa, Leghorn, and Pisa. He was apparently in Florence (a prime target for his journey) by June 28 (July 8) when he seems to have visited the Svogliati Academy. He may have been elected to the Academy on July 5 (15). He says he stayed in Florence for about two months, though it was closer to three (July–September). Many whom he met there became good friends, for example, Carlo Dati*. At the Academy he recited poems from memory, apparently in Latin, "trifles" he had written before he was twenty, to the praise of his hosts. The encomia from his Italian friends prefacing the Latin poems in the 1645 edition (except for Manso's*) may have been written about this time or during his second sojourn in Florence. Another tribute may have been the gift of *La Tina,* sonnets written by Antonio Malatesti* in the year before. They seem to have been published first in the mid-eighteenth century. In *An Essay upon the Civil Wars of France . . . And also upon the Epick Poetry of the European Nations from Homer down to Milton* (London, 1727), Voltaire* alleged that Milton saw here a performance of Andreini's* *Adamo;* in a revision he placed the city as Milan. Milton also visited Galileo*, perhaps at Arcetri, outside Florence, as Alfred Stern* conjectured (1, i, 276), or at Vallombrosa according to various local traditions. A letter to Benedetto Bonmattei*, dated September 10 (August 31?), exists, and there is a record at the Academy of Milton's having read a Latin poem in hexameters on September 16 (6?).

Next Milton went to Siena and then to Rome, where he stayed perhaps during October and November. Here he met Lukas Holste* and Giovanni Salsilli*, to whom he wrote a poem in November. French also dates Milton's meeting with Cardinal Barberini* and his attendance at a concert at the palace at this time although more probably these events occurred during Milton's return visit in February 1639. Milton was entertained at the English College on October 30 (20?). Discussions in Rome often concerned religion.

He progressed to Naples, where he met Manso, around December. Manso wrote a distich praising Milton, which is printed in the 1645 *Poems,* and Milton composed *Mansus,* which he sent to his host. He entertained the thought of traveling to Sicily and Greece, but hearing news at the docks of the civil disorders in England, he decided to forgo this and to retrace his steps through Italy as apparently originally planned. Milton's remarks in *2Def* about the rejection of the trip to Sicily and Greece and his subsequent continued stay in Italy have frequently been misinterpreted—largely, it seems, because of a lack of attention to the Latin (see Rose Clavering and John T. Shawcross, *Studies in English Literature* 5 : 49–59).

Before leaving Naples sometime in January and returning to Rome for about two months, Milton reports that he was warned of plots against him by English Jesuits in Rome because of earlier remarks on religion. Tradition has it that he met Andrew Marvell* in Rome, although Marvell seems not to have left England before 1642. Again he saw Holste and heard Rospigliosi's *Che soffre speri* at the Barberini palace, visiting with the Cardinal on the following day. He also

heard Leonora Baroni* sing and wrote three epigrams to her. It is unlikely that she sang at the Barberini palace even though tradition has often alleged this to be true. In March Milton was again in Florence, where he read at the Academy on March 17 (7?) and March 24 (14?). He wrote to Holste on March 29 (19?) and attended the Academy on March 31 (21?). Around this time Milton also visited nearby Lucca, the ancestral home of the Diodatis* and of Italian Protestantism.

Moving northeast, Milton crossed the Apennines, passed through Bologna and Ferrara, and arrived in Venice, where he remained a month, probably April and part of May. Books that he had accumulated were shipped home from Venice, a common procedure. Phillips tells us that some were music books, including Monteverdi. An important English embassy and thus community existed in Venice at this time. From Venice Milton moved toward England overland by going through Verona, Milan, Lombardy, and by crossing the Pennine Alps and Lake Leman, to Geneva. He was in Geneva by early June. Here he stayed with the noted theologian John Diodati*, his friend Charles's uncle. He wrote in the album of Camillo Cardoyn on June 10 (May 31?). From Geneva he returned to England through France, retracing his route out. When he arrived back in England is uncertain. In *2Def* he says it was "a year and three months, more or less" from the time of his departure, or around the end of July; and adds that this was almost at the same time that the second Bishops' War was begun. The second Bishops' War began around August 20. Thus we may assume that the return was about the beginning of August, which would be "almost at the same time."

One further question hangs over the Italian journey; that is, when did Milton learn of Charles Diodati's death, which the headnote to *EpDam* says occurred when he was abroad? One conjecture has been in Naples at the end of December 1638 in letters delivered there; but the indefiniteness of the itinerary and the short period of four months since the death seem to throw this into doubt. The trip to Lucca in March (?) has been read as being provoked by knowledge of Diodati's death. Another conjecture has been in Venice in April since it was normally the last port in Italy visited by traveling Englishmen before their return. The trip to Geneva and sojourn with John Diodati has been read as reflecting knowledge of Diodati's death. Or it is possible that Geneva was originally on Milton's itinerary and that he learned of Diodati's death from his uncle. (See Clavering and Shawcross for fuller discussion and references.) [JTS]

ITALIAN POEMS. Milton's Italian poetry consists of *Sonn* 2–6 and the *Canzone* (between *Sonn* 3 and 4), composed probably 1629–30 and first published in the 1645 *Poems*. The poems are generally regarded as a group; *Sonn* 1, "O Nightingale," and 7, "How soon hath Time," are linked to them as a kind of prologue and epilogue (see F. T. Prince, *The Italian Element in Milton's Verse* [1962], p. 96).

Sonn 2 addresses a lady, "Donna leggiadra," in the periphrastic manner of Italian poets; the references were deciphered by J. S. Smart (*The Sonnets of Milton* [1966], pp. 121ff.), who deduced that the lady's name was Emilia. The poem describes her eyes and her dulcet voice. *Sonn* 3 begins with a long simile of a shepherdess at evening watering a foreign plant, uneasy in its new surroundings, and compares to this the effects of Love on the speaker—moving his tongue, producing "a new flower of foreign speech." Both 2 and 3 end with a glance at divine love and express the fear that worldly love may become entrenched in the speaker's heart. The *Canzone* describes how young men and women mock him for his daring use of an unknown tongue to tell of his love : he ought to be looking to other banks, other streams, a different laurel; in response, he alleges that what he speaks is the language of love—"Questa

è lingua di cui si vanta Amore" (a line Carducci thought worthy of Dante and Petrarch).

In 4, addressed to Diodati*, the speaker confesses that he has indeed fallen in love—with a strange, exquisite beauty, a "new idea" of beauty, so powerful that he cannot successfully defend himself against it. *Sonn* 5 describes the woes of the smitten lover; both poem and speaker are overpowered by Petrarchist conventions. The final poem avers that, though he is a naive, plain lover, his character is sterling and strong, his heart is armed "with solid adamant."

The date of composition remains uncertain. Educated guesses by Masson and others linked the six poems to the Italian journey, but this hypothesis had to ignore Diodati's death and could not account for *Sonn* 4, the setting of which is clearly England. Since Smart's extended study, the general consensus has been ca. 1629, though E. A. J. Honigmann disagrees in his *Milton's Sonnets* (1966). But all attempts at dating remain conjectural; the guesses are based generally on other guesses. There are no persuasive reasons not to accept 1629–30, perhaps with Sergio Baldi's inventive modification that the poems may have been revised during the Italian journey (*Studi secenteschi* 7 : 103–30).

In the fullest and best study of these poems, Baldi bases his suggestion mainly on the remarkable control of language that Milton shows in these poems—the very point on which many critics have underrated Milton's accomplishment. Baldi shows that Milton's verses are comparable to the *canzionieri* of Petrarch*, Bembo, and Tasso* read in sixteenth-century editions and not "in the most accurate modern texts." He compares them with the works of minor Italian poets of the *Cinquecento* and with the Italian poetry written in England early in the seventeenth century by Italians or by Englishmen who were "masters of Italian" and finds a remarkable "linguistic maturity" in Milton.

Baldi's detailed study demolishes the

view that Milton's Italian, while more or less correct, suffered seriously from inevitable infelicities of prosody and style*. As Shaw and Giamatti remark, independently of Baldi, "Milton's mastery of the language is amazing!"—particularly for a young man of twenty-two "who had never yet been away from his own country" (*Variorum* [1970], 1 : 375).

The poems suggest broadly Milton's interest in Bembo, Della Casa*, and Tasso*, as well as in Petrarch. Milton purchased the Venice 1563 edition of Della Casa's *Rime et Prose* in December 1629 (H. F. Fletcher, in *The Intellectual Development of John Milton* [1961], 2 : 301–4, describes the volume, which includes Dante's* *Amoroso Convivio* and Varchi's *Sonetti*). His knowledge of Tasso, "illustrious Italian poet" (*2Def* 8:125), is evident from many direct references. Bembo is a more elusive figure, but the evidence of allusions, particularly as adduced by Baldi, argues that Bembo wielded a larger influence on the Italian poems than did Petrarch (Smart's view) or Della Casa (as Prince believes). The Petrarchan strain is felt, in other words, by way of the Bembist influence.

At first sight, the poems appear Petrarchan in several respects—the general theme of love, the recurrent conventions, the complications of human love in tension with divine, and the specific form that the sonnet takes in this group. The versification deserves particular mention. Working in the basic "Petrarchian stanza" (12 : 322), Milton varied the sestets : 2 and 6 rime CDEDCE while 3, 4, and 5 rime CDCD EE. But this latter "Petrarchian stanza" is also peculiarly Miltonic; this early in his career, Milton adopted the Tassonian precept of "*the sense variously drawn out from one Verse into another*" (2 : 6), breaking through the Petrarchan practice to a greater extent than Bembo or Della Casa did. Even in the three sestets formed by quatrain and couplet, Milton overrides the prosodic boundaries, eschewing English practice and modifying Italian models.

The *canzone,* relatively rare in English verse (Spenser's* *Epithalamion* and *Prothalamion* are striking exceptions), was the oldest Italian lyric form, popularized by the *dolce stil nuovo* poets, dominant in the fourteenth century, and revived and widespread in the sixteenth. Characterizing it as the noblest form of song, Dante defined it (*De vulgari eloquentia* 2. 3—a *congiunzione* of stanzas, each stanza a *compagine* carefully organized) and Petrarch enlarged its scope to include moral and political subjects. The *canzone* ordinarily consisted of a series of stanzas in hendecasyllabics interspersed with shorter lines, fully rhymed and complexly ordered, and concluding in a short stanza, the *commiato* or *envoi*. Only occasionally is it found in single-stanza form. Milton's *canzone* consists of fifteen lines, concluding with the three-line *commiato*, and so has puzzled scholars, who have called it a *ballata,* a madrigal, or, reasonably, a *stanza di canzone.* Carducci, recognizing the young poet's vigorous independence and untroubled by the unusual form, praised "this short Italian canzone."

Interpretation of the poems has generally been slight. Most commentators and scholars have regarded them merely as insignificant love poems, autobiographical* excursuses, or linguistic exercises, or some combination of these. The biographical approach is tenuous at best, as the dating problem itself suggests; here, speculation must build only on speculation. Cleanth Brooks and J. E. Hardy, doubting the lady's existence, have suggested as theme the "poet's consciousness that his medium is foreign" (*Poems of Mr. John Milton* [1951], pp.148f.). In an ingenious but inconclusive argument, John T. Shawcross has attempted to give primacy to a larger theme of divine love operating in the poems (*University of Windsor Review* 3 : 27–33).

The theme of love itself is less evident in the poems as a group than are the interlocked questions of the speaker's relationship to love, his relationship to language and the poetic art, and his vocation as poet. The first poem, "Donna leggiadra," develops the Renaissance

Neoplatonist* motifs of beauty and its power ("virtù") to inspire love—and therefore love's potential danger, against which the speaker seeks divine aid. In this poem, the fascination with speech and expression—to recur throughout the poems—is strong; it is supported by the image of the ears, an image that returns in *Sonn* 4, where the persona feels more deeply the perils of love's language.

The persona is also fascinated with his power as word-maker. In *Sonn* 3, he imputes to himself a nimble tongue ("lingua snella" : the phrase is quite unusual, as Baldi points out), and this fascination is intensified by self-consciousness, the fact of dealing with "strania favella" (foreign speech) in which he is "dal mio buon popol non inteso" (not understood by my good countrymen). Free of convention and attractively original, *Sonn* 3 leads to elusive complexities. The simile points up the problem : the persona can hardly be like the shepherdess; rather, the parallels must be between the shepherdess and love, the watering and the new flower quickened by Love, the rugged mountain and the poet's nimble tongue (by implication, neither is *really* appropriate to the fragile flower), and the unfamiliar clime for the plant and for love's flower. These parallels are extended by the final lines on the Divine Gardener and the persona's slow heart, and the hope that He may (though not certainly) bring forth good from His planting there.

Despite the spiritual and vocational problems uncovered in 3 and emphasized by the opening words of the *Canzone* —"Ridonse donni e giovani amorosi" (amorous young men and women)—the persona plunges on. He persists in the face of the truth his friends utter and repeat, that his real aim must be "L'immortal guiderdon d'eterne frondi" (the immortal guerdon of deathless leaves) (echoed perhaps in "fair Guerdon" and *"Fame* is no plant that grows on mortal soil," *Lyc* 73, 78), the plants of "altri rivi/Altri lidi" (other streams, other shores) (see again *Lyc* 174). The speaker's serious, almost solemn proclamation at the end—"il suo dir è il

mio cuore" (her words are my heart) and "Questa è lingua di cui si vanta Amore" (this is the language that Love boasts about)—contrasts sharply with this underlying truth that he would like, for the moment, to forget.

Sonn 4 opens with a brilliant Virgilian allusion, "Quel ritroso io ch'amor spreggia soléa" (I, that stubborn one who used to laugh at love) echoing the "Ille ego qui quondam" of Renaissance editions of Virgil and Annibale Caro's translation (published posthumously in 1581), "Quell' io che già tra selve. . . ." While in that famous if now excised passage the poet of the *Aeneid* was announcing his ascent from lower to higher things, Milton's "ritroso io" has now fallen—"Già caddi." Language has largely accomplished this fall, though it goes further than that, as the concluding elliptical metaphor suggests. He would like to believe that "Amor" is the vision of True Love seen by Socrates or by Castiglione's Bembo (*Il Cortegiano* 4) and calls it "nova idea" and "Pellegrina bellezza che'l cuor bea," but the lady's singing could draw the laboring moon (see Virgil, *Bucolics* 8. 69 and *Georgics* 2. 478). Against this enchantment, he might protect himself as Odysseus did against the Sirens' song, but the fire sparked by her beauty would still consume him.

Sonn 5 develops out of this subtle image. Most commentators have rightly viewed 5 as a melange of conventions, lacking originality. The poem is highly artificial. In context, however, the very banalities are to the point. The heavy phrases and images are cloying in themselves; the point is that the persona's condition is accurately and even devastatingly portrayed here by his floundering attempts to immerse himself in the love tradition. The most derivative of the six poems, this one exposes the persona as he tries to surrender to the condition of Petrarchist lover.

The final poem recovers from that condition. Damp ardor, burning cold, teary nights yield to the person himself. (*Sonn* 6 has been called the most "Miltonic" of the group.) The persona's self-portrait is framed by a modest, restrained, unconventional address to the lady. The portrait itself demolishes the momentary infatuation of *Sonn* 5, the balmy picture of would-be lover dolefully trying to learn his art. The portrait is assertive and daring in scope and in articulation. The persona emphasizes both a sense of worth and the sounding lyre; he can state directly that his heart is not soft but hard, disciplined, and suited for large tasks, that he is free from chance or vulgar hopes or fears. Though the infatuation did indeed reach him, his word is not gracefully love-poetic.

The various conflicts in the poems are generally resolved by *Sonn* 6. Probing love, language, and vocation, by way of the conventional and useful fiction of Emilia, subject at times to irony, the persona emerges his own man and may now go on "to fresh woods and pastures new." While the accomplishment is not great and these are minor poems, they are more than linguistic exercises. So far as we know, Milton wrote no other Italian verse, perhaps because the language did not appear to have the universality necessary. But in the poems we have, Milton is already the bold experimenter, attempting the language and the demanding form of the Italian sonnet, mastering them, and then moving on, all the while developing the style that is uniquely his own. In one sense, at least, the poems may indeed be viewed as autobiographical. The probing of the poetic life in these poems fits well with the probings in *Lyc* as well as in *El* 6, and in the largest terms of language and style the road leads, as Prince has observed, to *PL*. [MADC]

ITHURIEL. The angel* Ithuriel appears in only one episode of *PL*. He and Zephon detect Satan "Squat like a Toad, close to the ear of *Eve*" (4. 800), and Ithuriel brings the devil back to his proper form with a touch of his celestial spear. The two conduct Satan to their leader, Gabriel, commander of the angelic guard over Eden. Ithuriel's spear is a frequently used metaphor in later literature for miraculous action. The Hebrew of Ithuriel means "discovery of God," and the name does not appear in either the Bible or the Pseudepigrapha. It does appear obscurely as of an angel in some cabalistic works of the sixteenth century, but they have no evident connection with Milton's use. The role of Ithuriel and his partner seems, aside from their slight service to the plot, to be that of foils for Satan. Their moral serenity and steadfastness in the face of his effort to subdue them by scorn and the assertion of his rank contrast with his despairing fury. These youthful good angels, says Irene Samuel, when matching Satan's scorn with scorn of their own, do it without anger (*Dante and Milton*, p. 179). Satan is, of course, by far the more "human" and moving character; his contrast with these innocents of God, who humiliate him with their notice that his brightness is diminished, helps build our sense of his ruin. [RHW]

IVEMAY, JOSEPH: *see* INFLUENCE ON THE LITERATURE OF NINETEENTH-CENTURY ENGLAND, MILTON'S.

JAMES I (1566–1625), King of England from the death of Elizabeth (1603) to 1625, and author. Milton's initials and notes were reported to be in a copy of James's *A Remonstrance . . . for the Right of Kings . . . against an Oration of the Cardinal of Perron* (French, *Life Records*, 5 : 127). The poet makes frequent mention of King James in his work. In his early poems *QNov* and "In Proditionem Bombardicam," Milton refers to "good King James" as "blessed" and as "bringer of peace." His attitude changes, however, by the time of the political tracts; he accuses Charles* of learning kingcraft and religious principles from his father James (*Eikon* 5 : 181), and Milton says James would not put confidence in God (5 : 196). Milton goes so far as to suggest openly uncertain paternity for James (*1Def* 7 : 141). [WM]

JANE, JOSEPH: *see* ANTAGONISTS.

JANSSEN, CORNELIUS: *see* PORTRAITS.

JAVELLO, CHRYSOSTOM: *see* PROLUSIONS.

JEFFREY FAMILY: *see* BIOGRAPHY.

JENNENS, CHARLES: *see* ADAPTATIONS.

JEROME (342–420), Doctor of the Church. Jerome was known for scholarship unsurpassed in the early Church. His greatest achievement was the translation of the Bible into Latin from the original tongues, the still authoritative Vulgate. In addition to his translation, he wrote innumerable biblical commentaries wherein he brought a wide range of linguistic and topographical material to the interpretation of the texts. He was the first Christian Father to understand the relationship of the Apocrypha to the books of the Hebrew canon. His passionate nature led him to throw himself into many controversies and to attack Arianism*, Pelagianism*, and Origenism*. In his letters, which are of great interest and historical importance, he advocated extreme asceticism. His *De Viribus Illustribus* is a bibliography of ecclesiastical writers.

Milton considered Jerome "the most learned of the Fathers" and found in the Father's writings support for his ideas on divorce*, civil government, and freedom of the press. Arguing that incompatibility was grounds for divorce, Milton says that even Jerome, who preached for the single life and condemned second marriages after death of either party, defended Fabiola, a noble matron of Rome, who divorced her husband and married another. Jerome maintained, writes Milton, that the man was hainously vitious, and that if an adulterous wife may be discarded, an adulterous husband is not to be kept" (*Bucer* 4:29). And when she remarried Jerome defended her, using the words of St. Paul: "It is better to marry than to burn." The Father felt, according to Milton, that the height and perfection of

the Saviour's precept might be remitted to those that burn; God exonerated her because she was young and could not live in widowhood. It was necessary for Fabiola to remarry, Jerome asserted, in order to avert the danger of fornication. In *DDD*, wherein are enumerated various other reasons for divorce besides the "contrariety of minds," Milton singles out fornication and the suspicion of it as grounds for the dissolution of marriage; and he cites Jerome's dictum, "Where fornication is suspected, the wife may lawfully be divorc't" (3:487). In *Tetra* (4:212), Milton registers disgust over the idea that two people could be externally forced to live together where fear and suspicion exist; and again he cites Jerome's assertion that "divorce is free not only for actuall adultery, but for any cause that may encline a wise man to the just suspicion theof." In *RCG* (3:208), Milton, prescribing a system of presbyters as being part of the original church, avers that Jerome did not hide his opinion that custom "was the maker of Prelaty; before his audacious workmanship the Churches were rul'd in common by the Presbyters," and in *Eikon* (5:230) Milton gives further support to this contention by quoting Jerome's commentary on the Epistle of Titus, which declares that bishops and presbyters were one and the same. From Jerome's words Milton concludes that upon the instigation of Satan, partialities grew up in the church, and bishops, rather by custom than by any ordinance of the church, were exalted above presbyters. Milton invokes Jerome in two other matters: in his condemnation of licensing of books and in his defense of the new government's execution of Charles I. In *Areop* (4:312) Milton contends that if there must be licensing, men would not be able to read Jerome, for Jerome "lists more heresies in his books than he actually refutes, or lists a heresy to bring forth a truer opinion." In *1Def* (7:201), Milton, insisting on the tyranny of Charles I*, maintains that the situation was very unlike the slaying of Gedaliah by Ishmael, which offense Jerome called "a parricide for the ruler of Judea was not a tyrant but a just man." [PAF]

JOHNSON, SAMUEL (1709–1784), major author, critic, and biographer. The most famous and most quoted commentator on Milton is Dr. Johnson, the influential and acerbic arbiter of eighteenth-century opinion. His own excellent creative efforts illustrate the taste and literary criteria of his age; his numerous essays, diaries, travel works, biographies, editions, and letters portray a keen sense of observation, sensibility, and nicety in the older meaning of balanced discernment. Too frequently, if not almost always, Johnson's remarks about Milton have been taken out of full context and the real point he was making has often been obscured. This is not to say that Johnson read all of Milton's works with perceptions that the modern age would approve or that he was not influenced in many of his attitudes by his own beliefs. Certainly his monarchic and religious ideas were opposed to Milton's, and he allowed them to color his remarks as had others (like William Winstanley* or Addison* as far back as 1694) and as would others (like Liljegren or T. S. Eliot*).

Johnson was born on September 18, 1709, in Lichfield, and attended Pembroke College, Oxford. He moved to London in 1737 to pursue, along with David Garrick, a life in the theatrical world. Important works like the *Life of Richard Savage* (1744), *Irene* (1749), *The Vanity of Human Wishes* (1749), *The Rambler* (1750–1752), the *Dictionary of the English Language* (1755), *The Idler* (1758–1759), and *Rasselas* (1759) followed in the next two decades. He met his well-known biographer and friend James Boswell on May 16, 1763, and his friends Henry Thrale and wife Hester (later Mrs. Piozzi) in 1764 or 1765. The Club, a group of literary intellectuals led by Johnson, was established in 1764. His edition of Shakespeare appeared in 1765; that of Milton in 1779 (it was often reprinted in England and America). The *Lives of the Poets,* produced as *Prefaces,*

Biographical and Critical to the Works of the English Poets, was published in 1779 and again under the more familiar title in 1781. Johnson died on December 13, 1784. Boswell's *Life of Samuel Johnson* was published on May 16, 1791. Other important biographies are those by Sir John Hawkins (1787) and Arthur Murphy (1792).

Milton and his works enter the Johnson canon frequently by way of quotation, allusion, illustration, and brief and long discussions. To date there has been no study pulling together all of these items from the diaries, letters, ephemera, books describing Johnson's walking tours, et cetera. The writings in which Milton's work looms large are a prologue to *Comus* (1750), a preface to William Lauder's* *Essay* (1750), a rebuttal to John Douglas passed off as Lauder's (1751), four papers on versification in *The Rambler* (1751), two papers on *SA* in *The Rambler* (1751), the *Dictionary* (1755), and *The Life of Milton* (1779). In 1750, having heard of the financial plight of Milton's granddaughter Mrs. Elizabeth Foster*, Johnson proposed to David Garrick, manager of the Theatre-Royal in Drury Lane, that a benefit performance of John Dalton* and Thomas Arne's* *Comus* be given. Johnson supplied a prologue, spoken by Garrick, for the performance (once postponed) on April 5, 1750. His verse is a "Prelude" of "perpetual Praise"; "each Candidate of Fame/ Ambition catches at [Milton's] tow'ring Name," but it is the audience's "Charge . . . to crown Desert—beyond the Grave!" Yet about the same time he contributed a preface to *An Essay on Milton's Use and Imitation of the Moderns in His Paradise Lost* (1750), a revision of the articles in *The Gentleman's Magazine* the year before, by Lauder. His connection with Lauder came about because of his editorial connection with the magazine and Lauder's realization that he needed such bolstering of his views from someone of Johnson's stature. The preface is made to appear as if it came from Lauder's pen—a kind of forgery in itself; its burden is that *PL* had been unduly heaped with "lavish praises and boundless veneration," for it is a version of an "original" and "collateral relations, which it . . . contracted, in its progress to maturity." Johnson seems to have been won over by Lauder's allegations uncritically, although his willingness to accept them was undoubtedly a result of his dislike of Milton the "regicide" and republican. After Lauder's forgeries were exposed, Johnson was instrumental in getting Lauder to publish *A Letter to the Rev. Mr. Douglas, Occasioned by his Vindication of Milton* (1751), which was written at Johnson's dictation. "But for the violation of truth," says Johnson-Lauder, "I offer no excuse, because I well know, that nothing can excuse it." The reason, however, is given earlier as "anger" over the treatment of Lauder's *Poetarum Scotorum* in Pope's* satiric couplet in the *Dunciad* that compared Milton as foil, and Milton's great fame and its attendant idolatry. In the *Dictionary* Johnson quoted Milton everywhere and discussed his use of language here and there. It is a totally different view of Johnson's attitude toward Milton.

The articles in *The Rambler* on versification*—nos. 86 (January 12, 1751), 88 (January 19, 1751), 90 (January 6, 1751), and 94 (February 9, 1751)—show Johnson's attempt to cover all facets of his subject as he saw them and to offer full evaluation even though that evaluation be partially negative. For example, "The heroic measure of the *English* language may be properly considered as pure or mixed"; he defines *pure* as having the accent on every other syllable of a line. "Of these mixed numbers every poet affords us innumerable instances, and Milton seldom has two pure lines together, as will appear if any of his paragraphs be read with attention to the music." The discussions involve only the verse of *PL*. The inferences that can be drawn from such comments are that pure versification is best; that totally mixed versification is less highly evaluated; and that Milton's versification is therefore not without fault. In later papers, since he analyzes

the uses of language, syllabification, stress, hypermetrics, et cetera, Johnson reaches similar negative conclusions : "Milton therefore seems to have somewhat mistaken the nature of our language, of which the chief defect is ruggedness and asperity, and has left our harsh cadences yet harsher"; "If the poetry of *Milton* be examined, with regard to the pauses and flow of his verses into each other, it will appear, that he has performed all that our language could admit"; "Those who are determined to find in *Milton* an assemblage of all the excellencies which have ennobled all other poets, will perhaps be offended that I do not celebrate his versification in higher terms." But such remarks are taken out of context or illustrate Johnson's adherence to the criteria (or dicta) of his own age : "There are, in every age, new errors to be rectified, and new prejudices to be opposed," he had noted toward the beginning of the first paper. Many positive statements appear in these four essays, which place Milton at the head of comparisons with other poets, which observe his rhythms and "music," and which conclude that he had, indeed, a greater and nobler work to perform, that is, "to vindicate the ways of God to man." In all, Johnson's view of versification and particularly of Milton's versification may not always be very perceptive, but it evidences an approach of a particular age in literary history and, with unintended aim, suggests to a modern reader what some of Milton's metric achievements were.

Better known and more quoted are the two papers on *SA* (*The Rambler*, nos. 139, July 16, 1751, and 140, July 20, 1751). Arguing from his interpretation of Aristotle's* comments on tragedy, Johnson finds the dramatic poem "to want a middle, since nothing passes between the first act and the last, that either hastens or delays the death of *Samson*. The whole drama, if its superfluities were cut off, would scarcely fill a single act; yet this is the tragedy which ignorance has admired, and bigotry applauded." A modern audience understands much that occurs as the "middle," whether one accepts Samson's regeneration in the poem or not. What instead is clear from Johnson's comment is that he did not understand what the poem was concerned with and doing, but then neither did his contemporaries. And besides, some of the "faults" are still to be refuted to everyone's acceptance; for example, the versification of the choruses*, which Johnson found "often so harsh and dissonant, as scarce to preserve whether the lines end with or without rhymes, any appearance of metrical regularity." Johnson's commendations, on the other hand, though few, have often been overlooked : for example, "The beginning is undoubtedly beautiful and proper, opening with a graceful abruptness, and proceeding naturally to a mournful recital of facts necessary to be known"; or "It is not easy to give a stronger representation of weariness of despondency than in the words of *Samson* to his father [lines 594–98]." The six *Rambler* papers on versification and *SA,* coming as they do in 1751 at the height of the Lauder controversy, reflect much of Lauder's excuse : "nor can my attempt produce any other effect, than to strengthen their shoots [Milton's laurels] by lopping their luxuriance."

The Life of Milton falls into two parts : a basically biographical section and a long critical discussion of the poems. The biography* is a wide-ranging compendium of prior lives and pertinent incidental information. It certainly is much more than "the addition of a few notes to Mr. Fenton's elegant Abridgement" that he said he might have been contented with, and it is even much more in some details and in critical biography than was Dr. Thomas Newton's*, the standard life from 1749 until nearly the end of the century, when Johnson's became important and others, like William Hayley's*, appeared. Thus we find details like this concerning the sale of the rights to *PL* : "Simmons* had already agreed to transfer the whole right to Brabazon Aylmer* for twenty-five pounds; and Aylmer sold to Jacob Tonson* half,

August 17, 1683, and half, March 24, 1690, at a price considerably enlarged"; "The sale of thirteen hundred copies in two years, in opposition to so much recent enmity, and to a style of versification new to all and disgusting to many, was an uncommon example of the relevance of genius." But the biography is also given to expressions of dislike for the public Milton and his prose works, his political and religious beliefs, and even to the acceptance of the fairly well refuted charge that Milton had forged Pamela's prayer* into *Eikon Basilike*.* (Lauder, apparently learning of this charge surprisingly late, raised the issue again in 1754 in his *King Charles I. Vindicated from the Charge of Plagiarism Brought Against Him by Milton, and Milton Himself Convicted of Forgery, and a Gross Imposition on the Publick.*)

The survey of the poetical works touches the juvenilia (though not *Nat* specifically), *Lyc,* the companion poems, *Mask,* the sonnets, and the three major poems. Little space is devoted to those things he disliked; most discussion centers on the companion poems, *Mask,* and *PL,* the works that were most well-read, often imitated, most influential and quoted during the eighteenth century. Only *Lyc* also had a notable number of readers and imitators. The estimates devolved on the juvenilia are these : "Of the Italian [poems] I cannot pretend to speak as a critick; but I have heard them commended by a man well qualified to decide their merit." "The Latin pieces are lusciously elegant; but . . . [t]hey are not all of equal value; the elegies excell the odes; and some of the exercises on Gunpowder Treason might have been spared." "The English poems . . . have this evidence of genius, that they have a cast original and unborrowed. But their peculiarity is not excellence :" they are worse than the verses of others, they have a "repulsive harshness," the words are not pleasing, and "the rhymes and epithets seem to be laboriously sought, and violently applied."

Of *Lyc* he writes : "The diction* is harsh, the rhymes uncertain, and the numbers unpleasing. What beauty there is, we must therefore seek in the sentiments and images." It has no real passion because it uses "remote allusions and obscure opinions"; "Where there is leisure for fiction there is little grief." Jonson's literary prejudices and literary obtuseness may best be seen in the next, often quoted lines: "In this poem there is no nature, for there is no truth; there is no art, for there is nothing new. Its form is that of pastoral*, easy, vulgar, and therefore disgusting: whatever images it can supply, are long ago exhausted; and its inherent improbability always forces dissatisfaction on the mind." Coloring his view of the poem would still seem to be the alleged excessive fame of its author: "Such is the power of reputation justly acquired, that its blaze drives away the eye from nice examination. Surely no man could have fancied that he read 'Lycidas' with pleasure, had he not known its author."

Johnson, rather typical of his age despite the literary examples of Thomas Edwards, William Lisle Bowles, and Thomas Warton*, among others, disliked the sonnet, and so Milton's "deserve not any particular criticism." One can say only "they are not bad." *PR* comes off well although only a brief paragraph is given: "it is in many parts elegant, and every-where instructive." *SA*, as would be expected from Johnson's earlier work, has been too much admired; but a reason for Johnson's attitude emerges in his remarks here, that is, a dislike for classic drama as contrasted with that of the French and English stage.

The balance that Johnson tries to achieve in his criticism is seen in the four poems he admired and found pleasing. In *L'Al* and *IlP* "the images are properly selected, and nicely distinguished," although the characters seem not to be kept sufficiently apart. "A work more truly poetical is rarely found" than *Mask,* but "As a drama it is deficient." Johnson praises the verse, the images, the sounds, the "message," but he deplores the action, the supernatural intervention, the prologue to the audience, the long

discourses and "tedious" soliloquies, and the lack of decorum. *PL,* "considered with respect to design, may claim the first place, and with respect to performance the second among the productions of the human mind."

The aim of epic, for Johnson, is the moral; this must be conveyed by "a *fable,* a narration artfully constructed, so as to excite curiosity, and surprise expectation. In this part of his work, Milton must be confessed to have equalled every other poet." But even the "must be confessed" sounds some reservations. Johnson moves through subject, characters, the probable and marvelous of epic (his acceptance of the religious matter does not allow him any modern-day denigration of the poem in this area), machinery, episodes, integrity, and sentiments. The major defect and fault of *PL* is: its plan "Comprises neither human actions nor human manners," such that there is a "want of human interest." Thus, Johnson can write that *"Paradise Lost* is one of the books which the reader admires and lays down, and forgets to take up again. (None ever wished it longer than it is.) Its perusal is a duty rather than a pleasure." Second, "it requires the description of what cannot be described, the agency of spirits." Thus, the War in Heaven* is incongruous, "and the book, in which it is related, is, I believe, the favourite of children, and gradually neglected as knowledge is increased." Third, there is the allegory* of Sin and Death, "one of the greatest faults of the poem." And further, the conduct of the narrative, the unequal flats among the elevations (Dryden's phrase), the attempts at levity and punning* are noticed in turn. Johnson completes his critical survey of the poems in the *Life* with a discussion of diction, style*, and versification. It is good that Milton was not a "rhymer," he admits, "for I cannot wish his work to be other than it is."

Johnson's praise of *PL,* the companion poems, and *Mask* was quoted frequently in the eighteenth century and later. But even in his own time his adverse criticisms of Milton received strong reactions; some few critics cited him approvingly, many disagreed with sharp retorts. Francis Blackburn (1705–1787) in *Remarks on Johnson's Life of Milton* (1780) is largely concerned with Johnson's political antipathies, stressing the importance of Milton's republicanism and his contribution to educational thought and the defeat of censorship. John Scott (1730–1783) was concerned with Johnson's having mistaken the nature of *Lycidas*, taking up his strictures on the poem one by one. He concludes, " 'Lycidas' is a noble poem : the author's name is not wanted to recommend it : its own enthusiasm and beauty will always make it please, and abundantly atone for its incorrectness"; see *Critical Essays on Some of the Poems, of Several English Poets* (1785), pp. 37–64. Richard Cumberland (1732–1811) was not so strong an analyst of *SA* as Scott was of the pastoral elegy, but he does attack Johnson's "middle" through discussion of Aristotle and argument that "to say that nothing passes between the first act and the last . . . is not correct, because the very incidents are to be formed, which conduce to the catastrophe, and but for which it could not have come to pass." "Of the castastrophe," he concludes, "there remains only to remark, that it is of unparalled majesty and terror"; see his essay in *Observer*, no. 76 (1785). William Mickle's "A Critique on the *Samson Agonistes* of Milton in Refutation of the Censure of Dr. Johnson" appeared in *European Magazine* 13 (1788):401–6. Mickle (1735–1788) chalks up Johnson's "force of prejudice" to be "conceived, most probably from a dislike of Milton's political creed." Philip Neve makes the same point in his remarks on the *Life*: "let every reader in the mean time remember, that prejudice, envy, nay malignity, have throughout this work, ever extinguished the candor of its author : in all cases determined his will against his subject, and in some misled his judgment." (See *Cursory Remarks on Some of the Ancient English Poets, Particularly Milton* [1789], "Milton," pp. 109–46.) Even his friend Sir John Hawkins (1719–1789) criticized Johnson in his biography

(1787) for the views of *SA*, although Hawkins agrees that Milton's "style in controversy was sarcastic and bitter, and not consistent with christian charity" (p. 244).

James Burnet, Lord Monbaddo (1714–1799), was particularly bothered by Johnson's work, not only that on Milton. To Monbaddo, concerned as he was with language and its use, Johnson had not "formed his taste of good writing upon the antient masters of the art. It was no wonder, therefore, that such a critic as Dr. Johnson, who, in my opinion, was neither a scholar nor a man of taste, should pronounce, among the other oracles which he has uttered from his tripod, that Milton does not write English . . . but a Babylonish dialect" (see *Of the Original and Progress of Language* [Edinburgh, 1773–1792], 5 : 253–69). Monbaddo does not even accept the commendation of *PL*, which he thinks "more absurd than his censures of him, and so ridiculous that, if I had had a better opinion of the Doctor's critical talents, I should have imagined that he said it by way of irony and ridicule of Milton." What Johnson thought was a fair balance in ranging *PL* with other epics, for instance, struck Monbaddo as denigration by too faint praise.

Whatever the strictures of Johnson's criticism of Milton and whatever the censure leveled against Johnson, we do see a deep appreciation of Milton and an eye, if not always an approving eye, cast on Milton's departures from "proper" prosody, standard form, and subject treatment. His strictures seem to arise from his prejudice against Milton the man and political advocate, and from some disagreement with Milton's so-often breaking of rules and use of genres unacceptable to an eighteenth-century taste. We note, for instance, how frequently Johnson uses the word *proper* in tandem with some criterion of writing. Perhaps it should no longer be necessary to return to Johnson's criticism as a springboard into modern criticism; perhaps an amplification of what he commends would be a more meaningful course. [JTS]

JOHNSON, SAMUEL (pamphleteer): *see* ADAPTATIONS.

JOHNSON, THOMAS: *see* PUBLISHERS.

JONES, KATHERINE: *see* RANELAGH, LADY KATHERINE.

JONES, RICHARD: *see* RANELAGH, VISCOUNT.

JONSON, BEN (1572/3–1637), critic, poet, and dramatist. He was born in or near London, probably in June 1573 and not before October 1572, one or two months after his father's death. According to Thomas Fuller* in his *History of the Worthies of England* (1662), the youth received his early education in a private school at Martin's Church and then at Westminster School, where he was taught by the famous classical scholar and historian William Camden*. After leaving Westminster, Jonson worked in London as a bricklayer, served for a short period with an English military expedition in the Netherlands, and then, returning to London, began his career as an actor and dramatist in the 1590s.

Through a favorable reference to "Jonson's learned Sock" (132) in *L'Al* (1631?), John Milton first openly acknowledged the elder writer's erudition and dramatic talents. Jonson at the time *L'Al* was written had gained fame, not only for his learned comedies, but also for his neoclassical verse, court masques, tragedies, and anti-Puritan satire; and Milton, as his early and later writings reveal, appears to have reacted markedly to the general literary and cultural influence of the aging author.

Milton may initially have been drawn to Jonson's works while studying at St. Paul's School* under Alexander Gill*, the younger. In 1632, the younger Gill penned some mocking allusions about Jonson following the failure of the playwright's drama *The Magnetick Lady*. Because Milton relates in a letter dated 2 July 1628 that he had "almost constant conversations" with the younger Gill while at St. Paul's, it is likely that the school-master had something to say to his student about Ben.

One of Jonson's commendatory poems, *To the Memory of My Beloved, the Author, Mr. William Shakespeare*, printed in the first folio edition of Shakespeare's *Works* (1623), may well have influenced Milton in his writing of *Shak*, a poem that appeared in the second folio edition of 1631. Both poems are written in couplets, and both contain lines stating that Shakespeare's art is a monument without a tomb.

The colloquial tone, smooth rhythms, and pastoral figures and theme of the songs to spring in Jonson's masque* *Chloridia* (1630) are paralleled in Milton's lyrical *May* (1630?). The symmetry and rational clarity of *May* became features of later poetry by Milton composed under the general influence of Jonsonian neoclassicism. Milton's companion poems (1631?), for example, are written in the lilting style and iambic tetrameter common to some of Jonson's masque dancing songs. In the first of the poems, the dance of Mirth and her crew reflects a similar dance in Jonson's *The Haddington Masque* (1608), in which Mirth frolics with the figures Games, Laughter, Sports, Delights, and Pretty Lightnesses. However, the younger poet's *EpWin* (1631), a verse Milton composed while perhaps aware of a similar epitaph for the same person by Jonson, has a metrical smoothness and cool elegance that is lacking in segments of Jonson's sometimes harsh elegy. Milton's entertainment *Arc* (1631–1634?) contains themes and character types that can be traced generally to those in Jonson's *The Entertainment at Althorp* (1603) and *The Entertainment at the Blackfriars* (1620). *Mask,* in its structure, character types, and themes discloses Milton's indebtedness to the court masques of Jonson, perhaps in particular mirroring elements in the older poet's masque *Pleasure Reconciled to Virtue* (1618).

Jonson in his dedication to *Volpone* and Milton in *El 6* both express a belief in the spiritual purity of great poets and the ethical and didactic function of poetry. Jonson asserts in his dedication that the poet is the supreme teacher of those "things divine, no less than humane" which can "effect the businesse of man-kind," and he insists upon the "impossibility of any mans being the good Poet, without first being a good man." But unlike Milton, Jonson usually veiled possible "divine" Christian meanings beneath the outward fabric of pagan or secular themes and images. Moreover, the elder writer's position in the Establishment and the hostility of the Puritans to any kind of drama led him to attack them. The comedy *The Alchemist* exposes the greed of the characters Tribulation Wholesome, a dissenting pastor from Amsterdam, and Ananias, his deacon, both of whom seek out the alchemist Subtle in the hope that base metal can be profitably changed into gold. In *Bartholomew Fair* Jonson satirizes the character Zeal-of-the-Land Busy, a blustering Puritan preacher who lashes out against a drama being performed by other figures in the play. In general, Milton responded to such anti-Puritanism and pervasive, surface paganism not by attacks upon specific writings, but by the positive act of making Christian themes supported by classical allusions the central focus of his major and many of his minor works. When in *Apol* Milton defended his former teacher Thomas Young* and other Puritans against the attacks of Bishop Joseph Hall*, the poet proclaimed the primacy of Christian writings over classical and adopted a Puritan religious position quite different from the more traditional Christianity of Jonson. On the other hand, he differed from strict Puritans who opposed all forms of drama, first conceiving the subject of his epic* *PL* as a religious closet drama, "Adam Unparadiz'd" (1640–1642). In the completed epic, Adam and Eve, exhibiting a pronounced sense of duty and dedication to physical labor, emerge before the Fall as admirable figures embodying many of Milton's Puritan values, characters who stand in opposition to the comic Puritan types in Jonson's comedies. Although the elder author's tragedies are centered upon figures and events in Roman imperial history, Sejanus and Cataline, Milton's tragedy *SA* features an Old Testament hero and is based upon biblical accounts. Its understanding of Aristotelian* theories of the drama is quite different from Jonson's in its employment of a chorus* and strict adherence to the unities. Milton's was conceived as a closet drama; Jonson's were meant for the stage. In the younger poet's brief epic *PR,* the figure of Christ, in an extended statement that would have scandalized Jonson, denounces the sages of Greece and Rome as men "ignorant of themselves, of God much more" (4 : 310).

Both Jonson and Milton, stimulated by ethical concern, employed a wide spectrum of satirical techniques to mock the presumptions and sins of mankind; but Jonson's special achievement lay in his creation of comedies such as *Every Man in His Humour* (1598) and *Every Man out of His Humour* (1599), works in which the chief human traits leading to folly are revealed economically and precisely in memorable character types. Milton never wrote a "comedy of humours" after the caustic manner of Jonson, but in his voluminous prose writings proved himself, like Jonson, a master of satire* by exhibiting an easy control over such devices as scorn, irony, sarcasm, ridicule, and contumely. Yet, in one mode of satire Milton displayed unique ability : the sweeping, divine irony used by an omniscient God the Father in speaking of Satan in *PL* has no counterpart in the writings of the older poet.

Jonson spent the last years of his life in retirement. On September 18, 1634, the city of London, at the request of King Charles*, granted the playwright a pension without commitments. With this allowance to support him, Jonson, who had suffered a severe stroke, wrote almost nothing more. He died on August 6, 1637, and was buried in Westminster under a small stone slab marked with the simple inscription, "O Rare Ben Jonson." In this year Milton contributed an elegy to the memory of Edward King*. [JGD]

JOSEPHUS, FLAVIUS (37–ca. 100), Jewish statesman and soldier, whose most famous work, *Antiquities of the Jews,* is an early history of the Jews up to A.D. 66. His *War of the Jews* is an account of Jewish wars from the capture of Jerusalem in 170 B.C. by Antiochus Epiphanes to its destruction, which he witnessed, by Titus in A.D. 70. He earned the esteem of Vespasian and Titus and attained Roman citizenship.

Milton had an excellent grasp of the works of Josephus and spoke of him as "a qualified interpreter of Hebrew law, and best government." Milton's tracts on divorce* and civil government reecho Josephus's sentiments; and passages from the three major poems reveal the influence of Josephus's *Antiquities.* In *DDD* Milton, arguing that fornication is grounds for divorce, cites Josephus's affirmation of this just cause, especially when there is implied in the partner's conduct "a continual headstrong behaviour, as tends to plain contempt of the husband." In the case of the Levite wife in Judges 19 : 2, Josephus saw that she not only "plaid the whoor against him" but displayed in addition a "stubbornesse and rebellion against her husband." In *Tetra* Milton, discussing Christ's condemnation of Herod's marital state, which cost the Baptist his life, refers to the Herod-Herodias story as he found it in Josephus's *Antiquities* and concludes, "That much we gain from hence to inform us, that what Christ intends to speak here of divorce, will be rather the forbidding of what we may doe herin passionately and abusively, as Herod and Herodias did, then the discussing of what herin we may doe reasonably and necessarily." In the same work, Milton insists on a just cause for divorce, unlike the Pharisees who, according to Josephus, held "that for every cause they might divorce, for every accidental cause, any quarrell or difference that might happen." In *1Def* Milton asserts that God himself bears witness to the right possessed by almost all peoples and nations of enjoying whatever form of government they wish, or of

changing from one to another; and he cites Josephus's dictum : "An aristocracy is the best form of government; wherefore seek ye not any other; it is enough to have God for your ruler. But if huge desire of a kind have seized you, let him yield to the laws and to God more than to his own wisdom; and let him be restrained if he offer at more power than is proper to your affairs." In the same work, Milton says that the commonwealth of the Hebrews, in which God was sole ruler, was a theocracy, and, according to Josephus, only in God's anger were the Israelites given a king.

In *PL,* Michael's description of the Tabernacle (12. 255–56) as having "Seven Lamps as in a Zodiac representing / The Heav'nly fires" is reminiscent of Josephus's account (*Antiquities* 3. 6 : 7) of the golden candlestick, having "seven lamps . . . in imitation of the number of planets." In *PR,* Satan tempts Christ to accept riches with which to buy power, as did Antipater : "Money brings Honour, Friends, Conquests, and Realms; / What rais'd *Antipater*" (2. 423); in the *Antiquities* 4. 1, Josephus recorded thus the rise of Antipater : "who was very rich, and in his nature an active and seditious man." Furthermore, during the Parthia temptation, Satan mentions the plight of the leaders, Antigonus and Hyrcanus (*PR* 3. 367–68); and Josephus, in *Antiquities* 14, chronicles the consolidation of Antigonus's power by Parthian support against his uncle, the High Priest Hyrcanus, who had Roman help : after a three-year reign, Antigonus was executed by Herod, as was Hyrcanus some time later. In *SA* Samson's words about the foretelling of his birth by an angel who in the sight "Of both my Parents all in flames ascended / From off the Altar, where an off'ring burn'd / As in a fiery column charidting / His Godlike presence" are reminiscent of Josephus's *Antiquities* 5. 7, wherein he says that after Manoa had sacrificed, "the angel ascended openly, in their sight, up to heaven, by means of the smoke as by a vehicle." Later Samson, speaking to Harapha of his nuptial feast, says the "ill-meaning Political Lords, Under pretense of Bridal friends and guests, / Appointed to await me thirty spies." Here Milton all but paraphrases Josephus, "the people of Timnath . . . gave him during the time of the wedding feast . . . thirty of the most stout of their youth, in pretense to be his companions, but in reality to be a guard upon him" (*Antiquities* 5.8.6). [PAF]

JOVIUS, PAULUS (1483–1553). Italian bishop and author of *Historia Sui Temporis*, cited in *CB* from the two-volume Basle 1578 edition on the subjects of "Gluttony" (or Englishmen), of "Kings" (the crowning of Charles V), of "Military Discipline," and of "City Sieges." In the Preface to *Mosc* (10:327f.) Milton adds that he "had much the advantage of Jovius concerning Moscovia," reflecting that Jovius's account was limited because he could not know the reports of the English voyages. [WBH]

JOYCE, JAMES: *see* INFLUENCE UPON TWENTIETH-CENTURY ENGLISH LITERATURE, MILTON'S.

JOYNER, WILLIAM. *See* ASSOCIATES, PERSONAL.

JUDGEMENT OF MARTIN BUCER, THE. Milton's second tract on divorce*, *The Judgement of Martin Bucer, Concerning Divorce,* was entered in the Stationers' Register on July 15, 1644, licensed by John Downham*, and published by Matthew Simmons* (who had assisted in the publication of *DDD*) in London on or before August 6 (the date on Thomason's* copy). Milton's statement (*Tetra* 4:66) that the work was published "*about a week before*" Herbert Palmer's sermon of August 13 supports this likely date. The author's name does not appear on the title page, but his full name appears at the end of the address "To the Parlament." The tract, originally printed on forty-two quarto pages, was not reissued during Milton's lifetime. The first critical edition was *CM*. Arnold

Williams prepared the first annotated edition for Yale *Prose* 2.

The pamphlet opens with a series of "Testimonies of the high approbation Which learned men have given of *Martin Bucer,*" the views of thirteen eminent men (including Calvin*, Cheke*, Beza*, and Fox*) on Bucer*, followed by several testimonies on Paulus Fagius (1504–1549). Milton's intention here is to establish the authority of these two men and the acceptance of their ideas by leaders of the Reformation.

In the address "To the Parlament" that follows, Milton continues his praise of Bucer. He apparently did not learn of Bucer's work until May 1644, several months after the publication of the second edition of *DDD*. Milton is especially pleased to note that he arrived independently at ideas close to those of Bucer: "*For that I ow no light, or leading receav'd from any man in the discovery of this truth, what time I first undertook it in the* doctrine and discipline of divorce, *and had only the infallible grounds of Scripture to be my guide, he who tries the inmost heart, and saw with what severe industry and examination of my self, I set down every period, will be my witnes. . . . When the book [DDD] had bin now the second time set forth wel-nigh three months, as I best remember, I then first came to hear that* Martin Bucer *had writt'n much concerning divorce: whom earnestly turning over, I soon perceav'd, but not without amazement, in the same opinion, confirm'd with the same reasons which in that publisht book without the help or imitation of any precedent Writer, I had labour'd out, and laid together. Not but that there is some difference in the handling, in the order, and the number of arguments, but still agreeing in the same conclusion. So as I may justly gratulat mine own mind, with due acknowledgement of assistance from above, which led me, not as a lerner, but as a collateral teacher, to a sympathy of judgement with no lesse a man then* Martin Bucer" (4:11–14). This address, unlike that of the second edition of *DDD*, is not directed to the Westminster Assembly*, in which Milton had apparently already lost confidence.

The body of the tract is a translation and epitomizing of those chapters of Martin Bucer's *De Regno Christi (Of the Kingdom of God)* that parallel *DDD*. Bucer (1491–1551), Professor of Divinity at Cambridge, wrote *De Regno Christi* about 1550 for Edward VI; it was first published posthumously in 1557, but Milton used the second edition that appeared as part of *Scripta Anglicana* (Basle, 1577). In addition to advocating *divortium a vincolo matrimonii* (divorce from the bond of matrimony, i.e., absolute divorce with the possibility of remarriage) over *divortium a mensa et thoro* (divorce from bed and board, i.e., mere separation, as allowed by Canon Law), Bucer supported incompatibility as a valid ground. The ideas that Milton found of special interest in Bucer's work were his support of civil as opposed to ecclesiastical control over marriage*, his interpretation of the New Testament prohibition of divorce except for adultery as merely a warning against easy and unwarranted divorce, and the tradition that the early church accepted grounds for divorce other than adultery. Of these concepts, only the third was new to Milton, since the first was already common Protestant doctrine, and he had already expressed views similar to the second in *DDD*.

Milton's translation is an efficient, practical, nonliteral rendering of what he regarded as the relevant portions of *De Regno Christi*, chapters 15 through 47, somewhat less than half the text. In it, Milton acts "as an advocate, not as a scholar" (Williams, Yale *Prose* 2 : 817), occasionally "omitt[ing] materials . . . not merely useless but positively prejudicial" (p. 816). Milton translated only those passages that support his own views. On the whole, however, he is true to his original, aiming always at compression and succinctness (with occasional additions for clarification), qualities necessitated by both the nature of Bucer's prose and Milton's specific intentions, in marked contrast to the usual Elizabethan practice of expansion and elaboration. As Milton notes in his "Post-Script," he has *"epitomiz'd"* Bucer, "observing a well-warranted rule, not to give an Inventory of so many words, but to weigh thir force" (4 : 60). The omissions of sentences, paragraphs, and even entire chapters may indicate, however, that the translation was hastily prepared.

In the "Post-Script," Milton asserts that on the basis of what he has presented of Bucer's tract, as well as the views set forth by Erasmus* and Peter Martyr, he is clearly not a "forger of new and loose opinions," as his detractors have claimed. Because his ideas in *DDD* are in harmony with those of the writings of such eminent reformers, he sees his own works as having the right to be as freely published, perhaps implying that he had attempted unsuccessfully to have *DDD* licensed. W. R. Parker, however, sees in this complaint the possibility that a planned reprint of the second edition of *DDD* had been censored. Milton recognized that in translating Bucer's tract he was presenting nothing new to the English public; he uses the material not in the nature of proof but "as a sort of character witness against [his] traducers" (Williams, Yale *Prose* 2 : 418), who in slandering him had unwittingly slandered one of the most highly regarded of reformers.

Milton's plans for justification of the second edition of *DDD* went awry from the start, however, and the translation of Martin Bucer's work had no effect whatever on his detractors. On August 13, probably exactly one week after *Bucer* appeared, Herbert Palmer of the Westminster Assembly, preaching to both houses of Parliament, condemned the "impudent" man who had authored a "wicked book" on divorce as "deserving to be burnt." [AA]

JULIAN THE APOSTATE: *see* ADAPTATIONS.

JUNIUS, FRANCISCUS. Philologist and antiquarian, Franciscus Junius (1589–

1677) was born in Heidelberg, the son of the elder Franciscus Junius (1545–1602), who assisted John Immanuel Tremellius* in translating the Bible. His name also appears as Francis or Franz Junius or François Du Jon. He went to England in 1621 as librarian and tutor in the household of Thomas Howard, Earl of Arundel, and maintained his connection with this family for thirty years. He devoted himself to the comparative study of Teutonic and northern languages, notably Old English. In 1651 Junius left England to live in the Netherlands with his sister Elizabeth, the widow of G. J. Vossius*. He returned to England in 1674 and was residing with his nephew, Isaac Vossius*, when he died of a fever in 1677.

Scholars have long been interested in the close similarities between *PL* and the Anglo Saxon* version of Genesis now known as *Genesis B,* a passage of some 600 lines (235–825), apparently dating from the late ninth century and interpolated into an older (late seventh century?) account, the *Genesis A.* The two parts of the Old English Genesis run to 2,936 lines and are contained in a manuscript now catalogued as Bodleian MS. Junius II. The general parallels between *PL* and the *Genesis B* probably reflect the common tradition of paraphrases of the Fall* rather than indicating direct indebtedness, but the two poems also contain several striking similarities of detail, in Satan's speeches to the fallen angels, the journey through the abyss from Hell to Earth, the temptation and sin, and the subsequent dialogue of Adam and Eve.

The Anglo-Saxon manuscript was given to Junius by his friend Archbishop Ussher* around 1651. Junius published a transcript at Amsterdam in 1655 as *Caedmonis monachi paraphrasis poetica Genesios,* a 106-page quarto in Anglo-Saxon characters and without metrical breaks or translation. Nineteenth-century scholars frequently speculated about the possibility of Milton's having known Junius and thus perhaps having been introduced to the Old English poem by the philologist, but the first firm evidence that the two men

were indeed acquainted was the publication in 1911 by Stephanie von Gajsek of a letter from Junius's nephew, Isaac Vossius, dated July 8, 1651, to his friend Nicholas Heinsius*. Milton and Junius were acquainted much earlier, during Milton's marital separation in 1642–1645, according to Parker.

Milton himself apparently had no more than a rudimentary knowledge of Old English. The thirty-three Anglo-Saxon topics in his list of possible epical subjects have citations from Speed*, Holinshed*, Bede*, Malmesbury*, and Geoffrey of Monmouth*, but no references to Old English sources. Milton's discussion of the Old English poem on the battle of Brunanburh in *Brit* (10 :233) also indicates that he had difficulty reading Old English, even with the aid of Whelock's* word-for-word Latin translation. But since Milton did know Junius, it is possible that he may have examined the Old English Genesis with Junius's assistance prior to the departure of Junius from England with the mauscript in 1651. [JJR]

JUSTA EDOVARDO KING. In 1638 there was published at Cambridge, in keeping with the custom of the time, a two-part collection of verse dedicated to the memory of Edward King*, who had died in the previous year. The first part consists of twenty poems in Latin and three in Greek and entitled *Justa Edovardo King.* There is also on the title page a motto from Petronius : "Si rectè calculum ponas, ubique naufragium est" (If you reckon rightly, shipwreck is everywhere). The second part of the volume, which has separate pagination and is printed mainly in italic type, is entitled *Obsequies to the memorie of Mr. Edward King,* and contains thirteen poems in English, of which the last and longest is *Lyc,* signed simply "J. M."

"The poets who wrote on the death of Edward King were a limited Cambridge group, among whom, besides Milton, only Cleveland and Joseph Beaumont of the English elegists later rose to any pretension as poets." Ruth Wallerstein's statement (*Studies in Seventeenth-Century Poetic* [1950], p. 97) should be modified by Ernest Mossner's remark that the contributors were "a distinguished company of academics" (*Justa Edovardo King* [1939], p. xiv). Mossner provides a list of contributors to the volume (pp. xii–xiii), but a number remain unidentified. The editor, who presumably contributed the opening Latin poem and the handsomely set Latin panegyric in prose that precedes it, is unknown.

The Greek poems are limited in interest, though one of them (p. 24) is by Henry More, later celebrated as one of the Cambridge Platonists*. However, the poem by William Iveson (p. 13) is of some note, since its meter is an imitation of the Greater Asclepiad meter of Callimachus from an ode to a drowned mariner (frag. 400 Pfeiffer). In the Latin poems there are a number of passages that seem to be echoed in *Lyc,* though certain mythical expressions and allusions are perhaps inevitable in any classically inspired treatment of shipwreck. Thus in the elegy by Richard Mason (pp. 9–10) there occur the lines : "Hei mihi ! jam meus occubuit demersus aquosum / Phoebus in Oceanum, nunquam exhibiturus apertos / Ore mihi radios" (Woe is me ! Now my Phoebus sleeps sunk in watery ocean, never to display for me the radiance plain on his face). Lines 165–71 of *Lyc* read like a reply to this in their assertion that the day-star (Phoebus) rises again from "the Ocean bed." Similarly, the poem by R. Brown (pp. 14–16) has references to Hippotades and Orpheus* (cf. *Lyc* 96, 58–63).

"Where were ye Nymphs?" (*Lyc* 50) and "the blind *Fury*" (*Lyc* 75) seem to come together in Christopher Bainbrigge's lament, "Amphitrite / Decessit Furiis" (Amphitrite [wife of Neptune and chief among the Nereids—cf. *Mask* 921] has given way to the Furies) (p. 33). And John Hoper's poem (pp. 20–23) contains an unsurprising reference to Elysian shores, which nevertheless recalls *Lyc* 174–75. Perhaps the most interesting connection is found in a poem by an unknown called Coke (pp. 19–20), written in alcaics, which laments the absence of lifesaving dolphins from the Irish Sea (stanza 4) (cf. *Lyc* 164) and then goes on in the sixth stanza to chide the unfriendly ship ("navis inhospita"), the faithless pine ("insida pinus") whose impious sides let in the waves (cf. *Lyc* 101–5).

The most extreme example of the axiomatic assumption that the English poems in the volume are all inferior to *Lyc* is Sir Charles Oman's patronizing and condescending essay (*Cornhill Magazine* 156 : 577–87) ; in fact, though the elegies are fulsome and far-fetched at times, the level of competence is fairly high. Ruth Wallerstein devotes a surprising amount of space (pp. 97–102) to analysis of Beaumont's involved poem of compliment, commenting on the careful balance of "the two elements of Beaumont's design, lament and allegory" (p.99) and on "the blending of Latin attitudes and of the Anglican ideal of social order with personal religious intensity" (p. 101). Cleveland is given much briefer treatment by her, but his poem is a fascinating example of the witty, ingenious, "conceited" manner ; he concludes it with a preposterous image of King's fellow-academics as islands in an ocean of their own tears :

When we have fill'd the rundlets of our eyes,
We'll issue't forth, and vent such elegies,
As that our tears shall seem the Irish seas,
We floating Ilands, living Hebrides.

William Moore (More) "comments overtly and adversely on other poems in the collection" (Lloyd, *Notes and Queries* 5, n.s.433), and seems particularly to have Cleveland in mind when he says :

Nor do I like their pietie, who to sound
His depth of learning, where they feel no ground,
Strain till they lose their own; then think to ease
The losse of both, by cursing guiltlesse seas.

But it is difficult to question the authenticity of the emotions of Henry

King, Edward's younger brother, who contributed both Latin and English poems to the volume. His English poem, which opens the *Obsequies,* though it does curse "guiltlesse seas," has a certain Donnean force and integrity that avoid the excesses of Cleveland. Here, he is reminiscent of "A Nocturnal upon St. Lucy's Day":

Mean while let me poore, senseless, dead, alone
Sit and expect my resurrection,
To follow him; two sorrows sure will do,
That he is dead, that I am not dead too.
Yet dead I'm once already: for in him
I lost my best life.

The inferiority of such verse to *Lyc* is not in question, but the significant aspect of *Lyc* in relation to the other English poems is that Milton avoids, by elaborate indirection, the straining after novel effect that characterizes the greater part of the other elegies. *Lyc* is different in kind from them, as well as in execution, though it may well be that it is part of "a unified work within a flexible comprehensive design" (Lloyd, p. 432). There are certainly echoes in it of the poem by Hall, with its "fatall bark," and "Olivier's Arethusa, his Peter walking the waves, and his 'officious dolphine' recall Milton's contribution" (ibid.). Evidence adduced above from the Latin elegies also suggests that the entire volume may be considered "a unified work." [JD]

JUSTIFICATION is one stage in the Christian psychology of salvation, whereby God, having called the elect, justifies and then glorifies them (Rom. 8 : 29–30). Such justification does not literally make the elect righteous; rather it pronounces them to be righteous. By doing so God acquits man of his sins, imputing to him the merit* of Christ's sacrifice. Article 11 of the *39 Articles* asserts that men "are justified by faith only." In the Reformed tradition (see *Westminster Confession,* 10ff.), God effectually calls to leave their naturally sinful state all and only those whom he has predestined for salvation. He then justifies them, "not by infusing

righteousness into them, but by pardoning their sins" (11 : 1). Thenceforth they are "adopted" and "sanctified," or made holy forever.

Milton's understanding of the idea asserts that all mankind hear such a call; this is the Arminian* position. "The rest," God says, "shall hear me call, and oft be warnd / Thir sinful state" without avail (*PL* 3. 185ff.). For Milton, justification happens as a result of the faith of the believer, which issues not in "works of the law" (*CD* 16 : 31) but in works of faith*—"inasmuch as a living and true faith cannot consist without works, though these latter may differ from the works of the written law" (p. 39). Such faith and its resultant works, however, ultimately owe to the operation of the Spirit in each believer, who thus cannot take pride in or receive merit from them (p. 41). The same idea appears in *PL,* where Michael explains to Adam that "by Faith imputed" mankind

> may finde
> Justification towards God, and peace
> Of Conscience, which the Law by Ceremonies
> Cannot appease.
> (12. 295–98) [WBH]

JUSTIN MARTYR. Born ca. A.D. 100, Justin was brought up as a Greek, taught at Rome in the reign of Antoninus Pius, and was martyred under Marcus Aurelius, probably between 163 and 167. Of the many works formerly attributed to him, only three are now regarded as genuine; all of them are found in MS Paris 450, dated A.D. 1363. The Paris MS was published in Greek by Stephanus in 1551; a Latin translation appeared three years later. Milton seems to have used the 1615 Paris edition, in Greek and Latin.

The *First Apology,* addressed to Antoninus Pius, refutes various anti-Christian slanders and shows the positive values of Christianity. The *Second Apology* (sometimes referred to as "Pro Christianis"), which is much shorter, contains references to the first. The *Dialogue with Trypho,* written a few years after the Apologies, is a real or purported record of a debate between Justin and a Jew named Trypho, in which Justin relates his conversion and upholds Christianity as the true philosophy.

Although Milton links Justin once with some other Fathers as containing errors and heresies* (*Ref* 3 : 21), he cites him with respect in the divorce* tracts: Justin's apparent approval of a woman who was divorced from an ungodly husband gives "the judgment of the Church in those pure and next to Apostolic times" (*Tetra* 4 : 207–8; see also 4 : 171 and 249). In the antiprelatical tracts Justin's description of liturgical practices is invoked in support of spontaneous prayer (*Animad* 3 : 125), and Milton contends that the "Presbyter" described by Justin as leading the worship is not necessarily a bishop (*PrelE* 3 : 86). Justin's distinction that we worship God but give service to a ruler is cited from the *Second Apology* (now known as the *First*) in *CB* (18 : 173), and in the same place there is a reference to a statement in *Trypho* about polygamy* (ibid., p. 149).

Milton's familiarity with Justin's works is evident from these direct citations, which, except in one instance, are used to support Milton's own views and which are in keeping with his usual cautiously respectful, though independent, attitude toward the early Church Fathers. It is possible that he derived some other ideas from Justin (e.g., the metaphor of the sun and its beams as an analogy of the Trinity), but since these appear in other Fathers also, no further definite influence can be demonstrated. ([MCP]

JUSTINIAN (527–565), emperor of the Eastern Empire, who attempted to reestablish the glory of Rome by winning back western sections lost to the Goths, by codifying and reforming its legal system, and by bringing the various Christian sects into peaceful coexistence. Milton judged him to be a man "of high wisdom and respected piety" in *DDD* (3 : 487), a customary evaluation. His importance for the Middle Ages and later periods lay especially in his abridg-

ment of Roman law, the *Digest,* from which was excerpted the *Institutes,* a major legal text with which Milton was certainly familiar. He recommends Justinian as part of his educational program (*Educ* 4 : 255) and had himself drawn extracts from the *Institutes* in *CB* on the subjects of slaves (three times), law, the king, and liberty (twice). Justinian's authority is especially employed in the divorce* tracts, from *DDD* through *Tetra,* showing that Roman law permitted divorce with far greater leniency than the Christian interpreters of the New Testament would. Milton admits that, since he had repealed divorce by mutual consent, Justinian is "noted by judicious writers for his fickle head in making and unmaking laws" (4 : 216). *Eikon* also quotes him to show that the law is superior to the crown (5 : 298), and brief claims upon his authority appear in *1Def* and *3Def.* [WBH]

KEATS, MILTON'S INFLUENCE ON. The subject of Milton's influence on Keats has been discussed at great length by critics—and rightly so, because it is through his response to Milton that Keats's development can best be traced. While valuable observations are to be found in every biography and critical study of Keats, the most extensive considerations of Miltonic parallels are in Ernest de Selincourt's edition of Keats's poems (1936) ; W. J. Bate, *The Stylistic Development of Keats* (1945), pp. 66–91, 171–82; R. K. Gordon, *Modern Language Review* 42 : 434–46; and F. L. Jones, *Keats-Shelley Journal* 1 : 71–72. The reason for the comprehensive correspondence between the work of both poets can be traced to the friendly conspiracy practiced by Keats's mentors and friends: from 1813 to 1818 Clarke, Haydon, Bailey, and Dilke personally urged Keats to read and study Milton. The effect of this Miltonic inundation was to fill the sensitive and retentive mind of Keats with images and structures that appear throughout his poetry and range from bare echoes of Pandemonium's creation

(*PL* 1. 670–798) in his "Castle Builder" (1818) to an extensive imitation of the language and syntax of *PL* in his Hyperion poems. Some of the claims about Keats's borrowings from Milton, however, must be considered at least questionable and the similarities more properly attributable to their common affection for Elizabethan sources. For example, the description of Satan on his throne at the beginning of *PL* 2 is frequently cited as the origin of the description of Neptune in Keats's *Endymion*, 3. 832–87; it is likely, however, that Keats is recalling, as indeed Milton was, the house of Pride in Spenser's* *Faerie Queene* 1. 4. 4–10.

What benefit Keats derived from his tutelage to Milton is a sensitive question and has divided critics not quite neatly down the middle. The debate began in earnest with John Middleton Murry's *Keats and Shakespeare* (1926) and *Studies in Keats: New and Old* (1939): Murry argued strenuously that Milton has been a stultifying taskmaster and that only Keats's repatriation to Shakespeare's realm in September 1819 saved him from poetic dissolution. E. M. W. Tillyard in *The Miltonic Setting* (1938) contended persuasively, if with not too wide an acceptance, that Murry's attempt to make Milton "the Cyclops of Keats's Odyssey" (p. 30) was misguided and that it was only natural that Keats would turn away from Miltonic (and Shakespearean) influences to find his own voice.

The matter is not altogether clarified by Keats's own remarks about Milton in his poems and prose. His comments, more or less chronologically, move from excited wonderment (see, for example, "Ode to Apollo," 1815; "On Seeing a Lock of Milton's Hair," 1818, and his annotations to *PL*, 1818, in Joseph A. Wittreich, Jr., *The Romantics on Milton* [1970], pp. 553–60) to outright condescension and hostility: Milton "did not think into the human heart. . . . [H]is Philosophy, human and divine, may be tolerably understood by one not much advanced in years" (1818; Wittreich, *Romantics*, p. 552);

"Miltonic verse cannot be written but in an artful or rather artist's humour. . . . English ought to be kept up"; "The Paradise lost . . . is a corruption of our Language. . . . I prefer . . . native music . . . to Milton's cut by feet [and] I have lately stood on my guard against Milton. Life to him would be death to me" (1819; Wittreich, *Romantics,* pp. 561–62).

These last strictures came in September 1819, when Keats apparently abandoned his attempts at completing *Hyperion* in its recast Dantesque form, *The Fall of Hyperion. A Dream*: it is generally accepted that the remark in the letter to Richard Woodhouse, "I have given up Hyperion—there are too many Miltonic inversions in it" (1819; Wittreich, *Romantics*, p. 561), applies to both renderings of the poem (cf. Robert Gittings, *John Keats* [1968], p. 350). The pervasiveness of Milton in both versions of the Hyperion poems is undeniable; so steeped was Keats in imitating the epic style*, theme, and techniques of *PL* that even the attempted revision, *The Fall,* contained additional Miltonisms, despite Keats's attempt to excise those already there. (See, in addition to the notes in Selincourt's edition of the poems, M. R. Riddley, *Keats' Craftsmanship* [1933], pp. 266–80; Bate, *Stylistic Development,* pp. 66–91, 171–82 and his *John Keats* [1963], pp. 338–410 passim; Stuart M. Sperry, Jr., *Publications of the Modern Language Association* 77 [1962], 77–84; and Brian Wilkie, *The Romantic Poets and Epic Tradition* [1965], pp. 156–87). There are many urgent and constraining reasons why Keats would have discontinued his efforts at concluding the Hyperion poems (cf. John D. Rosenberg, *Keats-Shelley Journal* 6:87–95, and M. H. Abrams, *Natural Supernaturalism* [1971], pp. 127–29), which makes Keats's remark about "too many Miltonic[s]" more impatient and peevish than definitive. Keats himself had written earlier in another letter that "The Genius of Poetry must work out its own salvation in a man: It cannot be matured by law & precept. . . . That which is creative must create itself"

(1818; *The Letters of John Keats*, ed. Hyder E. Rollins [1958], 1 :374). Keats could not, after all, entirely have foreseen how abbreviaeted his poetic career was to have been, but the growing awareness of the seriousness of his illness might have encouraged him to end his discipleship to Milton's technical authority; but to make Milton Apollonius to Keats's Lycius is only to be reminded that dalliance with a Shakespearean Lamia would have been as harmful to a growing poetic mind seeking its own region—and it is to be noted that Hyperion is as Lear-like as Apollo and the Poet are Christ-like.

What Keats did acquire from Milton, however, must not be minimized or misprized. Without the rigorous apprenticeship he served to Milton (although it was always more than that), Keats would have become what he heartily despised: a mannered and "versifying Pet-lamb" (1819); *Letters*, 2 : 116). Nowhere in Shakespeare's life or work would Keats have found an example of a poet overcoming personal abuse and physical adversity, or a constant reiteration of the importance of poetry as he did in Milton's life and work. When Keats wrote in "Sleep and Poetry" (1817) that he must overcome the temptations of sensual poetry, "the realm . . . / of Flora, and old Pan" (101–2), and dedicated himself to a "nobler life" (123), it is certain he had in mind Milton's remarks in the Latin Elegies 5 and 6. Some months after his declaration in "Sleep and Poetry," Keats described Milton's achievement in terms pertinent to himself :

> [Milton] had an exquisite passion for what is properly in the sense of ease and pleasure, poetical Luxury—and with that it appears to me he would have been content if he could so doing have preserved his self-respect and feel of duty performed . . . [but] . . . he devoted himself rather to the Ardours than the pleasures of Song . . . [he broke] through the clouds which envellope [*sic*] so deliciously the Elysian fields of Verse, and committed himself to the Extreme. . . . (ca. 1818; Wittreich, *Romantics*, p. 553)

Not only did Keats's metaphor for poetic creativity derive from Adam's dreams in *PL* 8. 291–311, 460–90 (cf. *Letters*, November 22, 1817), but Milton's life itself satisfactorily answered the question that Keats posed repeatedly to himself in 1818—how can a poet do the world some good through his creative endeavors? (cf. *Letters*, 1 : 267, 271, 293, 387). "[T]he great end / Of poesy," wrote Keats, is "that it should be a friend / To sooth the cares, and lift the thoughts of man" ("Sleep and Poetry," 245–47); in Milton Keats found a poet who had been "an active friend to Man all his Life and has been since his death" (Wittreich, *Romantics*, p. 550), and Keats repeated this sentiment as the noble attribute of the Grecian Urn whose message defines the very function of art in human life ("Ode on a Grecian Urn" [1819], 48).

Basing his remarks on Keats's annotations to *PL*, Claude Lee Finney summarized what Keats had learned from Milton as "restraint, brevity, intensity, and grandeur" (*The Evolution of Keats' Poetry* [1963], 1 : 338). Only one important virtue can be added to this excellent epitome : what Keats himself called "Miltonian tenderness" (1817; "Epistle to Charles Cowden Clarke," 58). It is this chiefest of Keats's own disposition that brings round a consideration of "To Autumn" (1819), that most magnificent of poems long catalogued on the Shakespearean side of Keats's ledger. There is no doubt that the poem is filled with humility, joy, serenity, calmness, and fullfillment, and these are unmistakably qualities inherent in the Shakespearean vision : "Ripeness is all" (*King Lear* 5. 2. 11), as Murry and others have appropriately reminded us (*Keats and Shakespeare*, p. 189). We have only to recall, however, Gittings's observation that the stanzaic form of "To Autumn," with some slight variation, is composed of a Shakespearean quatrain and a Miltonic sestet (*John Keats*, p. 311) to admit the presence of another more consummate vision given to Adam by Michael : while "beyond is all abyss, / Eternitie, whose end no eye can reach," there is "A paradise within thee, happier farr" (*PL* 12. 555–56, 586–87). "To Autumn" is a poem that acknowledges human life to be but a segment on the eternally regenerating cycle of Nature, but imbues that understanding with a poignant sorrow and an immense tenderness. As Clemene says of Apollo's music, "To Autumn" fills us with "joy and grief at once" (*Hyperion* 2. 289). With an amplitude of mind, it balances against a Shakespearean freedom a Miltonic awareness "that the world is full of Misery and Heartbreak, Pain, Sickness and oppression" (3 May 1818; *Letters* 1 : 281). "To Autumn" represents Keats's final abandonment of the pastoral* garden of innocence and a heroic acceptance of mortality; it is a grave and meditative hymn for the dispossession of Adam and Eve, sung beneath the light of Michael's sword. *See also* INFLUENCE ON THE LITERATURE OF NINETEENTH CENTURY ENGLAND, MILTON'S. [APA]

KENNET, WHITE. *Brit* was reprinted in 1706 and 1719 in an edition by John Hughes in *A Complete History of England*, 1 : 1–82 (without the index or the 1698 alterations). The third volume in this collection gave an account of the reigns of the Stuarts and was written by the historian White Kennet (1660–1728), who has thus frequently and erroneously had his name attached to the edition. *A Register and Chronicle, Ecclesiastical and Civil* (1728), which he compiled, refers to Milton or his works frequently (pp. 23, 73, 96, 170, 180–81, 189, 189–90, 230, 239, 270, 711, 776–77); pp. 318–19 also notice the reprint of *Smectymnuus Redivivus*. It is a helpful corroboration of bibliographic matters.

Kennet is also the source of a fantastic story of reunion after death, which Milton hoped for at the burial of his second wife. He had heard the tale from a Mr. Harvey of Petty France (November 14, 1730), who in turn had been told it by a Mr. Lounds (see Anthony Wood*, *Fasti Oxonienis,* ed. Philip Bliss [1815], 1, col. 486). A tantalizing bibliographical problem

results from another item of marginalia written by Kennet in *Athenae Oxoniensis,* which Bliss picked up. Kennet mentions a Latin translation of chapter 1 of *Eikon* by Lewis du Moulin (brother of Milton's antagonist Peter*), which he supposedly owned. It seems to be printed, for he notes it as "Londini, 1650, 4to" (see Wood [1820], 4 : 126). Adding to the confusion, Gui Patin wrote in a letter to André Falcourt on July 5/15, 1660, that *Peter* du Moulin had turned *Eikon* into Latin (see *L'Esprit de Guy Patin* [1710], p. 64). No Latin translation is known, whether of the first book or the whole, by Lewis or by Peter du Moulin, in print or in manuscript. [JTS]

KENOSIS. St. Paul has written at Philippians 2 : 7, *allà heautòn ekénosen.* The verb *kenóō* means literally "to empty out" and metaphorically "to make of no account." From the Greek noun *kénosis,* "an emptying," comes the English word *kenosis,* Christ's action of emptying himself of godhead to become man. The Vulgate translates St. Paul's clause as *sed semetipsum exinanivit.* From the Latin verb comes the English noun *exinanition,* a synonym for *kenosis.* The translation of the idea into English is difficult, for the choice between the literal and metaphorical meaning *kenosis* betrays a translator's theological position. The "made himself of no reputation" of the A. V. supports the orthodox view that Christ in coming to earth lost none of his essential nature. To translate the phrase by "emptied himself" introduces the possibility of a heterodox interpretation : Christ gave up his essential nature in coming to earth.

Until the Reformation theologians held generally that the kenosis supported the doctrine of the dual nature of Christ and of the unity of his person. Milton has used St. Paul's verse in explaining the dual nature of Christ the God-man, and the sacrifice of the God-man (*CD* 15 : 259–61, 303, 307–9, 293). When Christ accepted humanity, he did not relinquish his divine nature, for by *nature* is to be understood "the essence itself" (15 : 269). In Milton's view, the mystery of the will and understanding of Christ's dual nature remains to man a mystery. That mystery he illustrates by bringing together Luke 2 : 52, and Philippians 2 : 7 with John 21 : 17 : Christ could grow in wisdom; yet, after he emptied himself, he had the faculty to know all things (15 : 275). This view of the kenosis follows the main course of patristic exegesis.

However, Milton's view of the Son* as subordinate to the Father* taints his view of the kenosis with heterodoxy. William B. Hunter argues that Milton in treating of the kenosis profits from the Nestorian hypothesis that the divine nature of Christ entered the human form at some time after the human form had been begotten. "Since for him two *persons* are united, he may interpret the 'emptying' as being a renunciation of the divine power by the Son as he becomes incarnate" (*Journal of the History of Ideas* 21 : 367). Indeed, Milton uses the doctrine of the kenosis in forming an argument that refutes the unity of essence between the Son and the Father. The infinite God, he argues, cannot be said to empty himself (*CD* 14 : 343). Though Christ's divine and human natures were both slain in his death (15 : 309), at the exaltation the divine nature was restored to its manifestation of glory, a glory "only next in dignity to God," which that nature had forfeited at the kenosis; and at the exaltation the human nature acceded to that glory (14 : 337; 15 : 309–15).

Outright statements of the kenosis in Milton's poetry are orthodox. The Father addresses the Son in *PL*:

Nor shalt thou by descending to assume
Mans Nature, less'n or degrade thine owne.
(3. 303–4)

There is an explicit catalogue of the divesting of glory in *Nat,* where "He laid aside"

That glorious Form, that Light unsufferable,
And that far-beaming blaze of Majesty.
(8–9)

Form is not essence : ". . . the sacred writers nowhere use the word 'form' for actual being" (*CD* 14 : 273) ; though form, Michael Lieb maintains, "implies 'essence' or 'nature' " (*ELH, A Journal of English Literary History* 37 : 348).

More general is the statement in *Circ* :

. . . for us frail dust
Emptied his glory, ev'n to nakednes.
(19–20)

Other statements of the doctrine are: "this glorie next to thee / Freely put off" (*PL* 3. 239); "Thenceforth the form of servant to assume" (*PL* 10. 214).

See Barbara Kiefer Lewalski, *Milton's Brief Epic* (1966), pp. 133–63, for a study of the kenosis and its bearing on an interpretation of *PR*. See Michael Lieb's article for a study of the nature of the kenosis and the implications of that doctrine in Milton's poetry and prose. [WA]

KEPLER, JOHANNES: *see* SCIENCE, MILTON AND.

KERYGMA. The kerygma is the message of the Gospel through which God declared that Christ had been incarnated to save man. After seeing Christ's risen spirit, Peter proclaims the redemptive nature of the life, death, and resurrection of Christ (Acts 2 : 14–40). The kerygma is, then, "the solemn and public proclamation of salvation in Christ made in the name of God to non-Christians; it was accompanied by an appeal to signs and wonders to dispose the hearers to faith, conversion, and a return to God" (*New Catholic Encyclopedia* [1967], 8 : 167).

According to Milton in *CD*, "the Gospel is the new dispensation of the covenant of Grace . . . announced first obscurely by Moses and the prophets, afterwards in the clearest terms by Christ himself, and his apostles and evangelists, . . . containing a promise of eternal life to all in every nation who shall believe in Christ when revealed to them"

(16 : 113.) This statement, though not an explicit definition of kerygma, exhibits Milton's belief in the kerygmatic purpose of the Holy Scriptures.

In the poems *PL, PR, Lyc,* and *Nat,* Milton teaches and preaches the kerygma. To do this, he, as narrator, assumes the role of *kerux,* the divinely inspired messenger or herald, asserting the providence of God, proclaiming the glory of Christ, and revealing the possibility of salvation through Him. This role as *kerux* proclaiming the kerygma is particularly apparent in *PL.* The narrator receives divine inspiration and revelation from the Spirit (the muse), and the content of the poem after the invocation is in effect the word of God. *PL* proposes to teach the kerygma so that man may find salvation through Christ. As Michael was the *kerux* to Adam, so Milton is the *kerux* to readers of *PL. PR, Lyc,* and *Nat* display the same relationship between the narrator and the Spirit; each poem becomes a means by which Milton proclaims the message of the Gospel. Although he does not specifically mention the term, the divinely inspired kerygma is of central importance to Milton's poetry and his theology. [PTW]

KIEFFER, ERHARD: *see* CRITICICSM.

KING, EDWARD, the "Lycidas" of Milton's poem, was born in Ireland in 1612. He was admitted to Christ's College*, Cambridge, in 1626, and appointed to a fellowship in the college by royal mandate in 1630; the mandate speaks of King's "present sufficiency and future hopes." In 1633–34 he was praelector of his college. He sailed for Ireland on a family visit in 1637, but on August 10 "that fatal and perfidious bark" struck a rock and sank; King was last seen kneeling on the deck in prayer.

Though obviously favored by those in authority, King does not seem to have been an exceptional young man; he had little opportunity to make his mark in university life or as a Christian minister. His surviving poems are all Latin con-

tributions to various Cambridge collections of occasional poems, similar to the collection *Justa Edovardo King**, which was published in commemoration of his death, and in which *Lyc* first appeared. It is not certain how well Milton and King knew each other, and there is no evidence for the assertion that Milton had a prior claim to the fellowship that King received; it is clear enough that Milton shared in the general esteem for King and the shock at his untimely death, or he would not have contributed to the memorial volume. [JD]

KINGSHIP. Milton's conception of kingship was dual : there were earthly kings in wide variety, he admitted, but only one *divine* ruler. Throughout his career he was consistent in his belief that ideal kingship belonged solely to Christ, "the heavenly and eternal King," who alone was to be "honored, worshipped, glorified." Christ came as a liberator, Milton thought, and His statements concerning worldly kingship indicated that obedience* to such kings should be given only when that obedience concurred with Christian faith* and freedom. Earthly kings ought to be the servants of their people, subordinate and responsible to the nations that they served.

Milton's theories of politics* in general contained a large element of Aristotelian rationalism tempered with Christian idealism. He agreed with Aristotle* that all peoples could not be governed by the same principles at all times; hence various kinds of government would at different times be best for a given nation. Monarchy for some people was the best form of government, Milton acknowledged, but absolute monarchy always was to be considered dangerous. By 1649 Milton had firmly concluded that it was political folly to repose all power in one person.

In his early writings, however, Milton had taken a position favorable to the Stuart kings. Not even ancient Sparta or Rome, he wrote, had been ruled with more justice and harmony than England. In principle, he insisted in *Ref,* the throne of a king "*is establisht in Justice,* which is the universal *Justice* that *Aristotle* so much praises, containing in it all other *vertues.*" But as he involved himself in the antiprelatical polemics of the 1640s, his apprehension grew. The English king was being seduced by the prelates, he thought. "We cannot serve two contrary masters, God and king," he insisted, as his perception of the inherent weaknesses of the monarchical theory of government developed. In *Tenure* he wrote, "How great a good and happiness a just King is, so great a mischeife is a Tyrant." And a short time later he firmly stated, "I hate not kings, but Tyrants."

By the time that Charles I* was brought to the executioner's block, Milton's conception of kingship had developed into what was to be its definitive form. He outlined his new definition of a king in the opening pages of *Tenure*: "A King governs to the good and profit of his People, and not for his own ends." Conversely, "A Tyrant is he who, regarding neither Law nor the common good, reigns onely for himself and his faction." The statement is Aristotelian, but Milton adds in this passage his own seventeenth-century qualifications drawn from the laws of Nature*. Those laws decreed, Milton insisted, that no man could be a true king except him who excelled in wisdom and courage. Men without those qualities became kings only by force or by favor. Milton's political philosophy included the conception of the abstract office of monarchy: "Who knows not," he questioned rhetorically in *Tenure,* "that the King is a name of dignity and office, not of person?" It was from this line of argument that Milton could contend that the execution of Charles I had been the execution of a guilty man, not of a king, because Charles had been deposed from his monarchical office *before* his death upon the scaffold.

Milton also turned to the laws of Nature for his theory of the origin of kingship. From the beginning of civilized societies men bound themselves together in common league for protection against injury and destruction. In Milton's version of the social contract free men voluntarily delegated their *innate* and *immutable* natural powers of self-government to one whose "eminence of wisdom and integritie" made him their choice for king. Unlike the submissive Royalist version of the social contract, which contained the idea of an "irrevocable alienation" of the people's power, Milton's conception included a qualified idea of popular sovereignty. The people gave their power to the king only provisionally, he insisted, because the law of Nature forbade their surrendering it absolutely. The original grant of power was made only for the sake of the welfare and freedom of the people. The king, therefore, by the laws of Nature was a magisterial officer, a servant of the people, bound by laws and limitations. Milton acknowledged that in England kingship was hereditary, but this, he declared, was mere "courtesie or convenience." To say that the king had as much right to his crown and dignity as any man to his inheritance was to make "the Subject no better then the kings slave, his chatell, or his possession that may be bought or sould." If monarchy were to be acceptable, Milton concluded in 1649, it should become an elective office.

In *1Def* Milton came to grips with the problem of the king's rights, prerogatives, and duties. It followed from his interpretation of the social contract that sovereignty might be both limited and divided, limited by the scope of the king's mandate, and divided as a result of the retention of certain rights by the people. Some of the Royalists had insisted upon the doctrine of *rex legibus solutus* (a king is above law): the laws of England, they said, were the king's laws, in word and in deed. Milton, of course, denied this conception of royal power. He insisted, as many of the seventeenth-century common lawyers had done, upon the supremacy of positive customary law in England. Such laws were the "laws of the land" and "the laws of the people," and Milton proved his point linguistically in *1Def* by tracing such terms to Anglo-Saxon* usage. Milton believed in the separation of powers : in his opinion Parliament was the true legislative body, the lawgiver of England, and acted (he insisted) with the power of the people. The king was formally bound by his coronation oath to observe and uphold the laws and customs of England. For a monarchy to be acceptable (by 1649 Milton thought the English people had advanced beyond such a form), the king and Parliament must function harmoniously in a mixed government to express the will of the people.

In the seventeenth century the royal prerogatives were classified as *regale et legale*, "absolute and ordinary," and "inseparable and separate." Outstanding jurists such as Coke*, Bacon*, and Fleming had advanced the political philosophy of the king's prerogatives in the early years of that period. But by 1640 the common lawyers were arguing that the king's absolute and inseparable prerogatives must be subjected to the common-law test of precedent. Such a test, of course, made all royal prerogative "ordinary" and "separate." Milton's position on this important question was the Parliamentary one; he insisted that the king held no transcendental powers, that the royal powers of arrest without naming a cause, of taxation, of dispensing with statutes, of convening and dissolving Parliament must be limited by English law. Milton believed that the royal prerogatives were given to the king only to be legitimately used for the *salus populi* (welfare of the people). "A king exists for the people, not the people for the king," he wrote in *1Def*.

The same maxim was true concerning the private actions of a king, Milton thought. A monarch's private life as well as his public should be exemplary of Christian virtue. A king must acquire first the governance of himself, Milton wrote. Salmasius* had argued in *Defensio Regia* that Charles I's private life was his own personal affair, that in general a king's private life need not necessarily be related to his public actions. Milton vehemently denied this precept by insisting upon a universal morality for both politics and ethics*. He thought a bad man could no more become a good prince than a bad man could become a good poet. The personal and the public elements were (he concluded) indivisible in the life of a king.

Finally, Milton insisted upon the conception of the conditional obedience of subjects to the king. The *jus resistendi* (the right to oppose) was a natural right of the people of England, he declared. When a king grew incorrigible, when he vitiated the bond of fidelity with his people, he should be deposed *and punished*. Many of the Puritans agreed in 1649 that Charles was rightly deposed, but they balked at punishing him. Milton contended that the same English laws that provided for the punishment of a magistrate guilty of maladministration should be used to punish the royal tyrant. Indeed, Milton proclaimed, a king might be punished with even more justice than a private man! He developed this idea further in *1Def*: the people could remove a king from his office and alter the government *even without cause* "merely by the liberty and right of free-born men to be governed as seems to them best." In the case of a tyrant the people possessed a natural right to depose him before or after his formal trial *"in whatever way they can."* By the law of Nature a king who had become an unbearable burden to his country should be removed from his position of power to destroy an entire people. It was legal, Milton argued, to resist illegal authority. Tyrannicide therefore should be praised by enlightened men.

At the end of his political career Milton conceded reluctantly in *BN* that England in its debased state might require a temporary king or protector (General Monck* appears to have been his choice), but this expedient statement was the result of the pressure of the times. In *Way* (1660) he stated that even the most virtuous and enlightened despot would find it impossible to establish true liberty*. Milton deeply mistrusted single rule. His hopes lay in his belief that universal education in England would develop a spirit of freedom too strong to admit the return of kingship to the isle. [ALS]

KLOPSTOCK, FREDERICK GOTT-LIEB (1724–1803). Milton's influence entered the German literary mainstream by way of Klopstock, who in 1745 joined the group of young rebels who had broken away from Gottsched's journal, *Belustigungen des Verstandes und Witzes,* to form their own. These young men, among whom were Christian Fürchtegott Gellert and Johann Adolf Schlegel, resolved to avoid disputes, to use materials that were between seriousness and joking, to publish their own works, and to publish translations*. With the publication of the first three songs of Klopstock's *Messias* in issues four and five of *Neuen Beiträge,* the young rebels had in effect joined the battle for Bodmer*. Taking full advantage of the new rights won for poetry through Milton and the Swiss, Klopstock rejected rhyme, freeing German verse from its former jingle. Though having himself no epic talent—his gift was lyrical—Klopstock inspired epic writing in Germany. His influence is most clearly seen in four major disciples: Friedrich Leopold Graf zu Stolberg, Johann Heinrich Voss, Matthias Claudias, and Franz von Sonnenberg. [MM]

KNOWLEDGE. The purpose of knowledge or learning, Milton says in *Educ,* "is to repair the ruins of our first parents by regaining to know God aright . . ." and out of that knowledge to learn how to love and imitate God so as to possess true virtue. For Milton, knowledge is not simply the mastery of information but learning that seeks to correct the effects of original sin and enable one to live righteously. The value of knowledge is determined by how well it serves that end, and is one of God's ways of renewing man's "lapsed powers" (*PL* 3. 176). Knowledge that may be discovered by human faculties includes both natural and moral philosophy (science* and ethics*).

Although human understanding is corrupted by the effects of original sin, God's purpose is still that we should study "the visible and inferior creature" so that we may arrive "to the knowledge of God" (4 : 277).

Such knowledge as man may acquire by the use of his natural faculties is not, however, sufficient in itself to achieve "the highest perfection" (4 : 277), such as the knowledge of God, for "No one . . . can have right thoughts of God, with nature or reason alone as his guide, independent of the word, or message of God" (*CD* 14 : 31). The word of God was the divine revelation of Holy Scripture, before which all other knowledge of whatever provenience gave place. The Bible, rightly perceived, was the absolute authority in all matters public and private. To read Scripture competently, one had to be a man of learning, industry, and good conscience, but these qualities were within the grasp of ordinary men, for the means God had given of acquiring "necessary knowledge" was "in proportion as may bee weilded and manag'd by the life of man without penning him up from the duties of humane society" (3 : 139). The revealed word of God supplied all the "necessary knowledge" one should have in order to lead a God-fearing life, although such sufficiency did not exclude the knowledge of God that could be drawn from nature and the human mind (14 : 25). As Jesus said in *PR,* ". . . he who receives / Light from above, from the fountain of light, / No other doctrine needs, though granted true" (4. 288–90).

A third kind of desirable knowledge may be added to that which is revealed (biblical) and that which may be discovered by human faculties. It is properly described as a kind of innate knowledge, which Adam apparently possessed when he found himself capable of naming whatever he saw (*PL* 8. 271–72), and in doing so understanding its nature with "such knowledg" as God "endu'd" his sudden apprehension" (8. 352–54). In *CD,* Milton calls this innate knowledge wisdom : "Certainly without extraordinary wisdom he [Adam] could not have given names to the whole animal creation with such sudden intelligence" (15 : 53). That prelapsarian Adam possessed a very high order of knowledge was not an idea original to Milton. Aquinas* believed that Adam had an angelic understanding, capable of perceiving the essence of things instantly (*Summa Theol.* 1. 94. 2–4). Likewise, Andrew Willet explained in his commentary on Genesis (*Hexapla,* 1608) that the ability to name implied great knowledge, for "names were given at the first according to the severall properties and nature of creatures" (p. 37). The Greek cognate of this idea is found in Plato's *Cratylus* (p. 422).

The desire for knowledge was dangerous, however, and Milton was at some pains to show the disastrous consequences of pursuing it improvidently. One is allowed "knowledge within bounds"—indeed, encouraged to acquire it—but "beyond abstain / To ask . . ." (*PL* 7. 120–21), for "Knowledge is as food, and needs no less / Her Temperance over Appetite, to know / In measure what the mind may well contain, / Oppresses else with Surfet, and soon turns / Wisdom to Folly, as Nourishment to Winde" (7. 126–30). Forbidden knowledge is thus a proscription against trying to know what one cannot know because of man's limited capacity. Basically, it is dubious speculation or the sin* of curiosity, which sought "with wandring thoughts, and notions vain" (*PL* 8. 87) to comprehend the inapplicable. The idea was shared by many, as John Donne's description of a vainly curious man suggests : "He that desires knowledge only that he may know, or be known of others to know; he who makes not the end of knowledge the glory of God, he offends in curiosity . . ." (Grossart, ed., *Works,* 6 : 96–97). Indeed, the Fall of Man is the direct consequence, as Adam admits, of seeking "Forbidd'n knowledge by forbidd'n means" (*PL* 12. 279). The Miltonic economy prescribed that Adam be "lowlie wise" (8. 173), secure in the knowledge that God had

revealed what was needful "to live / The easiest way" and enjoy "the sweet of Life" (8. 182–84). "Know to know no more" (4. 775). Put another way, the need to obey was the sole necessary knowledge in prelapsarian Eden.

Acquiring the knowledge of good and evil*—knowing good by knowing evil—is central to the climactic action of the Fall of Man. As a test of their fidelity, God forbade Adam and Eve to eat from the Tree of Knowledge. As Milton explained in *CD,* the test was an act in its own nature indifferent, and the tree "was called the tree of Knowledge of Good and Evil from the event, for since Adam tasted it, we not only know evil, but we know good only by means of evil. For it is by evil that virtue is chiefly exercised and shines with greater brightness" (15 : 112–14). Eve especially wants to know what it is that God had forbidden them, and yields to Satan's temptation "through expectation high / Of knowledge . . ." (*PL* 9. 789–90), in the mistaken belief that the knowledge she hoped to acquire would transform her into a god. Eve aspires too high and falls by trying to be more than her nature allows. As evil diminishes original goodness, it paradoxically defines what is lost. Forbidden knowledge is thus a proscription against attempting to know the unknowable. Ironically, to eat from the Tree of Knowledge is also to eat death (*PL* 9. 792), a killing of the body and spirit in the pursuit of a phantasy of life. As Sebastian Franck wrote in *The Forbidden Fruit* (1640), like Eve, all men "doe eate death, and yet . . . thinke themselves to eate life, and hope to be Gods."

In *PR* 4. 285–364, Jesus rejects Satan's temptation to the learning of ancient Greece. Many readers have found this rejection curiously at odds with the enthusiasms of *Educ,* and it is possible that sometime between 1640 and 1660 Milton changed his mind about the means and ends of education. Jesus very clearly condemns Greek philosophy as "false, or little else but dreams, / Conjectures, fancies, built on nothing firm" (*PR* 4.

291–92). But seen from a dramatic and structural point of view, Jesus' words need not be taken as expressing Milton's own views, and Jesus' rejection of classical learning parallels and corrects Adam's desire for forbidden knowledge (*PL* 8. 66–178). Milton had, moreover, always insisted on the sufficiency of the Scriptures to provide all the knowledge essential to the good life, of being "learned without letters" (*1Def* 7 : 69).

But Milton may have had in mind a commonplace distinction between knowledge (*scientia*), which derives from the study of the things of the world, and wisdom* (*sapientia*), which comes only from God. Milton's authority would have been Augustine*, who separated wisdom from human knowledge and thus set up the direct opposition of *sapientia* and *scientia*. Wisdom is the knowledge of the divine things of God; absolute wisdom is God Himself. Human wisdom is piety, faith in and worship of God according to His revelation. Knowledge of temporal human things or of mere moral virtue is not wisdom but human knowledge and prudence. Milton's Jesus may thus be seen as asserting and defending the sufficiency of divine wisdom against the vanity and ultimate irrelevance of human knowledge.

In contrast to his measured attitude toward knowledge in *PL* and *PR*, Milton's youthful *Oratio pro Arte* (*Prol* 7) is a euphoric witness to the joys to be found in learning and art. The *Oratio* answers the question whether learning makes men happier than does ignorance with an emphatic yes. "Knowledge is the fairest ornament of youth, the strong defense of manhood, the glory and comfort of old age." And with typical humanist* faith in the "godlike might and power of the human mind," Milton proclaimed a creed that only time and experience would temper : ". . . when universal learning shall have completed its cycle, the spirit of man, no longer confined by this dark prisonhouse, will reach out far and wide until it fills the whole world and the space beyond, with a divine expansion of magnitude. . . . He will seem to be one

whose power and dominion the stars will obey, to whom the land and sea will hearken, the winds and tempests defer; one to whom Mother Nature herself will surrender. . . ." [PEB]

KNOX, JOHN (ca. 1505–1572), Scot reformer. After a time in Catholic orders Knox became a Protestant preacher. In 1551 he was appointed chaplain to Edward VI, helping to revise the Second Prayer Book. He was probably responsible for the controversial "Black Rubric," an unauthorized addition questioning the Real Presence in the Eucharist. On the accession of Mary he fled to the Continent, where he met Calvin*. He drew up the *Scottish Confession* (1560), the standard confessional of the Reformed Church of Scotland till the Westminster Confession of 1647, consisting of twenty-five Calvinistic articles, including justification* by faith*, election, and supreme authority in Scripture. His *Treatise on Predestination* (1560) takes a rigid predestinarian* position. The principal work of his life was the *History of the Reformation of Religion within the Realm of Scotland* (unfinished, suppressed, complete ed. 1644).

G. P. Gooch traces a gradual four-stage radicalization of Knox's political philosophy from 1552, when he called for patient suffering of tyranny, through 1558, when he advocated armed resistance against evil rulers (*English Democratic Ideas in the Seventeenth Century* [1927], pp. 37–39). Milton elaborately cites his authority on this issue in *Tenure* (5: 28–29). [EFD]

KROUSE, F(RANK) MICHAEL (1916–1955), scholar who after earning his doctorate at Johns Hopkins University returned to his native state of Ohio as a member of the faculty of the University of Cincinnati. There he published *Milton's Samson and the Christian Tradition* (1949), a major investigation of the background of the play, especially as Samson had been interpreted in church history. His early death kept him from editing *SA* for the Milton Variorum. [WBH]

LABADIE, JEAN DE (1610–1674), French Jesuit who turned to Calvinism* about 1650, after being persecuted for putting into practice some of his views. He fled to the Netherlands, where he established the Labadists, a group dedicated to simple living and communal property. However, wherever he settled, Labadie was plagued by scandal over supposed sexual laxity, and was continually harassed. In 1651 he published an account of his suffering and conversion, *Lettre de la Communion Romaine,* a copy of which he sent to Milton around 1658. In *Epistol* 28 (April 21, 1659, a date that Parker says is in error, perhaps for April 27), Milton wrote to Labadie, first apologizing for the delay in acknowledging Labadie's book and letter (a delay caused by the slowness of their mutual friend, [Giles?] Dury), then stating the poet's admiration and sympathy. Labadie apparently was seeking an invitation to England; Milton wrote that he had secured Labadie a position succeeding Jean d'Espagne as minister of the Somerset House Chapel, and urged him to come at once. Milton either had not heard the scandalous rumors concerning Labadie or did not believe them. Labadie did not come to England but went instead to Geneva. [WM]

LACTANTIUS (ca. 250–ca. 330). Lucius Caecilius Firmianus Lactantius, born in Africa, taught Latin rhetoric at Nicomedia about 290, and became a Christian in middle life. He sought by the charm of his Ciceronian style*, the breadth of his interest in history and antiquity, and the use of frequent citations from the classical writers to propogate Christianity among the intellectuals. To this end he wrote *De opificiis dei, Divinae institutiones, De ira dei,* and *De mortibus persecutorum.* The second of these, written between 305 and 313, is the first known systematic presentation of Christian thought in the Latin language. Lactantius's abridgment of it is entitled *Epitome.* Though Lactantius's works lacked the penetration to make him important as a theologian, his style and learning later endeared him to Renaissance humanists; Gabriel Harvey referred to his writings as "elegant," and Pico della Mirandola gave him the title "Christian Cicero."

That Lactantius was to Milton one of the most interesting Fathers is evidenced (1) by six references to him in Milton's prose works and marginalia, two in *Ref* (3 : 29) and one each in *Tetra, 3Def, Logic,* and marginalia (4 : 209–10; 9 : 111; 11 : 49; and 18 : 304, respectively); (2) by seven entries from Lactantius's works made in *CB,* two under the heading "Moral Evil" (18 : 128–29), and one each under the headings "The Good Man," "Lust," "Courage," "Love of Country," and "Spectacles" (18 : 129, 132, 134, 164–65, and 206–7, respectively); and (3) by numerous echoes of Lactantius's ideas in Milton's works, which Kathleen E. Hartwell, in *Lactantius and Milton* (1929), and Ruth Mohl, in *John Milton and His "Commonplace Book"* (1969), have attempted to trace.

Though Dean Colet in his instructions of 1518 for St. Paul's School* included Lactantius among others in a projected curriculum, there is no proof that Milton read Lactantius there (see Hartwell, pp. viii, 67, 80–81, 133, 161–62; and Donald L. Clark, *John Milton at St. Paul's School,* p. 125). Ruth Mohl (p. 36) prefers to think that Milton studied the Fathers carefully during the Horton period, and Parker (*Milton,* p. 841), that he was reading Lactantius "in the autumn of 1639." On the basis of handwriting, the *CB* entries are dated 1639–40 or 41, after his return from Italy.

Of the ideas in Milton that may conjecturally be traced to Lactantius, two stand as examples. (1) Milton's two citations in *CB* (18 : 128–29) from Lactantius (*Institutes,* Bk. 5, chap. 7, and *De ira dei,* chap. 13) and other uncited passages from the *Institutes* relative to the need to test virtue are, Hartwell argues (pp. 21–34), the sources of Milton's "I cannot praise a fugitive and cloister'd vertue, unexercis'd & unbreath'd . . ." (*Areop* 4 : 311), a recurring Miltonic theme (*RCG* 3:223; *Apol* 3:311; *Areop* 4:311; *CD* 17:247). (2) Milton's emphasis upon the virtue of patience, perhaps most memorably stated in *SA* 652–59 and 1287–96 (see Mohl, pp. 49–53), can be observed in the comment on "the greatest of the virtues, namely, patience," which Milton cited in *CB* (18:129) from Lactantius (*Institutes,* Bk. 6, chap. 18). [MCJ]

LAERTIUS, DIOGENES, the reputed author of a work of great importance to Renaissance humanism*, a compendium on the lives and thought of philosophers from Thales to Epicurus, known as the *Lives and Opinions of Eminent Philosophers.* A book of no outstanding merit whether literary or philosophical, its value is due to the chance that it alone, of the many similar works written in the early centuries of our era, has survived intact.

Almost nothing is known of the circumstances in which the book was written, or of its author. Even the date of composition is only approximately known, and various theories based on its content exist. With the revival of letters Diogenes Laertius naturally assumed great importance. There were further translations into Latin and into Italian, and annotations were provided by scholars of the stature of the Casaubons, Aldobrandinus, and Ménage; Vives, Scaliger*, and Montaigne are among the admirers of the book. The *Lives and Opinions of Eminent Philosophers* thus took its place as one of the indispensable books of humanist culture.

Like any educated man of his time, Milton knew his Laertius thoroughly. Many of his passing references to ancient philosophy can be readily traced to the *Lives,* which he values in true humanist fashion as a work not of intellectual interest merely but of moral usefulness. It is on these grounds that he recommends the book in *Educ* as a text for young scholars. After three years of elementary studies, he writes, they will be fitted to contemplate with some judgment moral good and evil*. At this point there will be required "a speciall reinforcement of constant and sound endoctrinating to set them right and firm, instructing them more amply in the knowledge of Vertue and the hatred of Vice : while their young and pliant affections are led through all the moral works of *Plato, Xenophon, Cicero, Plutarch, Laertius,* and those *Locrian* remnants." At the same time such pagan training in virtue should be firmly related to Christian doctrine, should be "reduc't in their nightward studies wherewith they close the dayes work, under the determinate sentence of *David* or *Salomon,* or the Evangelists and Apostolic Scriptures" (4:284). Milton is not unusual in regarding the *Lives* as an important educational text. Joseph Mead*, who held the Greek lectureship at Christ's College* in Milton's time, lists purchases of Laertius, apparently in Greek though there were also Greek/Latin editions for college use. Also at Cambridge Richard Holdsworth of St. John's, in his "Directions for a Student in the Universitie," recommends the reading of Laertius among others after the regular work for the degree is completed, "being such as no one that pretends to be an University scholar ought to be unacquainted with" (H. F. Fletcher, *The Intellectual Development of John Milton,* 2:647).

This acquaintance Milton shows in such passages as Uriel's account of creation in Book 3 of *PL* and on several occasions in the prose works where he draws on Laertius for support of his own positions. For example his reference in *Prol* 1 to the fabrications of Democritus or in *Prol* 7 to the "Not-Being" of the Epicureans would have their standard source in the *Lives,* and in *PrelE* there is a witty reference to the same source. Here Milton accuses his opponents of inventing in their support a "Leucippean *Ignatius,*" the pseudo-Ignatius supposed to have been a contemporary of St. Peter. To make his satiric point Milton depends upon his readers' knowledge of Laertius's tenth book, in which we are told that Epicurus denied the very existence of the philosopher Leucippus, said to have been the teacher of Democritus. More extended use is made of Laertius's authority in *Areop,* where the freedom from legal censure of "*Epicurus,* or that libertine school of *Cyrene,* or what the *Cynick* impudence utter'd" is brought forward as an argument, and where Plato's "wanton epigrams," of which Laertius gives examples in his third book, are also cited. In some matters Milton prefers other authorities to Laertius; for example, he does not share the latter's admiration of Epicurus and his followers. But the *Lives* was clearly a work with which he had an easy familiarity, and with which he expected a similar familiarity in his readers. [KW]

LAFAYE, L. R.: *see* TRANSLATIONS OF MILTON'S WORKS.

L'ALLEGRO AND IL PENSEROSO. Milton's companion poems do not appear in *TM.* They were printed, undated, in both the 1645 and 1673 editions of *Poems,* where they follow the two short pieces on the death of Hobson* the University Carrier (died January 1, 1631). Until our own time, the composition of *L'Al* and *IlP* was placed early in the so-called Horton* period, 1632–1638 (actually, from 1632 to 1635 Milton was in residence at Hammersmith*), on the basis of the many references to nature and descriptions of country scenery that were assumed to derive from direct observation. But it is now customary to date them in 1631 (see Tillyard, *The Miltonic Setting* [1938], pp. 1–28, which reprints views of the dating first set forth in 1932), because they seem intended for a university audience and bear close resemblance to the mood and rhythms of Milton's graceful Jonsonian performances in *May,* the Hobson poems, and *EpWin.* Though opinion has generally settled upon Milton's last Cambridge summer of 1631, other dates, earlier and later, continue to be advanced. F. W. Bateson (*Seventeenth-Century News Letter* 7:10) and Harris

Fletcher (*Intellectual Development of John Milton* [1961], 2:479ff.) argue for the late summer of 1629 on the basis of *El* 6, addressed to Diodati*, where Milton is supposed to speak of some poems he wishes to show his friend. Both insist that *cicutis* (line 89) must be translated as *pastorals* and therefore refers to *L'Al* and *IlP* rather than to *Nat.* This argument poses its own difficulties—that we accept the companion poems as less mature productions of Milton's art than *Nat,* a position that requires one to believe that after the extraordinary variety and suppleness of the tetrameter couplets of *L'Al* and *IlP,* Milton moved to the heavier rhythms of *Nat.*

The differences between the 1645 and 1673 editions are few and minor, confined chiefly to accidentals of orthography and punctuation. The only substantial variant occurs in *L'Al,* at line 33, where 1673 prints "trip it as you go," and 1645 prints "trip it as ye go." In 1673, an obvious misprint in 1645 at line 57 of *IlP* ("Id her sweetest" for "In") is corrected.

Compared to Milton's other poems, *L'Al* and *IlP* would appear to offer few obstacles to appreciation and comprehension. Even Dr. Johnson*, who usually found as much to censure as to admire in Milton and condemned *Lyc* so roundly, could find nothing but cause for praise in these twin poems. And if influence is an accurate guide to literary reputation, they bore an impress upon the poetic vocabulary and imagery of the following century that was a measure of their high esteem. Indeed, their very success in appealing to eighteenth-century taste has been in our own time reason enough to raise questions about their poetic vitality, because Dr. Johnson's preference for the generalized image, to name only one issue, is exactly at odds with the romantic and post-romantic demand for concrete particularization. So despite the fact that they are probably the most accessible of Milton's poems for the modern reader, they have been subject to divergent analyses that, while not really undermining their critical reputation, have certainly shaken any final view as to the nature of their success.

If we begin with the primary consideration of genre, we find no such clear-cut relation as with *Lyc* (pastoral elegy), *Mask, PL* (classical epic*), *SA* (classical tragedy*), or *PR* (brief epic) that can guide our expectations as to the meanings and effects that come out of a proper response to genre. While pastoral* setting and imagery are evident, especially in *L'Al,* and a pastoral choice is suggested, neither poem exploits primarily some distinction between urban and rural, elevated or low modes of existence, nor do they focus in any central way upon pastoral figures or activities. The hindsight of literary history encourages us to view *L'Al* and *IlP* as important progenitors of the descriptive-reflective poetry of the eighteenth century. However, within the context of Milton's milieu none of the literary genres, as ordinarily defined, makes for a very exact fit. It is usual to talk about the companionate relationship of the two poems as defining their genre, shifting the question to rhetorical* and intellectual substance. Mirth and Melancholy may function as ideas, as embodied ideals, as goals of existence, or as protagonists.

Tillyard* has found in *Prol 1* —"Whether Day or Night is the More Excellent"—the pattern and the substance after which the poems were modeled. He assigns them to the medieval and academic tradition of debate*, which gave rise to so many poems debating the relative excellence of action and contemplation, the body and the soul, et cetera. The relevance is evident to both demonstrative rhetoric (the rhetoric of praise, which magnifies its subject in an encomium or diminishes it in a diatribe) and to deliberative rhetoric (which seeks to persuade to wise and worthy choices of action and to dissuade from those lacking in wisdom and moral worth). Tillyard suggested in *The Miltonic Setting* that each poem opens with bombast and intentional burlesque in the dismissal of its opponent by offering a gross and defamatory caricature. Later critics have emphasized that both the negative portrayal of Melancholy in *L'Al* and the praise of it in *IlP* refer to well-established concepts: the dreaded disease "loathed Melancholy" and the "divinest Melancholy" identified with contemplation and the intellectual endeavors of genius. No concomitant polarities have been advanced for Mirth, which is seen in *L'Al* as the innocent spirit of delight and in *IlP* as pleasure judged to be empty and frivolous. The way we read the 10-line openings of each poem, with their elaborate stanzaic pattern (a3, b5, b3, a5, c3, d5, d3, e5, e3, c5), setting them off from the tetrameter couplets which make up the body of each poem, is of crucial importance. But whether we see them as burlesque, as a witty pointing to the negative underside of Mirth and Melancholy, or as both, these openings do establish the patterns of parallel and contrast that organize the images and demand a simultaneous reading. While the body of each poem is a self-contained praise, a distinctly deliberative edge emerges when we compare actions and images associated with Mirth and Melancholy. The three major trends in interpretation correspond to how the rhetoric is perceived. For critics who see the poems as debate in the strict sense, *L'Al* and *IlP* offer mutually exclusive choices, or, at a more inward and subtle level, represent the tug-of-war in a mind attracted to both Mirth and Melancholy. For critics who see the rhetorical direction as primarily demonstrative, the respective praises of Mirth and Melancholy issue in either a complementary relation of equal "goods" or in a hierarchical ascent from a lesser good to a higher.

We do best, however, to leave these final questions in abeyance until we have explored the poems' intellectual and artistic substance. In recent years, critics have turned increasingly to intellectual history as a starting point, focusing especially upon Melancholy. As early as 1940 Lawrence Babb (*Studies in Philology* 37: 257–73) attempted to clarify the differences between the Melancholy that is the subject of praise in *IlP* and the Melancholy exorcised at the opening of *L'Al*. The latter is the disease of Galenic tradition, an affliction associated with depression and madness. The former is the enviable condition of the intellectually superior person.

As we turn to the poems themselves, we find that their structure cannot be considered apart from their images. From the outset we can see imagery supporting rhetorical strategy and preparing us for the figurative actions of Mirth and Melancholy. Each poem opens with a dismissal followed by an invocation. Out of this is generated first a parallel of "loathed Melancholy" to "vain deluding joyes," and then a double contrast between the positive and negative versions of each. The exorcism of Melancholy in *L'Al* is an anti-encomium or diatribe that attributes parentage, "homeland," and mental and physical traits that are all reasons for dispraise, and in which images of blackness and hell predominate. Melancholy is assigned *Cerberus* (the three-headed dog that stands at the doorway of hell) and "blackest midnight" as parents, a "*Stygian* Cave forlorn" as birthplace, and is urged to banish herself to some "uncouth cell" presided over by "brooding darkness" and the song of the "night-Raven." The horror of this disease is properly confined "under *Ebon* shades" and in "dark *Cimmerian* desert." In contrast, the inviting invocation to Melancholy in *IlP* transforms the images of darkness into something altogether appealing. Since in Platonic* and Christian thought light is traditionally associated with virtue, knowledge, and truth, darkness with evil, ignorance, and falsehood, a special extenuation is required to make blackness the more suitable symbol for wisdom. In hermetic tradition and in various kinds of occultism, however, the profoundest knowledge is assumed to be obscure and hidden from ordinary view. Darkness becomes a material appearance concealing the spiritual truth that is too bright for the carnal eye :

But hail thou Goddes, sage and holy,
Hail divinest Melancholy,
Whose Saintly visage is too bright
To hit the Sense of human sight;
And therefore to our weaker view,
Ore laid with black staid Wisdoms hue.
(11–16)

And to counter the scandalous parentage cited in *L'Al*, Melancholy here is the daughter of "bright-hair'd *Vesta*" and "solitary *Saturn*." Likewise, the Mirth invoked in *L'Al* as the "Goddes fair and free," *Euphrosyne* is the daughter (along with her "two sister Graces" (Aglaia and Thalia) of Bacchus and Venus, not the "brood of folly without father bred," that the devotee of Melancholy would banish to "Dwell in some idle brain, / And fancies fond with gaudy shapes possess."

The assigning of noble and praiseworthy forebears is followed by a description of the gait of each. Mirth is invited to "trip it as ye go / On the light fantastick toe"; Melancholy to "keep thy wonted state, / With eev'n step, and musing gate." As her chief companion Mirth has "The Mountain Nymph, sweet Liberty," while Melancholy brings the "Cherub Contemplation." The liberty associated with Mirth is freedom from care, all the sorrow-denying, blameless pleasures; contemplation is the characteristic activity and goal of divinest Melancholy. The images of both poems substantiate figurative universals valued as modes of absorbing play or study that enable us to reach beyond the limits of routine existence. Through Mirth one enters into a direct sensuous and aesthetic response to experience "that wrincled Care derides" —that liberates from everyday concerns. And divinest Melancholy pierces beyond the common light of every day into "secret shades" of intellectual and religious experience. Their different substances embody differing forms of ideally complete and self-sufficient *pleasure,* the term that Milton explicitly ascribes to the experiences of both poems. Whatever relation "finally" obtains between these ideals—the conundrum to which so much criticism has been addressed—one must first recognize that both Mirth and Melancholy are ideals. As such, both stand apart from the ordinary. So far from comprehending the entire range of possible human pursuit (the implicit assumption of much criticism), they represent two emphatically ideal choices, about which, as with all ideals, the prime questions are likely to be, "How can they be realized? Can they be sustained?"

The foregoing seems indispensable in considering the imagery of the poems. It is highly relevant, for example, to the issue raised by T. S. Eliot*, who complained in *Essays and Studies* (1936; p. 34), that Milton's generalized images lacked Shakespearean particularity, that in *L'Al* one does not see a particular milkmaid. The most persuasive answer to this charge is provided by Rosemond Tuve, who insists that the images "are not 'individuals,' unique sights seen by one man's eye, but particulars, irradiated by the 'general' which they signify" (*Images and Themes in Five Poems by Milton* [1957], p. 22). Moreover, as Miss Tuve also pointed out, "the unindividualized character of the images is matched in the time-structure of the poems." As Milton conveys a sense of realized ideality by not portraying single objects, so the scenes of the poems are not represented with dramatic and temporal particularity. *L'Al* does not follow the dawn-to-sunset pattern of a single day, *IlP* a night to morning pattern. Instead, the scenes are drawn from various days and follow no strict time sequence. The temporal references are typical and unspecified, rather than particular and immediate. Some details are observed, others participated in directly, while still others are speculatively proposed by the imagination as typical activities outside any given time. The temporal setting of the poems is an eternal present of "Oft" and "Som times" in which present and future moments are hardly differentiated, since the action does not consist of a particular series of narration. To approach the imagery and the temporal organization with this awareness is to become skeptical about inter-

pretations that assume and impose a narrative order that progresses from a beginning, through fixed stages, to a final destination. This quality of the images and of the time scheme also contributes to the self-contained completeness of each poem. The universality for which they have been so admired is convincing exactly because the details that convey that universality are memorably concrete without being narrowly particularized.

After its introductions, *L'Al* continues with an idyllic pastoral scene that incorporates responses to nature, human society, and the arts of poetry and music*. The song of the lark signals "From his watch-towre in the skies" the course of l'Allegro's many refined pleasures. Then follows the "lively din" of the more mundane and domestic cock. An earthy English rusticity and an idealized hellenic pastoralism are introduced and mingle throughout the poem. The images of domestic agriculture—the Plowman, the Milkmaid, the Mower, and "every Shepherd tell[ing] his tale"—combine a generalized, yet solid, fecundity with an elegance, each of which strongly ballasts and leavens the other. Before seeking out the parallels these or other images have in *IlP*, the reader should perceive the wide spectrum of feeling the imagery of *L'Al* compasses. The eye moves to compose a series of contrasted landscapes, turning from nature awesome and remote in the "barren brest" of mountains to nature familiar and amiable in "Meadows trim with Daisies pide." Leaving nature for the works of man, the eye again ranges from romantic towers and battlements that stir the imagination to the chimney of a nearby cottage in which modest human contentment dwells—Corydon and Thyrsis partake of their "savory dinner," dressed by "the neat-handed *Phillis*." The rich promise seen in the fields and in country labor is fulfilled in plentiful "Country Messes." Instantly the scene shifts out-of-doors again, as Phillis joins Thestylis, another country girl, "to bind the Sheaves," but there is no determinable, literal movement of l'Allegro, whether as actual observer or participant, or as imaginary viewer or actor, from one scene to another or from one role to another. Scenes, activities, and images beget each other in his mind and are no less vivid to his imagination than to his actual presence.

From pastoral occupations the scene shifts to the musical and social entertainments of "up-land Hamlets." The daylight hours of the "Sunshine Holyday" are given over to "Dancing in the Chequer'd Shade," to song, and to play. The pleasures of the evening are "the Spicy Nut-brown Ale" and "stories told of many a feat," tales of *Faery Mab* drawn from the native folklore, with their echoes of Mercutio in *Romeo and Juliet* and of *A Midsummer Night's Dream.* This evening of innocent country conviviality ends with the tellers of the tales and their audience all creeping to bed. "Towred Cities please us then," l'Allegro notes, but there is no reason to literalize the adverb. We do not proceed physically from the country to the town as an actual movement at a particular moment. Rather, the *image* of the participants in country pleasures all "lull'd asleep" begets associationally the *image* of the still ongoing and more sophisticated pleasures of the City. A world of courtly manners is summoned up—"throngs of Knights and Barons bold . . . with store of Ladies"— quite removed from the homespun of the pastoral world. The romantic sights of "pomp, and feast, and revelry, / With mask, and antique Pageantry" spiral away from the pleasures of pastoral everyday or pastoral holiday to a world of imagination exalted above previous experiences of the senses in nature and society. "Such sights as youthfull Poets dream / On Summer eeves by haunted stream" are no more visible to the merely physical eye than are the rapturous visions of Penseroso. The experience that l'Allegro here glimpses is not, however, mystical or even meditative, but aesthetic and humanistic, enhancing the senses rather than abandoning them. From this intense level of

sensation l'Allegro relaxes, as he leaves the haunted stream for the "well-trod stage," the most social of all the arts. The plays he looks forward to viewing are appropriately enough comedies, both the classical "learned Sock" of Jonson* and the "native Wood-notes wilde" of Shakespeare's* romantic comedy.

Finally, all the activities of body and mind, sensuous and aesthetic, culminate in a great incantation to music—

And ever against eating Cares,
Lap me in soft *Lydian* Aires,
Married to immortal verse
Such as the meeting soul may pierce. . . .
(135–38)

The fact that Lydian music is unrelated to the sounds of universal harmony and order, to the Platonic music of the spheres that figures in *IlP* and elsewhere in Milton's early poetry, does not mean that it should be judged as vitiating, as it was by Plato. Its peculiar power is truly to liberate us from care, and hence even from restless pursuit of further delight. So great is its re-creative power that it exceeds that of Orpheus* and "would have won the ear / of *Pluto.*"

Insofar as *L'Al* is related to Epicureanism at its philosophical best, to authentic liberation from care and pain because the pleasures pursued leave no bad aftertaste or reproof, the poem is also inevitably related to variety as distinct from the One, which is the goal of the religious contemplative. Accordingly, the music into which the action dissolves, though superior to that of Orpheus, is not a resolved harmony that composes the soul into a stasis. Under the aegis of Mirth, the highest good is fittingly heard as,

many a winding bout
Of lincked sweetnes long drawn out,
With wanton heed, and giddy cunning,
The melting voice through mazes running;
Untwisting all the chains that ty
The hidden soul of harmony.
(139–44)

This volatility and emotional directness of the solo aria become ominous only when judged from the standpoint of the "pealing Organ" and "Anthems cleer" of *IlP*; however, within the frame of norms established in *L'Al* they are felt as altogether appropriate and desirable.

The mode of ideal concepts embodied in *L'Al* are not logical propositions. Its norms are unique and yet intelligible because they function through objects (the images) that have both a concrete and a generic identity. Of course, the special circumstance of twin poems complicates as well as enriches our response. Accordingly, a great danger in reading the beautifully paralleled and contrasted images of *L'Al* and *IlP* is that of isolating them from their respective poems and viewing them primarily within the context of intellectual presuppositions. Such a procedure more often leads to foregone conclusions than to an exploration of poetry. It is safe enough to assume that for Milton—the dedicated young student who argued the superiority of learning to ignorance in *Prol* 7—as well as in the cultural milieu of the Renaissance, contemplative Melancholy holds a higher place than does Mirth.

Discussion of *IlP*, like that of *L'Al*, proceeds from a starting point like that which Miss Tuve posited from a somewhat different perspective: "[Milton] portrays not pursuer or pursuit but that bodiless thing itself which the freely delighting mind or the meditative mind tirelessly seeks to ally itself with" (*Images and Themes*, p. 15).

Following the praise of Penseroso's noble ancestry and association with blackness, the goddess is invoked as a pensive Nun, "Sober, stedfast, and demure." The gravity of mien and fixity of mind evident in Penseroso's succeeding activities are established as the goddess's characteristic physical and mental posture. The pursuit of the One, though it ends in *exstasis,* must proceed with deliberation: "keep thy wonted state, / With eev'n step, and musing gate." Images of discipline and detachment—"calm Peace, and Quiet, / Spare Fast, that oft with gods doth diet"— are decorous to Penseroso's quest of the

pleasures of contemplation, just as spontaneity of movement and response decorously govern l'Allegro. As suggested earlier, both poems take pleasure as their value and destination; it is a simplistic distortion to confine the idea of pleasure to Mirth and to posit contemplative Melancholy as pleasure's opposite or even coordinate. Rather, Mirth and Melancholy are both subsumed under pleasure, but as different modes requiring differing patterns of decorum. This becomes explicit as Milton summons up the Horatian* ideal of "retired leasure, / That in trim Gardens takes his pleasure." Withdrawal from the active world of affairs into the self-contained pleasures of the garden is a traditional emblem for both the Epicurean and Stoic-Platonic happy life. The kind of "busy-ness" that pursues what is external to man's inner contentment—erotic gratification, wealth, or power—and is therefore inimical to true delight, is alien to the norms of both poems. Scriptural, philosophical, and literary traditions reinforce the ideal of leisure in a pastoral world or in a formal garden as the appropriate setting for the highest, and least vulnerable, pleasures of body, mind, and soul. This broad range of experience is encompassed by the images of each of Milton's companion poems, making for the basis of their parallel relatedness, though with strikingly different emphasis, providing their patterns of massive contrast. The operative norms of *L'Al* and *Ilp* accordingly do not collide as mighty ethical opposites, but are juxtaposed as contrasting perspectives.

To return to the images themselves, Philomel, "Sweet Bird that shunn'st the noise of folly," signals the start of Penseroso's activities—a nocturnal walk as he moves unseen through the landscape, gazes at the moon, and hears the far-off curfew sound. Whereas l'Allegro glances at towers from his position in intimate relation to the landscape, Penseroso is "in som high lonely Towr," his isolation from nature and society providing the vantage point for his pursuit of mysterious knowledge. The scenes of social intercourse in

L'Al have no counterparts here. When the scholar seeks respite from his intellectual quest he turns not to light refreshment but to the highest humanistic pleasures of Greek tragedy, which he enjoys as a solitary reader rather than as a member of a theater audience. The diverting music of *L'Al* is holiday song and dance; here the speaker hopes for music of miraculous power—

But, O sad Virgin, that thy power
Might raise *Musaeus* from his bower,
Or bid the soul of *Orpheus* sing
Such notes as warbled to the string,
Drew Iron tears down Pluto's cheek,
And made Hell grant what Love did seek.
(103–8)

Folktales recounted in *L'Al* over a cheerful mug of ale have in *IlP* a weightier counterpart in Chaucer's* unfinished *Squire's Tale*, "The story of Cambuscan bold," continuing the theme of the quest for intellectual prowess. The arts convey in *L'Al* direct sensuous delight; the pleasures of poetry and music in *IlP* are more oblique and have the appeal of "Where more is meant then meets the ear."

The glorification of darkness at the expense of light, so insistently argued in the opening, runs throughout the poem. In the first scene, Penseroso finds during his night walk refuge in a "removed place,"

Where glowing Embers through the room
Teach light to counterfeit a gloom. . . .
(79–80)

And after the "pale career" of a night devoted to music and poetry, he seees "civil-suited Morn appeer, / Not trickt and frounc't as she was wont, / With the Attick Boy to hunt, / But Cherchef't in a comely Cloud . . ." (121–25). "When the Sun begins to fling / His flaring beams," Penseroso seeks out "twilight groves," unknown to the woodsman, where "in close covert by som Brook," and hidden "from Day's garish eie," he finds refreshment in sleep and dreams.

The consummating experience of Penseroso, like l'Allegro's, is couched in music. As he wakes from "som strange mysterious dream," he hears music sent perhaps by "th'unseen Genius of the Wood." His final vision, however, removes him from this natural setting to the "studious Cloysters pale." Dedicated study of nature's innermost secrets and man's highest wisdom issues ultimately, according to Christian and Platonic philosophy, in an absorbed contemplation of the Creator, in experience that approaches the mystical. The conclusion relates the intellectual endeavors of Penseroso to his religious dedication through music so exalted that it can dissolve him into ecstasies and "bring all Heav'n before [his] eyes." And such a contemplative existence, long enough pursued, may even enable the adept to "attain / To something like Prophetic strain."

These visionary final images are succeeded by the two low-keyed concluding lines adapted from Ralegh's* "The Nymph's Reply to the Shepherd," which remind us that a choice of pleasures is being offered:

These pleasures Melancholy give
And I wish thee will choose to live.
(175–76)

As with the parallel conclusion of *L'Al*, the reader may well wonder: after so utterly convincing a realization of Melancholy why need such a question be even implied, as it is by the subjunctive of the verb "give." Surely the entire poem is the most vivid proof that Melancholy can and does give these pleasures. And the same, of course, applies to Mirth in *L'Al*

These delights, if thou canst give,
Mirth with thee, I mean to live.
(151–52)

The foregoing discussion has already suggested some of the major lines of interpretation. Earlier views of debate between opposed life-styles or values, and contrast between complementary moods, are currently giving way to more intellectually complex (but less emotionally subtle) interpretations. Of these the most influential is a hierarchical relation, first fully developed by Don Cameron Allen*, for whom the poems "describe a progress from an enslaving dissatisfaction to an ultimate gratification" (*The Harmonious Vision* [1954], pp. 8ff.). For Allen the "dynamic symbol of the poem is the tower," which figures the ascent from the common experience of *L'Al* to the contemplative experience of *IlP*. Another account of the companion poems sees them as one poem, as a "vertical structure" that traces sequentially a progression of experience, indeed a progress of the soul (David M. Miller, *Publications of the Modern Language Association* 86: 32–37). In the remedies for diseased Melancholy prescribed in Burton's *Anatomy of Melancholy* (see W. J. Grace, *Studies in Philology* 52 : 579–91, for Milton's use of Burton* in *L'Al* and *IlP*), Miller sees just those activities which make up the body of *L'Al*. From the superior height of divine contemplation, however, Mirth is dismissed as vain deluding joys and superseded by golden Melancholy, yielding a four-step progression of the soul from desperate Melancholy, to the "neutral middle ground achieved at the close of *L'Allegro*," which is then rejected as vain, and proceeding finally to "a more positive state: as near to the contemplation of God as man can achieve on earth." The difficulty with this attractive and convincingly argued thesis, as with the older thesis of Tillyard about a debate between day or night (extendable to other pairs of polarities), has already been set forth : it substitutes foregone conclusions—clearly predictable once the intellectual frame of reference is announced—for the process of poetic discovery. Moreover, with this same four-step progression in mind, one could replace the hierarchical assumption with a cyclical one by citing, for example, Rosemond Tuve's attractive and widely accepted idea that "We need make no trouble about a division, no fanfare about a unification, that every man daily makes,

within the bounds of his own personality" (*Images and Themes,* p. 19).

In conclusion, it is important to resist the tendency to seize upon a single pattern of imagistic or thematic explanation with a view toward breaking down the complex separateness-and-relatedness of the companion poems. The relation of balance and contrast between the two interacts with the self-coherence of each ; the companion poems are precisely that —inseparable companions, not a single poem composed of two movements or divided into two parts. The richest thematic issues are probably not to be found in the contrast of images of Mirth and Melancholy and cannot be expressed in some abstractly defined relation between them. The more interesting tension seems to lie with the question whether these companionate ideals can be possessed and sustained in all the perfection of their pleasures without deteriorating into something the mind must reject. Accordingly, it is best to consider the habits of formal discourse and thought that the poems clearly do employ—debate, encomium, progress of the mind or soul; Epicureanism, and Platonism—as materials employed in the making of a lyrical object whose forming principle cannot be accounted for by a thematic formula of any kind. [LN]

L'ALLEGRO, IL PENSEROSO, ED IL MODERATO: *see* ADAPTATIONS.

LAMB, CHARLES. Lamb acquired his wide and lasting knowledge of Milton's poetry as a boy at Christ's Hospital. A few years later, in *Biographia Literaria* (1817), when his schoolfellow Coleridge* recalled his education at the hands of Upper Master Boyer, he revealed an aesthetic problem in diction that he and Lamb debated in the 1790s : ". . . [Boyer] made us read Shakespeare and Milton as lessons . . . the lessons, too, which required most time and trouble to *bring up,* so as to escape his censure"; while "in our own English compositions . . . he showed no mercy to phrase, metaphor, or image, unsupported by a sound sense, or where the same sense might have been conveyed with equal force and dignity in plainer words. . . . In fancy I can almost hear him now exclaiming, 'Harp? Harp? Lyre? Pen and ink, boy, you mean! Muse, boy, Muse? Your nurse's daughter, you mean! Pierian spring? Oh aye! the cloister-pump, I suppose!' " In one hour, that is, Boyer was drilling the boys in Miltonic elaboration, in the next preaching simplicity.

Coleridge and Lamb spent several years talking and writing themselves toward a practical and theoretical resolution of this opposition, which in the 1790s took the form of a debate about poetry. Coleridge usually wrote the poetry; Lamb usually wrote epistolary reviews of it. The main issue was elaboration versus simplicity. Milton was the model for elaboration, and the poetic aim was elevation. While Coleridge was attempting to elevate his verse by "Miltonizing" it—to use Humphrey House's word (*Coleridge* [1953],p. 65)—Lamb was scolding Coleridge's elaborate, and praising his simple verse, thus : "Cultivate simplicity, Coleridge, or rather, I should say, banish elaborateness; for simplicity springs spontaneously from the heart, and carries into daylight its own modest buds and genuine, sweet, and clear flowers of expression. I allow no hot-beds in the gardens of Parnassus" (8 Nov. 1796; *The Letters of Charles Lamb*, ed. E. V. Lucas, 1 : 55–56). Curiously, however, Lamb alternated his demands for simplicity with praise for Coleridge's Miltonic successes. Some lines in Coleridge's part of *Joan of Arc* are "worthy of Milton" (*Letters,* 1 : 10), Lamb says at first, then later compares them with Milton again "for fullness of circumstance and lofty-pacedness of Versification" (1 : 13).

At this point in his life Lamb was unable to reconcile his appreciation for Milton, and the kind of "sublime" poetry that Milton exemplified to Lamb's generation, with the standards of simplicity and spontaneity. Thus Lamb's response to the sublimer efforts of young Coleridge was ambiguous. First Lamb censured Coleridge's *Religious Musings* (1796) for being "elaborate." Then, having had a chance to "re-read it in a more favorable moment," he did not hesitate "to pronounce it sublime" (*Letters,* 1 : 8). Eight months later, having looked the poem over once again, he was prepared to say that *Religious Musings* is "the noblest poem in the language, next after the Paradise Lost; and even that was not made the vehicle of such grand truths" (*Letters,* 1 : 93).

No one today puts *Religious Musings* in the company of *PL*. The ambiguity of Lamb and his friends Coleridge and Wordsworth* toward Milton and the sublime clouded their judgments both of their own poetry and the poetry of others. Lamb was not sure whether to blame *Religious Musings* for its tumidity or praise it for its sublimity, nobility, and grand truths. This aesthetic confusion led Lamb to pass notorious judgment on Southey, whom "on the whole" he expected "one day to equal Milton"(*Letters,* 1 : 15). Lamb's judgments on the more grandiose poetry of the eighteenth century were also bad for the same reason, and with Milton's name again at the center. In 1802 Lamb criticized Cowper's "damn'd blank verse [which] detains you every step with some heavy Miltonism" (*Letters,* 1 : 326–27). But Lamb's poem "To the Poet Cowper," written in July 1796, placed Cowper* in a line of poets with Spenser*, Sidney*, and Milton, and ended with the call to "take up the mighty Epic Strain, / Cowper, of England's Bards, the wisest & the best" (*Letters,* 1 : 36). Almost simultaneously Lamb was claiming—in a slightly evasive sentence—that parts of Beaumont and Fletcher "exceed Milton, and perhaps Collins, in sublimity" (*Letters,* 1 : 29). Lamb's hierarchy of sublimity—Beaumont and Fletcher first, Collins second, and Milton third—is not the expression of a sound aesthetic.

Lamb and his circle of friends finally resolved their dilemma by exchanging the ladder of literary decorum, which they had inherited in a rigid form from the eighteenth century, for a sliding scale of literary values based on a much more liberal interpretation of "appropriateness." The new scale would accommodate virtually any literary experiment, including not only mixed genres but also new ones—or what were seen as new ones. Lamb and Coleridge's confused encounters with Miltonic sublimity were clarified by a new vision of sublimity based on what in terms of the old scheme is paradoxical: that the simplest may be most sublime. Thus a ballad could be sublime, as Lamb, Wordsworth, and Coleridge, along with many readers, realized when *Lyrical Ballads* was published in 1798. Coleridge's contributions to *Lyrical Ballads* show that for the most part he had taken Lamb's advice about simplicity. But Lamb had also learned something about sublimity, and never again would he try to spur Coleridge with the ghost of Milton as he had early in 1797: "Coleridge, I want you to write an Epic poem. Nothing short of it can satisfy the vast capacity of true poetic genius. . . . By the sacred energies of Milton, by the dainty sweet and soothing phantasies of honeytongued Spenser, I adjure you to attempt the Epic" (*Letters,* 1 : 185). By 1800 Lamb and his compatriots had learned to apply to poetry the lesson that Lamb did not state in print until 1821: "You may derive thoughts from others: your way of thinking, the mould in which your thoughts are cast, must be your own. Intellect may be imparted, but not each man's intellectual frame" (*The Works of Charles and Mary Lamb,* ed. E. V. Lucas [1903–5], 2 : 53).

After the poetic advances made in *Lyrical Ballads* were augmented and consolidated in the second and third editions of 1800 and 1802, neither Milton nor ideas of the sublime had been banished, but both were now sitting easier in the hearts and minds of Lamb, Wordsworth, and Coleridge. For one thing, there was a new feeling of kinship between the new generation of writers and the writers of the seventeenth century. There is a clear sense of victory over the poets of the eighteenth century—especially the later part of it—who had been uneasily admired and disdained before 1800, as in Lamb's ambiguous criticism of Cowper, who is mentioned frequently in Lamb's letters before the turn of the century but almost never thereafter. The new subjects of conversation are not Collins, Cowper, and Bowles, but Shakespeare and the Elizabethan and Jacobean dramatists, and Milton and the seventeenth-century poets and prose writers. To a certain extent Milton continued to haunt and even intimidate the poetic aims of Wordsworth, and the philosophical, theological, and political aims of Coleridge, but Lamb was able both to admire Milton as Milton deserved and to keep Milton in his place. To do so was easier for him, however, because in the long run he relinquished most of his ambitions as a poet, playwright, and thinker.

As to the latter, he put out disclaimers early and late. Early, in 1800, he said that "Public affairs—except as they touch upon me, and so turn into private, I cannot whip up my mind to feel any interest in. . . . I read histories of the past, and I live in them; although, to abstract senses, they are far less momentous than the noises which keep Europe awake" (*Letters,* 1 : 176). Late, in 1820, speaking as Elia he said that he was "not the man to decide the limits of civil and ecclesiastical authority" (*Works,* 2 : 8). Lamb's disinterest sets him apart from Milton, Coleridge, and even Wordsworth in their concern with political philosophy. And Lamb thought of religion as "a solitary thing" (*Letters,* 1 : 86), mainly for individual consolation, as when his sister Mary murdered their mother in 1796. He wrote much about religion during the months after the murder, and perhaps it was the tragedy that led him to find supra-Miltonic sublimity in Coleridge's *Religious Musings* upon rereading it four months after the stabbing. But the rate of religious discussion soon dropped considerably in Lamb's letters and remained at a low, quiet level for the rest of his life.

Thus after his youthful enthusiasms, his family tragedy, and the publication of *Lyrical Ballads* and its initial effect on the English literary climate, Lamb as a man of thirty had put a significant distance between his way of life and Milton's, and after 1808 there is almost nothing in Lamb's life that leads naturally to comparisons. Among his friends he was certainly not the Milton of philosophical concerns that Coleridge was.

Nor was he the Milton of poetry that Wordsworth—"the best Knower of Milton" as Lamb later called him (*Letters,* 3 : 372n)—was. Between the death of his mother in 1796 and the publication of *Specimens of English Dramatic Poets* in 1808—his first major work of literary criticism—Lamb spent most of his time as a writer learning that he was not cut out to be a poet or a playwright. Unlike Coleridge and Wordsworth, he seems to have had no trouble laying the ghost of Milton in his poetry, if he had ever been haunted. One reason is probably that Lamb's poetry is so mediocre as not to be haunted by any ghosts whatever. It is that peculiar brand of workmanlike but colorless verse with few hints of influence from other voices. Milton is echoed occasionally, and occasionally quoted (see the Appendixes and Bibliographies in R. D. Havens's *Influence of Milton on English Poetry* [1922] for convenient lists), but he seldom affects the poetry substantially. Of "A Vision of Repentance" Lamb says to Coleridge that "the latter half aims at the *measure,* but has failed to attain the *poetry,* of Milton in his 'Comus' and Fletcher in . . . the 'Faithful Shepherdess' . . ." (1797; *Letters,* 1 : 106). This is the only indication that Lamb ever attempted to emulate Milton in his verse.

Milton was of little use to Lamb as an exemplar because Lamb's poetic aims were seldom Miltonic. Lamb was characteristically self-restraining, even self-demeaning, in his poetry as in most other endeavors. It is remarkable that he spent as many years as he did trying to write successful poems and plays. At any rate, the evidences of Milton in Lamb's major

works are slight. In *Rosamund Gray* (1798), usually called a novel, there is something of *Mask* in the forest setting and moral situation, but more of *Clarissa.* Milton is more apparent in *Rosamund Gray* by the absence of his works from the small collection of devotional literature owned by Rosamund and her grandmother. The collection is mainly of seventeenth-century works, but no Milton. In a letter to Southey in 1799 Lamb explicitly rejected Milton as a model for the blank verse* of his new tragedy, *John Woodvil,* on the grounds that Milton's way with blank verse is too formal for the drama (*Letters,* 1 : 148). In 1806 Lamb became a professional dramatist for the first and last time with *Mr. H—,* a farce produced unsuccessfully at Drury Lane. Its plot turns on a witticism based on Adam's lament in *PL* 10. 891–92, when he calls Eve "this fair defect / Of Nature." Mr. H's "cursed unfortunate tongue" causes what we might call his Fall from Grace in the Garden of Eden at Bath, and the slip of his name—"Hogsflesh"— elicits "an universal scream" from the polite company of heretofore eager eligible ladies and envious gentlemen. There is a Miltonic allusion or two in the quips and cranks of *The Wife's Trial* (1827), a play that Lamb called "A Dramatic Poem" when he failed to get it produced at Covent Garden (see *Works,* 5 : 260, 269). Milton is a major presence in only one of Lamb's larger creative efforts, *Amicus Redivivus* (1823), one of the *Last Essays of Elia.* It is an extended prose-parody of *Lyc* based on the near-drowning of a nearsighted scholar, "G. D.," in real life Lamb's friend George Dyer. In *Amicus Redivivus* Lamb combines the prose style of his persona Elia, well developed by this time, with Milton's elegiac manner, and the result is an extraordinarily rich earful, even for Elia.

The publication in 1808 of *Specimens of English Dramatic Poets Who Lived about the Time of Shakspeare,* an anthology of excerpts from Elizabethan and Jacobean plays with commentary, marked a new stage in Lamb's literary career. From then on he devoted himself to impressionistic criticism and quasi-reminiscence in the magazine essay. Milton is no more obvious in Lamb's maturity than earlier, but he was still important as a touchstone for certain kinds of poetry, mainly the pastoral* and the sublime, and Lamb still quoted Milton as often as ever, which is to say, more often than he quoted any other writer outside the drama.

In *Specimens* Milton was used repeatedly as a source of comparison. Lamb mentioned Milton in the company of Marlowe and Samuel Richardson as one of those "holiest minds [who] have sometimes not thought it blameable to counterfeit impiety in the person of another. . . . Milton in the person of Satan has started speculations hardier than any which the feeble armory of the atheist ever furnished . . ." (*Works,* 4 : 34). Lamb compared Chapman's "Greek zeal for the honour of his heroes" to "that fierce spirit of Hebrew bigotry, with which Milton, as if personating one of the Zealots of the old law, clothed himself when he sat down to paint the acts of Sampson against the Uncircumcised" (4 : 83). These two passages display Lamb's keen perception of dramatization—"counterfeiting," "personating"—in Milton. Lamb's interest in fictional dramatization is a part of the larger Romantic interest in the "poetical character" and "negative capability." His view of Milton's Satan should not be forgotten when we generalize about the vicious Romantic strain that slipped its way into Milton criticism.

Examples from *Specimens* and from other essays in which Milton appears show clearly that Lamb saw him as a convenient source of authoritative dicta and comparisons, as when he used Milton in testifying to John Ford's "sublimity" (*Works,* 4 : 218), or *Mask* in describing the pastoral-morality genre (4 : 312). But of necessity Milton is secondary in those places. We wonder what Lamb had to say about Milton during those nightlong conversations with friends such as Hazlitt

and Coleridge, when Milton, Shakespeare, and Homer were the subjects.

But we shall never know, because Lamb chose not to write about Milton at any length greater than a paragraph or two. The only piece devoted to Milton alone is both a doubtful attribution and a trivial one (*Works,* 1 : 376–77), consisting mainly of a long quotation from *Mask*. The thesis of the article is that Milton is not a popular poet and probably never will be. Perhaps the thesis explains why Milton's works are not in the library of Rosamund Gray and her grandmother, but little else. The second most extensive record we have of Lamb's reactions to Milton's poetry is the marginalia in his copy of Milton. The most significant of these have been published in an appendix to E. V. Lucas's *Life of Charles Lamb* (1905), 2 : 446–49. They reveal the astounding supply of seventeenth-century poetry that Lamb knew by heart, his method of annotation being to match Milton's lines with lines from other poets.

The most interesting lines among the marginalia come from the editor, who says that "Procter [a friend of Lamb], telling us of some of Lamb's unexpected tastes in reading, says he preferred *Paradise Regained* to *Paradise Lost*" (*Life,* 2 : 449). Lamb's only recorded criticism of *PR* appeared in the essay "Grace before Meat" (it was also reported by Hazlitt*), where he offered the opinion that Milton "wants his usual decorum" when he has Satan tempt Christ with luxurious food (*Works,* 2 : 94). But Lamb's preference for *PR* over *PL* tells us that, although he would not be thought "an undervaluer of Milton" (*Letters,* 2 : 73), he would not value him as others did either. The evaluation is oddly like that purported (erroneously) throughout the eighteenth century to be Milton's.

For Lamb, the result of contemplating Milton's greatness was the depersonalization of Milton. Though he owned a portrait of Milton, and spent good times with the Hazlitts in the house where Milton once lived, Milton was always a distant universal voice for Lamb. His praise of

Milton is typified by his early comment on *1Def,* that it is "uniformly great, and such as is befitting the very mouth of a nation speaking for itself" (*Letters,* 1 : 329). But Lamb liked best the unique human voice, and he did not have much of an ear for the sounds that the mouth of a nation might make. Milton's poetry fits into the class of "Great Nature's Stereotypes" (*Works,* 2 : 173), but Lamb loved the individual rather than the species. When he saw the manuscript of *Lyc,* he decided that the "written hand" is "repugnant" to one's notion of poetry. But the more likely truth is that Milton's poetry, not poetry per se, repelled Lamb in its rawest, most personal state : "I had thought of Lycidas as of a full-grown beauty—as springing up with all its parts absolute . . ." (*Works,* 2 : 311). Milton was not one of the persons that Lamb wanted to see and talk to (*Life,* 1 : 523). Whereas Blake* sat and talked to Milton in his imagination nightly, Lamb found Milton like King Lear, too universal for personation. Milton was less a person than a book of Great Poems, virtually a whole culture. But for Lamb—unlike Blake— whole cultures had no outlines, no shape; his sight was for small or novel things. Thus he asks, "Shall I be thought fantastical, if I confess, that the names of some of our poets sound sweeter, and have a finer relish to the ear—to mine, at least—than that of Milton or of Shakespeare? . . . The sweetest names, and which carry a perfume in the mention, are, Kit Marlowe, Drayton, Drummond of Hawthornden, and Cowley" (*Works,* 2 : 174).

The sweet smells that Shakespeare and Milton do not give off are *humors.* In Lamb's mature aesthetic, all artistic styles and modes are essentially humors, expressions of dominant individual traits. Thus he can characterize Sir William Temple's prose style as his "humour of plainness" (*Works,* 2 : 201). The perception of styles as humors is well suited only to an aesthetic that is very broad in its tastes and, if not egalitarian in its view of literary kinds, then at least flexible in its

hierarchical arrangements. In other words, Lamb's idea of styles as humors is well suited to his Romantic view of decorum. But as Lamb heard him, Milton, "staled and rung upon in common discourse" (*Works,* 2 : 174), does not fit well into the scheme, and neither does any other writer who becomes a voice of the culture, because the individual voice will be blended away. From this point of view it is easy to see why Lamb preferred Hogarth to Reynolds and Leonardo to Michelangelo; why he loved the "homely versification" of George Wither's satires and compared it to Milton's sublimity on equal terms (*Works,* 1 : 182); why he loved the seventeenth-century writers; and why he would say to Coleridge, "I am glad you love Cowper. I would forgive a man for not enjoying Milton, but I would not call that man my friend, who should be offended with the 'divine chit-chat of Cowper' " (*Letters,* 1 : 66; the latter phrase is Coleridge's). Lamb applied to literature his view of life, which was that "Common natures do not suffice. . . . I want individuals. I am made up of queer points and I want so many answering needles" (*Letters,* 2 : 319). *See also* INFLUENCE ON LITERATURE OF NINETEENTH-CENTURY ENGLAND, MILTON'S. [ME]

LAMBARDE, WILLIAM (1536–1601), jurist and historian. Milton cited two statements from Lambarde's *Archeion,* a history of the high courts of England, in *CB.* The first states that laws were devised to limit the power of government; the second asserts that Parliament had the power, according to ancient custom, to elect and depose the Lord Chancellor, the Chief Justice, and the Treasurer (*CB* 18 : 165, 179). In *1Def* "Milton's use of the word *lust* to describe the tyranny of rulers seems to echo Lambard's phrase (7 : 547; Ruth Mohl, *John Milton and His "Commonplace Book"* [1969], p. 237). His references to the laws of Ina, Alfred, and Edward, as well as his allusions to the fabulous conquests of Arthur are probably drawn from his reading of Lambarde's *Archaionomia* (1568), edited by

Abraham Wheloc* in 1644.

Lambarde's career as a jurist on various levels of the Elizabethan judicial system provided him material for his handbooks and histories of the English courts; his interest in the ancient customs of Kent resulted in his producing one of the very first county histories, *A Perambulation of Kent* (1576). [RMa]

LANGBAINE, GERARD. In *An Account of the English Dramatick Poets* (Oxford, 1691) Gerard Langbaine (1656–1692) recorded favorable accounts of *Mask* and *SA*, pp. 375–77, while also noticing Sir Robert Filmer's* criticism of *1Def* in *Observations concerning the Originalls of Government* (1652). Under his entry on John Dryden*, Langbaine observes the use of *SA* in *Aureng-Zebe*, p. 157 and n. The volume was reprinted as *The Lives and Characters of the English Dramatick Poets . . . First Begun by Mr. Langbain, Improv'd and Continued Down to this time by a careful hand* [Charles Gildon] (1698?), where the entry on Milton is found on p. 100 and that on Dryden on pp. 42–43. In addition Milton's alleged aid to Sir William Davenant* is recorded on p. 33 (under Davenant), *The State of Innocence* is noticed on p. 47 (under Dryden), and there are further allusions on pp. 74 and 151. This edition was reprinted in 1751. Langbaine had earlier listed "Sampson Agonistes" as a tragedy in octavo in *Momus Triumphs: or, The Plagiarie of the English Stage* (1687; i.e., 1688), p. 17. [JTS]

LANGHORNE, JOHN. The earliest translations* of Milton's Italian poems were made by John Langhorne (1735–1779), who published them as *Milton's Italian Poems Translated, and Addressed to a Gentleman of Italy* (1776). In addition to prefatory remarks, there are allusions* in a "Poem of Address to Sign^r. Mozzi, of Macerata"; later editions of Langhorne's poetry reprint these poems. "The Pastoral Part of Milton's *Epitaphium Damonis*" is translated into couplets, the first rendering into English

of that poem. Allusions and influences will also be found in Langhorne's "Le Sociable, partly in the manner of Milton," "To the Memory of Mr. Handel," "The Viceroy: Addressed to the Earl of Halifax," and "The Fables of Flora, IV" ["The Garden Rose and the Wild Rose"]. In *Letters Supposed to Have Passed between M. de St. Evremond and Mr. Waller* (1769), 2:18–21, Langhorne commented on *Lyc*, with an imitative poem, and *PL* in Letters 28 and 29. Although these are entirely fictitious, various commentators have treated them as the authentic work of Waller and St. Evremond, respectively. [JTS]

LANGUAGES, MILTON'S KNOWLEDGE OF. Besides, of course, English, Milton wrote prose and/or poetry in Greek, Latin, and Italian; in addition he transcribed French from his reading; and sometimes he translated from Hebrew*. In *AdP* he mentions learning Latin and Greek, then French, Italian, and Hebrew, and we may suppose that this was the order order of learning through his early school and college years. In his commendatory ode Antonio Francini* cites Milton's command of French, Tuscan (Italian), Latin, Greek, and Spanish (thus dating acquisition of this language before 1638); and Phillips lists Greek, Hebrew, Syriac(?) Latin, French, Italian, and Spanish. The transliterations from the Hebrew given as marginal notes for *Ps* 80–88 suggest that he spoke Hebrew with a pronunciation common among Spanish scholars. His Latin pronunciation came to be continental, rather than English, that is, showing influence from the Italian. (See remarks in *Educ* and the preface to *Grammar*.) His work with Thomas Ellwood* in Latin stressed such differences in pronunciation. As Secretary for Foreign Tongues*, Milton would seem to have had to know Latin, French, Spanish, German, and Dutch; but there is no evidence of work in German. Testimony from Deborah Milton, through John Aubrey* or John Ward*, indicates that Milton taught her Latin and to read

Greek and Hebrew, and apparently also French and Italian, while Milton himself also knew Dutch. This latter language was acquired around 1652, when such knowledge would have aided Milton in dealing with documents related to the involved negotiations between the United Provinces and the Commonwealth. Roger Williams*, founder of Rhode Island and controversialist for free conscience, read Dutch to Milton and apparently instructed him in the language. See a letter to John Winthrop of Massachusetts, dated July 12, 1654. Williams was in England from December 1651 through early 1654. [JTS]

LATIN SECRETARY: *see* SECRETARY FOR FOREIGN TONGUES.

LAUD, WILLIAM (1573–1645), Archbishop of Canterbury, chief architect of policies opposed by Milton and the Puritans, and chancellor of Oxford University. He was born at Reading, received the B.A. and the D.D. from Oxford in 1594 and 1608, took orders in 1601, and rose through church and college offices and the friendship of the Duke of Buckingham to the deanery of the Chapel Royal in 1626, the chancellorship of Oxford in 1630, and the archbishopric of Canterbury in 1633. His contributions to Oxford and its library were fundamental to its development. His energies as a churchman were devoted to requiring outward ceremony, repair of church buildings, and conformity extending to Scotland, Ireland, and English colonies abroad. As his power developed years before he became archbishop, he was partly responsible for the suppression of Puritanism that influenced Milton's decision not to enter the priesthood. His severity early became evident in his attitude toward the assassin of Buckingham and toward one who approved the deed, Alexander Gill* the younger, Milton's friend and teacher and the son of his headmaster. Milton's Greek lines on a philosopher's message to a king may refer to Gill's pardon by Charles I after two years of imprisonment. With Thomas Wentworth, Earl of Strafford, Laud embarked upon *Thorough*, a ruthless effort to impose uniformity upon Ireland and Scotland as well as England. Milton blamed the massacre of English Protestants in Ireland upon preliminary private assurances by Laud and Strafford that it would go unpunished (*Eikon* 5 : 189). Despite the Scottish uprising, Laud caused the Short Parliament of 1640 to pass seventeen new canons, including the controversial "etcetera oath." He was impeached and confined by the Long Parliament, and was conveyed to the Tower on March 1, 1641. At about the same time, Milton decided to devote all his energies to the struggle for religious liberty* and within a year produced five anti-prelatical tracts, terming Laudian "decency" ostentation, arguing the identity of presbyter and bishop, advocating elective episcopacy, opposing the enforcement of uniformity by the magistrate, deploring the persecution that caused emigration to America, attacking the tyranny of the bishops, and approving their punishment. Although Milton did not write two comparisons of Laud and Wolsey mistakenly attributed to him, he did denounce Laud in particular, not altogether fairly, in *Ref*, where he maintained that the canons of 1640 claimed an "unquestionable *Patriarchat*, independent and unsubordinate to the Crowne." He called Laud an office-scrambler; a pontifically proud seeker of carnal precedence; "a dayly incroacher" upon the King; "a strong sequester'd, and collateral power; a confronting miter, whose potent wealth, and wakefull ambition [the King] . . .had just cause to hold in jealousie" (3 : 7, 12–13, 57–58, 63). Milton's denigration of the "privat Psalter" attributed to Charles before his execution in 1649 extended to Laud's breviary as well, "lipwork . . . clapt together and quilted out of Scripture phrase" without diligence or judgment (*Eikon* 5 : 83–84). In 1645 the archbishop had preceded the King to the block. [ETM]

LAUDER, WILLIAM (d. 1771), a Scots-man, classical scholar, and academician, known primarily as a literary forger because of his relationship with Milton criticism. In 1739 he published *Poetarum Scotorum Musae Sacrae,* two volumes, which included a preface and a life of Arthur Johnston, a Scots poet who wrote in Latin. Lauder called Johnston, whose work appeared in this edition, a better poet than George Buchanan*. "A Letter to a Gentleman in Edinburgh," signed "Philo-Buchanan" (by John Love, a rector of Edinburgh High School), charged Johnston with inaccuracies and Lauder with critical ineptitude. Lauder's reply appeared in 1741. He tried to bring Alexander Pope* into the controversy on his side by sending him a copy of John-ston's work, which he thought would unquestionably acquit his judgment. Pope responded the next year with a scathing couplet in *The Dunciad* (3.111–12), which compares Johnston unfavorably with Milton. Pope became Lauder's scape-goat for the poor sales of *Poetarum Scotorum,* and his anger was directed against Milton.

In 1747 he published in *Gentleman's Magazine* "An Essay on Milton's Imita-tions of the Moderns" (17:24–26, 82–85, 189, 285–86, 312–14, 365–66); the title is adapted from *An Essay upon Milton's Imitations of the Ancients, in His Par-adise Lost, with Some Observations on the Paradise Regain'd* ([Edinburgh], 1741). This study of classical sources, rather than of plagiarism, has been inaccurately assigned to Lauder; it probably was written by C. Falconer. In his *Essay* Lauder charged that Milton had pla-giarized his epic from eighteen Latin authors, particularly from Jacopo Masenio's *Sarcotis,* Hugo Grotius's* *Adamus Exul,* and Andrew Ramsay's *Poemata Sacra.* (In 1732 Lauder had published an English blank-verse transla-tion of one of Grotius's poems.) Rebuttals soon appeared in various places, includ-ing a letter in the *Gentleman's Magazine* from Richard Richardson (17:22–24). It is reprinted with other discussions as

Zoilomastix: or, a Vindication of Milton, from all the Invidious Charges of Mr. William Lauder with several new remarks on Paradise Lost (Cambridge, 1747). Lauder revised his work in 1750, now called *An Essay on Milton's Use and Imitations of the Moderns in His Paradise Lost.* Passed off as part of Lauder's work was the preface written by Samuel John-son*, one of the editors of *Gentleman's Magazine.*

In a letter dated January 28, 1749, but not published until December 1750, Richardson argued that Lauder had inter-polated parts of William Hog's Latin translation* of *PL* (1690) into his quota-tions from Masenio and Staphorstius. (The editors withheld publication because they could not "admit a suspicion of so gross a forgery, and in copies which came through [their] own hands, [they] con-cluded that the lines in question were in *Masenius,* &c. and that Mr *Hog* had thence copied them to save himself the unnecessary trouble of translating *Mil-ton.*") Hog also translated *PR, SA, Mask,* and *Lyc* into Latin, and Lauder had included paraphrases of the Bible by Hog in *Poetarum Scotorum.* In the meantime, however, between the writing of Richard-son's letter and its publication, John Douglas (1721–1807), bishop of Salisbury, proved Lauder's forgeries by parallel texts in *Milton Vindicated from the Charge of Plagiarism, Brought Against Him by Mr. Lauder, and Lauder Himself Convicted of Several Forgeries and Impositions on the Public* (1751, *recte* 1750); it was revised in 1756 as *Milton No Plagiary; or, A Detection of the Forgeries Contained in Lauder's Essay on the Imitation of the Moderns in the Paradise Lost.* Another reaction was *Pandaemonium, or A New Infernal Expedition Inscrib'd to a Being Who Calls Himself William Lauder* (1751), by "Philathes."

In the second edition of his variorum *Paradise Lost* (London, 1750), Bishop Thomas Newton* added a "Postscript" to vol. 2, dated December 5, 1750, in which Lauder's charges are discussed. To this are added nineteen specific forgeries or interpolations, to which Lauder had publicly confessed. Newton says that "Soon after I published my proposals for printing a new edition of the Paradise Lost [1749] with notes of various authors, Mr. William Lauder, a Scotchman, came to me, exclaiming horribly of John Milton, and inveighing most bitterly against him as the worst and greatest of all plagiaries." Newton advised him to publish his findings, but not to write with the acrimony and rancor with which he spoke. As a result of this communication with Lauder, Newton included citations from Grotius's* Adam Exul in his first edition, 1749. After Lauder's Essay was published, Newton found that there were "not above half a dozen passages" from other authors that he could add to his second edition. To complete his remarks, he relates that John Douglas, who had been at Oxford during the last summer, could find only Staphorstius's Triumphans pacis, which did not, however, contain passages and lines given by Lauder. "This discovery incited the Gentleman to make farther researches, and farther researches produced more discoveries," which eventuated in Douglas's book.

Meanwhile Dr. Johnson elicited a confession from Lauder and dictated A Letter to the Reverend Mr. Douglas, Occasioned by His Vindication of Milton (1751), in which Lauder's culpability is asserted, the reason for his act is set forth, and testimonials praising his earlier scholarly work attempt to recoup some favorable reputation. An Apology for Mr. Lauder, in a Letter Most Humbly Addressed to His Grace the Archbishop of Canterbury (1751) repeats the reason for producing "An Essay": to reduce the idolatry of Milton and the imitations of his poetry. Lauder never gave up the allegation that Milton had plagiarized. In 1752–53 he published the work of Masenio, Grotius, and Ramsay as Delectus Auctorum Sacrorum Miltono facem praelucentium; the fuller 1757 Paris edition of Masenio is Sarcotis. Carmen. Volume two of Delectus lists ninety-seven authors allegedly used by Milton in his epic. In 1754, in a apparent attempt to regain face, Lauder raised the issue of Pamela's prayer in Eikon Basilike* again by publishing King Charles I. Vindicated from the Charge of Plagiarism Brought Against Him by Milton, and Milton Himself Convicted of Forgery, and a Gross Imposition on the Publick.

Lauder emigrated to Barbados, where he ran a grammar school and then a general store. He died there in 1771. [JTS]

LAW, CIVIL. In Areop, Milton called upon the Parliament then sitting to obey the voice of reason, "from what quarter soever it be heard speaking," and to be as willing to repeal any of their own acts as any set forth by their predecessors (4:296). Reason would keep civil law in harmony with the law of nature*, described in Way as "the only law of laws truly and properly to all mankinde fundamental, the beginning and end of all Government" (6:113). For the individual who would be subject to the laws made by a sovereign Parliament, the Reformation principle of Christian obedience* prescribed that he not obey any law that his conscience could not accept. Ideally, the collective conscience of Parliament as well as the conscience of the magistrate and the citizen would be governed by the same set of principles, and tyranny would become an impossibility.

Christians believed that Mosaic law, the epitome of a comprehensive and highly specific legal code, had been entirely abrogated by the Gospel. Milton wrote in RCG that the "whole Judaick law" was either political and so rendered unnecessary by the Gospel, or moral, so that it had always been in agreement with eternal law, written and unwritten (3:197). Thus, the fewer laws the better. Parliament should pass only those laws that were necessary to frustrate the wicked but should be careful not to "prohibit what, to honest men, should be freedom from all restraint . . . for laws have been provided only to restrain malignity; to form and increase virtue, the most excellent thing is liberty" (8 : 237).

Milton was opposed to church involvement in civil law, a position consistent with his reliance upon the law of nature as the way to man's regeneration. Arguing for the separation of church and state, he noted in *CivP* that under Mosaic law priests and Levites judged in all cases, both ecclesiastical and civil, but that under the Gospel such practice was "forbidden to all church-ministers, as a thing which Christ thir master in his ministerie disclam'd *Luke* 12. 14; as a thing beneathe them I *Cor.* 6. 4; . . ." (6 : 25).

Although he believed that religious reform took precedence over civil reform, Milton's devotion to individual liberty* separated him from those sectaries who wished for government by the elect, in which reform of all others would be achieved by coercion. Neither could he accept a system of many positive laws, in which individual rights would inevitably be based to a considerable extent upon the ownership of property, and in which the law would be argued by lawyers and decided by judges.

A society regulated by eternal law would have little need for positive laws. An individual might forfeit his exercise of free will* through ignoring the dictates of right reason*, but as Milton explained in *2Def*, there would always be guidance available for the ignorant from those who were their superiors in wisdom* and virtue* (8 : 265). Thus a society with democratic ideals would be dependent to a degree upon aristocracy. The sin of ignoring reason would, in a society that was not reformed, invite tyranny, a fate that Milton believed ignorance fully deserved.

Don M. Wolfe summarizes Milton's attitude toward the civil law in *Milton in the Puritan Revolution* (1941) : "A poet, not a practical statesman, Milton was unable to see in English law a reflection, however dim, of the law of nature. The law was 'norman gibbrish' to him. Nor did he understand that reform could come only by making that reflection

brighter, not by destroying the old surface and creating the reflection anew on a bright and shining one" (p. 336). *See also* CHANCERY PROCEEDINGS. [GDM]

LAW, ECCLESIASTICAL. Milton was concerned with three major aspects of ecclesiastical law : its legitimacy, especially as asserted by the bishops of the Church of England; its application in divorce*; and its separation from civil law*, to be concomitant with an effective separation of church and state.

Many of Milton's comments on ecclesiastical law were in reaction to the *Constitutions and Canons Ecclesiasticall* as newly revised and published in 1640. They had been authorized in the sixteenth century and most recently revised in 1604. The young Milton's religious life had been in part directed by them. The seventeen articles prepared by the Archbishops of Canterbury and York and approved by Charles I state the exclusive powers and functions of the Church as exercised by its episcopacy. Three articles (III, IV, V) treat of popery, Socinianism*, and sectaries, threatening book burning and excommunication for infractions, and warning (Art. VI) against innovations of doctrine or discipline by either clergy or laymen. The clergy are placed under oath to eschew popish doctrine and support episcopal rule, and in Article VIII are directed to preach for conformity at least twice yearly. Permission of a bishop is required for the commutation of any penance (Art. XIV). A communicant may be freed of any citation from an ecclesiastical court by denying it upon oath, except when accused of schism, incontinence, disturbing divine service, or "obstinate inconformitie" (Art. XVII). These severe strictures ran counter to Milton's desire for reform, which he at first expressed against the episcopacy and later against government by presbyters* as well, for he regarded both sorts of control as inimical to separation of church and state.

The antiprelatical tracts express Milton's concern with the bishop's application of ecclesiastical law. In *RCG* there is support for Presbyterian* government in the assertion that "All that was morally deliver'd from the law to the Gospell in the office of the Priests and Levites, was that there should be a ministry set apart to teach and discipline the Church, both which duties the Apostles thought good to commit to the Presbyters" (3 : 197). Milton did not think this moral obligation was satisfied by the bishops, whose origin was, according to Bishop Ussher*, "fetcht partly from the pattern prescribed by God in the old Testament, and partly from the imitation thereof brought in by the Apostles" (3 : 196). Milton's view of the Mosaic law, an extreme one very much like Luther's*, was that its political parts had been entirely abrogated by the Gospel, and that all the remaining moral part was "perpetually true and good" (3 : 197), existing in the unwritten law of nature* or in the Gospel. His later disillusionment with presbyters was accompanied by an even stronger feeling for separation of church and state.

In writing of divorce, Milton used the term *canon law* for that part of ecclesiastical law dealing with private individuals. The title page of *DDD* expresses a hope to see the process of divorce freed "From the bondage of Canon Law, and other mistakes, to Christian freedom, guided by the Rule of Charity." Canon law was against nature in that it provided only for the right of the body, not of the mind and spirit, by perpetuating those marriages in which the wife was not "a help meet" for her husband. Such a law was therefore against the will of God, who "cannot be pleas'd with any vast unmeetnesse in marriage" (3 : 424).

The problem of identifying those parts of Scripture relevant to divorce law did not seem difficult to Milton. He excluded not only Mosaic law, including the Decalogue, as restrictive laws out of keeping with the Gospel, but also what he termed "Christ's Evangelic precepts" (*Tetra* 4 : 220). That which Christ had said persuasively Milton did not believe should be converted into a judicial constraint, especially when used against a divine law.

No laws, and least of all ecclesiastical laws, should be unduly restrictive. In *CivP* Milton asserted that there could be no real separation of church and state while there was "force and fining in religion" (6 : 10). Ecclesiastical courts he condemned as extortionate and endowed with powers more appropriate to Parliament (*Ref* 3 : 55, 70). Most ecclesiastical canons, anyway, were "meer positive laws, neither natural nor moral" (*Way* 6 : 113). They should be subject to repeal at any time by Parliament and were hardly worth serious consideration as viable laws in harmony with the spirit of a reformed society. [GDM]

LAW OF NATURE, THE. The law of nature was for Milton an unwritten law, a set of moral absolutes identical with the will of God. Whereas the Decalogue, the only written law "taught of God," was set down on tablets of stone, the law of nature was "in the hearts of all mankind" (*CD* 16 : 101), a law given originally to Adam, and of which mankind still had some remnant. In the regenerate, influenced by the Holy Spirit, there was daily progress toward renewal of its primitive brightness.

Milton's faith in regeneration distinguishes his interpretation of natural law from Richard Hooker's* more orthodox view of it as simply a part of a supremely rational system : "The general and perpetual voice of men is as the sentence of God himself. For that which all men have at all times learned, Nature herself must needs have taught; and God being the author of Nature, her voice is but his instrument" (*Of the Laws of Ecclesiastical Polity,* 1. 8. 3). Yet both would have agreed that man, using reason* to apprehend the law, was reaching the highest good within his capacity and that this could not be accomplished unless faith* transcended reason.

In his antimonarchical and divorce* tracts, however, in order to support his case Milton appealed from human to natural laws, insisting that the inadequacies and errors of man-made laws, both civil* and canon*, exhibited the inadequacy of reason and could be rectified only by reference to the law of nature. In his view that divorce *"restrain'd by law"* was *"against the law of nature and of Nations"* (*DDD* 3 : 504), he found support in John Selden's* *De Jure Naturali et Gentium, Juxta Disciplinam Ebraeorum* (1640), a work that he praised for its recognition of "the clear light of nature in us, & of nations," and "the pure and solid Law of God" (*DDD* 3 : 505).

In the divorce tracts Milton asserts repeatedly that those laws of men that go against the law of nature are invalid. By forcing incompatible persons to stay wedded, he wrote, such laws turn nature upside down. In interpreting the law, he wrote in *Tetra,* the "wisest magistrats . . . lookt not peevishly at the letter, but with a greater spirit at the good of mankinde, if not always writt'n in the characters of law, yet engrav'n in the heart of man by a divine impression" (4 : 75). Moses, he finds, never thwarts "the fundamental law book of nature," but "commands us to force nothing against sympathy or naturall order" (*DDD* 3 : 419). In *Tetra,* Milton urges that man follow "the first and most innocent lesson of nature, to turn away peaceably from what afflicts and hazards our destruction; especially when our staying can doe no good, and is expos'd to all evil" (4 : 117).

In *Milton,* E. M. W. Tillyard* complained of "flagrant sophistries" (p. 128) in *DDD* where the words of Christ on marriage and adultery are explained away as subordinate to a law "deeper engraven in blameless nature" (3 : 482). Other writers, however, such as Herschel Baker, Douglas Bush, and C. A. Patrides, find in Milton's concept of the law of nature an expression of his belief in man's essential capability of reaching toward the highest good through reason exercised according to the dictates of conscience*.

Following the law of nature did not require for Milton the deep study of books other than Scripture, but rather that exercise of the faculty of reason possible only for the faithful, and distinguished from sophistry as right reason*. Knowledge of "natural causes and dimensions" was a "lower wisdom" (3 : 229); rather than strive after such knowledge, man should heed Raphael's counsel in response to Adam's inquiry about astronomy, and "be lowly wise" (*PL* 8. 173).

The law of nature exacted an obedience* from man that he, however, should give willingly and lovingly. Abdiel's reproof of Satan for calling him servile emphasizes the free will* with which one should serve God, and makes clear at the same time the identity between the law of nature and God's will: "Unjustly thou deprav'st it with the name / Of *Servitude* to serve whom God ordains, / Or Nature; God and Nature bid the same" (*PL* 6. 174–76).

Although the law of nature was unwritten, Milton asserted that covenants "have ever the more general laws of nature and reason included in them, though not express'd" (*Tenure* 5 : 35). On this ground he argued that Charles I* had by his tyranny broken the law of nature, thereby invalidating the covenant with his subjects. The laws and covenants of men are always subservient to the law of nature, but the law of nature is itself in perfect harmony with any other part of eternal law. If, however, man at any time cannot find within himself the law of nature, he is then to turn to the Gospel, "those written records pure" (*PL* 12. 513) that have escaped the taint suffered by other parts of the Scripture. [GDM]

LAWES, HENRY (1595–1662), one of a group of English song writers commonly designated Carolines because they were attached to the court of Charles I* both officially, as members of the King's Musick or the Chapel Royal, and unofficially, as occasional instructors and performers in the households of various noblemen. Their characteristic solo airs and dialogues established in England a new, declamatory style inspired by the Italian *stylo recitativo*, which emphasized word values and sharply curtailed musical ones. When the Court was dissolved as a social reality by the fall of Oxford to the Puritans in 1646, most of the musicians returned to London, where they supported themselves during the Commonwealth period by private teaching and commissions. Those who survived into the Restoration years saw their particular style of song writing superseded by the more vigorous French Baroque style established at court by the Francophile Charles II.

Lawes himself was both a Gentleman of the Chapel Royal and a member of the King's Musick. He was employed at various times by John Egerton*, first Earl of Bridgewater, and several members of his family, including his stepmother and mother-in-law, the Countess-Dowager of Derby. It is possible that he also served in his early years William Herbert, third Earl of Pembroke, whose estate at Wilton was near Lawes's native Salisbury. As a member of the King's Musick, Lawes would have sung countertenor roles in many court masques in the period in which this form of entertainment achieved its most elaborate development. He wrote songs for some of them, perhaps more than the four songs which have survived, and for plays presented at court. He wrote some sacred music, including anthems for the Chapel Royal (Brit. Mus. Add. MS 31434) and settings for metrical paraphrases of Psalms intended for private meditations (George Sandys, *Paraphrase upon the Divine Poems* [1638], and *Choice Psalms* [1648]). His principal work as a composer throughout his career was the solo songs, mostly written for private performance by himself or his aristocratic lady pupils. He set the poems, mostly love lyrics, of many of the best poets of a rich poetic period—Carew, Herrick, Herbert, Milton, Lovelace, Suckling, Waller— as well as many lesser lights, such as William Cartwright, Sir John Mennes, Francis Quarles, Aurelian Townshend,

and others recommended more by their aristocracy than their talents.

By birth Lawes's background was musical and ecclesiastic, accordingly high church and royalist. His father was a lay vicar, later vicar choral, in the choir at Salisbury Cathedral. Henry Lawes and his brother William (b. 1602), who was to become the preeminent instrumental composer of his generation, grew up in the cathedral close and presumably began their musical training in the chorister's school. William is known to have been taken as a musical apprentice into the household of Edward Seymour, Earl of Hertford, another Wiltshire nobleman noted for his patronage of musicians. Both Alfonso Ferrabosco and Giovanni Coperario were in his employ for many years, and evidence remains of Coperario's particular interest in William Lawes. It is tempting to believe that Henry Lawes preceded his brother in the patronage of the Earl and the tutelage of Coperario and Ferrabosco, but his apprenticeship is not documented, and his subsequent musical style does not reflect the rigorous contrapuntal training he would have received there. An allusion by John Birkenhead in a dedicatory poem written forty years later indicates that Lawes was in London before he was twenty, presumably studying or beginning a career or both.

Lawes's known preferment at court came more than a decade later, in the early months of Charles I's reign, possibly through the influence of the Earl of Pembroke. On January 1, 1626, he was made Epistoller, a probationary title, in the Chapel Royal, and by warrant of October 26 was given a position as Gentleman of the Chapel. On January 8, 1631, he was appointed to the King's Musick as musician for voices, and a livery warrant of August 9, 1632, refers to another appointment as musician for both lutes and voices. His association with the Court may go back even further than 1626 if Murray Lefkowitz's speculation is correct that both Lawes brothers were members of a group led by Coperario in the service of Prince Charles before he came to the throne (*William Lawes* [1960], p. 11).

The origin of Lawes's association with either Milton or the Egerton family is not known. In the small world of London music everyone is likely to have had the opportunity to know everyone, and the prominence of Milton's father among amateur musicians creates a strong presumption that Lawes came to know the younger Milton at his father's house. Lawes's introduction could well have come about through Coperario or Ferrabosco; the latter's acquaintance with the elder Milton is specifically suggested by the fact that they published songs in the same collection (William Leighton's *Tears or Lamentations of a Sorrowful Soul* [1613]).

Coperario could also have been the link between Lawes and the Egertons; his acquaintance with the Earl of Bridgewater is attested by a copy of his *Rules How to Compose* which was in the Earl's library before 1617. Lawes must have been employed by the Earl for some time before 1626, the date of the marriage of Mary, the elder of the two daughters he is known to have instructed; and he may have been the musician who was hired to teach the Earl's eldest daughters in 1615, a date that fits well with Birkenhead's reference to Lawes's coming to London.

In any case, it is clear that Lawes had had a prominent place in the musical life of this family for a number of years before the performance of Milton's *Arc* for the Countess-Dowager of Derby, in which several of her grandchildren, Lawes's pupils, took part. That Lawes was the composer for *Arc* is therefore a very reasonable assumption, though the music is not extant and the only direct evidence of Lawes's involvement is a general statement on the title page of the 1645 edition of Milton's poems that "The Songs were set in Musick by Mr. Henry Lawes." (It should be noted in passing that this statement could also mean that

Lawes had set *May*, which is specifically labeled SONG in the 1645 volume. Again, the music is not extant.) If Lawes was involved with *Arc*, he is likely also to have been the producer and the actor who played the Genius of the Wood, a part that has clear resemblance to Lawes's role as the Attendant Spirit in *Mask*, both roles seemingly suggestive of his role as tutor of the children. It would also follow that Milton had in mind Lawes and his music in *IlP*, lines 151–54, as Miss Willa Evans has suggested (*Henry Lawes* [1941], p. 65).

The name of Henry Lawes has been known to later centuries primarily for his collaboration with Milton on the masque, later called *Comus*, written for the installation of the Earl of Bridgewater as Lord President of the Welsh Council on September 29, 1634. He wrote five lyric settings for the piece, four of them for the dual role of Attendant Spirit and Thyrsis played by Lawes himself: "From the heav'ns now I fly," "Sabrina fair," "Back, shepherds, back," and "Now my task is smoothly done." The fifth is "Sweet Echo," sung by Lady Alice Egerton as The Lady. These songs were, surprisingly, not included in any of the printed collections of Lawes's lifetime, and the music has survived only in two manuscripts. One of these (Brit.Mus. Add Mus 53723) is Lawes's own manuscript book and the other (Add. MS 11518) probably a scribe's copy from it, there being only slight musical differences and no significant textual ones between them. The heading in the Lawes manuscript, "The 5 songes followinge were sett for A Maske presented at Ludlo Castle, before the Earle of Bridgwater Lord President, of the Marches. October, 1634"—repeated almost exactly in Add. MS 11518—would seem to identify these versions explicitly as those of the original performance. The poetic texts differ from all the manuscript and printed sources of the whole masque in a few details, most strikingly in the absence of six lines in

"From the heav'ns now I fly," in addition to those lines which are otherwise missing only in *BrM*. The wording of the first line (instead of "To the Ocean") indicates that the song occurred at the beginning of the masque, as it does in *BrM*, rather than the end, where all other sources have it.

No music survives, and it seems unlikely that Lawes ever wrote any, for "By the rushy fringed bank," which Milton clearly wrote to be sung by Sabrina, or for the Attendant Spirit's speech at lines 922–37, which a marginal addition to *BrM* identifies as a song, though it is nowhere written or printed in the format of a song, as all the others are. Neither songs nor lyric speeches are accorded the roles taken by Lord Brackley and Master Thomas Egerton, who may not have been set to acquiring the grace of singing as their sisters were.

By the time of *Mask*, Lawes, at 38, had an established professional reputation, while the 26-year-old Milton was still unknown. Lawes, as a member of the King's Musick, would have participated in most of the great masques of the period, whereas Milton may never have seen one. Lawes is accordingly assumed to have been the guiding spirit in the production of the masque. As Parker has observed, at the first performance of *Mask* the high point of the entertainment occurred not at the dramatic climax of the plot but at the point when the music master, having guided his pupils through the performance, finally presented them to their parents for the recognition of their accomplishments (*Milton*, pp. 130–31). Lawes was responsible for the first publication of *Mask*, in 1637, though, as studies of *TM* have shown, Milton must have prepared the text, his refusal to put his name on the title page notwithstanding.

Evidence exists of sporadic but significant contact between Lawes and Milton for many years after the *Mask* collaboration. An extant letter from Lawes to Milton in the spring of 1638 is a response to Milton's request for help in getting a passport to Rome. Lawes, no doubt through one of his musical patrons —Sir Edward Dering, Deputy Lord Warden, seems the likeliest candidate— successfully applied to the Lord Warden, bypassing the Secretaries of State. In 1646 Milton wrote his sonnet to Lawes though it did not appear until the 1648 volume of Sandy's *Choice Psalms,* with settings by Henry and William Lawes. The 1653 volume of Lawes's *Ayres and Dialogues* contained commendatory verses by Milton's nephews, Edward and John Phillips, who may therefore have been pupils of Lawes. The association reflected by these pieces of evidence does not suggest intimate friendship or strong mutual influence, nor would one expect such a relationship between men so strongly divided politically as Milton and Lawes were. It does suggest, however, a continuing mutual interest and respect, no doubt deriving from their earlier collaboration and Lawes's early encouragement of Milton's career as a poet.

John Playford, the principal music publisher of the time, brought out between 1653 and 1658 three books of *Ayres and Dialogues* solely by Lawes, the only one of his contemporaries so honored. As late as 1669, seven years after Lawes's death, Playford was sure enough of an audience to include a fresh compilation of Lawes's airs in *The Treasury of Musick,* an expanded edition of his miscellany, formerly titled *Select Musicall Ayres and Dialogues.* These Playford publications and other contemporary miscellanies put into print about 250 songs, more than half the number Lawes is known to have written, and some others occur in various manuscript sources. The largest collection of his songs is the autograph, fair-copy manuscript (Brit. Mus. Add. MS. 52723) of 325 songs, including most of those found in the other sources, plus about 130 songs unique to this manuscript. Approximately chronological, it spans his career until about 1652. The songs at the beginning have strong affinities with the Jacobean period in the style of both the poetry and the music. The Elizabethans Sidney* and Spenser* are represented, and otherwise most of the first fifty entries set the works of poets active at the beginning of the seventeenth century, including Donne, Jonson*, and the Earl of Pembroke. Much of the anonymous poetry is reminiscent either of the lyrical style of Campion or of the introspective melancholy affected by John Dowland, and the music also remains close to the style of the lutenist-songwriters. Declamatory characteristics begin to dominate the older style with songs that can be assigned to the early 1630s. The *Mask* songs are entered as a group (nos. 74–78), and in the same sector of the manuscript are songs from other masques and court plays, including Cartwright's *The Royal Slave* and Davenant's *The Triumphs of the Prince d'Amour.* If Lawes wrote, as is usually supposed, music for Milton's *Arc* and Carew's *Coelum Britannicum,* he did not, for some reason, enter them into this fair-copy manuscript which he generally seems to have kept carefully and faithfully.

Taking the manuscript songs as a reasonably accurate representation of Lawes's development as a song-writer, one may see that the *Mask* songs occupy a fairly early place in the development of his own characteristic style. His mature achievement is best exemplified by the songs of, roughly, the later 1630s and early 1640s, spanning the period of the Court's last, expansive—though not untroubled—years under the "King's peace" and of dispersement and disaster ending in the King's captivity. Outstanding among these are a large group of settings of poems by Carew and more than a dozen by Herrick.

Lawes's style of verse setting too often is understood only in terms of Milton's sonnet, in which he said that Lawes

First taught our English Music how to span
Words with just note and accent, not to scan
With *Midas* ears, committing short and long.

In its claim for Lawes's primacy in

accommodating musical stress and quantity to the corresponding verbal values, Milton's witticism is gracious hyperbole. English musicians had been concerned to do just that since at least Thomas Morley's "Rules to be observed in dittying" in his *Plaine and Easy Introduction to Practical Music* (1597). Though Lawes, by using greater variety of note values and dotted rhythms, did scan individual words somewhat more precisely than his predecessors, his distinction lies more truly in his handling of the larger units of the verse. His generation of songwriters abandoned the symmetrical cadences and the rhythmic and melodic conventions of Renaissance style along with its contrapuntal texture, allowing the melodic line to follow freely the pace of the verse as it would be declaimed (hence, "declamatory airs"). The characteristic praise accorded to Lawes in commendatory verses is that he was preeminent in conveying the "sense" and "wit" of the poems he set. Insofar as "sense" can be understood as syntax, Lawes carefully constructed his melodic lines in phrases that varied in length to accommodate the syntactical phrasing through verse units of unequal length or run-on lines, in the latter case using musical punctuation within the phrase to mark the rhyme. "Sense" understood as meaning and, in particular, the "wit" of the meaning were both exposed and complemented by the wit of Lawes's music. He used extensively the traditional devices of word-painting (such as dissonances, melodic leaps, triple patterning, slurs, etc.), but more crucially, he also called upon a new flexibility of rhythmic movement to imitate or otherwise underline the details of image and idea and the play of feeling in the poem. His melodic line, with its varying phrase lengths and rhythmic patterns, moved easily against a freely felt tactus and above a simple chordal accompaniment improvised by the lute.

That Lawes's music was soon eclipsed and has remained so is not difficult to understand. It was a highly refined soloist's art in which, moreover, the inherent sensuous powers of musical structures were deliberately pruned back to favor the exposure of the wit of the verse. Its appeal was to the cultivated, hence largely to the Court; and it flourished under the active encouragement of both the King and the Queen. When court taste changed, the Caroline style quickly became a dead issue. Music historians of the eighteenth and nineteenth centuries, put off by its slender musical means, were not inclined to resurrect it. They saw the Carolines only as a low point between the great periods of English music—the Elizabethan and that of Henry Purcell. Furthermore, the Caroline songs have the even more fundamental handicap of belonging to the early, experimental phase of a major stylistic revolution in music, the great shift from Renaissance to Baroque* expressive ideals and techniques of both rhythmic and tonal organization then taking place throughout Europe, so that the music inevitably lacks the sureness of that which is produced in a period of thoroughly established practices. Lawes and his contemporary songwriters have the misfortune of seeming in retrospect something of a failed experiment in this process, and yet they produced many settings of genuine interest and charm that throw a special light on the lyric verse that they set. [JSA and JA]

LAWRENCE, EDWARD (1633?–1657), elder son of Henry Lawrence*, member of the Council of State*. Edward was known to Henry Oldenburg*, who in January 1657 requested Milton to deliver his greetings to the young man. First, this would suggest that Edward had been a student of Milton's, possibly in the later 1640s, and second, that he is the addressee of Sonnet 20, written probably around November 1655. The sonnet implies that "young Lawrence" visited Milton during the mid-50s, as Phillips says he did. Masson* had listed Edward's younger brother Henry as Milton's student and addressee of the sonnet, but John S.

Smart's* argument for Edward is now accepted. Edward was elected to Commons on November 11, 1656, but died of natural causes the next year. [JTS]

LAWRENCE, HENRY (1600–1664), Puritan statesman and member of the Council of State*. Lawrence was educated at Emmanuel College, Cambridge (B.A., 1623; M.A., 1627). He was distantly related to Cromwell*, who at one time was his tenant. During the early years of the Civil War, Lawrence and his family were on the Continent. Upon his return in 1646 he replaced a "disabled" member of Parliament for Westmorland. In 1653 he represented Hertfordshire. He was appointed to the Council of State on July 14, 1653, and was a member of the new Council, which met the day of Cromwell's installation as Protector, December 16, 1653. Lawrence was chosen Chairman, and on January 16, 1654, an order by Cromwell made him permanent Chairman, that is, "Lord President of the Council." Lawrence was returned to Parliament in 1654, again from Hertfordshire, and in 1656 he chose to represent Carnarvonshire until his elevation to the House of Lords in December 1657. He continued as Lord President after Richard Cromwell's* accession until July 1659. After the Restoration he lived in retirement in Hertfordshire.

Milton praised Lawrence in *2Def* along with eight other members of the Council (out of fifteen). Possibly Lawrence's eldest son Edward*, to whom Milton addressed *Sonn* 20, was a pupil of Milton's around 1647. Lawrence was author of several books that Milton would have been interested in: *Of Baptisme* (1646: 2d ed., *A Pious and Learned Treatise of Baptism*, 1649), *Of Our Communion and Warre with Angels* (1646), and *Some Considerations Tending to the Asserting and Vindicating of the Use of the Holy Scriptures and Christian Ordinances* (1649; 2d ed., *A Plea for the Use of Gospel Ordinances*, 1652). [JTS]

CONTRIBUTORS TO VOLUME 4

AA   Arthur Axelrad. California State University, Long Beach, Calif. 90840.
ACL   Albert C. Labriola. Duquesne University, Pittsburgh, Pa. 15219.
ALS   Alice L. Scoufos. California State University, Fullerton, Calif. 92634.
APA   Andy P. Antipas. Tulane University, New Orleans, La. 70118.
ARC   Albert R. Cirillo. Northwestern University, Evanston, Ill. 60201.
EFD   Edgar F. Daniels. Bowling Green State University, Bowling Green, Ohio 43614.
ERG   E. Richard Gregory. University of Toledo, Ohio 43606.
ETM   Elizabeth T. McLaughlin. 344W. 72nd St., Apt. 3R, New York, N.Y. 10023.
FTP   Frank T. Prince. Professor Emeritus of the University of Southampton, Southampton, England.
GDM   Gilbert D. McEwen. Whittier College, Whittier, Calif. 91608.
GdeFL   George deForest Lord. Yale University, New Haven, Conn. 06520.
GFS   George F. Sensabaugh. Stanford University, Stanford, Calif. 94305.
HB   Harry Blamires. King Alfred's College, Winchester, England.
JA   James Applegate. Wilson College, Chambersburg, Pa. 17201.
JAW   Joseph A. Wittreich, Jr. University of Maryand, College Park, Md. 20742.
JD   James Dale. McMaster University, Hamilton, Ontario, Canada.
JGD   John G. Damaray. University of Kentucky, Lexington, Ky. 40506.
JGN   James G. Nelson. University of Wisconsin, Madison, Wis. 33706.
JJR   John J. Roberts. The Westminster School, Atlanta, Georgia 30327.
JMS   John M. Steadman. Huntington Library and Art Gallery, San Marino, Calif. 91108.
JSA   Joan S. Applegate. Shippensburg State College, Shippensburg, Pa. 17257.
JTS   John T. Shawcross. City University of New York, New York, N.Y. 10031.
KW   Kathleen Williams. Late of University of California, Riverside, Calif. 92502.
LN   Leonard Nathanson. Vanderbilt University, Nashville, Tenn. 37235.
MADC   Mario A. Di Cesare. State University of New York, Binghampton, N.Y. 13901.
MBM   Maurice B. McNamee, S.J. St. Louis University, St. Louis, Mo. 63103.

MCJ	Milford C. Jochums. Illinois State University, Normal, Ill. 61761.
MCP	Mother M. Christopher Pecheux. College of New Rochelle, New Rochelle, N.Y. 10801.
ME	Morris Eaves. University of New Mexico, Albuquerque, N.M. 87131.
ML	Michael J.Lieb.University of Illinois, Chicago Circle, Chicago, Ill. 60680. 60680.
MM	Marian E. Musgrave. Miami University, Oxford, Ohio 45056.
MMu	Martin Mueller. University College, University of Toronto, Toronto 4, Ontario, Canada.
PAF	Peter A. Fiore. Siena College, Loudonville, N.Y. 12211.
PEB	Purvis E. Boyette. Tulane University, New Orleans, La. 70118.
PMZ	Paul M. Zall. California State University, Los Angeles, Calif. 90032.
PTW	Paul T. Wilson. Drawer A, Pensacola, Fla. 32503.
RCF	Roy C. Flannagan. Ohio University, Athens, Ohio 45701.
RCR	Richard E. Rierdan. Pepperdine University, Los Angeles, Calif. 90044.
RF	Robert Fox. St. Francis College, Brooklyn, N.Y. 11201.
RHW	Robert H. West. University of Georgia, Athens, Ga. 30602.
RMa	Rosemary Masek. University of Nevada, Las Vegas, Nev. 89109.
TAB	Thomas A. Brennan. University of South Alabama, Mobile, Ala. 36688.
TLH	Theodore L. Huguelet. Western Carolina University, Cullowhee, N.C. 28723.
WA	Ward Allen. Auburn University, Auburn, Ala. 36830.
WBH	William B. Hunter, Jr. University of Houston, Houston, Texas 77004.
WM	Willis Monie. P.O. Box 105, Hartwick, N.Y. 13348.
WS	Wayne Shumaker. University of California, Berkeley, Calif. 94720.